Rev. Francis R. Davis
Our Lady Of Lourdes
120 Fairmont Road
Elmira, N. Y. 14905

The gospels for preachers and teachers

The Gospels for Preachers and Teachers

FRANZ KAMPHAUS

Translated by David Bourke

SHEED AND WARD · LONDON

Copyright © 1968 by Matthias-Grünewald-Verlag. English translation copyright © 1974 by Sheed and Ward Ltd. First published 1974. All rights reserved. Originally published as *Von der Exegese zur Predigt* by Matthias-Grünewald-Verlag, Mainz 1968. *Nihil obstat* Lionel Swain Censor. *Imprimatur* David Norris Vicar General, Westminster 29 Dec 1973. This book is set in 11 on 13 pt Monotype Baskerville and printed in Great Britain for Sheed and Ward Ltd, 6 Blenheim Street, London WIY OSA by William Clowes & Sons, Limited, London, Beccles and Colchester

CONTENTS

Foreword   xi

1 **Introduction**   1

2 **The Easter stories: exegetical investigation**
    I Introduction   11
       1 The Easter witness considered as a medium of early christian preaching   11
       2 Discrepancies within the Easter tradition   12
    II The Easter narratives   18
       1 The grave stories   19
          (a) Mark 16:1–8   19
          (b) Matthew 28:1–10   22
          (c) Luke 24:1–12   24
          (d) John 20:1–18   26
          Excursus on the significance of the empty tomb   29
       2 The manifestation stories   33
          (a) Matthew 28:16–20   33
          (b) The Emmaus narrative (Lk 24:13–35)   36
          (c) The manifestation to the disciples assembled in Jerusalem (Lk 24: 36–49)   39
          Excursus on the bodily presence of the risen Lord   40
          (d) The departure of the risen Lord from the disciples (Lk 24:50–53)   45
          (e) The manifestation stories in John 20   49
          (f) The manifestation stories in John 21   56
          (g) The canonical conclusion of Mark (16:9–20)   58

CONTENTS

III Concluding implications 61
  1 The kerygmatic structure of the Easter narratives 61
  2 On the historical question 62

3 Preaching the Easter stories
I Basic considerations 66
II Treatment of individual pericopes 70
  1 The story of the tomb (Mk 16:1–8) 71
    (a) On the sermon literature 71
    (b) Suggestions for sermons on the story of the tomb 79
  2 The story of Emmaus (Lk 24:13–35) 83
    (a) On the sermon literature 83
    (b) Suggestions for preaching on the Emmaus story 87
  3 The story of Thomas (Jn 20:19–31) 90
    (a) On the sermon literature 90
    (b) Suggestions for preaching on the story of Thomas 97
  4 The gospel of the ascension (Mk 16:14–20) 103
    (a) On the sermon literature 103
    (b) Suggestions for preaching on the ascension 109

4 The miracle stories: exegetical investigation
I Introduction 114
  1 The conception of miracles among the ancients 114
  2 The rejection of the demand for signs in the new testament 115
II Interpretation of selected miracle stories 118
  1 The story of the healing of the paralytic 120
    (a) Mark 2:1–12 120
    (b) Matthew 9:1–8 124
    (c) Luke 5:17–26 126

CONTENTS

 2 The story of the calming of the storm   127
  (a) Mark 4:35–41   127
  (b) Matthew 8:23–27   130
  (c) Luke 8:22–25   134
 3 The story of the miraculous feeding   135
  (a) The Marcan stories (Mk 6:30–44; 8:1–9)   137
  (b) The Matthean stories (Mt 14:13–21; 15:32–39)   143
  (c) The Lucan story (Lk 9:10–17)   147
  (d) The Johannine story (Jn 6:1–15)   149
III Concluding implications   154
 1 The kerygmatic character of the miracle stories   154
 2 The historical question   156

5 Preaching the miracle stories

I Basic considerations   161
 1 The overthrow of the apologetic approach to miracles   161
 2 Overcoming the limited understanding of truth established by history   170
 3 Inadmissible attempts at 'playing down' the miracle stories   172
 4 Adhering to the real facts in preaching on the miracle stories   175
II Treatment of individual pericopes   176
 1 The story of the healing of the paralytic   176
  (a) On the sermon literature   176
  (b) Suggestions for preaching on Mt 9:1–8   189
 2 The story of the calming of the storm   192
  (a) On the sermon literature   192
  (b) Suggestions for preaching on the story of the calming of the storm Mt 8:23–27   200
 3 The story of the miraculous feeding   203
  (a) The sermon literature   203

CONTENTS

    (b) Suggestions for preaching on the story of the miraculous feeding   217
        (i) John 6:1–15   217
        (ii) Mark 8:1–9   220

6 The infancy narratives: exegetical investigation

  I Introduction   224
    1 The infancy narratives in the context of the apostolic preaching   224
    2 The literary form of the infancy narratives   225
    3 The relationship between the infancy narratives   226
  II Interpretation of selected narratives   227
    1 The Lucan infancy narrative   227
        (a) Special features and connecting lines in the Lucan infancy narrative   227
        (b) The annunciation of the birth of Jesus (Lk 1:26–38)   230
        (c) The birth of Jesus (Lk 2:1–20)   236
        (d) The prophetic witness of the presentation in the temple (Lk 2:21–40)   241
        (e) Jesus in the temple at twelve years old (Lk 2:41–52)   243
        (f) Conclusion   246
    2 The infancy narrative of Matthew   248
        (a) The special character of Matthew's narrative compared with that of Luke   248
        (b) The genealogy of Jesus and his birth (Mt 1)   249
        (c) The childhood of Jesus (Mt 2)   252
  III Concluding implications   257
    1 The kerygmatic character of the infancy narratives   257
    2 The historical question   258

7 Preaching the Christmas stories

  I Basic considerations   261

CONTENTS

   1 The structure of the preaching of Christmas as conditioned by the message of Easter   261
   2 Preaching as opposed to 'historicising' explanations   263
   3 The manifold aspects of the biblical message of Christmas   265
   4 The situation in which the message is proclaimed   266
II Treatment of individual pericopes   267
   1 The annunciation story (Lk 1:26–38)   267
     (a) On the sermon literature   267
     (b) Suggestions for preaching on Lk 1:26–38   275
   2 The story of Christmas (Lk 2:1–20)   278
     (a) The sermon literature   279
     (b) Suggestions for preaching on Lk 2:1–20   286
       (i) The gospel of the first mass of Christmas Lk 2:1–14   286
       (ii) The gospel of the second mass of Christmas Lk 2:15–20   290
   3 The story of the magi (Mt 2:1–12)   292
     (a) The sermon literature   292
     (b) Suggestions for preaching on the story of the magi   299
   4 The story of Jesus in the temple at twelve years old (Lk 2:41–52)   302
     (a) The sermon literature   303
     (b) Suggestions for preaching on Lk 2:41–52   306

8 Sermon composition
   I Hearers of the word   311
     1 The necessity of historico-critical exegesis for the preparation of sermons   311
     2 The relationship between exegesis and preaching   314
     3 The limitations of historico-critical exegesis   316

CONTENTS

- II The kerygmatic structure of the gospels in its significance for preaching — 319
  1. Preaching as address — 319
  2. Preaching as a disclosing of the truth of the gospels — 322
  3. Easter as the fountainhead of preaching — 326
- III The significance for preaching of the quest for the historical Jesus — 328
  1. Attempts to exclude the historical question — 328
  2. *Kerygma* and the historical Jesus — 333
  3. The unity of works and word in Jesus — 338
- IV The task of making the witness of the gospels relevant in the present — 344
  1. Preaching as a living mode of handing on the gospel tradition — 346
  2. Attempts at applying scripture to the present which are inadequate — 349
  3. A preaching which measures up to the realities of the existing situation — 359

Bibliography — 369
Sources of sermon material — 372
Abbreviations — 373
Tables of readings: Appendices 1–3 — 375
Index of biblical passages — 379
Index of authors and editors cited — 385

FOREWORD

How did this book come to be written? For some years I have had experience not only of the joy, but also of the burden involved in Sunday preaching. My studies in theology introduced me to the findings and methods of present-day study of the gospels. When, therefore, it came to the point of putting the insights thus acquired to practical effect for my preaching I often found myself more perplexed than enlightened for my task. I looked in vain for guidance that would help me to make the transition from the text of scripture to the sermon. When my bishop, Dr Josef Höffner, offered me an opportunity to make a scientific investigation into the questions with which I found myself confronted in my ministry of preaching I gratefully accepted the chance.

In the course of my work I have received assistance from many quarters. From the outset Professor T. Filthaut has helped the work forward with his wise advice and his dispassionate criticisms. He continued to work actively in order to ensure that it should be accepted as a thesis and published, but unfortunately he did not live to see this brought to fruition. In token of my gratitude for all that I owe to him as a man and as a theologian I hereby dedicate this book to his memory. Drs J. Gnilka, W. Kasper and J. B. Metz have made suggestions which were of great value to me in the course of their lectures and seminars, and also in private discussions. Over and above this, after the sudden death of Professor Filthaut, they took over the responsibility for my work. To them and to many friends at Münster who have helped me with their advice, I remain constantly indebted.

The thesis on which the following study is based was

FOREWORD

accepted by the faculty of catholic theology of the university of Münster under the title, *The Significance of Recent Study of the Gospels for Preaching, with Reference to the Easter Narratives, the Miracle Stories and the Infancy Narratives*. For this I now wish to express my appreciation to the professors of the faculty.

I was initially stimulated to write this book by the practical experience of preaching. If it is able to assist other preachers in our common ministry of the word, I shall consider myself well rewarded.

Franz Kamphaus

I
INTRODUCTION

The occasion and the purpose of this work
The church of Jesus Christ is a church of the word of God, that word which has gone forth and continues to go forth through him, that word which he himself is in his own person. Sacred scripture bears witness to this word in the unique, definitive and normative proclamation of the word which took place in the apostolic origins of the church. In renewing herself, therefore, the church takes as her primary starting-point a renewed awareness of the message of holy scripture. This applies first and foremost to the function of preaching, in however wide a sense this is taken. This is intended to renew, in the contemporary situation, that essential witness to the word of God which has gone forth definitively once and for all. It can succeed in fulfilling this task only if it allows itself to be guided by the original witness preserved in the bible. Thus the demand which is raised, ever more insistently, for a preaching that is biblical in character corresponds to the call for a renewal in preaching in general, and in the church as a whole.

There is a danger that this process of regeneration will stick fast right at the outset. At the point when preaching is turning back to renew itself at its own well-spring it finds itself barred from that well-spring. Hardly have preachers discovered anew the ancient treasure that is theirs than this treasure is, so it seems, torn from their hands. Scientific study of the bible, which has taught us to recognise the meaning of sacred scripture, seems itself in its historical and critical methods of research to deny the preacher access to scripture. It has rendered the text of the bible alien in that it makes it impossible for us to retain that view of it which is traditional and to which we have become habituated, the view, namely, in which we regard the text of scripture as supplying us with records which are factual and historically reliable. The result of this has been that preachers have been placed in a position from which, they feel, neither help nor guidance for escape is forthcoming. In this situation, therefore, they can approach their task only with reluctance and with a lack of conviction. They regard themselves as encumbered rather than enriched by the findings of exegesis. They feel that the value of their work has been called in question and rendered dubious rather than confirmed by these findings. They regard the whole process of historical and critical research into the bible as so much mischief-making, unpleasant and hostile in intent, and rendering the task of preaching more difficult. Scarcely have they become aware of the call for biblical preaching than they find the biblical critics making the bible itself more inaccessible to them than ever. The widespread attitude of mistrust towards the biblical science of this present day gives birth to a further attitude of mistrust towards scripture itself. Are we to take the gospels as true or not? There is a real danger that both together—scripture and exegesis—will be abandoned, and preaching will turn aside from the newly won insights offered to it, to follow the overworked paths of traditional theology.

In view of this situation a solution that is frequently recommended is to avoid encumbering the work of preaching with the problems of biblical criticism and research, to take this as a kind of esoteric discipline to be left to the custody of professional scholars and teachers, and to be reserved to a circle of specialists. On this view the proclamation of the christian message should be confined to the 'simple words of the bible', and the preacher must at all costs avoid disturbing or leading astray the faithful in their 'childlike beliefs'. This way of escape is cut off. Whether we welcome it or deplore it, it is a fact that not only preachers, but congregations too have finally caught up with the questions of current exegesis. These have been publicly can-

INTRODUCTION

vassed in reviews, in the press and on the radio and television. The effect of this has been that discussion of the bible has been forced out of the lecture-rooms and brought to the public notice, and has aroused the interest not only of theologians but precisely of enlightened laymen too. The question of whether ordinary congregations should be made aware of the problems of modern biblical science or not has already been decided. They already know more than their anxious pastors would like to have them know. In the contemporary situation the question assumes a different form: Should the uneasiness and insecurity of the faithful be rendered still more acute by the fact that those who preach to them are ignorant of the findings of critical research, or should these preachers rather make these insights their own, make good their past neglect, and make a positive contribution to clarifying the situation? It is idle to dispute the question of whether it would have been better for the faith and for the church had there never been any such thing as biblical criticism. A debate of this kind would be just as meaningless as a discussion of the question whether the world would have been better off if natural science had never found the clue to the secrets of the atom. Unreal speculations of this kind are mere evasions of the real responsibilities which confront us in the present hour.

Moreover the question of what our attitude should be to the findings of contemporary exegesis is a question of truthfulness. All too frequently, and often justifiably, the faithful receive the impression that they are being treated as ignoramuses and that the full truth is being withheld from them. The proclamation of the word is dragged down into the twilight of a 'double truth'. He who suppresses questions which are really open, or misrepresents their true urgency, stirs up an atmosphere of unease and a lack of frankness. The difficulties which have been suppressed very soon make themselves felt once more in different and more dangerous ways. They create an atmosphere of mistrust and undermine the strength of men's faith. 'Those from within the church who are authorised by her to preach her message cannot advance in this task one single step until they have found an answer to the problem of how to be honest enough in their preaching' (Dinkler, 437).

It would be foolish and irresponsible for preachers to ignore the problems raised by biblical criticism. Instead of setting themselves in opposition to the insights which such criticism affords, these preachers should seize upon them and make them their own in order to achieve thereby a new awareness of the word of God as attested in scripture, and one that is more conformed to reality. It can hardly be said that in catholic circles we have yet achieved this positive and constructive encounter between the biblical science of our own times on the one hand and preaching on the other. It is to be hoped that the work which follows will contribute to this end.

The enquiry itself: its limits and methods

The exegetical enquiry

There can be no doubt that the question of hermeneutics as applied to the interpretation of scripture is of decisive importance precisely in its bearing upon preaching. Nevertheless we have not felt it advisable to make this the basis for our enquiry. What has been discovered as a result of the current discussion of this problem is not merely that hermeneutics has a special relevance here. Also, and much more than this, it has been shown that there is a real danger of sticking fast at mere considerations of method, and so losing sight of the real subject under investigation. What we are attempting is to work out as clearly as possible what the 'real content' of scripture is in its significance for preaching. Due attention will be paid to hermeneutical problems to the extent that they have a subordinate contribution to make to this basic aim.

For the task we have set ourselves we do not propose to tie

INTRODUCTION

ourselves to any one system of biblical theology. In the particular field which we have set ourselves to explore this would have the effect of making us especially liable to fall into the danger of an over-systematised approach. The new testament cannot be forcibly fitted into a single uniform theological system. It embraces a 'whole series of theologians with very different fields of vision, points of view and ways of looking at things. The educational equipment which they can bring to bear upon their common subject is in fact extremely varied in degree, and often the levels of abstraction at which they can grasp it are widely divergent. They put forward a wide variety of topics, the treatment of which is often only rudimentary or incipient, and which differ greatly one from another in their basic lines of development' (Schlier 1964, 9). We are attempting, then, to educe the message of scripture from individual pericopes (the form-critical aspect), and thereby to indicate the basic lines of theology adopted by the particular scriptural author concerned (the 'redaction history' aspect). Now this approach will also serve as a preparation for the kind of preaching which we have in mind; one that is concerned first and foremost with enquiring into the message of a prescribed passage of scripture, taking due account of its position in the series of pericopes to which it belongs.

To this end we shall need to analyse a number of individual passages, and this means that we shall need to select a limited number of such passages for investigation. We shall opt for the narrative tradition of the gospels as our general field of enquiry, and from this we shall select as our examples the Easter stories, miracle stories and infancy narratives. Within these general groups of narrative material we shall be making a still narrower choice along the following lines: first, with regard to the Easter stories we shall be treating of those in particular which, as they stand in the gospels, have been brought into immediate connection with the actual events of Easter. Second, with regard to the miracle stories, in selecting certain special examples of these here we shall have in mind the differences in type which these stories exhibit. Third, with regard to the infancy narratives, in the case of the Lucan infancy narrative we shall confine ourselves to the stories about Jesus and leave aside those concerning the Baptist. It can be seen, therefore, that our choice of material from the narrative sections of the gospels is most closely connected with our central theme. For it is in this particular area that the problem of historicity becomes acute, and it is precisely here too that preachers are most of all disquieted and confused by the exegetical findings of the critics.

Our exegetical investigations will not be confined to those pericopes which are to be discussed in the homiletic section, for we must perforce adhere to the existing arrangement of pericopes which has come down to us in the gospels. The only way of interpreting the individual Easter stories and infancy narratives which does justice to the facts is to take them in the broader context of the general thematic current to which they belong, as this occurs in each particular gospel. Again for our understanding of the miracle stories the use of a comparative synopsis is indispensable. This broadening of the field of investigation is not only required for a sound exegetical approach, but is also justified from the aspect of homiletics in view of the new arrangement of the pericopes to be arrived at.

The exegetical investigations which follow have preaching as their aim. In saying this, however, we do not mean to imply in any sense that we are treating of a special kind of exegesis, a 'practical' kind, as it might be called, as distinct from—or even as opposed to—'scientific' exegesis. The widespread opinion that the interpretation of scripture with a view to preaching should be 'less scientific and more practical instead' is decisively to be rejected. It leads directly to an irresponsible dilettanteism. For the purpose of publicly proclaiming the christian message in the church we must not, in practice, dispense with scientific exegesis. On the other hand—a point which will become apparent in the course of this work—scientific exegesis by itself is not enough. It points us on beyond

INTRODUCTION

its own limits to the task of actually proclaiming the word. To that extent the process of orientating our exegetical investigations upon preaching is fully in accordance with the realities of the situation. Indeed at basis it is *the* realistic way of interpreting passages of the bible.

The homiletic aspects of the enquiry
Practical theology is particularly concerned to achieve as precise an understanding as possible of the outward form and expression which preaching assumes today. If the renewal of preaching is to be achieved on the basis of scripture then it becomes indispensable to analyse comprehensively the practice of preaching as it exists today in relation to scripture. For this reason the first question which we raise in the homiletic part of our enquiry is this: In what form are the Easter stories, miracle stories and infancy narratives preached today? Can we already discern any influence here of the fresh insights which biblical science has to offer?

In an attempt to answer this question we have reviewed the sermons and allusions to sermons published in sermon collections and periodicals belonging to the post-war period in Germany, and having a bearing upon our particular theme. Certainly they do not give an immediate impression of what the practice of preaching has been. Nevertheless the publication figures, which are sometimes very high, do permit us to conclude that some sermons at least were widely disseminated, and to assume that they had a decisive influence upon the proclamation of the christian message in general. We can accept this all the more readily in view of the fact, which we know from experience, that preachers are so fully occupied already that they seldom take the time for any really basic preparation of their sermons, and instead of this rely upon models of preaching already in existence. In order to give as comprehensive a view as possible of the situation with regard to preaching as reflected in written works we have investigated all the models of sermons available to us from the last two decades, which treat of the group of topics described above. The range of material reviewed (about 1500 sermons) is too great for it to be possible for us to enter in any detail into any one of the examples cited. Our purpose in this has been to indicate the prevailing trends. In our evaluation of these sermons we have confined ourselves for the most part to the aspects opened up by the findings of exegesis with regard to the particular passages of scripture concerned.

We have confined our homiletic investigation to the last two decades because to a large extent it is only in this period that catholic exegesis has been able to open itself to the findings of biblical criticism and that, on the basis of this, some degree of influence upon the practice of preaching has become possible. We shall further confine ourselves to catholic sermon literature, because otherwise the material for examination would be unmanageably great. In view of the fact that the available sermon material adheres almost without exception to the existing arrangement of the pericopes as found in the gospels we have felt it right in the homiletic part of our enquiry to confine ourselves to those passages of scripture which have been taken as texts in this sermon material.

While it is necessary, and highly instructive, to take stock of the sermon literature under investigation from the point of view of biblical criticism, our concern for the renewal of preaching should prevent us from ignoring certain secondary movements and influences as well. We shall attempt to indicate these in the subsections entitled 'suggestions for preaching'. In doing this we shall be thankful to avail ourselves of the few genuinely scriptural aids to preaching which have appeared from the catholic side, and also of certain valuable suggestions for preaching which come from the protestant side.

The 'suggestions for preaching' should not be taken as complete sermon models in themselves. To a large extent they are still lacking in the factor of 'actualisation' which must be present in the sermon in the concrete situation in which it is preached.

INTRODUCTION

They are neither intended to, nor capable of usurping the inalienable function of the preacher, that namely of proclaiming the gospel to *his* congregation. This exemplifies a principle of practical theology which is axiomatic throughout. It is not the function of practical theology to provide completed blueprints.

The plan of this work

The plan of this work is determined by the nature of its subject-matter, which comprises the three groups of the Easter stories, miracle stories and infancy narratives. We have deliberately avoided adopting that line of approach which is in conformity with the historian's outlook, leading from the infancy narrative through the miracle stories to the Easter stories. The early christian preaching takes Easter as its starting-point. The Easter event is the key to our understanding of the gospel tradition as a whole, right up to the infancy narratives themselves. For this reason the Easter narratives are deliberately accorded the first place even though from the traditio-historical aspect the miracle stories must in part have been still earlier. The stories of the infancy of Jesus, which from the traditio-historical standpoint are the most recent, follow in the third part. Finally the fourth and concluding section of the work comprises a discussion of the basic conclusions which arise from the new approach to the study of the gospels in their bearing on our concept of preaching.

In the three main sections the exegetical investigation has deliberately been placed before the homiletic one. This serves to indicate that the text of scripture provides the standard by which sermon literature must be judged, and that the suggestions for preaching constitute further and secondary applications in relation to this.

Note on the English edition

(1) Since the German edition of this work appeared, the Roman lectionary has been completely revised. In consequence the twelve readings discussed in the homiletic sections (four to each of the three parts) which were those prescribed for Sundays and feast days, so that sermon material on them would be available for analysis, are in certain cases now read on week days. This means that the final part of each section, the short suggestions for preaching on the reading, cannot in those cases be directly used. But that was never the intention. They were meant as models of how to use the main part of the study, the exegetical material, by contrast with the sermons analysed. For convenience, tables are given, showing where this material is now assigned in the new Roman lectionary for Sundays and feast days, and where these and related readings are found in the Roman and Anglican lectionaries.

(2) The German edition contained extensive footnotes. These have been treated in various ways.

(i) In the exegetical sections (chs 2, 4, 6) and in the introduction and conclusion (chs 1, 8) footnotes which were extended remarks have been incorporated into the text. Where they gave the source of quotation in the text a short reference follows the quotation; full bibliographical detail is given at the end of the book. Cross-reference to other German literature has been eliminated, since it is not useful to the English-speaking reader using this translation rather than the original.

(ii) In the homiletic sections (chs 3, 5, 7) quotation references have also been eliminated where they refer to the many awful examples of bad preaching. Only a list of the collections of sermon literature on which the author drew has been retained, at the end of the book. These authors are completely unknown to English-speaking readers, who will in any case be able to supply examples from their own experience. In the final section, ch 7, some of the examples themselves have been removed, to avoid wearying the reader.

2
THE EASTER STORIES: EXEGETICAL INVESTIGATION

I Introduction

1 The Easter witness considered as a medium of early christian preaching

'If Christ has not been raised, then our preaching is in vain and your faith is in vain' (1 Cor 15:14). The resurrection of Jesus is —this is what Paul is saying—the basis and, at the same time, the medium of the christian faith. By it the preaching of the christian message stands or falls. This preaching lives because Christ lives and is alive in it. Hence it is that the witness to the resurrection of Jesus has become, right from the outset, the heart and centre of the christian kerygma. This is not only true of Paul and the tradition on which he bases himself (for this cf Schmitt 37–61). In fact the speeches in Acts do not, in their existing form, go back to the apostle himself but are recognisable, rather, as 'central elements in the Lucan theology' (Wilckens 188). Nevertheless, even as they now exist they enable us clearly to recognise that the assertion of the resurrection was already available to Luke from pre-existing tradition 'as a basic formula of the early christian kerygma which was ancient and universally disseminated' (Wilckens 150). The Easter witness stands at the origins of christian faith and christian preaching. From this it may reasonably be supposed that it acquired fixed form not merely in brief kerygmatic formulae, but also in the accounts given by those witnesses to whom the risen Christ had appeared. But for all this 'there is an undeniable tension between the uniformity of the actual *message* of Easter on the one hand, and the Easter *narratives* on the other, which are ambiguous and, from the historical point of view, problematical' (Bornkamm 1963, 166).

2 *Discrepancies within the Easter tradition*

The differences set forth
The Easter traditions of the evangelists and of Paul cannot be brought together or harmonised so as to constitute a single uniform picture. Wide divergencies are apparent in them with regard to the number of the Easter manifestations, the persons involved and the place time and circumstances in which they occurred. No two narratives agree with one another.

This applies even to the story of the empty tomb. In the manner in which this has been handed down, the individual evangelists manifestly disagree with one another on notable points, and specifically in their timing of the events concerned, as also with regard to the number of women involved and the motive of their visit, the number of the angels and the precise tenor of their message, and finally the reaction of the women to what had taken place.

When we go on from this to compare the earliest record of Easter in 1 Cor 15:3-7 with those of the gospels, then it is not long before we become aware of notable discrepancies. Paul refers to Cephas as the first of those who witnessed the risen Christ (1 Cor 15:5). In fact this is confirmed by Luke (24:34) almost in passing, and is also reflected in the final supplementary chapter of John (21) although here it is Galilee rather than Jerusalem, as with Luke, that is assigned as the place of the manifestation. Nevertheless the gospels contain no record of any prior manifestation to Peter alone. The following narratives do suggest themselves as possible parallels for the manifestation to the twelve mentioned in 1 Cor 15:5—Mt 28:16-20, with its powerful description of the manifestation to the eleven disciples on the mountain in Galilee, in which they were commissioned to preach; Lk 24:36-49, according to which Jesus appears in Jerusalem in the assembly of the eleven and their companions, who have also been joined by the Emmaus disciples; finally Jn 20:19–23, the manifestation to the disciples at a time when Thomas was not present. These three pericopes differ so widely from one another that they do not admit of any clear or unequivocal picture of the manifestation of the twelve attested by Paul. As for the manifestations before more than five hundred brethren and before James referred to in 1 Cor 15:6, these go altogether unmentioned by the evangelists. Again it is extremely difficult to find any parallel in the gospels for the manifestation mentioned in 1 Cor 15:7 before 'all the apostles' (although this probably involves a greater number than the 'twelve', cf 1 Cor 15:5).

But if on the one hand Paul is aware of encounters with the risen Lord of which the evangelists seem to know nothing, on the other he is silent about several manifestations which these latter do record. In the list of witnesses in 1 Cor 15:5–7 nothing is to be found corresponding to the Emmaus narrative (Lk 24: 13–25) or the story of Thomas (Jn 20:24–29) while the manifestations of Christ to the women (Mt 28:9f) and in particular to Mary Magdalen (Jn 20:11–18) go unmentioned. Mark too tells us nothing of this, and Luke (24:22–24) actually seems to exclude any appearance of the risen Christ to women.

It has already been indicated above that the evangelists are also at variance with one another in assigning the places at which manifestations occurred. Mk (16:7; cf also 14:28), Mt (28:16–20) and the supplementary chapter of Jn 21 assign the manifestations of the risen Jesus to Galilee. Luke (gospel and Acts) and John (ch 20) represent them as taking place in and about Jerusalem. The directive of the risen Christ not to leave Jerusalem before receiving the Holy Spirit (Lk 24:49) absolutely forbids us to assign any manifestations to Galilee.

With regard to the times which they assign for these events the sources agree with one another on the point that the resurrection took place 'on the third day', yet if we turn our attention to the interval between the resurrection and the first manifestation of Christ new and important differences appear. According to Matthew the risen Lord appears to the women on Easter morning. Twice the charge is laid upon them (by angels and by Christ himself) that they shall tell the disciples to go to Galilee for a meeting with their Lord. Now since this is a journey of several days the manifestation to the disciples cannot have taken place on Easter day, something which Mark too and the supplementary chapter of Jn 21 exclude. But this is precisely what Luke and John (ch 20) do record, and they assign the first manifestation to the disciples to Jerusalem. Finally, the accounts differ very strongly from one another with regard to what actually took place in and during the manifestations. Mark (16:7) confines himself to stating that there was a meeting with the risen Christ, but tells us nothing of what took place in it. The conclusion to the gospel of Mark (which is canonical though inauthentic) simply gives a resumé of the Easter narratives of the other gospels, and plainly does not belong to the original form of the Marcan gospel. Whether or not Mark originally ended with a 'manifestation story', or what form this would have taken, cannot be satisfactorily answered. According to Mark (16:8) from motives of fear and panic the women tell nothing of their experiences at the tomb, whereas according to Luke (24:9) they execute their commission straight away. In this version some of the disciples immediately test out the information about the empty tomb and find it confirmed (Lk 24: 24). In the Johannine gospel these are Peter and John, who make all speed to assure themselves of the truth of Mary Magdalen's tidings (20:1-10). According to Matthew the disciples show themselves totally uninterested in the tomb itself, but straightway set out for Galilee (28:16), whither the Lord has directed them through the message of the women (28:8, 10).

We must not overlook the differences in the way in which the encounters with the risen Christ are described. According to Matthew (28:17) as soon as the disciples catch sight of their

EASTER STORIES: EXEGETICAL INVESTIGATION

Lord they fall to their knees in adoration. According to Luke (24:37) on the other hand, they believe that they are seeing a ghost or spectre, and they fall into terror and alarm, while according to John (20:20) they immediately rejoice. On the other hand Christ appears once more in Luke in a guise that is almost natural, as though he existed in an intermediary state. He walks with the disciples of Emmaus (24:13–35) has flesh and bones which can be touched (24:39), takes a piece of broiled fish and eats it before the eyes of the astonished disciples (24:41–43) imparts instruction and a commission to them (24:44–49) and finally leads them out of Jerusalem to take leave of them 'in a manner not very different from that in which he once led them from Galilee to Jerusalem to the scenes of his passion' (Grass 45). The ascension—significantly it is only Luke who provides a description of this (24:50–53; Ac 1:9–11)—brings the intermediary state in which the risen Christ has existed to an end. Whereas Luke (24:49) represents Christ as only having promised the Holy Spirit to the disciples, according to John he actually bestows the Spirit upon them straight away on the evening of Easter day in order that they may fulfil their mission and exercise their official function of forgiving sins (Jn 20:22f). Easter, Pentecost and the ascension too are very closely connected with one another here. Matthew simply records a single manifestation of the risen Christ to his disciples (28:16–20). Here there is no need to touch him in order to overcome the disciples' doubts. The majesty of the word of the risen Christ is enough. It proves him to be the glorified Lord. The ascension and the sending of the Spirit go unmentioned in Matthew. The appearance of the risen Lord is not terminated. It remains open in virtue of the presence of the Lord promised for the time of the church.

What is true of the appearances of the risen Lord must also be said of the words of commission. The versions of these vary widely, and it is difficult to reduce them to a single common denominator. No doubt Jesus did explicitly send his disciples forth, but it still remains an open question how the content of his commission to them is to be determined in more precise detail, whether it took the form of a command to baptise (Mt 28:19) or to call men to repentance and to have their sins forgiven (Lk 24:47), whether it imparted authority to them to forgive or to 'retain' sins (Jn 20:23), or finally whether it actually took the form of a promise (to those who believed and were baptised), and at the same time of a threat of condemnation (for those who did not believe) as presented in the resumé supplied by the conclusion to the Marcan gospel (16:16).

This comparison of the Easter traditions is provisional, and in no sense exhaustive. It would be possible to adduce many more examples of divergencies within one and the same gospel. But as its outcome it leaves us with the disquieting conclusion that these traditions diverge from one another in certain notable respects with regard to the precise questions of where, when, to whom and how the appearances of the risen Christ actually occurred. It is impossible to reduce all these traditions to a single uniform amalgam of historical fact. Are we to conclude that the fact of these manifest and important divergencies is the one factor that pervades and unites all these narratives? How is this to be explained?

Attempted explanations which are untenable
'Those who implicitly presuppose, or even explicitly declare that all these various presentations of the manifestations of Christ are faithful to the historical facts and therefore to be brought into harmony—let these, I say, put themselves to the least care and trouble . . .' (Vögtle 283). The attempt to produce this harmony has frequently been made, and continues to be made. And writers go to fantastic lengths in order to reduce these presentations to harmony. But the results are always unsatisfying. Certainly it is justifiable to point to the fact that even in the purely natural sphere the same event is recounted in various ways by those who witness it, and it is reasonable also to

EASTER STORIES: EXEGETICAL INVESTIGATION

assume that each evangelist has selected a specific number from among the manifestations known to him, and has recorded only certain particular features of these. Nevertheless is this of itself enough to explain adequately the important differences between the various presentations? The attempts at harmonisation in the name of historical veracity are—very often motivated by apologetic considerations—for the most part devised at the expense of an over-hasty glossing over of the passages concerned and for this reason they are an obstacle to an accurate and faithful interpretation of these passages. They fail of their very nature and because of the intention behind them in the same way as the rationalist critics of the bible who, since the time of Reimarus, have supposed that they could prove the message of the resurrection of Jesus itself to be unworthy of belief by pointing to numerous inconsistencies within the traditions. In both cases the way to a true understanding of these traditions is blocked from the outset because the horizon of thought is artificially narrowed by applying the categories of historical positivism. The Easter narratives remain closed to one who employs them as he would any kind of historical source, or who treats them as though they were reports of accurately observed events, and then either forces them into an order that is artificial and arbitrary, or else plays them off one against the other in a way that is merely destructive. They are far from being records of a fact belonging to the natural world, able to be expressed in terms of it, composed by neutral observers of this fact. They are intended not to satisfy our curiosity but to bear witness to Easter and so to awaken our faith in it.

The discrepancies and inadequacies which have been so harshly thrown into relief by the higher critics can actually afford access to a deeper understanding of the passages concerning the Easter event. For however ingenious these attempts at producing either harmony or discord between the various versions may be, they are all subject to the limitations of an over-preoccupation with historicity. But the scriptures are above and beyond all such attempts, and are still capable of disclosing to us the true intention that underlies these stories.

II The Easter narratives

The Easter stories of the gospels do not belong to the earliest tradition. The Easter preaching begins with the simple witness of those individuals whom the risen Christ has encountered and who confess their faith in him. In the beginning there are brief confessional formulae such as Paul and Luke too (cf the speeches in Acts) have access to and which have been incorporated into what is probably the earliest passage on the resurrection which has come down to us, that namely of 1 Cor 15:3b–7. They contain no mention of the empty tomb (the word *etaphe* in 1 Cor 15:4 is used to emphasise the reality of the death, not the tomb —cf Lohse 1963, 115) or any of the more detailed circumstances of the manifestation, but are confined rather to the simple message of the disciples, overcome by their encounter with the risen Lord: 'Jesus has arisen!' 'Only then—this is clearly perceptible in the later accounts—do those who undertake the tasks of preaching and theological reflection attempt to render worthy of belief, each in his own way, the simple (1 Cor 9:1) witness of one who has actually seen and heard for himself' (HTG I 139). Versions emerge which expand and embellish the contents of the brief confessional formulae in the interests of preaching. The Easter narratives have their origin in the Easter message. Right from their origins they bear a kerygmatic stamp. The task of the exegete, therefore, is to enquire into the kerygma which they embody.

The Easter stories can be subdivided into 'grave stories' and 'manifestation stories'. The two traditions originally existed as two distinct entities, and it is only subsequently—one can hardly fail to notice the stitches by which they have been sewn together—that they have been fused.

EASTER STORIES: EXEGETICAL INVESTIGATION

1 The grave stories

All four evangelists record that women (or a single woman, cf Jn 20:1) discovered the tomb of Jesus empty. Their manner of recording this is extremely varied. At this point Matthew and Luke are dependent upon Mark.

(a) MARK 16:1-8

Mk 16:1-8 is connected with the preceding passion stories by the reference to the temple and by the mention of the women (16:1). The names of the women agree fairly exactly with those mentioned in 15:40, but are in part different from those recorded in 15:47. Various traditions have been incorporated here without being brought into harmony. Nevertheless the threefold mention of the women appears 'like a chain of witness' which 'holds together the three basic facts of the kerygma: death, burial and resurrection' (Lohmeyer 353). The Marcan grave story breaks off abruptly at 16:8. The pericope of 16:9-20 is missing in the earliest manuscripts.

Factors in the narrative which are historically improbable
Purely from an historical point of view the grave story remains, in many of its features, enigmatic. This applies even to the motive assigned for the women going to the grave: 'The desire to anoint a dead body "on the third day", when it has already been laid in the tomb and wrapped in linen cloths is, however we may seek to interpret it, unprecedented by any custom known to us, and, in the climatic conditions of Palestine, in itself contrary to common sense' (Campenhausen 24). Moreover, this would imply a provisional and temporary burial, which is clearly contradicted by the account of the burial which precedes it (15:42-47). Although the women (at any rate Mary Magdalen) saw with their own eyes that Joseph of Arimathea had rolled a stone before the mouth of the tomb, it only occurs to them when they are already on the way thither that they

cannot move it aside by themselves (16:3). This 'betrays a degree of thoughtlessness that is more than we can credit' (Campenhausen 24). The angel appears, in the Marcan gospel (apart from the summary references in 1:13; 13:27, 32) only in this passage (16:5). His message is cast in the form of an early christian credal formula. The conclusion of the narrative (16:8) strikes one as particularly strange: the women fail to carry out the commission of the messenger of God. They are silent. However improbable the grave story does in fact appear in certain of its aspects (it is significant that Matthew and Luke have altered the text precisely at these points) it is narrated in a restrained manner, and avoids any tendency to the fantastic. Nevertheless so long as it is made the subject of questions of historical detail it remains enigmatic. At the root of it lies the Easter message. It is this that we shall be seeking to enquire into in it.

What the story tells us
Immediately after the sabbath is ended three women who have been witnesses of Jesus' death (15:40) buy spices and set out to show their reverence and love for the dead man by anointing his body. In this they display very great zeal. They actually arrive at the tomb 'very early on the first day of the week just as the sun has risen' (16:2). 'It is possible that the timing of the events recorded has a symbolic significance: they come to the tomb at a time when Jesus has already risen. The sun has risen beyond the power of the grave' (Grundmann 1965, 322). The great stone lies before the door of the grave barring their way to the achievement of their object. It serves as a reminder of the stern boundary that denies them, who are living, access to him, who is dead; but at the same time it also draws attention to the magnitude of the miracle. For in their anxiety about the vast obstacle before them the women find themselves overtaken by events. The stone is rolled aside, the grave stands open. The women 'look up' (16:4), but they do not yet notice that some-

thing unusual has taken place. They are, as the evangelist intends to convey to us, so dominated by the thought of death and the grave that they altogether fail to perceive the signs of life (the sun and the open tomb).

The narrator presses on very quickly to the centre of his story. The climax of it is the message of the angel to the terrified women. From the inside of the tomb, from the place of death, the tidings of life issue forth. As in the early christian credal formulae, the announcement of the resurrection is combined, in the angel's message, with a reference to the cross. Jesus of Nazareth, the crucified one, has been raised by God from the dead (16:6). This key sentence of the *kerygma* is followed by the reference to the empty tomb. The sequence of ideas here must not be overlooked. It has a special significance for the apostolic preaching. The reference to the empty tomb does not precede the resurrection *kerygma*, but rather follows it as though it were intended as a striking interpretation of it. The primary factor is the *kerygma*. The essential point here is not the discovery of the empty tomb at the purely empirical level, but the act of God's revelation to which the empty tomb supplies an interpretation. In the intention of the narrator, therefore, this latter feature has a subordinate function, and points us on to the central factor, the tidings of the resurrection itself. It has no independent significance of its own, and is not intended to serve as a proof of the resurrection which is sufficient in itself. Deprived of the message of the angel it would remain incomprehensible. It is only the indications which he supplies that serve to show that the crucified Jesus has not remained in the tomb but has undergone a bodily resurrection. The Easter faith does not emerge from the mere fact of the empty tomb. It is only secondarily and subsequently that the attention of the women is drawn to this. It is not to the empty tomb that they are to summon the disciples and Peter; rather they must direct them to that meeting with the risen Lord which Jesus himself has already announced (14:28), and which is to take place in Galilee (16:7)—which does not belong to the original form of the pericope; cf Dibelius 1961, 192.

The reaction of the women to their meeting with the angel and to his message is astonishing: 'But they went out and fled from the tomb, for trembling and astonishment had come upon them...' (16:8). Where God intervenes so directly man falls into fear and panic. The silence of the women is manifestly the opposite of what the angel has told them to do: 'And they said nothing to anyone, for they were afraid' (16:8). It can hardly have been Mark's intention to give the impression that the women refused to obey the angel's commission. What he seeks to convey in this verse is how strongly the apostolic preaching is based upon the true foundation of the Easter faith. It is neither the speech of the women that has led the disciples to the faith (the apostolic witness exists independently of this; it is sufficient in itself), nor has the news of the empty tomb in any sense been the occasion of their faith (it has not reached their ears at all. The women have said nothing about it). The basis for their Easter faith is their encounter with the risen Lord.

(b) MATTHEW 28:1–10

The Marcan grave story was already available to Matthew, and he has significantly altered it by introducing the narrative of the guard posted over the tomb from the special material proper to his gospel. This is appended to the account of the burial (27:62–66) and its influence extends throughout his entire Easter narrative. It relates how the high priest and the Pharisees initiate a major intervention (on the sabbath!) to secure the tomb of Jesus. They suddenly remember the prophecy of his resurrection (right down to the individual details, and that too before Easter—this formula 'on the third day' is only found from the time of the apostolic preaching onward), and on the pretext that the body may be stolen they demand that Pilate shall post a guard over the tomb for three days. The guards are eye-witnesses of the events on Easter morning.

EASTER STORIES: EXEGETICAL INVESTIGATION

There is a mighty earthquake. An angel of the Lord descends from heaven, rolls the stone aside, and sits upon it. In the meantime the soldiers shake and tremble as though struck by lightning, and fall helpless as though they are dead (28:2-4). When they are once more restored to consciousness some of them give a report of what has occurred to the high priests (not to their Roman officers! (28:11-15)). Having received a heavy bribe from these, they disseminate the lie that the body was stolen by the disciples. 'And this story has been spread among the Jews to this day' (28:15).

Nowhere in the new testament is the resurrection itself described. It remains a mystery of God. Matthew is alone in recording miraculous events at the tomb. In fact he represents two neutral observers (Gentile soldiers) as having been present at the opening of the tomb, but does not attempt to unveil the mystery of the resurrection itself. Admittedly we feel that he does pave the way for subsequent attempts to draw aside this curtain of mystery. The apocryphal literature has been the death of this process in that it has sought to penetrate the mystery from motives of curiosity. The Gentile soldiers with their captain and the elders are eyewitnesses of what actually takes place at the resurrection, and hear the voices from heaven. The angels are not only messengers of the risen Lord, but also his assistants. The difference between this and the gospel *kerygma* is unmistakable. This latter is concerned not with the manner in which the Lord is raised to life, but with the living Lord himself, not with the circumstances of the resurrection, but with him who has risen. All these questions as to the manner in which the resurrection took place have no basis in the gospel, and are therefore designed to lead us astray from the true issue.

It is in this report of the Jews that the key to a right understanding of the story of the guard is to be found. It is intended as a counter to the accusation that the body was stolen. Gentile soldiers are among the witnesses who were present at the tomb.

They confute all the calumnious attempts of the Jews. The story is manifestly stamped with apologetic motifs dating from the period after Easter. Matthew has expanded the grave story in order to establish the reality of the resurrection of Jesus and to refute the polemical attack of the Jews against Easter.

Apart from the story of the guards at the tomb and the connected account of the opening of the tomb, Matthew adheres for the most part to his Marcan model. The differences are of no great importance: Mt (28:1) is aware of two women only (Mark records three) who intend to see to the tomb (not to the actual anointing; the guards have already been posted there). The message of the angel (28:5-7) is the same as that in Mark's gospel, though admittedly there is no separate mention of Peter. The women leave the tomb in fear and great joy and carry out their commission to the disciples as quickly as possible (this is in contrast to Mk 16:8). This commission is once more reiterated in the actual encounter with the risen Lord (28:9-10). In Matthew's grave story, as in that of Mark, it is the Easter kerygma that is central.

(c) LUKE 24:1-12

Luke too, like Matthew, is dependent upon the Marcan gospel in his section on the burial. Nevertheless he still keeps his own conception of the event and gives the story more firmness and cohesion. The differences, which are more the outcome of Luke's way of telling the story, are less important. The women (the number and the names of these are different, cf 24:10) prepare the anointing immediately after the burial, and do not wait until Easter morning to do so (Mk 16:1). The moment they enter the tomb they see that it is empty, and do not need to have their attention drawn to this fact by the angel after the message of the resurrection as with Mark and Matthew. Nevertheless the sight of the empty tomb does not arouse faith in them, but rather bewilderment. While the women are standing there dumbfounded two men appear (Mark and Matthew know only of a single figure) in shining garments (Lk 24:4; cf 9:30; Ac 1:10).

By comparison with his predecessors Luke has made considerable alterations in the resurrection message of these angels (24:5-7). Mark and, under his influence Matthew too, conclude the angel's commission with the statement, 'He goes before you into Galilee; there you will see him' (Mk 16:7; Mt 28:7). Luke transforms this sentence and makes it convey something quite new. In his version the word 'Galilee' is retained, but instead of being associated with an encounter with the risen Christ, it is brought into connection with earlier prophecies (cf 9:22, 44; 18:31-34). It was while he was still in Galilee that Jesus foretold his cross and his resurrection. Now it had taken place. It 'had to' come to pass in this way not because fate willed it so, but because it was decreed in the counsel of God. The term *dei*, used for the most part in the context of scriptural references, has a central importance in the mind of Luke: the life of Jesus from its beginning (2:49) right up to its end (24:44) is subject to the will of God which finds expression in scripture. Jerusalem, the holy city, is the scene of the Easter event. Here the promises are brought to their fulfilment. All the paths travelled by Jesus lead to this place. It is from Jerusalem that the risen Christ sends out his witnesses to the ends of the earth. Jerusalem is the central point and the turning point in saving history. In accordance with his conception of Jerusalem, Luke alters the sending of the disciples to Galilee into a recalling of earlier promises made by Jesus in Galilee, which point them on to Jerusalem. According to Luke Jerusalem and the temple are the scenes of the promise and the fulfilment of salvation. It is in the temple that Simeon and Anna wait for and receive the consolation of Israel and the deliverance of Jerusalem (2:25-38). At twelve years old Jesus journeys to Jerusalem with his parents and stays behind in the house of his Father (2:41-52). Jerusalem is the goal of his great journey with the disciples (9:51-19:27), and the temple is the goal of his entry into the holy city (19:45-48). It is in the temple that the salvific event is brought to its consummation: the cross, the Easter event and the ascension take place in Jerusalem. It is from here that the mission goes forth (Ac 1:8), and it leads to Rome, the world capital, which finds its place at the end of the Acts of the Apostles (on the significance of Jerusalem in the Lucan writings cf Conzelmann ET 73ff).

In remembering these things (in Luke 'remembering' has great significance) the women arrive at belief in Easter and become conscious in this of the fact that they are called to hand on this faith to others. It is faith (and not simply a special commission imparted to them) that is brought to others in the news they bring. They do not flee in terror from the tomb, and keep silent about what they have seen (Mk 16:8) but bear the good tidings to the disciples, though the response of faith which they meet with among these is only slight. To the apostles their unheard-of tidings appear to be so much empty gossip (24:9-11). They have no trust in the news they bring, and do not even consider it necessary to go to the tomb and test the credibility of this news at the actual scene. If they have arrived at belief in Easter then (this is what the evangelist intends to convey as a counter to false accusations) this has been the effect neither of what the women tell them, nor of the empty tomb. Luke knows that the empty tomb cannot provide any basis for faith. He turns his readers' attention away from the tomb to the risen Christ: 'Why do you seek the living among the dead?' (24:5). Everything leads up to this message: Jesus is risen.

(d) JOHN 20:1-18

The combination of different traditions
In his account of the events at the tomb John has combined two different traditions together: the story of Mary Magdalen's visit to the tomb and her meeting with the risen Christ (20:1, 11-18), and the story of the race between the two disciples (20:

2–10). The tensions between the two pericopes, especially in vv 2, 11, where the actual joins occur, are unmistakable. 20:11 gives the impression that it is only at this point that Mary looks into the tomb (20:1 simply states that the stone has been rolled away). Yet already in v 2 Mary tells the disciples that the tomb is empty. According to v 11 she is standing at the tomb, yet we have been told in v 2 that she has left it. We hear nothing of her return to it, and nothing either of a meeting with the disciples on their way back from it. 'According to vv 11ff she is standing at the tomb as though the episode recorded in vv 3–10 had never taken place' (Bultmann, 1964, 528). Then when she looks into the tomb Mary sees two angels (20:12), of whom there is no mention whatever in the description of the disciples' visit. Finally the command to tell the news to the disciples (20:17) is deprived of its significance if in the meantime the two most important disciples have already been brought to believe in the Easter event.

These few indications show that the stories fused together in Jn 20:1–18 were originally independent of one another, and do not constitute a single integrated historical presentation of the course of events on Easter morning.

Mary Magdalen's visit to the tomb (20:1, 11–18)
In the story of Mary Magdalen's visit to the tomb, motifs belonging to the synoptic grave stories can clearly be discerned, though admittedly in John they have been freely adapted. The synoptics mention several women by name. John records the presence of Mary Magdalen alone, without mentioning the motive for her visit to the tomb (Mark and Luke indicate that this was to anoint the dead Lord). She sees that the stone has been rolled aside, and hurries in alarm to the disciples to tell them that the body has been taken away (20:1f). Then she stands once more at the tomb weeping (20:11). For her the empty tomb is anything but a reason for joy, and certainly in no sense an occasion calculated to awaken her Easter faith. As in

the synoptics the reaction it produces is one of bewilderment, a state of mind which not even the angels can dispel (20:12f). It is only the risen Lord himself who brings her to believe and to proclaim the good news of Easter (20:14–18).

The race between the disciples (20:2–10)
Mary Magdalen is not the first to believe. Peter and John (20: 2–10) arrive before her not only in a temporal sense, but in the degree of their faith as well. At Mary's news they hasten to the tomb. On the way the beloved disciple overtakes Peter, but when they arrive at the tomb he allows him to take precedence. It is not easy to throw light upon the deeper meaning of this race. It may be that we should look to the relationship between Johannine and Petrine groups within the early church for the background to it. (Bultmann [9]1964, 531, suggests that the race is an image of the relationship between Jewish and Gentile christians.) Both disciples believe in the resurrection and, moreover, without having to have the empty tomb pointed out to them (as it is in the synoptics) through the angels' message or (as in the story of Mary) by the risen Lord himself. Indeed they arrive at belief in the resurrection even before they have understood the message of the scriptures on this point (20:9). The mere 'vision' of the empty tomb is of itself enough to bring them to believe.

This does not mean, however, that the empty tomb is taken as a 'proof of the resurrection'. The empty tomb is not a proof, but a sign that brings him who 'sees' to belief in the risen Lord. We can have no true understanding of the Johannine concept of 'seeing' so long as we regard '*horan* (considered as sense perception) and *pisteuein* as radically opposed' (Bultmann [9]1964, 539 note 3). The 'vision' which brings the disciples to believe is not one that takes place at the purely optical level. Rather it is a vision which is already pervaded and empowered by that faith which follows upon the manifestation of the sign and enables it to extend 'to the power inherent in the manifestation of Jesus, which quickens and illumines all things, that is to his *doxa* or glory' (Schlier 1964, 281).

EXCURSUS: ON THE SIGNIFICANCE OF THE EMPTY TOMB
Attention has already been drawn to the fact that the Easter message takes priority over the Easter stories. There are two senses in which this is true. Our examination of the grave stories has established that the key sentence of the *kerygma* (cf the angelic message) takes priority in terms of time and, over and above this, has shown that in terms of content as well it deserves unquestionably to be regarded as the most important. This appears from its actual position in the stories, where it is placed not only at the beginning but also at the centre. The stories themselves are only to be understood from this key message at their centre. The empty tomb has no independent value of its own in the *kerygma*, and does not serve as a proof of the reality of the resurrection before the apocryphal gospels.

It is not the case at all that those who find the tomb empty believe in the resurrection. On the contrary, the sight of it arouses fear and terror. The empty tomb evokes not enthusiasm and joy, but rather alarm and bewilderment. The news of it is incapable of inspiring any fresh hopes (Lk 24:22-24).

Considered purely as a fact there are numerous ways of interpreting the empty tomb. It is open to misinterpretation and is, in fact, misinterpreted right from the outset. We can clearly recognise this from the gospels themselves in that they react against such misinterpretations (for instance that it was a trick of the disciples, or that the body was stolen, Mt 28:11-15; Jn 20:6f, 13). The message of the empty tomb is first and foremost simply: 'He is not here' (Mk 16:6). At most it can serve to indicate that a dead man has returned to this world. But this is still far from raising any question of faith in the resurrection of Jesus. It was not because of the empty tomb that the women came to believe, and far less did they have faith *in* the empty tomb. If they actually saw it for themselves then it was the object of their sensible perception and not an object of faith. The gospel narratives, therefore, enable us plainly to recognise that the empty tomb was neither a reason for, nor the object of belief in Easter. Its function of pointing on to the truth of Easter is only brought to our notice by the message of the angels: 'He has risen. He is not here' (Mk 16:6). Our notice is drawn not to the empty tomb, as though this could supply a reason for believing, but precisely away from the tomb: 'Why do you seek the living among the dead' (Lk 24:5). The angels point us on beyond the tomb to the risen Christ himself. The women are to call the disciples not to the tomb but to the encounter which they are to have with the Lord. 'In this sense the empty tomb directs us away from itself... and towards the centre of the event. It is not intended to be made a subject of speculation in its own right, but probably is intended to prepare the way for the unheard-of event of resuming relationships with him who has been laid in the tomb' (G. Koch, 163f).

That this is, in fact, the situation, is underlined by the fact that in the traditio-historical development of the grave story the connection is drawn ever more closely between the manifestation of the risen Lord and the tomb. Mark (16:5-7) and Luke (24:4-7) simply speak of an angelic apparition at the tomb. Matthew makes this angelic apparition (25:5-7) lead on to a manifestation of the risen Lord (28:9f) although he does not assign any special significance to this (Christ has no more to say than the angel). In John the angelic apparition (20:12f) is thrust into the background by comparison with the manifestation of the risen Lord (20:14-17) and comes to be almost devoid of significance.

The empty tomb has no independent message of its own to convey. It points to the risen Lord, and that too in a special respect. It serves to show that he who has risen is Jesus of Nazareth, the crucified one and no other. He is not a being who comes wholly from the other world, but is rather that Jesus who has lain in the tomb. However true it may be that the resurrection is a new and unheard-of event, and one that is outside all the categories of human experience, still it cannot be separated from the person of Jesus. Cross and resurrection are connected together and related to one another by the fact that one and the same person is their common subject.

The stories of the empty tomb have the function of contributing to the Easter *kerygma*. The message of the angel which points us away from the tomb to the manifestation itself defines the limits of its significance and these limits must not be overstepped. Faith in Easter did not emerge at the empty tomb, but rather in the encounter with the risen Lord. It is upon this that the apostolic preaching is based. Paul has found it possible to proclaim the gospel in full without ever mentioning the empty tomb.

If then the stories of the empty tomb assume a subordinate function within the Easter message as a whole, it follows that the question of its historical content should not be elevated into an *articulus stantis et cadentis* of the Easter faith. 'The headlong zeal with which some exponents of the apologetics of the resurrection have hurled themselves upon the empty tomb and the proof it allegedly supplies is to be rejected as unsound. To state the matter as sharply and explicitly as possible, we might express it by saying: we believe not in the empty tomb, but in the risen Lord' (Grass, 185).

In the researches of biblical criticism the grave stories are generally described as 'legends'. But this designation of literary form is intended neither as a decisive answer with regard to the historical problem involved, nor—and this must be emphasised above all—does it constitute a negative judgment on the essential message which these stories are intended to proclaim. The use of the term 'legend' is often based upon an extremely indiscriminate and inadequate understanding of this literary type, which gives occasion for confusions and is guilty of stoking the fires of the 'biblical controversy'. According to one view that which is designated as 'legend' or 'legendary' is *eo ipso* devalued as being unhistorical, or even quite untrue. 'This is an extremely superficial and inaccurate interpretation, which in itself prevents any serious form-critical consideration' (K. Koch, 209). Against this interpretation it must emphatically be stated that the legend is wholly capable of expressing truth, indeed that it can impart realities which are not available to the historian to grasp. Furthermore attention must be drawn to the fact that 'the concept of literary type as such does not imply any judgment, whether negative or positive, about the historicity of the particular account to which it is applied'.

In the case of the grave stories the historical question is not easy to answer. Those who regard it as self-evident that the verdict should be in the negative are often just as culpable in failing to provide proof for their view from an accurate and objective examination of the actual passages involved as those who show an exaggerated confidence in traditional apologetics. 'If we examine what is capable of being examined, we cannot, in my opinion, avoid the conclusion that the information we are given concerning the empty tomb itself and its discovery at an early stage must be allowed to stand. There is much to be said in favour of this view, and nothing compelling or decisive against it. Therefore the information is probably historical (Campenhausen, 42). Grass is prepared to concede 'that the gaps in the evidence required to establish the historicity of the empty tomb are extremely narrow' (184). Grass gives the impression that he maintains these narrow gaps in being not so much because of any historical findings as because of a specific preconception of what physical resurrection must mean (*totaliter-aliter*).

The grave stories have a subordinate contribution to make to the Easter message. They serve to illumine the message of the angels which occupies the central position in them. In this message witness is borne to the fact that the crucified Jesus of Nazareth has risen from the dead. The women receive the commission of announcing to the disciples that they are to meet the risen Lord. It is this meeting that we are told about in the second group of Easter stories.

2. *The manifestation stories*

If we abstract from the canonical conclusion of Mark, the direct literary interdependence of the synoptics ends at Mk 16:8. In the stories of the manifestations of Christ each goes his own way. At the same time the traditions upon which they draw do converge at various points. This applies not only to the content of the stories but to their formal structure as well (cf Nineham, 9–35). Above all they are united by their common subject: they bear witness to the fact that an encounter took place with the risen Lord.

(a) MATTHEW 28:16–20

Matthew has drawn together the various manifestations of the risen Lord to his disciples in the powerful concluding scene towards which the entire gospel is orientated, and which supplies the basic standpoint from which it is intended to be read. The scene of the event is Galilee (28:16) in accordance with the charge given by the angels (28:7) and confirmed by Jesus himself (28:10). For the disciples it is there that the Easter event begins. The place of the manifestations is disputed, but probably the first (official) manifestation should be assigned to Galilee. This view is supported by the earliest tradition (Mk 16:7; Mt 28:10, 16; Jn 21:1). After the disciples had returned to Jerusalem manifestations took place there also, as attested by Luke and John (ch 20). The exact geographical location of the mountain is not determined, but is understood to be a traditional scene of revelations (cf 5:1; 15:29; 17:1).

The story omits any precise details of how the event concerned took place. No word has been left to us in it concerning the manner and circumstances of the manifestation. Instead it takes all this for granted in the words 'when they saw him' (28:17). It is far from conveying any idea that the manifestation of

Jesus took a quasi-natural form. Any reaction on the part of the disciples (terror, Lk 24:27 or joy, Jn 20:20) to what they see remains unmentioned. Matthew confines himself to the bare statement that there are some who doubt. The motif of doubt constantly recurs in the manifestation stories (Lk 24:11, 25, 37f, 41; Jn 20:24–29; Mt 28:17; Mk 16:11, 13, 14). This reflects the problem with which the later community was confronted in that it was no longer in a position to 'see', and responded with scepticism to the statements of the witnesses. The witnesses to the resurrection are presented as individuals endowed with a critical judgment, whose own initial attitude of reserve and mistrust had to be overcome. It is this that makes their witness credible. This scepticism of theirs is not overcome by any assurances which the evidence of the senses can supply, but solely by the word of power uttered by the risen Christ himself. It is this that supplies the basis for the disciples' assurance of the reality of Easter. It is Matthew's answer to a question put to him by the community for which he is writing, at a time when the manifestations already belonged to the past; the question, namely, of what belief in Easter was based upon. Matthew's answer is to point to the word of the glorified Lord.

The brief narrative sections in 28:16f lead up to 28:18–20. These verses contain the word of power uttered by the glorified Lord (v 18b), his missionary charge (19, 20a) and the promise of his support (20b). One element in the word of power gives expression to the fact that the risen Lord has been inaugurated as *Kyrios* over heaven and earth. In comparison with the actual rising from the dead far greater emphasis is laid upon this element in the scene as a whole. The glorification brings salvation to its fulness and creates a new situation. While the *exousia* (power) of the earthly Jesus is still limited, it now undergoes its predestined expansion to a dimension that is world-wide. It gives him power for his missionary charge, and provides the basis for his command to preach to all nations. The manifestation of the glorified Lord and his summons to his disciples to preach to the Gentiles are closely connected with one another (v 19, *oun*). Mission implies proclamation of the dominion of Christ. It is 'not merely in a superficial and external sense' that the command to go forth and preach constitutes 'the centre of the whole group of sayings' (Dinkler, 175). The eleven are charged with the task of making disciples of all the nations. In a few brief and pregnant words the state of discipleship (the church) is more precisely defined in terms of baptism and obedience to the commands of Jesus. The reference to 'all that I have commanded you' (v 28) makes the church the upholder of the binding force of these words uttered by Jesus during his earthly life. The glorified Lord is no other than the Jesus who lived for a time upon this earth. Here, as throughout his gospel, Matthew sets his face against a purely 'pneumatic' type of christianity which is totally emancipated from law (cf Bornkamm *et al* ET 159–64). The reference to the giving of the Spirit is omitted, and instead of this greater emphasis is laid upon the commandments. We must not follow those dreamers and fanatics who pass over the earthly Jesus and make the Spirit a substitute for him.

He is with those who are his own right to the end of the world. Thus the disciples' meeting with their risen Lord in the present endures throughout the age of the church. In Matthew's version of this episode there is no mention of leave-taking or ascension into heaven. The Lord who appears here in the present is the glorified Lord and henceforward his presence in the church is continuously to endure. The glorification has taken place at Easter. 'Ascension and glorification as a separate episode taking place *after* the resurrection, as in the Lucan and Johannine Easter narratives, have no place in Matthew's version' (Dinkler, 173 note 16). Resurrection and glorification, glorification and mission, the historical Jesus and the glorified Christ, Jesus Christ and the church—all these are united to each other in the closest possible manner.

In Mt 28:16–20 the hand of the evangelist can clearly be

discerned. He has brought together the various traditions available to him, and fitted them into a single concluding scene in which he sums up his entire gospel. 'The individual statements are presented in a series of theological clauses which are carefully constructed in precise and polished terms' (Trilling ³1964, 48). They reflect the liturgical and missionary practice of the community, but also the theological conception of the evangelist himself. As is attested in v 20b the early church is assured of the presence of her Lord. For this reason she has felt able, here as throughout this gospel, to transform the tradition and to adapt and apply it to her existing situation in the sure conviction that in the proclamation of the christian message in which she herself is currently engaged the message of the risen Lord will be faithfully reproduced.

(b) THE EMMAUS NARRATIVE (LK 24:13-35)
The Emmaus narrative carries us into a conceptual world that is different from that with which we are confronted in the concluding scene of Matthew's gospel. In accordance with Luke's own way of thinking the story unfolds in and about Jerusalem. The risen Lord meets two disciples on their way to Emmaus. So far as his outward appearance is concerned there is no difference between him and a normal man. He converses with them and lets them invite him to supper as though he had reassumed, once more, the natural and physical mode of existence. It is not until he suddenly vanishes from their sight at the supper table that he exceeds the limits of this natural mode.

The two disciples leave Jerusalem. They turn their backs on the place of salvation to which Jesus had led them (9:51—19:27). So far as they are concerned their journey with him is at an end. They have separated themselves from him and go their own way. They are apostates. Their journey must be understood in the context of Luke's own ideas: he who does not remain in Jerusalem thereby forfeits the promise (cf Lk 24:49; Ac 1:4) his eyes are 'held' (24:16). Hence it is that once the disciples' eyes have been opened and they have recognised the Lord, in that same hour they return to Jerusalem (24:33). It is not until the 'power of the Most High' has come upon them (24:49) that they will be sent for from Jerusalem (cf Ac 1:8).

As they are proceeding on this journey of theirs Jesus himself draws near to them and accompanies them. They relate to this unknown companion of theirs the story of Jesus of Nazareth which still fills them with disquiet (24:19-21). The Jewish authorities have caused him to be crucified. Their hope lies buried with him in the tomb. Even the news brought by the women and confirmed by certain other disciples that the tomb is empty has done nothing to alter this state of affairs. The empty tomb has been incapable of freeing them from their state of bewilderment and loss, and even the message of the angels that Jesus is alive, brought to them by the women, has failed to arouse any fresh hope in their hearts. The stranger replies to the disappointed travellers by opening the scriptures to them (24: 25-27). It is in the light of the fact that the Lord has entered upon his glory and has risen from the dead that their meaning becomes clear. Easter is the key to the understanding of scripture. Proof from scripture is a factor which plays a significant part in Luke's theology, running like a scarlet thread through the Lucan Easter story (cf 24:26f, 44, 46).

On arriving at their journey's end the two disciples ask their companion to stop with them for the night (24:28f), and at the evening meal he takes the bread, gives thanks, breaks it and gives it to them (24:30). He is the same as he who took the five loaves and two fishes, and having looked up to heaven and blessed them, broke them and gave them to his disciples (Lk 9:16). And again that last meal which they ate together took the same form: 'He took bread, and when he had given thanks, he broke it and gave it to them' (22:19). United through this shared meal their eyes are opened and they recognise him (24: 31). Though in the selfsame moment he disappears from their view, they have experienced, in his word, and in the meal eaten in common with him, his own presence; and this inspires them to bear witness to him. Yet the community assembled in Jerusalem has already anticipated them in this: 'The Lord has risen indeed, and has appeared to Simon' (24:34: Peter has pre-eminence over the disciples of Emmaus, who are less important than he). The confession of the community confirms their own message (24:35).

The story of Emmaus is the most developed of the Easter narratives. Numerous parallels are to be found in the traditions of other peoples to that element which constitutes the dominant motif in this story: God comes in human form in the guise of a wanderer upon the earth, attaches himself to men in order to reveal himself to them, and then vanishes as soon as he is recognised. In Gen 18:2 this motif can plainly be discerned: three men come to Abraham at Mambre and are taken in by him as his guests. In their persons Yahweh himself imparts a promise and a prediction to Abraham. In respect of its form the Emmaus narrative stands extremely close to stories of this kind both within and without the sacred scriptures. Its narrative motif must have been derived from these. Admittedly, in that it is attached to the meeting of the disciples with their risen Lord, something which has taken place in space and time, it is no longer restricted to expressing religious promptings and experiences. In Jesus Christ it is made real, embodied in concrete history, and it is in this form that it becomes an element in the message of Easter.

The essential message of the Emmaus narrative is this: Belief in Easter and assurance of the reality of the Easter events on the disciples' part is based upon their encounter with the risen Lord. An encounter of this kind—this is what Luke intends to convey, with an eye to the needs of the post-Easter community —is not simply confined to the occasion of a public manifestation and reserved to the eye-witnesses alone. It is also possible today. Christ is journeying at our side even though perhaps he has long gone unrecognised there. In listening to his word and in the union achieved in the common meal our ears and eyes and hearts are raised to the point where they can recognise him and confess him.

(c) THE MANIFESTATION TO THE DISCIPLES ASSEMBLED IN JERUSALEM (LK 24:36–49)

The manifestation of the risen Lord to his disciples at Jerusalem is attached to the Emmaus narrative but the connection is rather loose. The point at which the actual join occurs is unmistakable: where the manifestation to Peter and the disciples of Emmaus evoked reactions of joy, here the dominant reactions are once more fear and alarm.

Like the Emmaus story this narrative too enables us to recognise that the disciples did not arrive at their Easter faith from their own resources, but were brought to it in spite of themselves. The initiative in bringing this about lies wholly on the side of the risen Lord. At first when he appears to them those gathered together believe that they are seeing a ghost. But they receive palpable signs which enable them to convince themselves that it is, in fact, the Lord. And when this is still not enough wholly to dispel the doubts of the disciples he eats a piece of broiled fish before their eyes (24:36–43). The risen Lord reminds the disciples of what he has told them during his earthly life, and solemnly reiterates once more: it 'had' to come to pass in this way (24:44). As in the case of the two travellers on the way to Emmaus, he discloses to them how the scriptures are truly to be understood. Once again he shows that suffering and resurrection are the fulfilment of what 'has been written concerning me' (24:44). From this point onwards too the task is laid upon them of preaching repentance and forgiveness of sins to all peoples, beginning from Jerusalem. Here the disciples are to wait until they receive the promise of the Father, 'the power from on high' (24:49). Here the promises are fulfilled, and from here their way leads out to the peoples to whom they are to bear witness. 'This commission constitutes Jesus' final word to his disciples in Luke's gospel, and the whole history of Jesus converges upon it. It was in Jerusalem that everything had to be consummated, and in Jerusalem that the history of the church begins' (Lohse 1961, 38). The Acts of the Apostles will recount how the witnesses carry out their commission, and how the way they have to travel leads from Jerusalem to Rome.

EXCURSUS: ON THE BODILY PRESENCE OF THE RISEN LORD

The description of the manifestation of the risen Lord in Lk 24: 36–43 is extremely full and detailed (the same is also true of Jn 19:19–29), and precisely with a view to the preaching of the word, this needs a more detailed explanation.

(i) What is true of the interpretation of the bible in general applies here also. The question of who the recipients are of a given section of scripture or a given narrative in scripture is of decisive importance for our understanding of it. As has been made apparent several times already in our expositions up to this point, the evangelists enable us plainly to discern that the Easter preaching met with the most strenuous resistance. They have, for instance, to counter the accusation that the body was stolen (cf Mt 28:11–15; Jn 20:1f, 6f) as well as the calumny that the news of the resurrection derives from the gossip of women (cf Lk 24:11, 22–24). Similar apologetic tendencies are also to be discerned in the background of Lk 24: 36–43 (as well as in that of Jn 20:19–29). The objection of the opponents of christianity which has prompted this extremely realistic presentation of the facts may be stated as follows: you have seen a ghost (cf 24:37) and have been following a phantom; or, put in modern terms, your faith is based upon a vision which is purely subjective in character. In reaction against this it is emphasised: a ghost has neither flesh nor bones (24:39). The risen Christ has allowed us to know him by physical touch (24:30–43).

The emphatic message which the narrative is intended to convey is that the risen Lord is one and the same as the crucified

EASTER STORIES: EXEGETICAL INVESTIGATION

Jesus of Nazareth (cf the touching of the hands and feet in Lk 24:40; Jn 20:20) and, against all tendencies to 'spiritualise' the resurrection after the manner of the docetists, it firmly insists upon the fact that he was present in the body. The resurrection is in no sense confined merely to the 'immortal soul', but embraces the whole man.

These, then, are the particular statements in these accounts of the manifestations of the risen Lord which are of special importance for the kerygma. They are apologetic in character and intended to counter false accusations, and in this way bear witness to the reality of the encounter with the risen Lord. This is a point which must not be overlooked. We shall misinterpret the narrative if we use it as an occasion for speculations about the exact constitution of the risen body of Christ. In these stories an attempt is made to hold together the two notions of the risen state, on the one hand, and the physical mode of existence on the other. This creates a tension which it is all but beyond our powers to control. But we must not, on that account, use these stories as a pretext for producing rationalising definitions intended to resolve this tension. The apologetic motivations should not be viewed in isolation or regarded as the point of departure for the Easter preaching, or even as the central factor in that preaching. Rather they must be interpreted in the light of what is in fact central to the apostolic *kerygma* of the resurrection.

(ii) A factor which is certainly not without problems of its own, yet which is, in certain respects, necessary as an aid to the interpretation of scripture, is the distinction between the form and the content of the statements in scripture. In the case of the Easter narratives we must not simply shrink from applying this distinction. However important it may be that the Easter message must be retained in all its fullness, it still remains true that in the Easter narratives we should not accept simply at their face value either the cryptographic symbolism of Jewish apocalyptic, which is subject to the conditions of a particular epoch, or those modes of expression which have an element of the mythological in them. We should not simply transfer these unaltered to our own modes of thought and expression, presenting them as statements which are binding upon us in faith. It cannot be claimed that ideas of this kind have binding force merely on the grounds that they represented dominant influences in apostolic times and for this reason found their way into the new testament. When the fresh insights which we have today achieved make it necessary to call these in question, this does not mean that we are throwing doubts upon the actual contents which they are designed to express. Those who fail to realise this distinction will, in their exaggerated apologetic zeal, regard faith itself as *ipso facto* called in question in cases in which it is only the mode in which it is expressed that is being discussed. It is precisely the apocalyptic ideas in scripture that must 'to a large extent be re-thought out, though this does not mean that the reality to which these images point need itself be discarded' (LTK I, 1050).

Apocalyptic ideas were current at that time which were influenced by a misinterpretation of Ez 37:1-14. According to these ideas the resurrection of the body entails a restoration of the earthly mode of life. The dead bones are knit together, covered with flesh and skin, and the whole rises out of the grave. All this does not belong to the actual content of Easter. Furthermore it entails the hidden danger of supporting and fostering those ideas in which the resurrection is conceived of as a return to the conditions of daily life upon this earth. Easter precisely does not imply a mere return of a dead man, a fresh beginning in which the former course of life is resumed and continued after a temporary interruption. Luke too, however full and vivid his presentation of the facts may be, attests the fact that the risen Lord has entered upon a new mode of existence. His startling manifestation of himself and his sudden disappearance plainly point to the fact that his present mode of existence is different from that of earthly life.

(iii) The new testament narratives do not yield any unified picture of the physical mode of existence entered into by the risen Christ (for instance cf Mt 28:16–20 with Lk 24:36–43). A wide variation is discernible between the statements on this point, and yet obviously they are set side by side in the new testament. From this it must be concluded that the narrator's ideas on this point have remained open, and that the details of the description are to be understood as expressing something possible but not something which it is absolutely demanded of the reader that he shall accept.

The manifest divergencies in the gospel presentations serve to point the difficulties involved in combining the two notions of resurrection and physicality, and in describing a reality for which there is no counterpart in our conceptual world (not even in the raising of the young man of Nain, the daughter of Jairus or Lazarus, all of which belong to a totally different dimension). Instead it is promised that there will be something to correspond to this reality of the resurrection in the future, namely the resurrection of the dead. 'Somewhere between the sheer solidity involved in this idea of physical existence on the one hand, and a spiritualising interpretation of the event on the other, lies the truth' (G. Koch, 231). Paul employs the paradoxical formula *soma pneumatikon*, spiritual body (1 Cor 15:44).

In interpreting the Easter narratives, therefore, a point that must not be forgotten is that '... what the apostles, being themselves as yet unachieved, were able to experience of this consummation, is a somewhat broken, translated experience, and that even then it still remains obscure' (Rahner 1956ff ET II, 214). The terms in which it is sought to give expression to this reality are not adequate to the reality itself in the same way that the description of a scientifically observable process of nature is equal to its subject. It is useful to bear this in mind as a safeguard against the erroneous idea that we can have the same kind of knowledge of the reality thereby expressed as we can have of some area of 'this-worldly' reality from the description that is given it. It is beyond the limits of our thought-categories to conceive of, or to express the mode of existence of the risen Lord. Closer investigation into this question must be rejected as futile.

(iv) The encounter of the risen Lord with his disciples is a personal event. The significance of this is not that 'something' is exhibited by way of demonstration; at the central point of the manifestation we find the words '*ego eimi autos*, it is I myself' (Lk 24:39). It is significant that in the gospels, unlike the apocryphal writings, Jesus manifests himself not to neutral observers or even to his opponents in order to win them over by confronting them with objective evidence. Certainly through their encounter with him the faith of the disciples is placed on a fresh footing. But what is unfolded to them before all else in virtue of the fact that their eyes are opened is that dimension in which alone such an encounter is possible at all. The risen Lord does not let himself be wholly grasped and comprehended as something which can be completely and clearly understood. He withdraws himself from the view of the disciples just as surprisingly and just as uncontrollably as he has revealed himself to them (Lk 24:31). However much the physical aspects of his manifestation are emphasised, this manifestation still evokes terror and doubt, and the effect of it, as we are told in paradox, is that the disciples do not believe for very joy (Lk 24:41). Moreover it is nowhere mentioned that the chance they are offered to touch him is in fact taken.

It is precisely the particularly realistic narratives of Lk 24: 36-43 and Jn 20:18-29 that convey to us that here it is faith that is in question. It would be to distort these narratives to the opposite of what they really mean if we were to conclude from them that the disciples were enabled to assure themselves by direct experience of the reality of the risen Lord, or that the supernatural proof offered them was so overwhelming that they were, in effect, spared the effort of believing. 'This would lead to the grotesque conclusion that those who were the first to preach faith were themselves not called upon to believe, but were rather dispensed from this duty by the fact that they actually saw' (Ebeling ²1965, 64). Their seeing is a seeing with the eye of faith.

(d) THE DEPARTURE OF THE RISEN LORD FROM THE DISCIPLES (LK 24:50–53)

The Lucan Easter stories lead on to the narrative of the Lord's leave-taking and ascension into heaven. The transition is abrupt. It has the effect of bringing the ascension into direct connection with the resurrection. It takes place on 'Easter day'. The scene of the event is Bethany, which for Luke was next to the Mount of Olives in the neighbourhood of Jerusalem (Schlier 1964, 229). In the act of blessing his disciples the risen Lord takes leave of them and is carried up to heaven. It is the completion of a process which began with the passion. 'From now on the Son of Man shall be seated at the right hand of the power of God' (22:69; cf Ac 2:33–36). Hence the disciples adore him. They fall prostrate before him and acknowledge him as their Lord. The manifestations, together with the entire earthly life of Jesus, have been brought to their close.

Even though Jesus has separated himself from his disciples, they are not filled with the pain of leave-taking: 'They returned to Jerusalem with great joy' (24:52). Not only have they seen their risen Lord, but they are also assured of his promise of the Spirit. They therefore praise God in the temple. The gospel of Luke begins and ends with this element of joy in the good tidings from God. It begins when these good tidings are announced to Zechariah (1:13–17; cf also 2:27, 37, 46) and it ends here with the praises offered to God by the disciples. Here the promise of the old covenant is fulfilled and, in the power of Christ, opens out into the age of the church. The messiah of Israel is the Lord of the church and the saviour of the world.

The ascension of Jesus
Where the gospel of Luke ends with an account of the ascension, the Acts of the Apostles begins with it. This serves to indicate the fact that in the Lucan writings taken as a whole the ascension 'represents a supreme milestone and turning-point' (Schlier 1964, 227). This indication is confirmed by other observations independent of the ascension narratives. In the structure of the third gospel 9:51 has a significant part to play. After the information given in this verse Jesus begins his journey to Jerusalem. 'As the days drew near for him to be taken up into heaven.' Certainly the term *analempsis* here refers not merely to the ascension but to the death of Jesus as well. For in fact it is with this that that exaltation of him actually begins (in Lk 22:69, 'from now on') which comes to its consummation in the ascension. Yet it is significant that this saving event of the death of Jesus is presented in the perspective of the 'taking up' of the ascension (cf the term *anelemphthe* Ac 1:2, 22) while this in turn is thereby made into an element of decisive importance in saving history itself. Luke then sums up the whole of Jesus' work as the 'time that the Lord Jesus went in and out among us, beginning from the baptism of John until the day when he was taken up from us' (Ac 1:21f). We can only rightly understand this central function of the ascension in the context of specifically Lucan ideas.

For Paul and Mark with the advent of Jesus, and above all with his death and resurrection, the final age is already present. The new aeon brings the old one to an end. The parousia is already imminent. Luke is dominated by an awareness of the delay of the parousia. The eschatological tension and compression of the time after Easter is relaxed, and the conception of time involved is extended. Mark speaks of the *coming* of the Son of Man (14:62), Luke of his coming *again* (cf Ac 1:11). His first advent is brought to an end with his enthronement at the right hand of God (cf Lk 22:69; Ac 22:33–36). This has its counterpart in the parousia, now understood as a second coming. The resurrection recedes into the background in its function as a turning-point by comparison with the ascension. 'Whereas in the other gospels the events after Easter are presented in a manner that is strangely abrupt and devoid of that continuity which belongs to our natural thought-patterns, dim and mysterious in the extreme, Luke prolongs the continuity of the life of Jesus right up to his ultimate manifestation' (Lohfink, 76). The manifestation of the risen Lord is described almost in the same manner as an encounter with the earthly Jesus. 'Nowhere does the risen Lord bear so few of those traits which belong to a Lord who has already been exalted into heavenly glory as he does in Luke' (Grass, 45). The same is true of the account of the ascension, correlative to the realistic presentation of the appearance of the risen Lord.

We can only rightly understand the ascension of Jesus if, while taking due cognisance of the fact that it has been incorporated into the Lucan scheme of ideas, we do not fail to recognise also its connection with the resurrection. It takes place in the course of a manifestation of the risen Lord. This in itself warns us not to think of it as similar in character to the ascension of Elijah (2 Kg 2:1–18). It is not Luke's intention to depict a mysterious 'taking away', a single continuous movement which leads from our world into the world beyond. (This is not to contest the fact that in the tradition of the ascension adopted by Luke in Ac 1:9–11 ancient ideas of 'takings up' in the manner of the ascension of Elijah or of figures of later Jewish apocalyptic such as Henoch would have been in the background and would have served as precedents.) He is proclaiming the exaltation of the Lord. Just as the witnesses have 'seen' the Lord in his risen state, so too they have seen him exalted or, better, they have 'seen' him exalted *in* his risen state. 'This means that taken in its precise meaning the ascension is the actual happening of the awakening of the dead to life. It is that awakening, made accessible to the witnesses involved, which their own natures are to undergo, and in which they are to be brought to their consummation. It is, as it were, "the obverse side of the resurrection" (Vilmar), and its final sealing' (Schlier 1964, 242). The transcendent event of the resurrection and exaltation of Christ is made manifest in the appearance of the risen Lord. Luke unfolds both aspects of this manifestation: the encounter with the risen Lord (resurrection) and his ascension (exaltation).

The fact that two different accounts of the resurrection exist side by side in the twofold work of Luke confronts his interpreters with a serious problem. Attempts have not infrequently been made to solve this by regarding one or even both of the accounts concerned as interpolations. But it is arbitrary and unjustified to force the text in this way, and fails to carry conviction. Those who take this view overlook the fact that the twofold account of the ascension is in conformity with the fact that Luke's own work is twofold, and that Luke's own central conception too envisages a basic reality. So far from representing a mere repetition one of another, each of these accounts has a function of its own to perform in its particular place, and gives expression to different theological aspects. This is not intended to suggest any sharp cleavage into two different epochs found side by side and completely separate from one another. It is precisely the ascension, considered as the exaltation of Christ to the right hand of God, that holds together the two aspects in what follows. It is the single 'way of the Lord' (ie of God) which finds its realisation in the way of Jesus and in the way of the christian mission (the church). This is by contrast with the widespread theory, deriving from Conzelmann, that Luke's gospel is constructed on a schematic plan based on a division of saving history into three epochs (the time of Israel; the time of Jesus at the centre of time; the time of the church). This is not in accordance with the mind of the evangelist himself.

In Lk 24:50–53 the ascension represents the point of conclusion appended to the earthly life of Jesus. Our gaze travels back to the essential stages leading up to it (death and resurrection 24:46). Jesus' earthly career and, included in this, his manifestations after the resurrection, have been brought to a close. Now follows the separation. Clear expression is given to the distance which this implies: '*dieste ap' auton*, he parted from them' (24:51) in sharp theological contrast with Mt 28:20, 'I am with you always'. In fact the mission mentioned in 24:47 already points on to the future, yet it is held back for the present by the explicit commandment to remain in Jerusalem and there to wait for the Spirit (24:49).

The account of the ascension in Acts 1:9–11 is dominated by a different theme. It has a second point to convey about the ascension over and above the fact that it constitutes the closing point of the gospel (Luke clearly refers to that in Ac 1:2). Thus what emerges here is a double truth: the ascension now opens up to our view a vision that extends forwards to the age of the church. It opens the way to the coming of the Holy Spirit. The exalted Lord sends out his disciples in the power of this Spirit to the ends of the earth (Ac 1:8). The dividing line which marks off the age of the church is precisely delineated: the ascension as the point of departure is set over against the second coming as the point of conclusion. The special importance of the ascension narrative in Ac 1:9–11 is constituted by its bearing upon the 'interval' that lies between these two points, the present age of the church. Now in the present, we are told, we must look not upwards to heaven (1:11) but forwards and outwards to the ends of the earth, and in our witness point to the exalted Lord as the living power of the present.

(e) THE MANIFESTATION STORIES IN JOHN 20

The most significant turning-point within the manifestation stories of the fourth gospel is marked by the division of the chapters. The gospel originally ended at 20:30f. Chapter 21, with its second conclusion in vv 24f, plainly reveals itself as a supplement. It expands the Easter tradition of Jerusalem in ch 20, to which Luke has already borne witness, by adding to it the Galilaean tradition on which Mark and Matthew also draw. This chapter evinces a special interest in the figure of the beloved disciple (cf 21:7, 20–23), and places the gospel as a whole explicitly under his authority.

The traditions which the fourth evangelist has incorporated in ch 20 are unmistakably related to those drawn upon by Luke. In this respect the Johannine gospel too enables us to discern here a stage which is later in terms of tradition history. The progressive intensifications of the motifs involved must not be overlooked.

The manifestation of the risen Lord to Mary Magdalen (20:11–18)
According to John the first appearance of the Lord on Easter morning is to Mary Magdalen on her second visit to the tomb. The angels have been unable to console her. When she turns back and sees Jesus, however, she fails to recognise him, and believes that it is a gardener with whom she has to deal. Her eyes, like those of the disciples of Emmaus, are 'held'. In order for her to recognise the Lord they first need to be opened. Mary must not hold the Lord; he has not yet ascended to the Father. She is given the task of telling the good news of his exaltation to the disciples.

The meeting of the risen Lord with Mary focuses upon the words which he utters and the message which she is told to convey to the disciples: 'Do not hold me, for I have not yet ascended to the Father, but go to my brethren and say to them: I am ascending to my Father and your Father, to my God and your God' (20:17). When Jesus appears to Mary he is already on his way to the Father. She must not hold him back, for this would constitute an obstacle to the paths by which each of them respectively has to travel: Mary would be held back from going to the disciples, Jesus from going to the Father.

EASTER STORIES: EXEGETICAL INVESTIGATION

Once he has passed on to the stage of exaltation and glorification with the Father it is no longer possible to have and to hold Jesus as it was in his earthly life. He has not simply returned from the dead (like Lazarus). With his resurrection a new mode of existence commences which, at the same time, makes possible a new mode of being with him. For his ascension to the Father opens the way for the sending of the Spirit and by that very fact bestows at the same time that fullness of union with him which has been promised in the farewell discourse. Thus 'the state of "not seeing and still believing" (cf 20:29) which constitutes the true encounter with Christ which is signified and intended, also represents the true fulfilment of the promise implicitly contained in 20:17' (Thüsing, 276).

Precisely when the ascension to the Father takes place is not established or even represented in spatial terms. The evangelist 'precisely refrains from recording this as a process which can be assigned a location in time or space. The reader of the gospel learns nothing whatever about any point in time for the going up to the Father' (Thüsing, 273). He, just as much as the evangelist himself, must refrain from speculating about the process by which this took place. The point of this account is the theological assertion that the descent of Jesus from the Father (Jn 1), his 'going forth' from him, has its counterpart in that movement which raises Jesus up already in his earthly life, comes to its climax on the cross (considered as the throne of Christ the king, cf 12:32), and terminates at the right hand of the Father.

Where Luke, dominated by his awareness of time as extending out into the future, characterises the ascension as the turning-point between the age of Jesus and the age of the church, the fourth evangelist understands the passing over (13:1) and going up to the Father (3:13; 6:62; 20:17) involved as a single overall process, and refrains from pointing out in any precise sense its individual elements. Both bear witness, each with his own special vision, to the fact that the exaltation of

Jesus is his way to the Father and that which makes possible the sending of the Spirit.

The manifestation of the risen Lord before the disciples assembled in Jerusalem (20: 19–23)
Attached to the manifestation to Mary Magdalen is that further manifestation which is granted to the group of the disciples. To some extent this is prepared for by Mary's own tidings (20:18). The story here is extremely close to that of Lk 24:36–49.

'At evening on the first day of the week' (Jn 20:19) in spite of the doors being closed, suddenly and in a miraculous manner Jesus is standing in their midst. He makes himself known to them by the marks of his passion. That he shows these marks in his hands and side, not his hands and feet (Lk 24:39) is a way of connecting the present scene with 19:34, the piercing of the side with a lance (cf Thüsing, 171–3). There is no doubt. The risen Lord is he who was crucified. He has not laid aside his earthly history. On the contrary, in his glorification this has attained to its goal, and it is only now that it achieves its full significance. The disciples rejoice to see their Lord (cf 16:22). After reiterating his salutation of peace he lays upon them the commission of continuing his mission in the power of the Holy Spirit. In this Spirit he also imparts to them authority to forgive sins.

Jn 20:19–23, in common with many other passages in the fourth gospel, shows that 'the presentation of a fact is an "image" for an all-embracing theological reality' (Thüsing, 267). This is not to say that the manifestations of the risen Lord have here 'only that relative value which the *semeia* (signs) have in general, or that their true significance "is" a symbolic one' (Bultmann [9]1964, 533). These manifestations are not on the same plane as the *semeia*. 'They are not merely signs of that which Jesus will be for those who believe when the age of the Paraclete comes. Rather, in a real sense, they actually introduce this age' (Thüsing, 287 note 1). And yet their reality is not that of mere external brute facts. 'The special style of the evangelists, with its meditative characteristics and its sense of imagery' (Thüsing, 267), renders the events which are presented transparent, and enables us to look through them to a deeper level of theological reality that lies beyond.

The crucified Lord, bearing the marks of the wounds as his distinguishing characteristics, lives and bestows life upon others. His manifestation is, as it were, a window through which we see the coming of the Spirit, and it inaugurates the age of the Spirit in which the promises (above all those of the farewell discourse) are fulfilled. He bestows upon his disciples that peace which is more than a private spiritual joy, or one that is merely 'interiorly' satisfying. This joy imports salvation (cf 14:27). The encounter with the Lord releases joy, and a joy, moreover, that is not the mere transient joy of a temporary leave-taking, but eschatological joy which is inspired by the fulfilment of salvation (16:22) From the wound in his side the stream of living water gushes forth. When he breathes upon them (cf Gen 2:7) the Spirit goes forth from his body. The body still has a function to perform as the medium of the bestowing of the Spirit, for in his exaltation Jesus remains wholly human. By the glorification this Spirit has been released, and is bestowed upon those who have come to believe (7:37–39). In the Spirit Jesus is present among his disciples, and continues to work in their mission, which is itself a continuation of his mission from the Father. Through the Holy Spirit the disciples are given authority to pronounce forgiveness for sins or to withhold it (20:23). Their mission, like the mission of Jesus himself, summons men to the radical decision: so long as the world believes it stands acquitted, but if it withholds itself in unbelief it stands condemned (cf 3:18f; 16:8–11).

It is the risen and glorified Lord bearing the marks of his wounds who bestows the Spirit. Good Friday, Easter, Ascension and Pentecost are viewed together and projected into one another. In this way an epitome of the whole gospel is provided, which 'opens our view to the age of the Paraclete without turning our gaze away from the figure of Jesus. The age of the Paraclete proceeds from the consummation of Jesus' earthly work' (Thüsing, 269).

The story of Thomas (20:24–29)
Jn 20:11–18 relates how the risen Lord encounters an individual person. Jn 20:19–23 tells us of his manifestation before the community. Jn 20:24–29 describes how he manifests himself to a single individual in the community. While in Jn 20:13–23—different in this from the manifestation stories of the synoptics—there is no mention of doubt, now this factor is 'presented in the instance of Thomas taken as a representative model' (Haenchen 1966, 558). Here, in fact, a special story is devoted to the subject of doubt. On the occasion of the manifestation to the disciples Thomas is not present. He refuses to be impressed by their witness. He demands that he himself shall touch the marks of the passion. The Lord agrees to his demand but there is no mention of the touching taking place. The renewed manifestation terminates with the pronouncement of a blessing upon those who do not see and yet believe.

In terms of realism the manner in which the manifestation of the risen Lord is presented and expressed is at its strongest in the pericope on Thomas. It has been available to the evangelist from a pre-existing tradition. It betrays clear apologetic interests. The term *ophthe*, see, is palpably directed against gnostics and docetists.

With regard to the meaning of the manifestation stories it is no part of the evangelist's mind to describe these as miraculous occurrences of the most extreme kind at the external level. The phrase 'Do not hold me' is by itself enough to give the clearest expression to this fact (20:17; see above), and the point is deliberately underlined through the criticisms of the faith of Thomas (20:29). Both passages make it clear that the evangelist 'is protesting against the idea that the resurrection of Jesus should be presented as a return to earthly life' (Haenchen THLZ, 896f) or that it is sought to provide assurances of its genuineness by purely empirical means. It does not render faith superfluous, but rather demands it: 'Do not be faithless but believing' (20:27). However unmistakable his rejection of mere miracle faith may be, the evangelist does not for one moment intend to present the Easter manifestations as 'dispensable', or to indicate in any sense that the word of Jesus 'alone' has power to convince (cf Bultmann ^{9}1964, 539f). Such an interpretation subjects the 'mode' of revelation to that modern axiom which deprecates every interpretation that is plain and straightforward as an overpreoccupation with brute fact, and seeks at any price to get rid of it. It fails to do justice to the contemplative style of the fourth evangelist, and his deliberately anti-docetist emphasis. 'With regard to the tension asserted by the modern exegete to exist between the sheer blunt presentation of facts on the one hand, and their inward kerygmatic significance on the other, he has not yet become aware of this, or at least not in the form in which they present it. Rather he has known how to unite both elements, the factualness of the facts and their inward meaning' (Grass, 62). The saying to Thomas bears not upon the manifestation (which in fact in this particular instance precisely does lead to faith) but the doubter himself, and that too because he demands this manifestation and because of the manner in which he demands it.

Abstracting from the supplementary chapter, Jn 20:29 is the final definitive word of the Lord in the gospel, and points on beyond Thomas to the age in which the risen Lord will no longer be manifest. In this age of the Paraclete, the age of the church, faith will be based on witness. Those who, in this age, still continue constantly to demand to see are condemned, and those who believe in the word of the witnesses into which the vision has entered ('We have seen the Lord' 20:25) are pronounced blessed. In his encounter with the risen Lord Thomas makes confession in the name of the community, and in their

words, that he is the true God: 'My Lord and my God' (20:28).
The gospel leads up to this concluding confession of faith. Here
Jesus is acknowledged for what he has been right from the beginning (1:1). Here the confession of faith of the church of
Jesus Christ as a whole is epitomised.

(f) THE MANIFESTATION STORIES IN JOHN 21
Whereas ch 20 tells of manifestations of the risen Lord in Jerusalem, in ch 21 the scene of the events is the Sea of Galilee.
21:1 and 21:14 represent a loose redactional connection with
the preceding episode. Originally the narratives in Jn 21 referred to the initial manifestations. It is only in virtue of their
present context in the gospel that they have been relegated to
third place (cf 21:14, where no account is taken of the manifestation to Mary Magdalen). It evidently presupposes that
'after the catastrophe the disciples have returned to their homeland and their former callings, and that they are astonished by
the appearance of the risen Lord at this point' (Grass, 76).

The manifestation of the risen Lord at the Lake of Tiberias (21: 1–14)
The pericope is extremely close to Lk 5:1–11. Both go back to a
single common tradition which Jn 21:1–14 relates as an Easter
story, whereas Luke presents it as a vocation story belonging to
the outset of Jesus' work.

As though the imparting of the Spirit and the mission had
never taken place at all it relates how, at Peter's suggestion,
seven disciples return to their craft as fishermen. During the
night they catch nothing. Yet the next morning, when all unrecognised (cf Lk 24:16) Jesus bids them launch out their nets
for a second draught, it brings them a success that is overwhelming. Then the eyes of the beloved disciple are opened and he
recognises: 'It is the Lord.' When Peter hears this he leaves the
boat and swims to Jesus. After the other disciples too have
brought the ship to the bank, and Peter has drawn the net to
land, Jesus shares a meal with them.

The narrative is thickly strewn with expressions which are deeply symbolical, though admittedly it is hardly possible to bring their significance to light down to the last detail. The catch of fish itself is indicative of the mission which the risen Lord bids them undertake. In spite of their barren toil during the night, next morning the Lord himself bids them launch out their nets for a second draught, and at this their nets are filled. The meaning of this is given clear expression in Jn 15:5: 'He who abides in me, and I in him, he brings forth rich fruit, for without me you can do nothing'. The beloved disciple is the first to recognise Jesus, and to utter his confession of Easter faith: 'It is the Lord' (21:7). Peter is the first to draw the right conclusions from this, and he hastens to him. As in the episode of the race between the disciples, so too here the relationship between Johannine and Petrine circles lies in the background of the narrative (cf Grass, 78). The fact that in spite of the great quantity of fish the net is not broken is a sign of the unity of the church and the fact that Peter draws it to land is an indication of the special authority accorded to him (cf vv 3, 7). A satisfactory explanation of the number of fish caught has hardly been arrived at so far.

There is a certain tension between v 12 and v 7, and v 12 serves to characterise the situation which the scene as a whole is intended to depict. It reflects the peculiar tension of the disciples themselves in relation to the risen Lord: 'It is he, and yet it is not. It is not he whom they have known hitherto, and yet it is he!' (Bultmann [9]1964, 549). The embarrassment of the disciples is only dissipated at the meal (21:13) which Jesus has prepared for them (21:9); at the Lord's supper he continues his fellowship with them through communion. 21:13 in the terms and expressions it uses plainly points to the eucharist.

Peter is vested with the authority of shepherd (21:15–19)
Jn 21:15–19 contains an originally independent element of tradition which is close to that of Mt 16:17–19. In spite of the

redactional note inserted at 21:14, the pericope is directly joined to the preceding passage. What is described here takes place 'after the meal' (v 15). Attention is concentrated upon one of the disciples, namely Peter. The others recede into the background.

A striking feature is that Jesus repeats his question as to whether Simon loves him three times (vv 15, 16, 17). Manifestly there is a play here upon the threefold denial of Peter (cf 18:15–18, 25–27) (cf Cullmann, ET 190), and it becomes clear that he who is here inaugurated as shepherd has himself gone astray and must first be brought back. He lives in the power of the Lord's forgiveness. It is no merit of his that he receives the office of shepherd. Furthermore the sheep whom he has to pasture are not his sheep, but the Lord's ('Feed *my* lambs (or sheep)!' vv 15, 16, 17). Peter is asked whether he loves the Lord three times. This love is the necessary prior condition, the decisive criterion for the fulfilment of his task. In this love he is summoned to follow the way of his master, and is to follow his leadership even to the point of martyrdom (21:18f).

(g) THE CANONICAL CONCLUSION OF MARK (16:9–20)

The Marcan gospel too has acquired a supplementary addition composed by another hand and telling us of manifestations of the risen Lord. The earliest and best manuscripts conclude with 16:8. It is here too that the course which the synoptics have all in common followed finds its conclusion. Even among the fathers of the church several (Eusebius, Jerome) are unfamiliar with this supplement. At the same time its antiquity must not be underestimated. Justin, Tatian and Irenaeus attest this. It would have been composed in the first half of the second century AD. Subsequently it would have been appended to the gospel of Mark, and thereby have found its way into the canon (the canonical conclusion of Mark).

Mk 16:9–20 is not conceived of as a conclusion to the gospel. The gospel itself breaks off abruptly and then the supplement begins immediately and without transition. 16:9 performs the same function as 16:1. The section provides a summary survey of the manifestation stories of the three other gospels, a kind of epitome. It is intended 'not to relate matters which are unknown, but to rehearse what is already known' (cf Lohmeyer, 361). It may be derived from the early christian catechesis.

Mk 16:9–11 tells of the manifestation of the risen Lord to Mary Magdalen, and is related to Jn 20:1, 11–18. 16:12f sums up the Emmaus narrative (Lk 24:13–35). The third manifestation in Mk 16:14 is concerned with the assembly of the eleven for a meal. Here Lk 24:36–49 (cf Jn 20:19–23) is being drawn upon. Mk 16:15–18 contains elements of an earlier tradition. 16:15f is related to Mt 28:16–20, but is not merely to be understood as echoing this. 16:19 presupposes the Lucan narrative of the ascension. The final verse reflects the missionary practice of the church as described in the Acts of the Apostles. Here the presence of the Lord (cf Mt 28:20) receives special mention.

The interpretation of the individual verses and groups of verses, loosely connected with one another as they are, must be conducted in the context of the corresponding Easter narratives in the rest of the gospel traditions. The relevant passages have already been treated of in the preceding pages, so that here we can dispense with any detailed analysis. Although Mk 16:9–20 arranges elements of various traditions in a loose sequence, its arrangement of these is, nevertheless, stamped by specific theological motifs. It is these that we propose to indicate in what follows.

The actual structure itself is composed with a specific end in view. The manifestations are arranged in climactic form. Mary Magdalen—the two travellers—the group of disciples. Special weight is also attached to the third manifestation in virtue of the fact that the missionary command is connected with it and that the ascension is attached to it. The 'process by which unbelief is brought to believe' (Grundmann ²1965, 328) is thrown into relief as the dominant aspect of the pericope. 16:11 and 13 lay emphasis upon the unbelief of the disciples in response to the Easter witness of Mary Magdalen and the disciples of Emmaus, and this brings about a tension between 16:13 on the one hand and Lk 24:34f on the other. According to 16:13 the risen Lord rebukes the unbelief and the hardness of heart of the eleven (cf 8:17–21). 16:16 represents faith and—as the outcome of faith and that for which faith is a prior condition—baptism, as necessary for salvation, and at the same time emphasises that unbelievers incur condemnation. 16:17f describe the (charismatic) signs which are to characterise the lives of the believers. It is a theme that is central to the second gospel that in his work Jesus constantly meets with unbelief and misunderstanding on the part of his disciples, that faith is not their achievement but his. This is a point which the conclusion of the Marcan gospel also brings out emphatically. A later reviser has still failed to understand the problems involved here, and has supposed that he has to excuse the disciples. Thus he has interpolated immediately after v 14 an apologetic defence of the disciples (the so-called Freer-Logion) in order to deprive the rebuke of the risen Lord of its sting.

A further theme, side by side with that of belief and unbelief and closely connected with it, is that of preaching, to which there is renewed reference in Mk 16:9–20. Both Mary Magdalen and the disciples of Emmaus are conscious that through their encounter with the risen Lord they have been called to bear witness. The manifestation of the risen and exalted Lord (cf 16:19) leads up to the missionary command (16:15f). The passage here draws on the Lucan tradition of the exaltation and dominion of Christ, treated of above. The effect of this is that the overcoming of unbelief and the task of preaching are brought into such close association that it actually appears that there is an intrinsic connection between them: Easter faith is made real in preaching. 'Thus the effect of the overcoming of unbelief and temptation, in brief the event of divine grace, is that man is taken into service and, precisely in virtue of this, inaugurated into faith' (Schweizer 1967, 218). Faith implies a bearing of witness. Thus the section is brought to its conclusion with a reference to the missionary activity of the church which, in the power of her Lord, proclaims his dominion everywhere.

III Concluding implications

1 The kerygmatic structure of the Easter narratives

The Easter tradition in the new testament confronts us—this was the point with which our investigations opened—with a problem which is disquieting. The Easter witness is, in fact, unequivocally to be recognised as the foundation, and at the same time the medium of the early christian preaching. Nevertheless ambiguities and discrepancies do occur between the Easter narratives, and these do create an undeniable tension. We have sought to avoid suggesting any premature solution to this tension. By setting out the divergent traditions side by side we have brought out this tension in all its sharpness. At the same time, however, this has had the effect of making visible the basic line of argument in each individual passage, and its overall intention. These passages will not yield any result if we adopt the sort of approach in which we institute comparisons and harmonisations on a purely historical basis. The basis of their unity is to be found in a broader and more comprehensive dimension: in the acknowledgement that God has raised Jesus of Nazareth the crucified one from the dead. The mode in which this universal witness is expressed varies. In a new age, under new circumstances, the ancient Easter message is not simply repeated. Matthew's view of it is different from Mark's. In the Johannine gospel it acquires a different form from that which it has in Luke. Each one proclaims it from his own standpoint and at the particular moment in history which belongs to him. This means that in proclaiming this universal witness he is occupied with the particular questions, objections and attacks which affect his own community and cause them disquiet.

Both factors, therefore, belong together: the witness itself, which is central and universal, on the one hand, and the form in which it is proclaimed, which varies in each individual case on the other. The Easter narratives comprise a unified proclamation which is dynamic and full of tension. They must be viewed in their historical contexts. Thus the conclusion to be drawn from the Easter tradition of the gospels themselves is that preachers today, unlike those of former ages, cannot simply reproduce the Easter message, but must express it as 'new'. The historical situation is an integral element in the reality of this message.

2 *On the historical question*

However important it is to recognise the kerygmatic structure of the Easter narratives this structure does not imply that Easter faith is 'not interested in the historical question' as Bultmann puts it, calling the argument of 1 Cor 15:3–8 'unfortunate' (in кuм, 47). This view is contradicted by the unequivocal witness of the new testament Easter tradition itself. In attempting an answer to the historical question certain distinctions have to be drawn. The new testament does not recognise (and in this it is fundamentally at variance with the apocryphal writings) any human witnesses of the resurrection itself. It knows only of witnesses to the risen Lord. The resurrection of Jesus, as the Easter narratives enable us to recognise is, in a strict sense, an eschatological event which exceeds the bounds of the conceptual horizon by which we are circumscribed. If it were an event on the level of 'this worldly' experiences, comparable to the return of Lazarus to his former mode of life, then death would have been something that Jesus constantly still had to face rather than something that he had put behind him. But according to the witness of scripture his resurrection is the deed by which he breaks through into a new dimension, one which 'leaves behind' the course followed by the old world, subject as it is to death. This is a 'new' world, a 'new creation'. There is no way within this present world which we can point to or win for ourselves which leads out of the 'old' creation into the 'new'. The resurrection of Jesus must not be thought of on the same plane as the purely historical processes of which we can have knowledge, nor even on the same plane as the events belonging to his earthly life, for instance that of the cross. One who knows what is meant by historical research, and what is being asserted in the resurrection of Jesus from the dead, cannot suppose that the resurrection can be proved by historical arguments. There is no way leading to the risen Lord which by-passes faith. As has been shown above, the empty tomb cannot be accorded any weight as a proof of the resurrection. Moreover scripture (and here again it differs notably from the apocryphal gospels) knows of no neutral observers of the manifestations of the risen Lord, but only witnesses who believe.

This is not to say that the resurrection of Jesus is simply a creation of faith. The Easter narratives of the gospels are not convictions *of* faith but witnesses *to* faith. They attest the fact that prior to any presence of Christ in the *kerygma* of the church he has risen as the crucified Jesus of Nazareth 'in himself' and apart from any witnesses. The force of this phrase 'in himself' is in no sense such that it is a mere prop or support for something that 'properly speaking' takes place within ourselves. Certainly it is not to be understood from a position of detachment or neutrality, but in faith alone. But at the same time the Easter event which is laid open to the eye of faith is not located in us, but rather rooted in the action of God which was wrought upon Jesus. The Easter narratives leave no room for doubting the fact that it was not of themselves that the disciples arrived at Easter faith, but that they were overcome from a position of disbelief and apostasy in their encounter with the risen Lord. It is not *kerygma* and church that provide the points of departure. Nor is it merely a question of the 'meaning' of Jesus continuing to make its impact. What is in question here above all and as the basis of all is the person of Jesus himself, and that too not as existing in some kind of 'prolongation' (prolongation of life, prolongation of the event). What is in question here, rather, is something radically new: the new creation which God has founded in him. However great the possible dangers may be of objectifying our modes of expression, the force of the expression 'in itself' as applied to the resurrection of Jesus must be maintained as the origin of the Easter event. Otherwise it would follow logically 'that in his death Jesus was abandoned by God and remained abandoned, that it was not God who was made present to him then but only ourselves. Then even as far as we are concerned we would be acting in a way that was unjustified and vain' (Kessler BiKi 22, 22).

What we can assure ourselves of as a matter of sheer historical fact is this: men bear witness that they have seen Jesus after his death. They have related his 'manifestation' to the resurrection of the crucified Lord, and have regarded this as the basis for their faith. The message that is brought to us under the sign of witness (not of proof) is this: the risen Lord did not remain hidden. He has encountered men in space and time. The 'new creation' has been manifested in the 'old'. Eyes have 'seen', ears have 'heard' and the hearts of men have been touched. The Easter event has entered into the dimension of 'seeing' and 'hearing', and into the words of the witnesses. It has been brought down to their limited human categories and possibilities of expression. These are never identical with the event itself, but surely do serve to indicate it and make it possible for something new to happen. Therefore the Easter narratives are not 'at basis dispensable' or mere 'concessions to the weakness of humanity' (Bultmann [4]1961, 409). They show that the Easter event is not merely an interior event of importance for the believer's own understanding of himself, but also an event that arises in space and time and is relevant to them; an event which makes it possible for objective statements to be made about the encounter which certain specific individuals had with the risen Lord. Through such statements the encounter itself is not simply made a pure statement of fact and objectified. The intention of the witnesses, in fact, is not that their narratives 'shall be understood as bearing upon the "matter in the abstract". By them they intend to point on as witnesses to him about whom and in the power of whom they have written and borne witness' (G. Koch, 205). As witnesses in this sense of the encounter with the risen Lord which has taken place in history and is itself historical, they are of fundamental importance. If they are eliminated and set aside as of no importance, then the danger can hardly be escaped of degrading the Easter proclamation to an unhistorical myth.

The Easter stories of the gospels 'preach in narrative form and present the history they relate as a sermon. The modern alternatives of whether they are to be taken as historical sources or as a kerygmatic summons to decision is alien to the gospels themselves, and no less alien to them is the modern practice of dividing factual truth from the truth of existence' (Moltmann, ET 188). Therefore that approach to them is correct in which they are viewed neither as confined to the level of historical fact, nor as constituting the 'pure' *kerygma*. Here, as throughout sacred scripture, history and the proclamation of the word constitute an indivisible unity.

3
PREACHING THE EASTER STORIES

I Basic considerations

The Easter narratives of the gospels enable us to recognise what is the fundamental significance of the Easter event: the basis of the christian faith is the encounter with the risen Christ. The earliest of the church's confessions of faith are paschal confessions (cf 1 Cor 15:3–5, and also Mk 16:6 par). Easter is the origin and the centre of the proclamation of the christian message. A new awareness of the fact that the Easter event has this central part to play has been awakened by contemporary movements in theology, and has been brought to the attention of the church as a whole by the *Liturgical Constitution* of the second Vatican Council. The effects of this new awareness are not merely confined to orientating the Easter preaching back to its origins. The most far-reaching renewal consists in the changes which have been brought about in our understanding of preaching in general: the function of preaching is not simply to impart instruction. The risen Lord himself is present in it, and bestows himself in its message. All preaching of the christian message bears a paschal stamp.

The presence of the Lord in the preaching of the christian message is a subject upon which we shall have occasion to speak at a later stage and in another context (p 326f). What we are immediately concerned with is the question of the renewal of the preaching of Easter in particular. Here a process of regeneration has already been going on for some decades. The form this takes is that the preaching of Easter 'as practised in the earliest age of christianity and in the age of the Fathers' has 'emerged as an ideal of christian preaching of Easter' on the basis of which 'it is held, the contemporary form of preaching must be theologically reappraised and shaped afresh' (Dreher, xii). Easter sermons which are considered to provide definitive and normative models for contemporary forms of preaching are, amongst others, those of Melito of Sardis, Hippolytus of Rome, Zeno of Verona and Pope Leo the Great. Naturally in the course of the four centuries which have elapsed since they were preached enduring differences have supervened and, in association with these, the liturgy has acquired fresh forms in history. But through and beyond all these differences we perceive a dynamic concentration of the saving event present in the celebration of the mysteries of the *Pascha Domini*. The early christian preaching of Easter—in which the liturgy provides a dominant influence—is 'basically a preaching that is mystagogical in character: it takes as its theme not the historical event of the Lord's victory through his passion and resurrection, but the fruits of salvation which he gained as a result of this, grace considered precisely as that which is gained in the liturgical mysteries of Easter night' (Dreher, 4).

There can be no doubt that this renewed awareness of the early christian preaching of Easter has resulted in a decisive advance in methods of preaching. The old traditional practice of preaching was to take Easter as an event of the past now completed and, to a large extent, this kind of preaching remained bogged down in the process of drawing edifying examples from history, adducing apologetic arguments in support of Easter, and in exhortations, independent of the central meaning of Easter, to receive the sacraments and to undergo a 'moral resurrection'. In contrast to this, as a result of this new awareness of the early christian preaching of Easter, the saving significance of the Easter event is accorded its full and all-embracing importance.

Unfortunately this process of regeneration—this is something which will be established in the enquiry which follows—has hardly penetrated into the sermon literature which is published. This state of affairs is to be ascribed primarily to the fact that those engaged in producing this literature prefer to continue on in the comfortable, well-worn paths of traditional styles of preaching. Nevertheless, over and above this, there are also real and just reasons, inherent in the very nature of the case, which warn us against committing ourselves totally and without reserve to responding to this call to return to the early christian preaching of Easter.

(i) Its idealism appears questionable when it includes characteristics such as those of the following example: 'Every element of the historical in the passion and resurrection disappears. Every concrete individual circumstance recedes into the background ... Properly speaking, it is not the night of the resurrection of the Lord, but rather the night of the paschal mysteries as celebrated by the community that is praised again and again as the festival which comes as the climax to all the christian mysteries. The subject treated of here is not the unique and "once and for all" event which took place at the tomb on Easter morning, but the work of redemption performed by the Lord upon his church and upon the entire world' (Dreher, 5). Certainly, as against an overhistorical and objectifying view of the Easter event emphasis should be laid upon its saving significance. But—this is a point that has already been touched upon—the ontological value of the resurrection of Jesus as a fact 'in itself' must not be dissolved into a purely redemptive significance 'for us'. Here the same danger threatens which is to a large extent present in the theology of the *kerygma* when this is carried to extremes. Emphasis is laid so one-sidedly upon the presence of the risen Lord in his community—now in the sacrament, now in the word—that the basic reference over and above this to the prior and pre-existing original event, to the act of God in Jesus 'recedes into the background' or even 'disappears'.

(ii) The mystagogical preaching of Passover is wholly concentrated upon the presence of Christ in the liturgical mystery. The element of faith rarely receives any explicit mention.

Evidently the preacher takes it for granted in his hearers. But this is, to a large extent, to misconceive the basic situation in which preaching has a function to perform on festival days in particular. Precisely for those christians who only still take part in the liturgy at Easter and Christmas (but not only for these) faith is anything but a factor to be taken for granted. The prior assumptions entertained by the exponents of the mystagogical approach go far beyond what their real dispositions are. Their ideas are received almost with bewilderment and are set aside as unrealistic.

The Easter narratives of the gospel reckon with individuals who are cast down and full of doubt, who no longer have faith to bring to bear, but rather need to receive it. The gospels allow time for faith to develop. The uncertainty and questioning of the individuals surrounding the risen Lord are relevant to the situation of the hearers of today. 'Even the disciples needed time, brought as they were under the shadow of death, until they understood the message of the cross as pointed out to them by the resurrection' (Fischer, GPM 19, 168). In the intention of the gospels Easter preaching is first and foremost a preaching of faith: they bear witness to faith and awaken it, that faith which is based upon the encounter with the risen Lord.

(iii) The early christian preaching of Easter to a large extent overlooks the basic connection between the Easter event and the missionary task. It remains enclosed within the sacred sphere of the celebration of the mysteries. By contrast with this the Easter stories of the gospels attest the fact that the encounter with the risen Lord lays a duty upon its recipients to bear witness; that Easter faith remains living only as made fruitful in missionary service. Only he who actually proclaims Christ's royal dominion acknowledges him as the exalted Lord.

(iv) Today more than ever before the manner in which the hearers are related to the liturgy has been upset. Over the centuries the liturgical forms have been rendered in many respects ambiguous and obscure through successive truncations and accretions. Over and above this a question which impresses itself urgently upon us is whether modern man is still capable of entering into the liturgy at all. From this point of view too it seems questionable to hold up the early christian mystagogical preaching of Passover as the prototype and ideal for Easter preaching today.

Certainly with regard to the preaching of Easter it is necessary 'to take what has evolved and trace it back through the decisive phases of its development right to its origins where the original outlines are clear and meaningful, and so where one can regain contact with the true meaning of Easter and that too without forcing or destroying anything, but rather in a true sense regenerating it' (Fischer-Wagner, 306). But having embarked upon this course we must not stop short a little before we arrive at the actual sources themselves, at what we suppose to be the origins of this Easter preaching. It is not the Easter sermons of a Hippolytus of Rome or a Zeno of Verona that constitute the normative origins of this preaching, but the writings of the new testament. These contain the earliest Easter sermons which have acquired fixed form in writing, and the *original* ones. The proclamation of the christian message of Easter in all ages draws its life from these origins and is to be measured by them. The question we shall be enquiring into in what follows is whether the Easter preaching of the last two centuries measures up to the standard of the gospels, and further how it can be brought into conformity with those standards today.

II Treatment of individual pericopes

As explained in the Introduction, the analysis and counter-suggestions are confined to sermons on those Easter stories which were prescribed in the pre-1969 arrangement of scripture sections for the Sundays and feast days of the paschal season. The day on which they were used is given in brackets.

The story of the tomb (Mk 16:1–8). (Easter Sunday)
The story of Emmaus (Lk 24:13–35). (Easter Monday)

The story of the manifestation of the risen Lord to the disciples and to Thomas (Jn 20:19–31). (Low Sunday)

The canonical conclusion of Mark (Mk 16:9[14]–20). (The ascension)

A table giving the present position of all the readings discussed in ch 2 will be found in Appendix 1.

1 The story of the tomb (Mk 16:1–8)

(a) ON THE SERMON LITERATURE

No very great preference is shown in the catholic sermon literature of the last two decades for the gospel of the first day of Easter. It is only rarely that the suggestions for preaching for this festival take as their starting-point either the biblical passages or the liturgy. Most of them opt for dogmatic considerations, and include the following themes in various combinations:

The resurrection of Christ as a victory over sin and death, proof of his divinity and the foundation of our faith. Not infrequently this approach includes apologetic tendencies.

The resurrection of christians (often understood as a mere prolongation of life after death) as a source of consolation.

Exhortation to receive the sacraments (Easter confession and communion) and to a renewal of morals, an ethical 'resurrection'.

It is no part of our task to adopt any general position on the subject of Easter sermons. They will be considered here only to the extent that they refer to the gospel previously assigned to Easter day or allude to statements contained in this gospel.

'Embellishment' of the text

Several authors do indeed take the Easter gospel as their starting-point, but find that its restrained presentation of the facts fails to satisfy their taste for story-telling and fantasy, and attempt to 'complete' it. For, so they allege, 'the Lord is not niggardly with his manifestations or niggardly with his words either'. Such authors therefore are generous in their use of words, and do not hesitate to discover new manifestations. 'The Easter sepulchre is situated about eighteen steps below the place of the crucifixion. Today we are going down those steps. There is something there for us to see that is unique. It is early morning. The sun is just rising and its rays illumine the hill of the cross and shine into the rock tomb in which the Lord lies. The morning breeze stirs trees and bushes. It is as though the branches were awakening and trying to whisper a secret . . .' In order to lift the veil from this mystery and to find a clue to the events at the tomb it is suggested to the hearers that they shall 'hide themselves in spirit' under a hazel-bush in order to see 'what it was like when Jesus rose victorious from the dead'. Before the tomb 'sit four Roman soldiers, their armour glittering in the first rays of the morning sun. A small fire is also burning, for it is still cold . . . But now—just look over there! Their faces have grown ashen pale with terror. What is that? The stone begins to tremble. The earth is heaving, and light! Light! Light! It is as though the sun were plunging headlong down upon them . . . Then a cry: Comrades, the tomb is empty . . .'. Another preacher attempts to invoke the resources of modern technical achievements to present his constructions in a form in which they will have contemporary appeal. From the Easter narratives emerges a 'show of lantern slides', in which the first picture can be described as follows: 'Over Jerusalem . . . lies the half light of dawn. The dwellers in the city are still wrapped in the deepest slumber. Only a few women shrouded in dark garments hurry noiselessly through the narrow streets'.

The excesses of fantasy are at their boldest in those cases in which new manifestations are discovered. 'Even though all four evangelists decide, from motives of reverence, to extend a veil of silence over the first meeting of the risen Lord with his mother, still our loving importunity may dare to lift it a little . . . Already soon after midnight on the third day it is becoming ever brighter in her chamber and in her own heart. Mary is surely aware of it, and believes in the fact that after three days Jesus will rise again from death and the tomb. She is ready. All at once he is standing there ... He himself in his whole being and personhood ... Drunk with bliss and happiness, Mary throws herself into the arms of her Son, newly restored to her, and tenderly he folds his mother to his heart.'

These innocent and edifying fancies lead directly to the apocrypha, and not seldom go beyond even these. They are just as remote from the gospel as the apocrypha themselves. Preaching is deprived of its meaning if it allows personal fantasy to prevail in place of the text of scripture. Unhappily it can be shown that the few sermon models which do take up the actual gospel story in their Easter preaching rarely manage to tell the story without introducing harmonisations and embellishments of their own.

Their loquacity is at the opposite pole to the restrained narrative of the gospel. This latter leaves no room for interests of a folklorist kind. Here there is no mention of either the morning breeze or the whispering of branches or of anyone being drunk with bliss and happiness. The women are not caught up in a mood of solemn reverence at the early morning. With the ointment in their hands they make their way to the tomb and to the dead man himself (16:2f). They have no thought for the joys of spring or the songs of the birds. Their concern, rather, is with the very great stone which lies before the tomb and reduces them to helplessness (16:3). It is the sharpest possible indication of the fact that death imposes a dividing line, and brings home to them, inexorably, the harshness and severity of death.

The empty tomb and the 'proof of the resurrection'
It is natural that in sermons on the grave story the empty tomb itself should be spoken of. Not infrequently it occupies a central position in the preacher's line of thought.

(a) 'Our gospel, therefore, is, in a true sense, the gospel of the empty tomb . . . Right from the beginning onwards the news of the empty tomb has been an integral part of Easter . . . Just as the prophet Isaiah (53:9) extolled the tomb of the servant of God, so too Jesus himself and the first christians have thought of the meaning of the death and resurrection of the Son of God only in the context of the mystery of the empty tomb . . . This is the goal in which the fulfilment of the will of God through the facts of history, through the words and works of Jesus himself, finds its culmination: the empty tomb.' It belongs to the 'foundation of rock on which rests our Easter faith'. 'The question that arises at the tomb is the question of to be or not to be. Here the Lord has interposed his power as creator in order to provide a firm foothold for our faith . . . Our hope for the blessings of eternity is founded in an empty tomb.' Certainly the 'fact of the empty tomb . . . is not the sole proof of the resurrection of Jesus. But within the general framework of the motives of proof it once became an indispensable factor, and to this present day it has remained indispensable'. 'Taken together with the manifestations of Christ it is henceforward the decisive argument by which the resurrection is proved.' It is faith's 'most sacred location'.

(b) Side by side with the 'historical line of proof' which appeals to the empty tomb we have the 'anthropological line of proof' in which we engage our own hearts as 'counsel for the defence' of the resurrection. 'When we rely not merely upon our senses and not merely upon our reason, when we let our heart speak, this heart which has hidden depths of its own, then it calls out, then it cries to us with the force which comes from having finally recognised something decisive: It is true! Christ has arisen! Otherwise what would life amount to . . ? I might almost say man would have had to invent it (the message of Easter) if God had not proclaimed it to us.' This way of adducing proof culminates in the appeal: 'Christians lay your hands upon your hearts! Why do we believe in the resurrection! I believe because I shudder at the prospect of nothingness and the despair it entails; because it drives me mad to imagine that with death everything is ended... We have a cloud of witnesses for the resurrection of Christ. Certainly that is true. But for me the best witness is I myself: I believe in the resurrection because I believe in me.'

On (a): Mk 16:1–8 is not 'the gospel of the empty tomb' to the extent that is alleged. At the centre of this gospel stands the message of Jesus' resurrection. The risen Lord, not the empty tomb, is the culminating goal of the will of God. In the earliest example of Easter preaching (1 Cor 15) it has not been found necessary to make any reference to the empty tomb. It should not, therefore, be presented as providing any proof of the resurrection or any basis for belief in Easter. It is an interpretative sign of the Easter message, not a self-subsistent factor in the process of proving it. The resurrection is in no sense deducible from the empty tomb. It cannot simply be assigned to the level of any everyday event.

To assign the resurrection a place among the events of world history is in contradiction to the express statements of the gospel, and the same is true of the attempts which have been made to provide assurances of its reality or to defend it on this basis. In the context of the resurrection the term 'proof' can only give rise to misunderstandings and should be avoided. The function of the Easter sermon is not to demonstrate but to bear witness. The angel points away from the tomb to the risen Lord. It is important to follow in this direction for it is only through the encounter with him that faith can be born.

On (b): far more questionable than the approach which seeks to adduce 'proof' on the basis of the empty tomb is that which attempts to appoint one's own self as an advocate in defence of faith in Easter and by this means to compensate for the elemental anxiety which lies at the roots of human existence. *Hybris* and cowardice go hand in hand and together tend to dissolve faith. This is not the place to expound in detail the consequences to which this line of argument can lead. We can say at any rate that the Easter gospel shows with all possible clarity that the tidings of the resurrection were not for one single moment experienced by the individuals involved as the fulfilment of their heart's desire or as a consolation in which their despair was overcome. Terror, trembling, panic and a headlong flight from the tomb—this is how the women react (Mk 16:5f, 8). In this one short section there are no less than four emphatic references to reactions of this kind. It is only by ignoring these statements that we can, in the name of edification, distort the tidings of the resurrection into something that is self-authenticating, something which man's own inward promptings lead him to expect, indeed almost as something which he would otherwise have had to 'invent'. This is to reduce it to the level of an obscure presentiment of a general survival after death, which should never be put forward as the true message of Easter.

The experience of the women at the tomb is that all their presentiments and expectations have been totally turned upside down. They find themselves no longer able to keep abreast of what is happening. It is something quite outside the world they know. For in fact Jesus is not simply 'present once more'. A new reality has broken in upon them. In Christ God is initiating a new beginning, and with the new aeon which he now ushers in he is bringing the old to an end. 'To bring home to these women, so anxious and on the point of flight, the full impact of the dominion of God now definitively asserted in the resurrection of Jesus—that is the closing message bequeathed to us by Mark the evangelist' (Schlier 1949, 126). Mark's presentation makes it quite clear that the revelation found the women totally unprepared, so that they betook themselves to terrified flight. Mark precisely does not seek for some point in the behaviour of the women to which to attach his own moralisings, but emphasises that the reality that is breaking in upon them is quite new and one for which humanity cannot make itself naturally suitable. It is only exceptionally that any trace of this message can be discerned in the sermon literature.

Festival of spring
'Surely that must have been the most brilliant sunrise of all, that sunrise of the first Easter morning in the history of the world...' 'Joseph of Arimathea's garden is resplendent with all the glorious hues of spring.' Thus 'the renewal of nature, the opening of all the blooms is turned into an exultant festival of scents and colours... a divinely willed symbol of the redemption wrought in Christ'. For God has 'deliberately placed the festival of Easter in the season of spring in order that we may have clear and palpable evidence before our eyes of how much the rejoicing of God is imparted to us in the glory of Easter'. 'That which is taking place out of doors in nature, in the fields and forests, in the vales and on the hilltops during these days and weeks—must not all this... not find an echo in your innermost soul? It is the victory of life over death, the victory of light over darkness, the victory of joy over sorrow. That which men dimly guessed at even in the ages before Christ, the "death and new becoming", the descent and the resurrection—that has now found its wondrous fulfilment in christianity, in Jesus Christ.' The springtime that is taking place in nature is turned into a 'springtime of human souls', a 'springtime of humanity' and a 'springtime of immortality', and the resurrection is related to the emergence of our people from the miseries of the war, to the 'regeneration of mankind' and the 'rebirth of a community', to the victory of the church over her enemies in the course of the history of the church, above all in the counter-reformation.

Concomitant with this devaluation of the resurrection goes a further devaluation, this time of the terrors of death. It becomes unimportant, is 'only one more penance' and (this is actually said of death!) 'the transition into the mode of existence of the resurrection'. Death and pain retain only a 'dominion over externals' for 'It is a reality and no mere beautiful and poetic idea: to the eye of faith there is a radiance that suffuses all things: the light of Easter. To the ear of faith comes the echo of an eternal alleluia from heaven. For everything that is harsh, terrible or evil has in principle been overcome.'

These quotations enable us to realise how great the temptation is to lay out about the tomb of the Lord 'a flourishing rock-garden in which all the shrubs, flowers and blossoms of human pride and human ambition grow rank and luxuriant. The first and most pressing task of christianity's Easter sermon is absolutely to resist this temptation and to give the lie to it' (Stählin, 207). A point that must not be overlooked, it is true, is that very many, though by no means all of the authors we have just cited do not stop short at this interpretation of Easter in terms of spring. What they are trying to achieve in their flight of springtime fancy is to draw their hearers out of their existing world and to lead them in spirit into the Easter event itself. They must be given due credit for making the effort. At the same time, however, the question must be put whether they really do succeed in this aim. The message of Easter is not simply something that can be fitted into the cycle of the seasons and brought into harmony with the laws of nature. Goethe's phrase about 'death and new becoming' (*Stirb und Werde*), so often cited in these sermons, may have its place in these contexts; but when it comes to throwing light upon the event of Easter it contributes nothing, but rather impedes the listener from arriving at it. What we are concerned with here is not a process of renewal in nature or a regeneration of mankind or of human nature. The constant alternation of the tides in the unfolding processes of the cosmos is broken across. It cannot therefore serve as an example for a reality which precisely goes beyond it and in the last analysis deprives it of its absolute dominion over all.

Insofar as a comparison is possible at all it is to the formation of the world that we should relate the resurrection. The resurrection of Jesus is the beginning of a new creation. It is an event that goes right down to the very roots of things. Instead of obscuring the reality of death and resurrection with a cloud of fantasy we must whole-heartedly accept that reality in all its radical importance. Only so shall we do justice to the message of the gospel of Easter. This message contains a warning for the preacher not to slip into an attitude of over-facile Easter euphoria or to be over-hasty in joining in the chorus of alleluias. This message conveys to us that the joy of Easter 'can only be true and authentic if it is accompanied by fear and trembling. Otherwise it is no true joy at all but mere temporary elation' (Schlier 1949, 126).

(b) SUGGESTIONS FOR SERMONS ON THE STORY OF THE TOMB

The preacher has to reckon with the fact that in not a few cases from among his hearers their faith is under attack; that they would probably like to believe yet cannot do so or at any rate imagine that they cannot. The 'unbelief of believers' is a factor which must neither be lost sight of nor drowned in the clamour of the preacher's own zealous but over self-assured outpourings. To adopt this approach would be to fail to do justice not only to the real situation of the congregation but to the intention of the Easter gospel itself as well. This gospel is aimed at individuals who are still making their pilgrimage through life, and for whom the first goal at which they arrive will in fact be the grave.

Jesus 'is not here' (Mk 16:6). 'He is not in that place in the sense that he can be sought there in purely historical terms. This means that the position with regard to the present-day experience of faith is basically the same as it was then: God is dead (F. Nietsche). He is no longer available to be discovered and experienced within the dimension of this present world' (Filthaut, 40). The weakness which is a factor in the history of Jesus ('You seek Jesus of Nazareth who was crucified' 16:6) is made strong by the omnipotence of God ('He has arisen'), who 'gives life to the dead and calls into existence the things that do not exist' (Rom 4:17). In destroying the securities that this world has to provide, God brings home to man his word, the word that summons him from death to life and sets him under his promise (16:7).

On the way to death
After the sabbath rest three women who have been witnesses to the death of Jesus (Mk 15:40) set out as quickly as possible on their way to the tomb to show the last honours to the dead man, a last gesture of gratitude for what he has been to them (Mk 16:1f). For this purpose no expense (the spices) and no trouble ('very early on the first day of the week') is too much. Their love is great; but it is meant for a dead man; their way leads to the tomb. They are seeking, as the angel tells us, for Jesus of Nazareth who was crucified—seeking the dead among the dead. Their concern is for the dead body and their intention is to banish the stench of decay with sweet-smelling herbs. This is all that is in their power to achieve. They have had to 'come to terms with death. For them Jesus has become a memory; he belongs to the past. So far as the future is concerned they can expect nothing more from him' (Eichholz, 136). The stone that lies in their way and prevents them from getting to him to anoint him marks clearly and unmistakably the dividing line of death which severs every connection with the living. 'Who will roll away the stone for us from the door of the tomb?' (16:3). This is the question which they ask in their helplessness. Death is irreversible. In the tomb life is finished.

In the light of this, then, it is all the more amazing that the great stone which denies them access to him should have been rolled away (16:4). It never seems to strike the women at all how amazing this is. Quite unimpressed by this circumstance they press on into the tomb itself. 'Their thoughts are so wholly taken up with the tomb and Jesus lying dead within it . . . The only difference it makes whether the tomb is closed or open is, at most, as to whether they can perform the service they have in mind for the dead man or not. The women have no eyes for any signs' (Schlier 1949, 125). The tomb itself claims all their attention.

The great turning point
It is not until they see the angel that they begin to be disconcerted (16:5). It is at this point on their way to the tomb that they are brought face to face with the new world. It is at this point that God himself intervenes in their finite world languishing as it is under sentence of death. It is at this point that heaven and earth meet and touch. How could the women react otherwise than to be beside themselves with terror, at this point where they are brought face to face with the vast power of the divine presence? God himself has to explain to them the significance of what is taking place through the medium of his messenger. The *aggelos*, angel becomes the proclaimer of the *euaggelion*, gospel. From the place of death within the tomb itself the tidings of new life issue forth. Those who come to seek Jesus of Nazareth who was crucified experience the fact that God has raised him from the dead (16:6). Now he is no longer to be sought as a dead man among the dead; he is living.

The risen Lord is that Jesus of Nazareth who was crucified. Cross and resurrection belong together. We cannot believe in the Lord that has risen if we pay no heed to the Lord who was crucified. The risen Lord has not cut himself off from his physical history. This is what the reference to the empty tomb insists upon (16:6). Easter is not a reality which is emancipated from earthly existence. 'God has meant it not merely for our soul, our religious feelings, our intellectual assent, our conscious and deliberate decision. He has meant it for our whole body in just the same way that it was not simply the "idea" of Jesus that he made to live on at Easter, but Jesus himself whom he raised from the dead' (Schweizer GPM 15, 123).

On the way to life

This then is the message which the tomb symbolically conveys. With this message its function in the story is ended. It is meaningless to dwell upon it any longer. The angel directs the women away from the tomb to the encounter with the risen Lord. Through his messenger God says to them and to us: 'That we shall fail to find Jesus if we seek him in the tomb where the most that our skill in anointing can do for him is to preserve his body for a period, perhaps for several centuries. This would imply that all that we see in him is a great figure of the past who still lives on in his message or in his work among those who revere him. God's message to us is that Jesus wills to come to us, and that we must make ourselves ready for this meeting with him' (Schweizer GPM 15, 123). The task of the women is to tell the disciples and Peter that this meeting is to take place. They do not remain dumb hearers of the tidings of the resurrection, but rather become witnesses to it. Easter is a summons to bear witness. The risen Lord does not remain hidden, for—this is the message which the women have to deliver—'There (in Galilee) you will see him' (16:7). He enters into the hearing and seeing of the witnesses and thereby into the gospel itself, in which he summons us ever anew to the Easter encounter with him.

The new aeon

When the women receive the news of the resurrection their reaction is not one of extreme joy about something which they have been able straightway to recognise and accept. On the contrary it is as though they have been struck by lightning. They tremble and flee in panic and are too frightened to speak (16:8). What is the source of this terror which strikes them dumb and reduces them to a far greater state of bewilderment than the death of their Lord? Death belonged to their world. It was a factor to which they could assign a place in their scheme of things. However cruelly they felt its impact, they could cope with it, come to terms with it. They could pay the dead man their last tributes, reverently cherish the memory of him. But if Jesus really has risen from the dead, and is not simply 'once more present' in their world, then this can only mean that the old world they knew has come to an end. The old has passed away and something new has come into being. In that case it is the Lord who confronts them in a second coming and their sole concern is with him. 'In him God confronts his world with the end of all the possibilities open to it, and begins to reveal to us the single possibility which is his to bestow, the possibility of redemption. With him God begins all things anew, and all we still have to do is to say yes or no' (Schlier 1949, 126).

2 *The story of Emmaus (Lk 24: 13–35)*

(a) ON THE SERMON LITERATURE

To a large extent Easter Monday was reckoned as a 'no sermon' day. In the relevant literature this is shown by the fact that the helps for preaching that are offered were only few in number by comparison with those for the first day of the festival. It must be admitted that such helps as were offered were at variance with the general practice in that they are predominantly concerned with the gospel. There is a general preference for the story of Emmaus. Here too however the story as it is presented fails to satisfy, and attempts are made to 'get beyond' the gospel itself (this is how the practitioners usually prefer to justify their approach) by adding fanciful embellishments. 'Unfortunately not all the lines have been sketched in.' Efforts are made, therefore to introduce the colours that are felt to be missing from the picture, and these 'false colours' have the effect of blurring the clear outlines of the story. 'Yet how human this Easter narrative is!... how full of traits from everyday life and observations which are psychologically accurate!' In accordance with this way of taking the story preachers for the most part concern themselves with a description of the individual characters of the story.

The unknown traveller
'After the terrible happenings of Holy Week, after the mighty event of Easter Sunday, the gospel relates to us an idyll. . . .' 'It shows that this mighty conqueror has not ceased to be a compassionate saviour. He has endured his gigantic struggle and emerged the victor from it, but in all this he has not for one moment forgotten us poor mortals.' 'The impression is that the warm-heartedness of his humanity was never so great as after the resurrection. The Lord exhibits the following qualities which are intrinsic to his nature:

1 The art of coming close to people.
2 The art of conversing with them.
3 The art of making them happy.'

'He has smiled at these two disciples of his who are so full of grief as they journey at his side and never recognise him at all. Perhaps it was gradually getting rather dark over the long wide road . . . And perhaps the Master had drawn his cloak across his face a little. Perhaps this was how it was when he put such searching questions to them. . . .' 'There is some music-like quality in the voice of the strange traveller.' It is 'as though everything that his sacred hands touched turned to gold'. 'He accompanies them. He listens to them. He speaks a few kind words. He breaks the bread.' This is all, and the application gives a no less over-simplified impression: Christ is always there when we need him; we must listen to others, give good advice ourselves, and receive holy communion.

Even the factor of recognising the Lord in the breaking of bread does not escape the general tendency to a superficialising interpretation: 'The meal at Emmaus was not a celebration of the eucharist.' 'No, it must have been some way of the Master's own of breaking bread that was typical of him for it to have made so deep an impression on the disciples: an act that was full of sweetness and love and self-giving.' Finally along with the breaking of bread go Easter water, Easter lamb, Easter eggs and Easter hare; these too are distributed as signs by which the risen Lord can be recognised.

These quotations enable us to realise what confusions interpretation can lead to when due attention is not paid to the literary form of the text. Our exegetical enquiry has shown that in the Emmaus story a motif has been taken up which is general in the history of religions, and that this has been made to contribute to the christian preaching of the message of Easter. In the sermons quoted this motif, which is really only a symbol, is taken to be the true essence of the story; that is why they remain at the level of purely formal considerations (cf the 'art of coming close to people'), and thereby positively impede their hearers from arriving at its kerygmatic message. They pose conundrums about what must have been especially typical in Christ's way of breaking the bread, and in doing so fail to recognise the fact that the point of the story is man's encounter with him in the eucharist.

A further factor which can lead to a false interpretation of the Emmaus story is the effect of dogmatic preconceptions. As a result of certain influences in scholastic theology the explanation of the doctrine of the eucharist has concentrated predominantly upon the real presence of the Lord in the offerings, which is said to depend upon the pronouncing of certain specific formulae. On the basis of this the meal taken at Emmaus cannot be accounted eucharistic in character. In the mind of the biblical author the real presence in the offerings is subordinated to the actual presence of the risen Lord at the meal. Christ sits at table with his disciples and shares a meal with them. Now this is precisely what we are told in the story of Emmaus. Lk 24:30f can only be understood—and this is something imposed by the very terminology itself—in a 'eucharistic' sense.

The two disciples

The story of Emmaus 'is redolent with a wonderful atmosphere'. It presents 'a picture which is, from every aspect, lovely ... It is springtime and Easter. The sun is shining bright and warm. Two disciples are on the way to Emmaus. Gentle breezes of Spring waft about them'. No wonder that the temperature outside warms them inside as well: 'Did not our hearts burn within us?'

'Unfortunately both in respect of time and in terms of our own interior dispositions we are far too remote to feel for ourselves how it must have felt to them.' The range of descriptive epithets used to characterise the disciples extends from 'honest well-meaning men' to sensible men equipped with 'the irony of those who know', and in all cases the story is applied to the corresponding type of christian or unbeliever.

Several sermons evince a special interest in the question of why the two travellers should have failed to recognise the Lord. Among the reasons suggested for this are their grief, disappointment, anxiety, and state of being 'closed in upon themselves'. All these attitudes, we are told, are to be condemned. They are tantamount to denials of him. 'Their thinking does not go deep enough'; and further 'their heart is too sluggish and unresponsive ... And finally their theology too is deficient'. On the one hand the example of the Emmaus disciples should serve as a warning to us, and teach us that God's plans must not be criticised. On the other hand their warm-heartedness and hospitality are held up as a praiseworthy example: 'This true humanity on the part of the simple disciples of Emmaus, whose hearts can still burn!' Their attitude bears witness to 'the virtue and the blessing of hospitality'. And the moral: 'We can all have a share in this blessing. We shall all have it provided that we take as much pains to practise hospitality as these two disciples did. We must make great efforts to revive the practice of hospitality once more as a christian virtue, and to exercise it as a work of mercy. . . .' 'The greater our love is for the Lord, the more our heart burns, . . . the nearer we are to that Emmaus that is God's revelation within us.' When they come to the entreaty, 'Stay with us for it is towards evening' some preachers depart from the narrative altogether; for they take this entreaty as a starting-point from which to develop their ideas on the subject of evening and evening prayer and, in connection with 24:17b, take sadness as a topic for preaching upon.

The literary form of the Emmaus story is also ignored when such preachers come to describe the characters of the disciples and their attitude. More than this, the kerygmatic content of the story is obscured by irrelevant moralisings. Certainly it is incontestable that great importance is attached to love and hospitality in the message of the bible. Nevertheless they are not the subject of the Emmaus story.

These departures from the text appear particularly crass in cases in which particular clauses or key words are arbitrarily torn from their contexts and wrongly made to act as pegs for the individual's own ideas. This procedure resembles the methods of biblical interpretation practised by many sects.

(b) SUGGESTIONS FOR PREACHING ON THE EMMAUS STORY

The Emmaus story has a bearing upon the situation in which we ourselves stand. It shows what Easter means for individuals who have not seen the risen Lord. It is in the meeting with the risen Christ that faith is born and made actual. He did not only appear to the eye-witnesses. He encounters us today on our way, even when we fail to recognise him for a long time and—scripture envisages even the disciples as liable to this—even if we are assailed by doubt and despair and so go astray from the path of faith. He bestows his word and his sustenance upon us. He is present in both. Both derive their force from the fact that he is present in them. This of itself brings out certain points which are important for our understanding of the eucharist. The word is presented as a concomitant of this sustenance and as a factor which is likewise essential and no less important than it. The eucharist is no longer thought of as consisting primarily in the 'changing' of one substance into another, but rather as a meal that we share with the risen Lord.

Disciples without hope

It is a characteristic of the Easter narratives that Jesus' manifestations are surprising and unexpected. The disciples are not prepared for his coming or in any sense disposed for it by faith. They are demoralised, dispirited, disappointed and in despair. Even after the Easter event many of them are still at the pre-Easter stage of understanding. This is the case with the Emmaus disciples. They have turned their backs upon Jerusalem, the place of promise and the fulfilment of salvation, and are in the act of returning home. For them the history of Jesus is finished, something that belongs to the past. They did have hope 'once upon a time', but now it is buried. This is their frame of mind as they travel their way together, thinking over and discussing the past yet once more (13f). And as they travel Jesus draws near and accompanies them on their way. In their state of hopelessness he is at their side even though they fail to recognise him (15f). They tell him what has happened in the recent past, which still moves them so much. About what has taken place in Jerusalem they are particularly well-informed (19–24): they know that Jesus was a prophet who by his works was held in esteem not merely in the eyes of the people but in the eyes of God as well. They know that Jesus has been crucified, and it is this that constitutes the final blow that they have felt so crushing, the scandal that they cannot overcome because they do not understand how God can allow a prophet of his to be brought to nothing in such a way. How could they understand this, seeing that so far as they are concerned Easter has not yet arrived? They know that the tomb is empty, and even that angels have actually told the women that Jesus is alive. 'They know all that can be "known" at all; but they can tell of all this "only with sorrow" . . . For in all this they still do not have Jesus' (Surkau GPM 4, 128). What they say of those disciples who went and saw for themselves that the tomb was empty applies to themselves too: 'Him they did not see' (24).

Encounter in the word
'The turning-point comes through what Jesus himself says to them, through their encounter with his word' (Dinkler GPM 15, 125). Jesus does not favour the two disciples with any open epiphany of himself by which to recognise him. He does not say: 'Look, it is I!' He discloses himself to them through his word. He refers them to the scriptures (25–27), and uses the statements contained in these to show them how the way of God does in fact lie through these events, which are so incomprehensible to them: 'In common with all the Jews you take scandal at the cross and suppose that God's plans have been brought to nothing. You look for a messiah equipped with external glories who will free Israel from alien domination. God wills not splendour but suffering.' The cross constitutes not the ruin of his ways but the point at which they all converge. All the scriptures lead up to this point. Christ must suffer in order to enter into his glory (26). The light that radiates from this glory falls upon the books of Moses and the prophets and reveals the cross as their fulfilment. It is the risen Lord who illumines the scriptures, so long familiar yet still misunderstood. It is in the encounter of the disciples with him that the meaning of the scriptures dawns upon them. It is only through him and in the light of him that their message can bring light. He is the medium that illumines them, the key that unlocks their meaning. Wherever the word of scripture finds expression there he is present in a hidden epiphany.

Encounter in the sharing of the meal
The story of this encounter does not end here. It presses on to a further conclusion. By itself the word is not enough to make the disciples recognise him. On arriving at the goal of their journey

they ask the unknown traveller to stay with them (29). This entreaty is crucial; without it the traveller would have journeyed on. He would have left them behind. He wants to be asked to stay. 'At the centre of the whole story comes this entreaty. It is as though it was the threshold which the two disciples must cross in order to enter into a new sphere, untrodden by them hitherto' (Stählin, 348). The stranger follows them and accompanies them inside. At the meal it is he, the guest, who becomes host. He takes the bread, pronounces the blessing, breaks it and distributes it to them (30). At this moment the eyes of the disciples, which have been 'held' up till now, are opened (31). God opens them for them and now they recognise him whom they had already given up hope of ever seeing again. Suddenly they know: He is alive! He is there! It is not in virtue of any special manifestation that it is given to them to know this. They recognise him, the risen Lord, in the meal that they share with him. They cannot lay hold of him or gain possession of him. He disappears from their view (31). He is not theirs to dispose of as a possession. But in this encounter with him they have been made sure of his presence. They have heard his word and shared a meal with him.

Witnesses to the resurrection
As a result of this they are impelled to bear witness to him. No other course is open to them but to return to Jerusalem (the centre of the event of salvation which they have left so far behind), and there to proclaim the truth of their experience. There, in confirmation of their own witness of faith and lending strength to it, they hear the confession of Easter faith made by the community: 'The Lord has risen indeed and has appeared to Simon' (34).

3 The 'story of Thomas' (Jn 20:19–31)

(a) ON THE SERMON LITERATURE
The sermons for Low Sunday refer for the most part to the

celebration of first holy communion and in this they are chiefly concerned to praise the 'day of life' and to awaken in the adult section of the congregation the memory of the children's paradise which they have lost. Those sermon models which do bear upon the gospel itself concentrate upon the three following subjects: Peace, confession, doubting Thomas.

Peace
'This, therefore, was his opening word, his Easter greeting to his disciples: "Peace be with you". This word flows like balsam into their wounded hearts. What liberation it must have brought from all feelings of guilt! Now, at the point at which the soul of Jesus himself is steeped in the victory of God's peace, now he wills to bestow this peace upon his friends as well.' It 'was an interior peace. It was liberation and redemption from the confusion and terror of the days which had just passed, a deliverance from anxiety . . .'. 'Your soul, which is tormented with doubts and tortured by the nagging thoughts of its own unfaithfulness, needs nothing so much as for God to bestow peace upon it'. 'They breathe more easily, and absorb this word of the Saviour's joyfully into their anguished souls.'

The conclusions drawn from the fact that peace has been bestowed are expressed in the following terms: 'A christian community must be constituted as a community of peace, as an island of peace in the midst of the brawls and quarrels of the multitudes. Shame to that christian who takes part in these brawls, who acts like the heathen or the beasts in striving for his desires with fists and elbows, nails and teeth!' In sermon literature the word 'peace' undergoes a similar fate as in politics. It is constantly being spoken of and yet no clear idea is provided of its meaning and its implications (see below pp 285–6). The psychologising interpretation misses the true significance of the biblical greeting of peace altogether. This is concerned not primarily with the state of the disciples' souls, but with their salvation. The risen Lord bestows upon them his eschatological gift of salvation, which opens to them, the believers, that new possibility of existence which consists in union with God. Peace, therefore, is neither primarily a psychic phenomenon nor yet primarily a question of morality. Those upon whom it is bestowed are indeed charged with the task of living by the gift they have been given. But precisely because peace in one's daily life grows out of the peace that is bestowed upon one, it represents something more than a mere moral appeal. Those who live this peace cannot withdraw into an island from which they can look out upon the 'brawling multitudes' and dismiss 'the heathens' (non-christians), equating them with beasts.

The fact that peace is so often wrongly interpreted is, to a large extent, due to the separatist outlook and attitude which christians adopt. The composers of sermons all too often tear the salutation of peace from its context in the pericope as a whole, and make it a peg on which to hang their own vague ideas and counsels, instead of paying heed to its true meaning as brought out in the context of the gospel.

Confession

The salutation of peace and the forgiveness of sins are frequently associated with one another (Jn 20:23), and are connected with an appeal to fulfil the Easter duty of confession. 'To this salutation of peace Christ has attached the institution of the sacrament of the forgiveness of sins. Thereby an effective remedy against the lack of peace in their hearts has been offered to all the sons of Adam . . . Oh that in this week of Easter we might feel once more in a truly lively way the message which this salutation of peace brings to us, and the effect which this sacrament of peace is intended to have and to bestow upon us!' Low Sunday should help to awaken in us a longing for peace: 'Oh that we might cleanse our hearts from all these perverse and evil matters, and regain once more the blessings of childhood! That we might be able to be once more as pure, as innocent, as eager, as faithful, as conscientious and as full of peace and happiness as these children are, and as we ourselves once were!' Since many do not prize such peace as this they must be '"compelled to come in" (Lk 24:23) to the confessional. Hence the commandment of the church. Properly speaking the message which this commandment is intended to convey is not: "At least once a year you must confess your sins", but "at least once a year you must have your peace" . . .'. 'What security this provides!' '"Confession eases the soul" (*Beicht' macht leicht*). So runs the proverb. How often we have experienced this for ourselves! If you do not experience it then make haste to make your Easter confession and bring upon yourself the peace of Christ. Afterwards you will feel like a man who has had to move a grand piano and has just finished his work! Throwing your burden into the corner you draw a long breath, and, joyful as a child dressed in white to make his first communion, you step out joyfully to the altar of God.' 'Yet how simple it is to make one's confession in this way! The repentant sinner acknowledges his sins and, in return for the payment of a small penance, obtains absolution. The priest who hears his confession listens to the acknowledgment of his sins, silently takes the decision whether to forgive or not to forgive, counsels the penitent, gives him his penance, and pronounces the words of absolution. How simple all this is! . . .'

The practice of isolating Jn 20:23 from its context in order to apply it to the Easter confession, and the practice of connecting it so closely with the salutation of peace are not in accordance with the message of the gospel itself. Jn 20:23 should not be restricted to confession. Its message is broader than this would imply. The disciples are sent out in the power of the Spirit to 'forgive' and to 'retain' sins. They confront the world with the decision between belief and unbelief . . . In their work it is not merely salutation but judgment too that is revealed. Hence it is no purely private peace of soul that is in question here, and certainly not the blessedness of childhood that is intended to touch us. Neither Jn 20:23 nor the sacrament of penance are to be understood in this individualistic and psychologising sense.

Certainly a material connection does exist between the salutation of peace and the word of authority. The risen Lord bestows upon his disciples, together with peace, that same eschatological salvation which they themselves in virtue of their mission impart in the form of forgiveness of sins. But this connection is not for one moment intended by the evangelist in so immediate a sense that it should occupy the foreground and dominate his message as a whole. The wrongness of this interpretation appears from the fact that the saying about the forgiveness of sins refers immediately back to the mission and the imparting of the Spirit, and is only rightly to be understood in the light of this. The fact that it is subordinated to these prior factors is hardly apparent at all from the sermon literature. Thus the conclusion is arrived at that the priests are 'authorised and empowered of their own authority to administer and impart these merits which he (Jesus) himself has gained through the shedding of his blood'. Pushed to its ultimate extremes, this conclusion leads, in the last analysis, to the blasphemous assertion that Jesus 'bows to the judgment of his servants'. The simplifying approach to the sacrament of penance is decisively to be rejected. Preaching should be aimed at destroying any tendency to 'automatism in one's attitude to confession' instead of positively demanding such an attitude.

Unbelieving Thomas
(*i*) *Psychologising descriptions.* Those sermon models which are concerned with the story of Thomas rarely get beyond the stage of historicising and psychologising considerations. They attempt to recreate the atmosphere of the moment when the risen Lord manifested himself.

His wounds 'are radiant with a consoling light which seems to come from another world. These marks of the bloody struggle against the prince of this world are now shining beacons of victory which suffuse the terrible and bloody cavities with a gentle radiance'. When it comes to depicting Thomas' character fantasies proliferate. The apostle is represented as 'a sanguine personality', 'a melancholic', 'a pessimist', 'one to whom everything is black and sickening'. He is represented as 'a sceptic in the modern sense' and a 'doubter who belongs to our own times'; as a 'rationalist' in the true sense, as 'an acute and far-seeing thinker, and a man who takes quick decisions', as 'the prototype of modern man with his critical attitude', and like him 'burdened with all that lust for power which proceeds from a self-assertive mind and all that spirit of rebellion which comes from a disposition of obstinate self-will'. 'He was no child. . . .' His encounter with the risen Lord is depicted in vivid hues. Here the motifs of the touching—familiar to us from the apocryphal literature but unsupported by anything contained in the gospel—is especially favoured. 'How his hands must have trembled at this point!' 'What does the trembling hand of Thomas feel in the wounded side of the Lord?' Even his confession of faith in the divinity of Christ does not escape from the psychologising process: 'In this one phrase, "My Lord and my God" Thomas gives expression to all that happiness which pervades his soul. This first encounter of Thomas with Christ is touchingly beautiful.' This emotional portrayal represents a departure from the character and intention of the gospel itself. It is no part of the intention of this gospel to analyse the psychic structure of Thomas. On the contrary John intends to provide an answer to the urgent question of the community as to how faith is possible in that time in which the risen Lord no longer makes himself visible. This is a point that has hardly been noticed in the sermon literature.

(*ii*) *Factual proof.* For not a few preachers the story of Thomas counts as an objective proof of the resurrection of Jesus. This is a false and hazardous course for apologetics to embark upon.

'One who doubts the reality of Christ approaches me. I draw his attention to the proofs from the historical facts for the resurrection contained in holy scripture.' 'Throughout the space of forty days' Jesus has '"compelled" his disciples to face the proof of the reality of his resurrection'. 'Even as a little boy that detail which the evangelist gives about the "closed doors" made a deep impression upon me. That the risen Lord, without further ado, should pass through all the doors that are closed and suddenly stand in the midst of his disciples—this is a fact which still strikes us of today as astonishing, and cannot fail to evoke reflections.' 'With regard to the visual and auditional impressions we receive, we can fall once more into doubt. Perhaps our vision or our hearing was at fault. But when anyone has become convinced through seeing, hearing *and* touching, then there is no longer any room for doubt ... The fact that Jesus had to supply such a wealth of proof in order to convince his disciples has had beneficial effects.' 'It is not Jesus' word, not his miracles, but his wounds that constitute the ultimate proof beyond all possibility of deception that he has risen glorious from the dead.' 'We need no further proofs than these in the sight of the world.'

In connection with the miracle stories we shall have to speak in detail about the fact that the apologetic approach which seeks to construct a 'factual proof' has no foundation in the central message of the gospel, but is rather quite peripheral to the miracle stories themselves.

Thus in the case of the story of Thomas too, it is no part of the evangelist's intention to supply a 'proof'. On the contrary, this story contains a manifest criticism of 'miracle faith' as such! The effort to arrive at objective certainty is explicitly rebuked at the end of the story (20:29). The encounter with the risen Lord which is presented in such realistic terms contains a summons to faith: 'Do not be faithless but believing' (20:27). Certainly the kind of faith that is demanded here is not in any sense 'blind faith'. It is constantly related to the confession of those who testify: 'We have seen the Lord' (20:25). But this 'vision' which is a vision of faith is not a purely optical process. Primarily, rather, it is an event which takes place within the person. Neither for Thomas nor for us today can there be any empirical assurance of faith. We do not have to prove Christ but to bear witness to him. This does not entail any diminution of the reality of the resurrection but removes it from the sphere in which attempts are made to prove it in terms of the natural sciences, and sets it in that unique personal dimension which alone is adequate to it, the dimension namely of faith.

(b) SUGGESTIONS FOR PREACHING ON THE 'STORY OF THOMAS'
The section of the gospel that was prescribed for Low Sunday fell into three parts. From the aspects of time and content alike the two sections of 20:19-23 and 20:24-29 are plainly separated from one another. The concluding verses of 20:30f do not refer exclusively to what has been said just before, but look back over the whole of the fourth gospel. The fact that the pericope has so many different levels in terms both of its external composition and of the development of thought within it means that it has a wealth of facets and ideas to offer which extend beyond the limits of a Sunday sermon and make it advisable to be selective. Here we provide suggestions for three sermons. These are based upon the threefold division of the pericope itself.

(i) The manifestation of the risen Lord to the disciples (Jn 20: 19-23)

The observance of Sunday
Even the opening words are significant. The manifestation to the disciples takes place 'at evening on the first day of the week' (20:19), and the encounter with Thomas follows 'after eight days' (20:26). The narrative serves to remind us of the origin of the christian Sunday, and to show what its real significance is. It is concerned with the encounter with the risen Lord. The observance of the Lord's day, therefore, is based not merely upon a remembrance of the resurrection of Jesus, but on the actual presence of the risen Lord himself. Against this background the individual traits in the gospel acquire their due

relevance and importance for the present day. They do not merely depict a scene in the past. They interpret the contemporary situation.

Encounter with the Lord
Jesus comes through closed doors. In this his divinity is manifested for by the exaltation the reality of this has been made actual. This divinity of his precisely does not signify any separation or remoteness in terms of distance. On the contrary it means that the Lord has overcome all external obstacles to draw near to us and freely to bestow himself upon us. It is precisely this that the salutation of peace implies as well. He bestows upon his disciples that salvation which consists in the presence of their Lord to them. Jesus shows them his hands and his side pierced with the lance. He is the same man who was crucified. In the resurrection he has not laid aside his earthly mode of existence. He has raised his own personal history to the state of exaltation, and has thereby perfected it. To say 'Christ' is to say 'Jesus who was crucified'. The risen Lord who bestows the Spirit is the 'historical' Jesus of Nazareth. He who wishes to share in the new life of this Jesus must not attempt to by-pass the historical facts of his earthly life up to and including his passion.

The sight of their Lord brings the disciples peace. As with the actual word 'peace' the state implied here means something more than a mere momentary state of mind. The disciples do not rejoice merely, for instance, because they behold once more the Lord whom they believed to have died. In their encounter with him a new dimension of existence opens up to them. Eschatological salvation is bestowed upon them. It is this that constitutes the real reason for their joy (cf 16:22).

The missionary charge
Jesus reiterates his salutation of peace, and this is followed by the missionary charge. The fact that the two are combined in

this way serves to emphasise the fact that the point of the encounter with the risen Lord is not that the disciples shall enjoy an interior peace, but rather that the world shall be saved. The mission is indissolubly united to the Easter event itself. As the Father has sent his Son into the world, so this Son in his turn now sends his disciples into the world (cf 17:18). They are to continue his mission. Their mission is based upon his, as laid upon him by the Father. It is he who brings about the salvation of men. Mission is first and foremost *his* work, not the work of men. Unless it maintains this intrinsic connection with its own origins it degenerates into mere propaganda.

The mission is not only referred back to its origin in God, but opened up to the future too, and carried forward by the Holy Spirit whom the risen Lord imparts to his disciples. Jesus does to them what the creator did to Adam (Gen 2:7): he breathes upon them. It is a new creation and a new birth that is taking place at this point (cf Jn 3:3ff). Here then begins a new aeon, the age of the Holy Spirit. Only in his power can the mission of the disciples achieve its goal.

Just as the mission of Jesus himself confronts the world with a crisis (3:18f; 9:39), and just as the Spirit as the promised one is he who not merely saves the world but also 'convinces' it (16:8) so too it is with the mission of the disciples. This imports salvation and perdition, forgiveness and judgment. Provided the world believes it stands acquitted, but to the extent that it closes itself in unbelief to the truth of the risen Lord it stands condemned. Jn 20:23 should not be restricted to the sacrament of penance. The actual statement in scripture shows that the entire mission of the disciples (in particular their preaching) has the character of an eschatological decision. In considering the bearing of this on absolution from sins we should not lose sight of the wider sphere of extra sacramental forgiveness.

The manifestation of the Lord to his disciples points on to the age of the church, and throws light upon the manner in which Sunday should be observed. It is in this observance that our encounter with the risen Lord takes place, that Lord who is the same as he who was crucified. The gifts of salvation which he bestows are peace and joy. They culminate in that one gift which embraces the whole of salvation, the Holy Spirit. The imparting of the Spirit serves not only to build us up in our interior souls, but also gives life to our mission to the world, a mission which is a continuation of Jesus' own, and, like his own, summons men to a radical decision. The liturgy, therefore, is not irrelevant to the present world, or purely 'other-wordly', but on the contrary is related to the world in a twofold manner: the risen Lord is the earthly Jesus. He directs the disciples and the community which is his to the world.

(ii) *The story of Thomas (20:24–29)*

The questions underlying the story of Thomas are such as are no less important to us of today than they were to the christians living at the end of the first century: How is faith possible in the period in which Christ no longer lets himself be seen by eye-witnesses? How can men living in this age of the church come to believe in him? What basis for faith can be found in this age? These questions are not simply themes, in some sense, of the missionary preaching, but rather, ever since the time of Thomas, have played an important part in the assembly of the community on Sundays in the inner room of the church ('After eight days his disciples were once more within and Thomas was with them' 20:26). The christian is never certain of his faith as of a sure possession. Rather, like Thomas, he is tempted by unbelief.

Thomas and the risen Lord

In the manifestation of the risen Lord to the disciples Thomas is not present. These others tell him of their experience and confess: 'We have seen the Lord' (20:25). But Thomas will not believe on the basis of their witness. He demands the same assurances as have been granted to the other disciples. Like them he wants to see and to touch for himself, and so to convince himself that the risen Lord is indeed identical with him who was crucified. Eight days after the manifestation to the disciples—this Sunday Thomas is among their assembly—his demand is fulfilled. This does not mean that he is given any objective proof. It is precisely in this situation, when Jesus is palpably near to him, that he receives the summons of faith: 'Be not faithless but believing' (20:27). Thomas is overcome by that which lies beyond his physical senses and can only be apprehended in faith: 'My Lord and my God' (20:28). This is his confession of faith, the confession of faith of the gospel as a whole and of the church in all ages.

'Blessed are they who have not seen and yet believed' (20:29)
Manifestly the assurance which Thomas receives in this encounter is to be regarded as exceptional, a concession to the doubter. Not that this means that the act of seeing is altogether set aside as inessential. It has a fundamental importance of its own. But it is a free gift which has been vouchsafed to the eye-witnesses. No-one has a right to demand it as a prior condition for faith. Thomas ought to have given his adherence to the witness of the disciples. That is why he is rebuked. In the age of the church faith is referred to the confession of the eye-witnesses. There is no room here for any arbitrary demand on the part of individual that he shall 'see'. Those are 'blessed who have not seen and yet believed' (20:29).

The foundation of faith
The story of Thomas contains statements which are of decisive importance for those who have neither had contact with Jesus during his earthly life nor yet seen him after his resurrection. This means that they are precisely relevant to our situation. We are just as incapable as the christians who lived about the year 100 of replying to those who ask us about Christ: 'See, here he is!' We cannot relate our faith directly to any act of 'seeing'.

Can this faith of ours, then, survive at all? Yes, says the gospel; those are blessed who believe without having seen. But is not faith of this sort suspended in mid-air? By no means. It points back to the witness of those who confess: 'We have seen the Lord' (20:25), and it is based upon and upheld by the risen Lord who lives on in his community. It is orientated towards him. Faith, therefore, is not simply an attitude in which one maintains the truth of certain past events. However much it may be related to these events, and however indispensable they may be to it, it is, nevertheless, made real in the encounter with the Lord present in the here and now. He is a believer who confesses with Thomas in this encounter: 'My Lord and my God' (20:28). The encounter between Thomas and Christ takes place in the assembled company of the disciples. In spite of his unbelief Thomas nevertheless frequents their assemblies and is accepted by them. Certainly community life is no less vital a factor today than it was then for the achievement of belief.

(iii) The original conclusion of the gospel (20:30f)
These two verses neither belong in any direct sense to the pericope on Thomas nor relate exclusively to the Easter narratives. They form the conclusion to the gospel as a whole, and sum it up in a brief and pregnant manner. A sermon concentrating on these verses in particular could serve to explain to the hearers the meaning and purpose of this gospel and to this end might concentrate on the following points:

1 Only a selection of the works of Jesus are contained in the gospel, for these works are innumerable. And yet nothing has been withheld from anyone. Small as it is, this selection is enough, if only we can see it for what it really is: a collection of signs representative of the whole. Each sign is transparent to him who has 'eyes to see'. It reveals Jesus himself.

2 By the word 'signs' here we refer not merely to the miracles, but also to the discourses. For this evangelist word and deed

belong together. The miracles are deeds which speak, and the words are events brought about by God himself.

3 The evangelist does not intend to present some kind of historical record of facts, and so to enrich the fund of knowledge of his hearers but rather to awaken the belief that Jesus is the messiah, the Son of God. It is belief that imports life, salvation.

4 The gospel of the ascension (Mk 16:14-20)

(a) ON THE SERMON LITERATURE

Even a survey of the various titles of sermons is enlightening. The composers present their considerations on the ascension under headings such as 'Revelry in Heaven', 'Action Father's Day', 'On the Ascension Commando', 'Necktie Day', 'Brothers it is Time', 'Joyful Ascension', 'The Human Spirit Which Dwells in Heaven', 'The Christian Way of Life', 'Consolation in Leave-Taking', 'Poor Consolation'.

The convulsive efforts to appear contemporary and to descend to the level of the television commercial in order to achieve a friendly atmosphere give a most unfortunate impression. They arouse the suspicion that the composers of these titles have little or no confidence in the power of the salvific event itself and the ideas connected with it to attract men, and that they are seeking to hide this deficiency by indulging in the most blatant forms of commercial advertising. Their ideas live up to the promise of their titles. They are for the most part preoccupied with the following two themes: the portrayal of Christ's ascension, the christian's longing for heaven.

The portrayal of Christ's ascension
Not a few composers of sermons come very close to pagan and Jewish ideas of ascensions into heaven, and present a highly emotional description of the ascension of Christ, one which is mythological through and through. 'Anyone who knows how to read between the lines can vividly picture to himself this

hour of our Lord's leave-taking. This is what we will attempt to do today....'

'After the meal is ended the saviour leads his faithful followers out to the Mount of Olives. But instead of taking the direct route there they make a little detour to go by Bethany. The saviour wants to pay a last visit there to Lazarus, Mary and Martha, the brother and the two sisters with whom he has stayed so often and so happily and by whom he has always been received so hospitably... On arriving at the crest of the Mount of Olives the saviour takes leave of all the scenes of his life both hidden and public, and says his last farewell to them. He sends a glance of joy and thankfulness in the direction of Bethlehem... His glance may have become sterner as he looked out over Jerusalem... And finally he may even have to announce one last deep farewell to the whole world, "Farewell thou sinful world! Truly thou hast not made it easy for me to redeem thee!"' 'Gently his feet leave the earth, softly his figure begins to disappear. Rays of light radiate out from him....' 'As he soars above the Mount of Olives he surveys once more the scenes of his earthly life: Bethlehem, where he submitted to the helplessness of the child; the roads of the Holy Land, upon which his sweat fell; the temple in which men sought to kill him; the way of pain along which he dragged himself to the mound of the cross and to death. Now he receives his reward. In this hour he demonstrates to the world that there is a justice....' 'What then can the mood of the disciples be as their Master mounts higher and higher before their eyes, raised above all earthly difficulties until he vanishes from their sight? They are full of grief as they gaze after him. And what is going on in the soul of the saviour himself? His work done, his sufferings endured, he goes to his Father in heaven in the happy consciousness expressed in the words "It is consummated"... Higher and higher he rises until a cloud hides him from the gaze of his disciples. All about him far and wide the invisible hosts of the souls which have been redeemed accompany him.

Legions of angels hover before him rejoicing and doing homage to him.' 'How well we can understand the apostles when they were unwilling to withdraw their gaze from the spot at which the Lord disappeared through the veil of cloud! . . . If at that hour the apostles had had the eyes of an angel then they would have seen that their Master took that way to the heights as a victorious liberator and the leader of a great triumphal procession.'

The advent of space rockets provides material for fresh speculations and comparisons: 'In the age of the space travellers it is important to understand clearly the difference between the ascension of Christ and a journey into space. Jesus ascended by his own power and the power of his Father, and went up perhaps six hundred metres from the earth. But once he had got to the other side of the clouds he altered the mode of his ascent. He withdrew from the world and entered heaven. Even if the cloud had moved away the disciples would still not have seen anything more of him . . . There is no intrinsic necessity why he should, so to say, have completed this definitive event when he had attained to a height of about six hundred metres. This is simply how it seemed to his disciples.'

Anyone who denies this mythology is counted a heretic by the over-zealous exponents of apologetics: 'Hands off the facts! . . . Anyone who does not believe what Mark and Luke write about the ascension of Christ [here the author is evidently referring to the alteration of place] no longer has his feet firmly planted upon the soil of the catholic faith. Besides he is making out that the evangelists are liars.'

As is shown from the title *Kyrios* and the quotation from Ps 110:1, what Mk 16:19 is intended to express is that Jesus has been inaugurated into the kingship of God. In this passage and in the Lucan tradition of the ascension upon which this verse is based the idea of a 'taking up' after the manner of the ascension of Elijah has been laid under contribution in order to give expression to the concept of exaltation. The sober realism of the narratives is designed to avoid awakening any mythological ideas. The mythical framework is radically broken. Its contribution to the *Logos* of revelation is merely that of an external figure of speech (The Lord 'was taken up into heaven' Mk 16: 19; cf 2 Kg 2:11).

In view of the fact that today the image of the world has been completely transformed it is unfortunate in the extreme that mythical ideas which have already been broken through in the new testament narratives should be re-introduced without any heed to the consequences, that they should be presented as the reality itself, and that to this end an unnecessary strain should be imposed upon men's faith. The truth of Jesus' inauguration into the dominion of God is thereby distorted into a journey upwards into the sky (Jesus 'soars higher and higher above'), combined with a romantic account of a leave-taking. Such presentations, with their exaggerated love of the miraculous, rightly evoke from those who hear them either contradiction or at least a pitying smile.

The idea that Jesus withdrew himself spatially from the world before the eyes of the disciples necessarily evokes a mood of leave-taking. Now precisely in the context of the ascension this is utterly misconceived. What the exaltation of Jesus implies is that he has drawn near to the world in a new way.

The christian's longing for heaven
Christ has vanished. 'He has escaped from time and broken out of its prison. . . .' He has gone before us into heaven and is waiting for us there. Thus there is only one conclusion which necessarily follows from ideas of this kind: Follow him there!

'"Longing for heaven"—that is the watchword for the present day.' By his ascension our saviour has opened up for us that most blessed way which leads out of all earthly sorrows to the heart of the heavenly Father'. Thus we see 'In the gospel of today . . . eleven men standing with shining eyes directed to the Mount of Olives, that mountain associated with the deepest sorrows and the most terrible anxieties. Why are their eyes shining? They have turned them away from the scenes of anguish. They are looking upwards and they know that there is another world there above. There above is home!' 'Is it too much to ask that at least once in the year we should leave behind us the mundane affairs and the turmoil of everyday life, and should soar upwards to the holy mount of the ascension to experience in spirit what took place there. . . ? It is important today to raise ourselves up above the clouds to the saviour, the hero of the day, and there above at his side take a wide survey as the Master himself has done. . . .' There all the longing for home will be aroused (we must not forget the romantic idyll of the traveller's return: Christ as the first home-comer). Here it is intensified to an eternal homesickness. '"I would I were at home". The earth still holds us firmly to itself, but we know that one day it will set us free, first our soul and then our body as well.' 'The situation is such that we can never cease to be astonished at it. Our home is with God. It lies far off from the world . . . We must not wait for death to separate us by force from the earth, but must do this in spirit already in the present . . . This is the support we need in order to transcend the world and its evils. Outside they believe only in that earthly happiness which belongs to the titillation of the flesh. They are buried in their own lust . . . We exist in order to go to heaven.' What do we care for 'the materialists of all ages? All these do not in fact merit the name "man" in the full sense of the word. They deny the most sublime longing that is in man, the aspirations of religion which cause us to seek God. Their life, in common with that of the beasts, moves forward only within the limits of earthly existence . . . It is only the doctrine of heaven, of eternal bliss, that has any answer to give to the deepest longings that are in man . . . It is joy in the thought of heaven that enables us to bear and to overcome the distresses to which our existence is subject'. The earth is the '"veil of tears" . . . Our home is not to be found here on this earth. Here we are in exile. "It is not

here; the home of our soul is to be found above in the light"'.
Here we have to earn our ticket to heaven. 'It is valid not merely
for a boring journey by a stopping train which stands puffing at
every molehill. Our train to heaven must be a swift express or
even a Trans-European! Mother church helps us to prepare for
the journey. She accompanies us on the journey and gives us
abundant provisions for the journey in her "dining car".' 'How
carefree we can be as we journey through life, much more
comfortably than with the "Touropa".'

Anyone who imagines that the unfortunate consequences
which follow from a type of piety that represents a flight from
the world have long since been overcome will find himself to a
large extent disappointed when he comes to look into the kind
of sermons that are commonly preached today. The quotations
we have given reveal that de-christianised attitude in which
hope for the kingdom of God is blended with the longing of the
soul that feels itself threatened, to escape from the evil tumult
of the world into a pallid spiritual heaven where hope is no
longer directed forwards but only upwards, and to an extent
that is unbalanced and one-sided. In this longing for heaven
nothing earthly is valued any longer except as a means of
earning one's ticket for the celestial train from which one looks
out contemptuously at the unbelievers, and above all at the
Godless materialists who do not deserve the name of 'man' at
all, and are to be regarded as on a level with the beasts.

This is not the place to enter into the manifold causes for this
distortion, or to indicate in any comprehensive way that
christian hope is not to be realised by by-passing the world and
the future it holds. For our present purposes we must simply
point out that the kind of 'other-worldly' christianity which is
reflected in these quotations cannot invoke the tradition of the
ascension in scripture in its support, and that so far from this it
is in flat contradiction to it.

The ascension of Christ does not for one moment mean a
taking leave of the world. On the contrary it implies that Jesus

is enthroned as Lord of the world. His exaltation has not made him remote and alien from the world, but has brought him near to it in a new way. Therefore the disciples and the church are exhorted to look forward to the future that this earth holds: 'Go into all the world and preach the gospel to the whole of creation' (Mk 16:15). The ascension of Christ and the missionary charge are united as closely as possible one to another. The church must continue the mission of God to the world which was initiated with Jesus. She must not take leave of the world. The biblical tradition of the ascension already contains within itself a criticism of that kind of christianity which devotes itself wholly to the other world and forgets that over and above the duty of waiting for the parousia it has a task assigned to it in this world: 'Men of Galilee why do you stand looking into heaven...' (Ac 1:11).

(b) SUGGESTIONS FOR PREACHING ON THE ASCENSION (MK 16:14–20)

The reading under consideration consists of the second half of the canonical conclusion of the Marcan gospel. This comprises a resumé of the Easter narratives contained in the other three gospels. It can be seen, then, that this gospel contains a wealth of statements which are full of significance for the *kerygma*. They all relate to the Easter event, and it is in the light of this that they must be interpreted in our preaching. For all the literary problems which this pericope entails it must be emphasised that the statements it contains provide a most effective summary of what took place at Easter. They are firmly rooted in the message of the bible as a whole and are meant to be preached today also. In view of the fact that the various traditions are simply arranged in a loose sequence several homiletic possibilities are open to us here. Every verse could be taken as a point of departure for a sermon. However the fact that this gospel is used for the feast of Christ's ascension makes it natural to begin with verse 19, which does not depict the actual ascension itself, but introduces it by means of two quotations from the old testament (2 Kg 2:11; Ps 110:1): 'The Lord Jesus was taken up into heaven and sat down at the right hand of God.' The preacher should first make it clear what is meant by this statement.

The horizon of ideas
Mark 16:19 clearly bears the stamp of the conception of the world entertained at that time. This is a point that must not be overlooked. It is no part of the preacher's duty to disseminate outworn cosmological ideas. His task, rather, is to proclaim the theological content of the ascension: Jesus has been enthroned as king of the world by God. His enthronement ('... and sat down at the right hand of God'), like the resurrection itself, transcends our dimensions of space and time. The fact that in Mk 16:19 (and similarly in Luke) it is expressed in spatial categories does not mean that it is to be taken as an empirically observable fact.

The comparison so much favoured nowadays between the ascension and a journey into space might be used to throw light upon the fact that in the ascension of Jesus totally different dimensions are in question than those into which the rockets are sent. 'Heaven is not a place beyond the stars. It is something much vaster and more breath-taking: it means that there is a place for man in God. This has its basis in the interpenetration of the human and divine natures in Jesus the man who was crucified and exalted ... What we call "heaven", therefore, is actually himself. For heaven is not a space or sphere but a person, the person of him in whom God and man are for ever indivisibly one. And we are going to heaven, are indeed entering into heaven to the extent that we go to Jesus and enter into him. To that extent the term "ascension" can be applied to a process that takes place in the midst of our everyday lives' (Ratzinger in GUL 40, 83).

The kerygmatic statement of the 'ascension'
In unfolding the theological content of the ascension our point of departure must be the fact that it is immediately connected with the manifestation of the risen Lord, in other words that it belongs to the events of Easter taken as a whole. The risen Lord shows himself to be the exalted Lord. The disciples experience the fact first that Christ lives, and second that Christ is Lord. It is precisely Mk 16:19 that makes it clear that the statement about the ascension derives its significance from the idea of Christ sitting at the right hand of God. Christ's ascension is the festival of Christ's kingship.

The festival of the ascension, therefore, is the celebration of the kingship of Christ as prescribed by tradition. The celebration of the festival of Christ the King on the last Sunday of the year raises problems, the more so since its introduction in 1925 was influenced by political events (cf Pascher, 450). Here the idea of kingship and the title of king are in the foreground, whereas in the ascension of Christ it is the saving event of the exaltation of the Lord that is celebrated. The festival of Christ the King might be saved from political and religio-political misinterpretations, and the festival of the ascension might have its original meaning restored to it if both festivals were combined and Christ's ascension were celebrated as the festival of Christ's kingship.

In transcending the limitations of the world he has not abandoned it but rather drawn closer to it and encompassed it. Hence every idea of leave-taking is to be eliminated from sermons on the ascension. Under no circumstances should the hearer be given any impression (such as will immediately arise if we give a spatial interpretation of the ascension) that Jesus is now far away from us. He does not abandon the world to its own fate. He fulfils all things. All power is given to him in heaven and on earth. His royal dominion consists precisely in the fact that he fills all things with his presence. Thus he is not merely a historical figure of the past who has taken leave of the earth. On the contrary he is present to it and to the entire cosmos permanently and all-pervasively.

The world mission
For this reason the disciples and the church are warned not to stand there looking up to heaven in a manner which betokens flight from the world (Ac 1:11). Rather they must look forwards into the future of this earth, and proclaim the gospel to all creation (Mk 16:15, the whole world, all creatures). The world belongs to Christ, and they must win it for him. There is a direct and immediate connection between the ascension and the world mission. 'In the period between the resurrection and the return of the Lord the proclamation of the gospel on a world-wide scale is the form in which the kingship of Jesus Christ (which is likewise world-wide in its extent) finds expression. For the word is the lowly guise in which Christ exercises his dominion' (Ratzinger in GUL 40, 83).

The church has a relationship with all creatures, and has to announce the claim of her Lord, a claim which is either responded to with faith (and, as a concomitant of this, by receiving baptism) or rejected in unbelief (Mk 16:16). All the world is faced with the eschatological decision as to whether it withdraws into itself and declares itself not subject to the dominion of Jesus, or whether it submits to this dominion. 'He who says yes at this point . . . he has pledged himself together with his entire life, to him who has become his Redeemer. He who says no at this point thereby forfeits not some edifying religious feeling, but his life before God. For he falls under the condemnation of the judge' (Weber in GPM 4, 157). Even the disciples are not exempt from this decision. They are not heroes of the faith but men threatened with disbelief and hardness of heart (Mk 16:14; cf 11:13), and precisely in their state of temptation they represent the pattern and prototype of all believers.

The signs

Signs will accompany those who believe (16:17) and confirm the word of the disciples (16:20), though admittedly not as instruments which prove that a divine intervention has taken place by supplying objective evidence to this effect. They have no independent autonomous function but follow upon faith and the word. In other words they do not occur prior to, or independent of faith. One cannot by-pass faith and press on directly to them. They are not for us to control or to dispose of, and cannot be used as advertisements. They are not magical powers but acts of the power of Christ who is the redeemer and liberator of creation and not only a 'saviour of souls'. His salvation bears upon our entire existence in all its aspects, and so upon its physical side too. It is not in any sense located merely in the purely interior and private sphere of our being.

According to this gospel to celebrate Christ's ascension means to celebrate Christ himself as Lord of the world and to assent to the world because it is his.

4
THE MIRACLE STORIES: EXEGETICAL INVESTIGATION

I Introduction

1 The conception of miracles among the ancients

Miraculous experiences are far from being a phenomenon that we encounter exclusively in the domain of early christianity. The same phenomenon is to be found, for instance, in Jewish and Hellenistic circles, and should be viewed primarily against the background of the ancient conception of the world. This does not envisage any sharp cleavage between this world and the other world, nature and supernature. Both constantly interpenetrate one another. The breaking in of transcendental powers into this world, which arouses astonishment and feelings of terror, is experienced as miraculous. 'Once one realises this one understands that the concept of miracle entertained by the ancients focuses (and in this respect it is unlike our own) not primarily upon the heightened causality involved, but on the event considered as divine epiphany' (Käsemann, 227). It bears not upon the element of the extraordinary in a given event but on the encounter with the divinity which it entails. Admittedly we are not infrequently in danger of considering the extraordinary as a phenomenon 'in itself', and of using it as an instrument, a piece of objective evidence by which to prove that a divine intervention has taken place. In this way the miracle is deprived of its epiphanic character, and degraded to the level of a mere piece of wonder-working. The ancient miracle stories provide material for examination.

MIRACLE STORIES: EXEGETICAL INVESTIGATION

*2 The rejection of the demand for signs in the
new testament*
There is a radical difference between the new testament conception of miracles and the general tendency apparent in the stories of wonder-working in late Jewish and Hellenistic traditions. This finds clear expression in the rejection of the demand for signs, in which a critical attitude towards wonder-working is apparent. This is a factor which does not merely appear almost accidentally in some isolated passage. On the contrary it pervades all levels of new testament tradition as an essential part of the message of the early christian preaching. The concept of sign involved in the rejection of the demand for a sign is one that is not included in the normal understanding of sign. It has not the positive meaning, full of theological content, of the Johannine sign, but the negative significance of a miracle performed in support of the message of faith (cf Schnackenburg, ET 517f).

(i) Paul
In his epistles Paul has neither handed down any miracle stories nor adduced them in support of his arguments. Certainly he bears witness to the experience of 'signs and wonders' (Rom 15:19; 2 Cor 12:12), but he also refers to the fact that the advent of Antichrist 'will be by the activity of Satan with all power and with pretended signs and wonders' (2 Thess 2:9). Nowhere does he enter in any greater detail into the nature of the 'signs and wonders'. These seem to have had little influence on his understanding of his faith. Even for the authentication of his apostolate it is hardly true to say that he ascribes to miracles importance even in principle. He refuses to prove his credentials by appealing to 'signs'. When the Jews demand that Paul's faith shall be attested by miracles of this kind, miracles which will assure them as neutral observers of the reality of the divine intervention, this is tantamount to a provocation offered to

God. It is an expression of that spirit of human self-assertion which believes that it has sure criteria for testing out the claims of revelation. Man attempts to summon God before his tribunal and is only willing to accord him any acknowledgement when he has authenticated himself there by means of assured proofs. Such 'accredited faith' is no faith at all but disbelief. It is as a counter to the provocation which this spirit of disbelief represents that Paul insists upon preaching the cross (1 Cor 1:22–24). God reveals himself not in the sort of sign that expresses self-assertion, but in that other kind of sign that expresses self-giving.

(ii) *The synoptics*
According to the synoptic tradition Jesus' reaction to the demand for a miracle to confirm his message of faith in the sense of an objective proof of this message is one of unambiguous opposition. The rejection of the demand for a sign on the part of his opponents finds unmistakable expression in the answer he gives to them as attested in all levels of the gospel tradition. In the version of Matthew, which approximates to the sayings source (Q), this answer runs as follows: 'An evil and adulterous generation seeks for a sign, but no sign shall be given it except the sign of the prophet Jonah' (Mt 12:39; cf Lk 11:29). Mark does not include this reference to the sign of Jonah, and thereby gives expression to Jesus' refusal of the demand for a sign in a manner that is peculiarly sharp: 'And he sighed deeply in his spirit and said: "Why does this generation seek a sign? Truly I say to you no sign shall be given to this generation." And he left them . . .' (Mk 8:12f).

The instances in which Jesus casts out devils and heals the sick are not enough for the Pharisees. They do not regard these as providing any adequate authentication of his mission. Jesus must prove himself authorised by God by performing a miracle to authenticate his message of faith which they are able to test directly for themselves. And this proof must be objectively evident, measurable by human standards and powerful enough to make it impossible to retain any doubt as to his divine authority. This is in accordance with the Jewish ideas of that time. Some striking event described beforehand must be provided in order to confirm beyond all doubt that God acknowledges him who appeals to him. Jesus radically rejects this demand for a guarantee given in advance, and thereby takes up a stand against the messianic expectations of his time. He grants no sign of this kind which is capable of being submitted to objective analysis and so enables his divinity to be tested out. This would amount to doing away with the decision of faith. If anyone seeks to make certain of the truth of his claim to revelation by testing it out empirically then Jesus rejects such a one and departs from him (Mk 8:13).

Even the sign of Jonah (Lk 11:29f; cf Mt 12:39f) does not hold out any prospect of providing the sort of miracle in confirmation of the message of faith which the Pharisees expect. It is originally (cf Lk 11:30) focused upon Jesus (or upon his preaching), and in a secondary (and mitigating) interpretation (Mt 12:40) upon his death and resurrection as signs of the fact that the kingdom of God is breaking in upon the world. 'The Matthaean version too has still managed to preserve Jesus' refusal to all disbelievers who demand a sign clearly enough' (Bornkamm GPM 13, 279).

(iii) John

According to John the Jews make two attempts to demand a 'sign' of Jesus. In connection with the cleansing of the temple they demand that he shows what authority he has for this proceeding by providing a miracle which will enable them to believe (2:18). And after the multiplication of loaves they want to see a sign from heaven (6:30f). His reaction, like that of the synoptics, is unequivocal: he rejects the demand out of hand. He himself *is* the new temple. He himself *is* the bread of heaven. There is no sign over and above these truths to authenticate his claims. He who makes his acknowledgement of Jesus dependent upon certain prior conditions which have to be fulfilled before he will believe manifests thereby that he is an unbeliever. Jesus demands a faith that is unconditional and unconditioned.

II Interpretation of selected miracle stories

Significant though the rejection of the demand for a sign is for our understanding of the new testament miracles, it must be remembered that exegesis is primarily concerned not with the miracles themselves but with the miracle stories. Its function is not primarily to discuss the possibility and reality of the miracle (a question which belongs rather to the systematic department of theology) but to investigate the literary data and so to determine the particular linguistic forms in which these stories are couched. This in turn enables the exegete to explain the particular message contained in these stories. The exegete, therefore, has to enquire into the underlying intention of the story-teller and the special characteristics of the stories themselves in which Jesus is depicted as possessing extraordinary powers which go beyond all human experience. Only when this is established can the historical question be embarked upon.

As with miraculous experiences so too with these miracle stories, they do not represent a phenomenon which is exclusive to sacred scripture. Miracle stories are narrated by many individuals in antiquity—including some who were contemporary with Jesus himself. A comparison of the available material reveals the fact that in not a few cases the authors of the miracle stories have undeniably adopted the parlance of the world they knew (the parlance of Jewish and Hellenistic miracle stories), and also that they draw upon the motifs of the old testament. Elements of style held in common lead us to suppose that there is some degree of formal dependence. Here as there the stories are introduced by a description of the perilous situation (nature miracles), or the long and severe suffering of an individual (miracles of healing). Next the development of the extraordinary event itself is described, and finally it is stated to have been successful (reaction of the bystanders, 'Greek chorus' type of conclusion).

In addition to the question of literary or pre-literary dependence on the part of several of the miracle stories in the new testament, a further point for consideration is that the route which they have followed from their original form in oral tradition to their final redaction in the gospel is often a complicated one. Probably most of them would originally have been told as isolated stories circulating among the communities, and so far as their form is concerned they would have been stamped with very different characteristics. Forms which are well adapted for describing some extraordinary act on Jesus' part are to be found side by side with others which manifestly have little interest in the actual performance of the miracles, and instead of this are primarily concerned with some saying of Jesus. In common with the rest of the tradition of Jesus these narratives have a history of their own, the development of which can be traced through its particular stages by a comparison of the various traditions incorporated in the gospels. 'The motifs occur at different points. Variants emerge. Heightened effects are introduced' (Bultmann [6]1964, 241). One question which arises is how great an influence we should ascribe to Jewish and Hellenistic parallels, and also to developments within the tradition with regard to the form of the miracle stories in the new testament. However in view of the fact that the material under investigation is so complex and has passed through so many different stages of development no general decision can be arrived at applicable to all these stories. We can only arrive at more detailed conclusions by considering each individual case in its own right. In any case the interpreter has to take into account as an indisputable fact that many influences have been brought to bear. In view of this it would be quite wrong to take up an *a priori* attitude, in which one immediately accepted the miracle stories as historical records. Nevertheless, as will be shown, it would be just as mistaken to force them into the general category of 'miracle stories of antiquity', and to deny that they have any historical value at all. A more precise comparison between the available traditions serves to warn us against premature judgments, and to remind us of how important it is to recognise the real and objective differences which do exist.

The selection of miracle stories which follow is based partly on the fact that they were formerly used on certain Sundays in the Roman lectionary, and thus preaching material on them is available, partly in order to cover a variety of types of story.

1 The story of the healing of the paralytic

All three synoptics record the story of the healing of the paralytic, and all three connect it with a controversy about the authority to forgive sins (Mk 2:1–12; Mt 9:1–8; Lk 15:17–26). Matthew and Luke are dependent upon Mark at this point, but display notable deviations from him in the manner of their respective presentations.

(a) MARK 2:1–12

Mk 2:1–12 in the context of the gospel as a whole
In ch 2 Mark introduces a collection of five conflict sayings. 'He was preaching the word to them' (2:1). This emphatic indication, which is also to be found in other passages of special importance in the gospel (4:33; 8:32), introduces a section which is of special theological importance. The predominant interest here is no longer the miracle and the manner in which it is performed, but the word of preaching. The gathering of the people (cf 2:2 once more) is already overshadowed by the great controversy in which Jesus defends himself (and his associates) against his opponents. He proves himself to have authority over sin and the law (the forgiveness of sins 2:1–12; association with publicans and sinners 2:13–17; the question of fasting 2:18–22;

breaking the sabbath commandment, on two occasions, 2:23–28; 3:1–6). At these decisive points, which are of central importance for his claim to divine authority, the Pharisees are roused to protest. Their opposition intensifies from episode to episode, until finally it culminates in their decision to do away with Jesus (3:6). In the act of rising superior to sin and the law the cross becomes visible.

According to 2:1 the conflict takes place at Capernaum, although it has been stated a little before that Jesus had departed from that place (1:35–38) and was preaching throughout 'all Galilee' (1:39). The apparent discrepancy between these two statements enables us to recognise that what we are being told should not be understood as the narrative of a journey, but is rather conceived of from the point of view of the *kerygma*. For the evangelist the scene of these happenings is no longer simply Capernaum (though perhaps the story of the healing of the paralytic was originally attached to this place) but the actual community.

Interpretation of Mk 2:1–12
A form-critical analysis reveals the fact that in this pericope two units of narrative which are different in respect of content and form alike have been combined together: the story of a healing and a conflict saying concerning the forgiveness of sins. This latter has been inserted into the pre-existing miracle story even though it 'has different presuppositions and a different origin' (Lohmeyer, 54). The 'joins' in v 5 and v 10 should not be overlooked. Even from a purely formal point of view they can be recognised as such from the fact that the phrase 'He said to the paralytic', which occurs immediately before the beginning of the insertion (2-5a) is taken up again word for word at the end of it by way of transition (2:10). In the light of this the conflict saying breaks in in a way that takes us wholly by surprise. The scribes make their appearance (2:6) without any previous introduction and in the conclusion (2:11f) they have

disappeared once more equally suddenly without leaving any trace of the controversy itself. Furthermore: 'the four men have not brought the paralytic to Jesus in order that his sins may be forgiven him but in order that he may be healed' (Haenchen 1966, 101). If we set the insertion temporarily aside then what we are left with is a narrative which exhibits all the elements which belong to the characteristic style of a miracle story.

The miracle story: 2: 1–5a, 11f
The details of the story are fully developed. Immediately following upon the description of the situation (Jesus preaches 'at home' in Capernaum 2:1f), the action of the four men in climbing up and breaking through the roof is described as an element of heightened intensity in the presentation as a whole. Those who seek to explain the story will find themselves faced with a riddle so long as they attempt to reconstruct it in terms of sheer historical fact. The aim of the narrator is quite different. He intends to bear witness to a faith which breaks through all obstacles and thereby arrives at its goal, namely Jesus himself. Jesus responds to this faith (2:5a, 11). The healing takes place without any gesture or external act on Jesus' part. The word of power is sufficient. It proves Jesus' authority. He is the prophet who performs the sign of the final age, the eschatological message of good tidings predicted in Is 51.

2:12 serves to confirm emphatically the success of the healing. Who could doubt it when the paralytic himself carries his bed home? Over and above this all the bystanders confirm that the miracle has taken place (the 'Greek chorus' conclusion). They praise God.

The conflict saying (2:5b–10)
In v 6 the opponents appear on the scene. They are the scribes. In fact they do not utter a word—to that extent this is a 'conflict saying' only in an indirect sense. Nevertheless Jesus knows

MIRACLE STORIES: EXEGETICAL INVESTIGATION

'in his spirit' (the Spirit of God 2:8) what they would like to say. They take scandal at the fact that Jesus pronounced the word of forgiveness (2:7). Their faith tells them that this is something that is for God alone to do. Jesus does not dispute this, but nevertheless puts forward the claim that he can bring to realisation the reconciliation between mankind and God upon earth (2:10). He acts in God's place. It is precisely against this that the protest of the scribes and their accusation of blasphemy is directed. They contest his authority. Yet—this is the question of v 9—if a man heals a paralytic by a word of power should it not be conceded that that same man must also be empowered to pronounce the forgiveness of sins? Both words of power have in fact their basis in the authority of the 'Son of Man' (2:10).

The manner in which the conflict saying has been combined with the miracle story

2:9ff combines the two narrative units together and does so in such a way that the miracle story is subordinated to the conflict saying. It contributes the force of its own argument to the actual controversy, though admittedly the changed situation in which it is applied does cause its message to be modified in certain respects. Thus in the existing form of the pericope the central point is no longer the healing of the paralytic, but the justification of Jesus' claim to authority. The purpose of the miracle now becomes not so much to provide evidence of Jesus' compassion for the sick man as to attest the fact that he has power to forgive sins. This alteration in the kerygmatic intention is emphasised by the context (see above p 120).

How has this unusual combination of two narrative units come about? One suggestion is that it is because the close connection between sickness and sin was current in Jewish ideas at that time (cf Schmid [5]1963, 57; Hahn [2]1964, 43 n 1). No intrinsic connection between sin and sickness is to be discerned in Mk 2:1–12. The question here is not simply the forgiveness of sins in general, but the authority to forgive them, and the healing is not intended to prove that the sins have been forgiven, but simply to bring out the authority of Jesus. Furthermore the healing is presented not as the outcome of the forgiveness of sins but as an independent action in its own right (2:11). Jesus has broken away from the opinion which prevailed in later judaism according to which a man's sickness was held to be the consequence of his sins; cf Lk 13:1–5; Jn 9.

This might in fact have been at any rate the occasion for a literary composition which, in its existing form, has been made to contribute to a different theme. Here it is concerned with the authority to forgive sins. Whereas the scribes (representing orthodox judaism) maintain that God (in heaven) alone can forgive sins, the christians confess that with the coming of the 'Son of Man' this authority is present 'upon earth' (2:10). This is not simply a question of a surviving practice in the church being projected back into the historical life of Jesus. It is a fact that belongs firmly to the history of Jesus that he made himself accessible to sinners and forgave them their sins (Bornkamm ET 64–95). In the background of this narrative we can already discern the practice of forgiving sins together with the invocation of Jesus' name and authority as exercised in the community of his adherents. Admittedly in Mark there is not yet any explicit reference to this practice.

(b) MATTHEW 9:1–8
Matthew has not simply confined himself to repeating the pericope in Mark which was known to him, but has told the story afresh with certain striking alterations. This has had the effect of bringing out its central theme even more clearly.

The immediate context has been taken over from Mark: Mt 9:1–17 contains three of the five Galilaean conflict sayings (Mk 2:1–3, 6), though admittedly these are included in the great cycle of miracles (8:1—9:34). Already in Mark, as we have seen, the miracle story is made subordinate to the question

MIRACLE STORIES: EXEGETICAL INVESTIGATION

which is the subject of dispute (even though here it still retains a distinct point of its own). But now, in Matthew, this process is pressed to its logical conclusion and 'the story is constructed round the saying about the power of the Son of Man to forgive sins as its clear and dominant central point' (Lohmeyer-Schmauch, 169). 'The conflict saying has, as it were, taken over those sections of the pericope which were originally designed to present a miracle story in the orthodox style' (Bornkamm *et al* ET 177).

Of the broadly developed exposition of the miracle story in Mark (2:1–5a) only one brief section has survived in Matthew to provide an introduction to the conflict saying (9:1f). The story advances directly and undeviatingly towards its central point. The bearers of the sick man and the multitudes receive only a passing mention. The climb onto the roof is eliminated altogether, with the result that the reference to the faith of those who accomplished it appears unmotivated. Jesus and the scribes dominate the theme as a whole. The controversy between them is presented in concise and polished sentences (9:3–6). A particularly significant point is the alteration of the conclusion (9:7f). Where Mark has retained the orthodox conclusion of a miracle story without reference to the conflict saying, Matthew has incorporated it in the centre of the pericope, which dominates the whole. The central word *exousia*, power, serves to establish the connection (9:6, 8). The 'chorus' of praise to God is no longer (as in Mk 2:12) called forth by the miracle, but rather by the manifestation of the power to forgive sins, which is now asserted not of the 'Son of Man' alone, but of 'men' as well (Mt 9:8).

A factor which already appears in the background to the story as told by Mark achieves clear and direct expression in Matthew: the point here is the authentication of the forgiveness of sins as practised in the community. The extension of the authority of the Son of Man (Mk 2:10 par) to 'men' (Mt 9:8) shows that the proclamation of the message does not remain fixed, but rather develops and advances, and takes the changed situation into account. The question of the scribes: 'Who can forgive sins except God alone?' (Mk 2:7) is omitted because it could lead to misunderstandings. God's power to forgive is in fact bestowed upon 'men' by Jesus, and is made actual in the community. The authority of the community derives from Christ. It only has this authority because he is its Lord and remains with it 'until the end of the world' (Mt 28:20).

Where Mark is primarily concerned with the question of Jesus' authority, Matthew is concerned with that of the community. Both deny that the claim of the scribes is justified. In the background of the conflict saying the controversy between the christian community on the one hand, and orthodox judaism on the other can be discerned. And it is apparent that in Matthew the two sides have already hardened in their opposition.

(c) LUKE 5:17–26
Luke takes over from Mark (2:1—3:6) the whole section of the five conflict sayings (5:17—6:11). Since it is precisely the journeys of Jesus that he records (Galilee–Judaea–Jerusalem) he strikes out the name of Capernaum at the outset (5:17).

Luke pays particular attention to the composition of the narrative. By introducing the Pharisees and scribes right from the outset (5:17), he creates an organic transition from the miracle story to the conflict saying. The abruptness of the change of scene is smoothed over. When he comes to the enterprise of climbing onto the roof the evangelist envisages (5:19) a roof of tiles, and thereby brings the story into line with the ideas of his Hellenistic hearers. In his treatment he attaches more importance than Matthew to the miracle story, conforming in this once more to the Marcan prototype, and actually going beyond it in this respect at certain points. The theme is set in the introductory sentence: 'The power of the Lord was with him to heal' (5:17; cf 4:36). The suddenness of the healing (5:25) and the enormous reaction produced in the bystanders—including the healed man himself (5:25) at the 'unheard of event' (5:26) is brought out in the manner of the Hellenistic wonder stories. The phrase 'today' used by Luke at central points (5:26; cf 2:11, 3:22, 4:21, and 13:33) serves to indicate that in the deed of power performed by Jesus the time of salvation has been inaugurated.

2 *The story of the calming of the storm*

Matthew (8:18, 23–27) and Luke (8:22–23), in dependence upon Mark (4:35–41) both include the episode of the calming of the storm in their gospels. In certain respects the evangelists do show notable differences in the manner in which they hand this story down, and these enable us to discern the particular kerygmatic intention in each case. It is important to pay due attention to this in what follows.

(a) MARK 4:35–41

Mk 4:35–41 in the context of the gospel as a whole
In the fourth chapter of his gospel Mark begins by presenting the first (and apart from ch 13 the only) instance of the major discourse, consisting of three parables and various groups of sayings woven together to make up the sermon by the lakeside. This is followed by a cycle of three miracle stories (4:35—5:43), which represent the acts of Jesus. Word and act are combined with one another in virtue of the unity of place and time. A single scene is set for all these events, and this is constructed by the evangelist himself. He has assigned the various narratives to a single place, the lakeside, and already in 3:9 and 4:1 prepares us for the situation by representing Jesus as 'in the boat' (4:36). In terms of time the cycle of miracles is combined with the sermon by the lakeside by the information given in 4:35.

Over and above these geographical and chronological determinations the narratives are related in terms of content too to a single central point which they have in common. This is the 'secret of the kingdom of God' (4:11), and therefore the secret of the messiah as well. His revelation meets with misunderstanding and so the section as a whole concludes once more (see above p 120f) with his being rejected, this time by his own fellow village dwellers of Nazareth (6:1–6a).

The miracle story
The whole course of the event is described down to the individual details (cf the mention of the cushion in 4:38). In his presentation Mark begins by describing in terse and urgent sentences the situation of peril: the boat is on the lake, the storm suddenly arises, the waves break into the boat and it fills with water (4:37). While the powers of nature are breaking in Jesus is asleep (4:38). This contrast, which is only rendered more acute by the outcry of the disciples, serves to heighten the tension. Jesus' word of power, by which he commands the storm and the sea to silence, occupies the centre of the narrative. 'He utters the same words as elsewhere in the healing of the possessed, as though the wind and waves were mighty demons or the tools of such demons. And at this word all is over' (Lohmeyer, 91). The 'mighty storm' (4:37) is followed by the 'great calm' (4:39). The success of the word of power and the significance of him who performs the miracle are underlined by the reaction of the bystanders (cf the 'Greek chorus' conclusion in 4:41). The narrative is constructed after the manner of the miracle stories of antiquity. It has parallels in the old testament and extra-biblical literature. But even though it may have been 'influenced by legendary material, it retains its own originality' (Lohmeyer, 92).

The question of faith (Mk 4:40)
However much the story may give the impression of an ortho-

MIRACLE STORIES: EXEGETICAL INVESTIGATION

dox miracle story, its message does not consist merely and exclusively in showing Jesus' power and transcendence over the elements of nature and in presenting him as the great wonder-worker and man of God. We shall arrive at a deeper understanding of the story if we notice the particular form in which it is cast. Jesus' word to the disciples (4:40) interrupts the flow of the narrative. One would have expected it—Matthew too has felt this (8:26)—to come before the miracle. In the structure of the pericope as a whole it is by performing the miracle that Jesus answers the despairing cry of the disciples (4:38). The question in 4:40 gives the impression of an afterthought. It is precisely this fact that makes it noticeable. In the intention of the evangelist it is in no sense a mere 'appendix' to the nature miracle, but rather imparts a new accent to the story as a whole in that it draws our attention to the attitude of the disciples towards Jesus.

Once a miracle has been performed a new situation arises in which Jesus turns reproachfully upon his disciples: 'Have you still no faith?' (4:40b). The disciples are rebuked because they constantly fail to arrive at any true understanding (cf 8:17, 21) 'because it has not yet dawned upon them who Jesus is' (Gnilka, 35). His question is intended to make them pay heed, and, in connection with the miracle, bring them nearer to an understanding of his messiahship. In fact a glimmer of light does begin to appear in the darkness of their incomprehension. The story leads to the question: 'Who is this...?' (4:41). In this passage they find no direct answer to their question. In spite of the miracle Jesus ultimately remains unrecognised. He remains a mystery.

This feature runs like a scarlet thread through the second gospel. Its message and significance is 'not so much historical as theological' (Lohmeyer, 92). This message has been described as 'the messianic secret'. Mark has constructed his gospel as a 'book of secret epiphanies' (Dibelius [4]1961, 232, 260). The messiahship of Jesus breaks through again and again in his words and deeds, but throughout his earthly life it remains a mystery, and must so remain (cf the command to silence 1:34, 44; 3:12; 5:43; 7:36; 8:26, 30, and the explanation of the reason for parables, 4:11f). Probably the disciples have been initiated into the secret (cf 4:11), but still even they can grasp it fully only in the perspective of the cross and the resurrection. Even after the vital turning-point marked by the confession of Peter (8:29) Jesus is faced with fresh instances of their lack of understanding (8:32f, 9:32). After his glorification he explicitly commands them not to preach his epiphany 'until the Son of Man has risen from the dead' (9:9).

However we may interpret the messianic secret in detail, it does show, at any rate in the context which we are considering here, that in Mark's mind miracles 'in themselves' do not provide any direct means of access to Jesus, and are not able to be handed down as assured conclusions in the purely historical sense. Only in the light of Good Friday and Easter do they come to make any contribution, for him who has received the vision of faith, to the revelation of the Son of God.

(b) MATTHEW 8:23–27

Matthew has included the story of the calming of the storm in his cycle of miracle stories (8:1—9:34). Again he renounces details which have a purely narrative value (the swamping of the boat, the fact that Jesus was lying in the stern, and the cushion, the exact form which the authoritative command took) and concentrates wholly upon a theme which has already made its appearance in Mark, though admittedly under a different aspect: the relationship of the disciples to Jesus.

The very context in which the story is placed serves to indicate the underlying intention of the narrator. The introductory verse is placed further back in the cycle of stories as a whole, and is already to be found in Mt 8:18 (cf Mk 4:35). Obviously we expect this to be followed by the continuation of the story of what took place on the lake. Instead of this we find Jesus discussing the question of discipleship, first with a scribe (8:19), and then with one of his disciples (8:21f). This insertion plainly interrupts the continuity of the pericope (and also of the cycle of miracle stories taken as a whole). But this is not accidental. The two discussions, which Luke includes at different points (9:57–60) are intended to introduce the leitmotiv of a story that is attached to them. Matthew underlines this intention of his by deliberately departing from the Marcan model (4:36) so as to introduce the 'stitchword', 'follow', into the story of the storm on the lake: Jesus is the first to enter the boat and his disciples follow him (8:23). In the mind of the evangelist the term 'disciple' is no longer confined to the twelve apostles or to a broader group of disciples (cf Lk 10:1), but is intended to have a wider application than it could have in the particular situation envisaged, and to signify the Christian community as a whole. The significance of what takes place on this particular occasion is that it provides a pattern of what discipleship should mean in general. This is confirmed by certain striking alterations to the text of Mark which Matthew introduces.

Whereas Mark speaks of a mighty storm of wind (4:37), in Matthew the atmospheric disturbance is described as a *seismos*, 'shaking' (8:24). This term, 'which it is quite unusual to apply to a storm at sea, but is frequently to be met with as a description of apocalyptic terrors' (Bornkamm *et al*, ET 56) serves to show that in principle we have already passed beyond the particular concrete situation of what took place on the lake, and it is transparently evident that Matthew is envisaging the perils involved in discipleship in general.

It is significant that in describing the beating of the waves in this story, and also in the story of the walking on the water (14:24), Matthew does not speak primarily of the distress this causes to the disciples who are in the boat. 'It is the ship herself which is imperilled by the waves' (Bornkamm *et al*, ET 266). This factor, taken in combination with the point which we have noticed in the foregoing observations with regard to the 'storm', makes it natural to suppose that already as early as Matthew's time the ship was understood as a figure of the church.

The disciples awaken Jesus not with a despairing cry, which draws down a rebuke upon them, but with an urgent prayer: 'Save, Lord, we are perishing' (8:25). The language of this appeal is cultic in style. The *Kyrie* embodies the credal confession made by the community to their Lord. The *soson*, save, does not merely refer to the external peril, but is 'the community's entreaty uttered to their redeemer and saviour'. And finally the last word of the verse is 'not a cry of terror wrung from them by the present peril, but also, and more than this, an expression of belief in a state of human need and danger that is constant' (Lohmeyer–Smauch, 163).

According to Matthew it is straight away, while the threat is still in being, that Jesus replies to the disciples' appeal (8:26) and not, as with Mark and Luke, only after the miracle. The effect of this transposition of details is to lay greater emphasis upon the dialogue between the disciples and Jesus (in the midst of the situation of peril). From the way Jesus' answer is introduced it is 'as though he were looking beyond the immediate situation of the moment in what he said, and addressing himself to every age as though present to the community in that age' (Lohmeyer–Smauch, 163). A further significant point is that the phrase 'O ye of little faith' is found only when Jesus is addressing the disciples, who have already constituted themselves as his followers (8:30; 8:26; 14:31; 16:8; 17:20). Their faith flags just at the point when it ought to be made strong amid the assault of alien forces. It is so weak that in time of temptation it fails. Whereas Mark, in accordance with his special conception of the messianic secret, emphasises the unbelief of the disciples of Jesus with regard to the revelation of the messiah, Matthew, with his concept of 'those of little faith', is already envisaging the situation of the community (after Easter) in which faith is threatened by disbelief. The motif of faith and discipleship is neither abolished nor weakened by this, but rather made relevant to the situation confronting Matthew himself.

The 'Greek chorus' conclusion in Matthew is not constituted by the disciples who have followed Jesus. Instead certain 'men' are introduced for this purpose for the first time (8:27). This has the effect of including in the story figures representative of those to whom it is being preached for the first time. 'The scene envisaged in the pericope is thereby expanded. Its horizon is extended and from being an account of discipleship in which Jesus' disciples experience temptation and deliverance, tempest and protection, it becomes a summons to embrace this state of discipleship and to become followers of Jesus' (Bornkamm *et al*, ET 56).

Admittedly the main emphasis in the narrative is not laid upon the appealing summons to become followers of Jesus. Matthew's principal aim is to remind those who have already become followers in this sense of how solemn this decision of theirs is, and thereby to emphasise afresh a point which has already been proclaimed in the sayings with regard to discipleship which immediately precede this pericope (8:19–22): The Son of Man who has nowhere to lay his head (8:20) does not guarantee that his disciples will have a peaceful journey in any sense. Those who decide to become his followers have to reckon with active hostility and danger. But this would not make them any less certain of the fact that with them in the boat is that Lord to whom the demonic powers are subject.

From the manner in which he presents the material it can be concluded that Matthew is not merely a transmitter of tradition, who has handed down the story of the calming of the storm unaltered, but is the interpreter of this story too, 'and in fact the first exegete who does interpret the voyage of the disciples together with Jesus through the storm and the calming of the storm by applying these events to the subsequent life of the church, and thereby to the church herself considered as a barque' (Bornkamm *et al*, ET 55).

(c) LUKE 8:22-25

Luke has taken over (Lk 8:22-56) the three miracle stories from Mark (4:35—5:43), but in doing so he has broken the immediate connection with the parable of the sower (8:4-18, his is an abbreviated version) by inserting the saying about the mother and brothers of Jesus (8:19-21). Mark's unified setting is abandoned. The lake is presented as geographically speaking the central scene in which the event takes place (the setting of the sermon at the lakeside has already been transferred to an earlier point in Luke's narrative, cf 5:1-4). According to 8:1 Jesus' whole life at this point is spent in continual journeyings. For this reason the introduction has been left general: 'It happened one day...' (8:22). There is no longer any mention of his taking leave of the people or of other boats (Mk 4:36). The lake appears as 'a border scene at the outer limits of the situation of loneliness', as 'the appropriate milieu for the epiphany of power'.

To a large extent Luke adheres to his Marcan model in his version of the story of the calming of the storm. Nevertheless here too certain significant alterations should be observed. In describing the storm he lays particular emphasis upon the factor of the weird and uncanny. It is as though a demon had descended (*katebe* 8:23) into the element appropriate to it. The appeal of the disciples includes the typically Lucan form of address, *epistata*, saying (8:24), and Luke has removed the note of reproach which was in it. Above all Luke has altered Jesus' rebuke to the disciples, though he follows Mark in placing this after the stilling of the storm has actually taken place. In altering this rebuke he has introduced a different interpretation of the central question of faith. Instead of: 'Have you no faith?' (Mk 4:40) this rebuke now runs: 'Where is your faith?' (Lk 8:25). Faith is basically presupposed. Luke means to convey 'That it was only in this moment that the disciples failed in their faith. Their failure is represented as an exception' (Gnilka

31). This alternation has had the effect of giving the pericope as a whole a quite different emphasis. It is made to conform to the distinctive outlook of the third evangelist. Whereas Mark, working from his central conception of the messianic secret, lays great emphasis on the disciples' lack of faith and their blindness to the secret of the messiah, Luke has restricted their lack of understanding to their attitude towards Jesus's passion, though admittedly here he has emphasised it. In other contexts he does not speak of any obstinacy or blindness on the part of those to whom it has been given 'to know the mysteries of the kingdom of God' (8:10), but on the contrary presupposes their faith. They should be in a special manner witnesses to the epiphany of their Master, who, in the power of God (cf Lk 11:20; Ac 2:22), has destroyed the dominion of Satan (cf 10:18). In his victory over the demonic powers the way is cleared for the kingdom of God to be ushered in. The time of salvation has arrived.

3 The story of the miraculous feeding

In the accounts of the miraculous feeding of a great number of individuals we are confronted with a new category of miracle story. As a title to these stories the description 'multiplication of loaves' is inaccurate. The central concern of these stories is not the multiplication of the loaves but the fact that through Jesus starving men are satisfied. The theme of feeding and partaking of meals appears as a third topic in addition to the healings and exercises of authority and power over the forces of nature. Even from a purely external point of view and without entering into the actual content of these stories, their significance in the early christian preaching can be recognised from the fact that no story in the tradition of the gospels occurs so frequently as the story of the feeding. It appears in six different versions: as the feeding of the five thousand in all the evangelists (Mk 6:30–44; Mt 14:13–21; Lk 9:10–17; Jn 6:1–15), and in addition to this as the feeding of the four thousand in Mark (8:1–9) and

Matthew (15:32-39). It is no longer seriously contested today among students of the new testament that all six accounts go back to a single common original.

The stories of miraculous feedings in the gospels follow patterns already found in sacred scripture. Accounts of miraculous feedings are found even in the old testament, and even here we can discern certain theological and literary influences in the way in which this same theme is worked out. The manner in which Israel received sustenance during the wilderness wanderings was experienced as a miraculous intervention of Yahweh, and in various ways she constantly returns to this experience to bear witness to it anew (Ex 16; Num 11). A further episode connected with the tradition of the miraculous feeding in the wilderness is the 'miraculous feeding of the hundred men' which occurs in the story of Elisha (2 Kg 4:42-44). The prophet is presented as a new Moses. Just as in the wilderness Yahweh caused his promises to come to fulfilment through the intervention of Moses as his mediator, so now he repeats this action of his, only this time through Elisha: 'Thus says the Lord, "They shall eat and have some left"' (2 Kg 4:43). In the course of tradition other motifs have come to be associated with that of miraculous feeding, and the chief of these are the motifs of the shepherd and the meal (cf, eg, Hos 13:4-6; Ps 78; Ps 107).

Israel's hope is deeply conditioned by her vision of her own past history with God. Just as Yahweh has fulfilled the promises which he gave through Moses and later through Elisha that he would bring his people sustenance, so too in her present afflictions he will, of his faithfulness, act in the same way. The acknowledgment of Yahweh's saving deeds in the past leads on to Israel's expectation for the future. In this connection Deut 18:15-18 has above all come to be understood as a prediction of the prophet who is to come in the final age. The eschatological prophet (or the messiah) is presented as the new Moses, 'as with the first redeemer (Moses) so too with the last (the mes-

MIRACLE STORIES: EXEGETICAL INVESTIGATION

siah)', as the new Elijah-Elisha. The miracles of the final age correspond to those of the first age, though admittedly they are characterised by the inexhaustible abundance of the age of salvation. The leader of Israel sent by God will lead his people as a good shepherd to fertile pastures, and will fill the hungry by giving them the new manna in the form of a meal of eschatological joy. The stories of miraculous feeding in the gospels are to be viewed in the context of this expectation.

(a) THE MARCAN STORIES OF MIRACULOUS FEEDING (6:30–44; 8:1–9)

(i) *The stories of miraculous feeding in the context of the gospel as a whole*

The tradition of the meal
The stories of miraculous feedings have an integral part to play in the message of the gospels as a whole. They belong to the context of the tradition of the meal. Jesus' message of the nearness of God finds concrete expression in the sharing of a common meal to which he calls his own disciples, the publicans and sinners and—it is precisely this point that is attested in the stories of miraculous feedings—the multitudes. In this act of sharing a common meal he anticipates the eschatological meal to be eaten in the kingdom of God, and gathers the new people of God together. This theme acquires special significance by reason of the final meal which Jesus shares with his disciples (Mk 14:22–25). With this meal he brings his fellowship with them in the partaking of meals as practised up to this point to a close, and promises that the fulfilment of this will be bestowed in the future (cf 14:25).

The context
In the introductory scene (6:30–33) Mark establishes a connection with something that he has already told us, and at the

same time creates the necessary conditions for the story of the miraculous feeding which follows. In 6:30 he harks back to an episode which comes before the judgment of Herod about Jesus (6:14–16) and before the news of the death of the Baptist (6:17–29), namely the mission of the twelve disciples (6:6b–13). These (and it is only in this passage in the second gospel that they are called 'apostles') have completed their mission and now render an account of it to Jesus. Galilee is in a state of excitement. The people are coming and going (6:31). They pursue Jesus in their multitudes even when he seeks to be alone (6:33). Thus the scene (which is enigmatic in the extreme) is set. The indications are imprecise. It is hardly possible to make out the locality that the author has in mind for the event. Any attempt at establishing the historical details from the setting as depicted here would be misconceived. 'What now takes place is Jesus' answer to the feelings which his emissaries have awakened' (Grundmann ²1965, 132). He reveals himself as the messiah.

If it is true that the introduction in itself conveys the broader context in which the story of the miraculous feeding in Mk 6:34–44 must be viewed, and only in which its deeper meaning can be appreciated, this is even truer of the still wider development of the gospel as a whole. In 6:51bff the fact that the story of the miraculous feeding is brought into association with the story of the walking on the water (6:45–51) is the evangelist's way of conveying to us that in both cases there is a deeper underlying meaning to be discerned. After all the very fact that the story of the miraculous feeding is repeated (8:1–9), though admittedly with a different emphasis, serves to indicate that it has a special significance. Finally in conversation with his disciples Jesus once more recalls the miraculous feeding to their minds: 'Do you not yet understand?' (8:21). It is more than the mere satisfaction of physical needs that is in question here. Yet the disciples are the same as 'those outside' (4:11b). Their eyes and ears are closed to the secret of the messiah (8:18; cf

MIRACLE STORIES: EXEGETICAL INVESTIGATION

4:12). They have to be opened for them by a miracle (8:22–26). This is the third climax in the gospel over blindness—the Pharisees (3:6), the men of Nazareth (6:1–4) and now the disciples (Schweizer 1967, 222f).

(ii) The feeding of the five thousand (Mk 6:34–44)
6:34 announces the theme of the story: when Jesus sees the great multitudes of people he is moved with compassion 'for they were like sheep without a shepherd'. In this instance it is not the concrete need of an individual man that he encounters, as elsewhere in the miracle stories. Rather his gaze is directed towards the whole people. He sees them as Moses saw them at the end of the wilderness wandering when, faced with his approaching death, he begged God: 'that the congregation of the Lord may not be as sheep which have no shepherd' (Num 27:17). Now the office of Moses is taken over by Jesus himself. The term 'compassion' is not the expression of any merely human emotion, but 'a theological characterisation of Jesus as messiah, in whom the divine mercy is present' (TWNT VII, 554). He is the new Moses, the shepherd of the final age, who takes up the cause of the leaderless people and constitutes the new people of God.

His compassion is manifested first in the fact that he teaches the people (6:34). But here, as so often in Mark, no further information is supplied as to the detailed content of his preaching. It reveals the mystery of the kingdom of God (1:15).

In 6:35 a conversation is initiated between the disciples and Jesus which is the first to occur in the Marcan gospel. In this the disciples take the initiative (6:35f). Throughout the whole episode they have a decisive part to play, and are even charged themselves with the task: 'You give them something to eat' (6:37). Subsequently (6:41) they do, in fact, do this. But at first they wholly fail to understand the meaning of the command. As so often (in Mark) they are blind with regard to the messiah. The question which they put in reply 'shows the total lack of understanding ... not merely with regard to the person and mission of their Lord, but also with regard to the task which he is laying upon them' (Bornkamm *et al*, ET 183).

At this question the action passes to Jesus himself, and from now on he is the initiator of all that takes place: He speaks (6:38), he commands (6:39), he takes the bread and breaks it (6:41). The division of the multitude into groups of fifty and a hundred is reminiscent of the arrangement of the Israelite camp (Ex 18:25) during the wilderness period. Just as Moses arranged the people in groups so now Jesus does the same. The reference to the 'green grass' (6:39) acquires a deeper significance in this context. It can hardly be intended as a reminiscence of past history, but rather underlines the eschatological character of the episode. Jesus is the shepherd who makes his flock settle 'on green pastures' (Ps 23:2).

He manifests his solicitude as shepherd not only in word (6:34), but in deed as well. He is the host. Like any Jewish father of a household he pronounced the blessing on the food which has been brought to him. He hands over the loaves and fishes and causes them to be distributed by his disciples (as mediators 6:41). They are made to play an active part in the episode which previously (6:37) they have failed to understand. There is a superfluity of food. Five thousand men have been satisfied and still there is more food left over than was there before (6:43f). This superfluity is a sign of the fact that the fullness of time has arrived. Jesus is the new Moses, the shepherd of his people, in the eschatological exodus. He performs the new miracles of manna, the counterpart of the miracles of the first age, and by it produces an inexhaustible fullness. He is the messiah, who gives his people a share in the banquet of eschatological joy of the final age.

The details of the exposition show that the story of the miraculous feeding in Mk 6:30–44 cannot be assigned to the category of the miracle stories in the purely formal sense, 'which are intended to bring out the miraculous power of Jesus, and thereby to strengthen the christian's trust in so powerful a Lord' (Haenchen, 250f). So general a characterisation fails to bring out the specifically christological statement which our story embodies. But neither is this specifically christological statement adequately expressed merely by referring to the Mosaic typology.

It is undeniable that 6:41 is, in the manner of its formulation, plainly assimilated to the story of the last supper (14:22). Already at a very early stage the primitive christian community has applied the story of the miraculous feeding to the celebration of the eucharist. Thereby it has not departed from its original message, but rather given it actuality and relevance. 'The sense of community with Jesus through the sharing of a meal as entertained in the earliest christian community and as interpreted eschatologically can again be discerned in the messianic meal of the story of the multiplication of loaves' (Heising, 63). The same Lord who has gathered the leaderless multitudes in the wilderness like a shepherd, taught them and fed them with a superabundance of food, now also assembles his people in order that they may hear his word and partake of his eschatological meal.

This eucharistic aspect, however, should not be taken in too absolute or exclusive a sense. Mk 6:34–44 remains a messianic story. Its central point is the revelation of the messiah. 'This provides the basis for everything else' (Gnilka, 38). The reference to the eucharist should only be understood on the basis of the eschatological fellowship through the sharing of a common meal which has been granted by Jesus.

(iii) The feeding of the four thousand (Mk 8:1–9)
In Mk 8:19f the stories of the miraculous feeding are brought into connection with one another. Jesus has both in mind when he asks his disciples, 'Do you not even now understand?' (8:21). The author of these verses has made the two instances of the 'feeding' story refer to two different events, and has even 'made

Jesus himself speak of these two instances of feeding thousands of individuals as of two different episodes'. (Haenchen, 289). It can hardly be established unequivocally how this reduplication has come about. B. van Iersel (183–90) holds 'that one and the same account of a miraculous feeding acquired two different forms because it was circulated in two different milieux, one Jewish christian and one Gentile christian'. Manifestly in both cases there is a deeper message to be understood, and in the light of this alone it is improbable that the evangelist's intention in including the second story is simply to record the miraculous feeding and nothing more. In other words it is highly improbable that his intention here is completely different from what it was in the case of the first story of a miraculous feeding.

Mk 8:1–10 taken as a whole is more concise in its presentation, and leads undeviatingly to the actual feeding itself. In contrast to 6:30–33 the setting is indicated only by means of a brief general redactional note: 'In those days ... again a great crowd ... nothing to eat' (8:1). The reference to the 'sheep without a shepherd' (6:34) is missing. The sole grounds adduced for Jesus' compassion for the people are that they have already remained with him for three days and have 'nothing to eat' (8:2). What is in question here is a state of urgent need, namely hunger: 'If I send them away hungry to their homes they will faint on the way' (8:3). This is why there is no reference to preaching here, although in 6:34 we are told that Jesus' first reaction on seeing the people is to preach. Here the story passes immediately to the subject of the feeding. In this Jesus himself takes the initiative (in 6:35f it is the disciples who do this). Once more (cf 6:37) the disciples show their lack of understanding (8:4). There is no mention here (8:6) of dividing the people into groups to sit down, or of the green grass (cf 6:39f). The loaves and the fishes that are eaten are presented as two separate 'courses' (8:6, 7, in contrast to 6:41), and a separate blessing is attached to each. The numbers in the second story of the miraculous feeding are different from those of the first. In Mk 6:34–44 fewer loaves and fishes are available, yet more people are satisfied and a greater quantity is left over.

In the second account of the feeding too the fragments that are left over serve to indicate the abundance of the food which was distributed. The superabundance of food is an eschatological sign. That age has been inaugurated in which the people will no longer suffer want of any kind. Admittedly the narrative ends with the statement: 'And he sent them away' (8:9). The feeding is an episode on the way. The final and definitive state of fellowship has still to be achieved.

While there are no direct references to the Mosaic typology (cf 6:34, 39f), still Mk 8:1–9 is likewise sustained by the consciousness that Jesus is the new Moses in whom God performs the signs of the final age. The general lines of the story are still more consistent in converging upon him (cf eg 8:3; he takes the initiative in the feeding). He is the leader sent by God who provides food in the wilderness for the new people of God in a miraculous manner.

The effect of separating the account of the feeding with loaves from that of the feeding with fishes (8:6, 7) is that 8:6b is assimilated still more plainly to the words of institution. A still closer connection has been established between the 'feeding' stories and the eucharist. Mk 8:1–9 attests the fact that Jesus invites men to fellowship with him in an eschatological meal.

(b) THE MATTHEAN STORIES OF MIRACULOUS FEEDINGS (14:13–21; 15:32–39)

(i) The 'feeding' stories in the context of the gospel as a whole
From 13:53 onwards Matthew follows Mark closely in the sequence in which he arranges the stories. In the great section of 13:53—17:23 (Mk 6:1—9:32) he has made very few alterations to the arrangement of material in the Marcan model either by omitting or by inserting pericopes. 'The high points of

the narrative are the miraculous feedings, Peter's confession of the messiah, the transfiguration on the mountain, and the events leading up to the messianic passion. In view of these it is justifiable to describe the section as a whole as progressive messianic revelation' (Trilling 1965, 54).

(ii) The feeding of the five thousand (14: 13–21)
In contrast to Mark (6:30–33) the introduction here (Mt 14: 13f) is not only abbreviated (the pericope as a whole gives the impression of being more precise). It has also been altered. The reason adduced for Jesus seeking for solitude is not so much the fact that the people are pressing in on him, but rather the news of the death of the Baptist (14:12f). Jesus withdraws for reasons of security. In his new presentation of the first story of miraculous feeding Matthew throws two themes in particular into relief: the position of the disciples and the eucharistic interpretation of the feeding. In contrast to the Marcan version the Mosaic typology no longer manifests itself explicitly here.

The position of the disciples
In his account of the conversation which precedes the feeding Matthew omits the question which the disciples put in reply to his own (Mk 6:37), and by which they manifest their own lack of understanding with regard to the task which Jesus lays upon them: 'You give them something to eat'. They immediately reply by pointing out how much food is available, and admittedly do not show overmuch trust in their Lord or their own resources: 'We have only five loaves here and two fishes' (14: 17). In the term 'only' here the deficiency of their faith can be discerned. In fact they are not (as with Mark) lacking in understanding, but of little faith. This interpretation is confirmed by a further observation. Those words which, in connection with the story of miraculous feeding, give such emphatic expression to the blindness of the disciples in Mark (Mk 6:52) are either omitted or taken in a different sense. These changes are in con-

formity with the new line of interpretation superimposed upon the stories of the feeding: the disciples are not presented as blind and unbelieving (Mk 8:17). Jesus rebukes them for their little faith (Mt 16:8), and in the end even this rebuke is deliberately mitigated by the remark 'then they understood...' (16:12). Matthew is speaking to disciples (in his own community) who do in principle 'understand' and believe, and yet are assailed by temptation and peril (see above pp 132f). Greater importance is attached to the function of the disciples, not only in the introductory dialogue, but also in the actual feeding itself. Significantly Jesus does not command them (as in Mk 6:39f) to arrange the people in groups and make them sit down: 'Manifestly Matthew intends to represent the disciples simply in their role as mediators at the meal' (Bornkamm *et al*, ET 184). Thus they receive the command (not as in Mark) to bring the food to Jesus, and they are active participators in the 'giving' (14:9, not simply in 'setting the food before' the people as in Mk 6:41). Jesus' act of 'giving' is extended and projected through them. The command 'You give them something to eat' (Mt 14:16) is literally fulfilled.

While Matthew emphasises the function of the disciples, nevertheless in his treatment too all the lines converge upon Jesus: 'It is quite manifest that the miracle takes place not through the disciples but through Jesus' (Bornkamm *et al*, ET 182).

The eucharistic interpretation of the feeding
The time assigned for the miracle, 'the hour is now late' (Mk 6:35) is altered (Mt 14:15) in such a way that it corresponds literally to that of the last supper (26:20). Furthermore the motif of the fishes is notably reduced. Mark (6:41–43) refers to the fishes in the blessing, in the distributing and in the gathering up. But in Mt 14:19 they are mentioned only in the thanksgiving. Interest is concentrated upon the feeding with bread.

By means of these alterations the narrative as a whole has been assimilated to the account of the institution of the eucharist and thereby to the Lord's supper itself. The emphasis on the mediatorship of the disciples is connected with this.

The Mosaic typology
It is striking that Matthew does not take over the old testament motifs present in his Marcan model. He will have omitted Mk 6:34 because he has already introduced this verse in a different context (9:36). Mk 6:39f goes unmentioned because of Matthew's concern to concentrate upon the actual feeding, in which the anticipation of the Lord's supper can be discerned. (This also has a relevance to the function of the disciples.) The Mosaic typology is not unknown to the first gospel (Bornkamm *et al*, ET 35), and even though it is not directly expressed, the mere fact that it is present in the Marcan model means that it should be regarded as present in the background of Matthew's version of the 'feeding' stories.

(iii) The feeding of the four thousand (15:32–39)
Matthew has assimilated the second story of miraculous feeding to the first. Hence the same general tendencies are apparent in both narratives. The function of the disciples is emphasised. The term *hemin*, to them, in 15:33 serves to convey that they are conscious of their responsibility for feeding the multitudes. According to 15:36 they are again (cf 14:19) directly involved in the actual 'giving' of the food.

Secondly, the effect of Matthew omitting the meal consisting of the fishes (the 'second course' Mk 8:7) is that the meal consisting of bread is made central and dominant (15:36). 'The significance of this alteration is undeniable: the miraculous feeding is now described more exclusively in terms which derive their clear and consistent connotation from the celebration of the eucharist' (Bornkamm *et al*, ET 186–87).

MIRACLE STORIES: EXEGETICAL INVESTIGATION

(c) THE LUCAN STORY OF THE MIRACULOUS FEEDING (9:10–17)

(i) The story of the miraculous feeding in the context of the gospel as a whole
Luke records only the feeding of the five thousand. In the general context of the 'great omission' (of Mk 6:45—8:26; cf Conzelmann, ET 52–55) he has not taken over from the Marcan model either the second 'feeding' story (Mk 8:1–10) or the dialogue about the feeding (Mk 8:14–21). He has also arrived at a new arrangement of the pericopes by connecting the miraculous feeding, the confession of Peter, the passion prediction and transfiguration with one another. Like Mark (6:30) he establishes a connection between this and the preceding pericope, the mission of the disciples (Lk 9:10). The lake setting (crossing, Mk 6:32) is abandoned (see above p 134), and Bethsaida (taken over from Mk 6:45 or 8:22) is inserted as the new indication of place in the story of the miraculous feeding.

(ii) The feeding of the five thousand (Lk 9:10–17)
In Luke's fresh presentation of the story of the miraculous feeding, tendencies are manifested which were already observable in Matthew, though admittedly in Luke they appear in a different way. In addition to this greater emphasis is placed upon the miracle itself.

The emphasis upon the function of the disciples
In the verse which introduces the feeding (9:12) Luke has substituted the term 'the twelve' for that of 'disciples'. In the concluding verse (9:17), in which we are told how much of the food was left over, the actual number 'twelve' is placed at the end of the sentence and so given special emphasis, having thereby been made the final word of the whole pericope. It can hardly be accidental that the two numbers correspond so strikingly to one another. By this device the evangelist succeeds

in conveying that the narrative depends for its meaning upon the symbol of the twelve. Further in 9:13 he assigns the word *humeis*, you, to an emphatic position, making it the final word with which Jesus' commission concludes, and imparts a double emphasis to it by the words *hemin* and *hemeis* which follow. Like Matthew he omits the sharp counter question of the disciples, which reveals their failure to understand (Mk 6:37). Instead of the indeterminate *ochlos*, crowd, he uses the specific term *laos*, people. 'The twelve' or the 'disciples' (9:14, 16) are ordered to the *laos*, people. In using this term Luke does not merely have Israel in mind, but is already looking to the christian community. These observations serve to indicate that in comparison with Mark the role of the disciples (or the 'twelve') as mediators has been more strongly brought out not only by the first evangelist but also by the third.

The eucharistic interpretation
Luke has replaced the introductory indication of time in the Marcan model by a formula which occurs elsewhere in his gospel only in the Emmaus story immediately before the supper at Emmaus (24:29): 'The day began to wear away...' (9:12). Through this indication of time alone, but above all through the formulation of the blessing of the bread (cf 9:16 with 24:30) the miraculous feeding is brought into association with a meal which in turn is directly associated with the celebration of the last supper. In accordance with this a direct connection with the account of the institution of the eucharist is discernible in the all-important verse, 9:16, and by comparison with Mark the motif of the fishes is thrust into the background. The distribution of the fishes and the gathering up of the fragments of them are no longer explicitly mentioned.

From these indications it can be concluded that in his story of the miraculous feeding Luke too is concerned to draw attention to the eucharist.

MIRACLE STORIES: EXEGETICAL INVESTIGATION

The miracle
Luke exhibits no interest in the old testament motifs in his model. He either passes over them or else historicises them; this is the sense, for instance, in which he takes Mark's (6:39f) arrangement of the people in groups (cf Heising, 75 note 4).

Luke emphasises the miraculous character of the event. Thus he does not wait until the conclusion of the story to tell us of the great number of those who were involved, but sets them directly side by side with the minute quantity of provisions available so as to draw the contrast between them as sharply as possible. Still greater emphasis is laid upon the numbers involved; in each case they are placed in the emphatic position after the substantives to which they refer.

Luke focuses our attention very strongly upon the miracle. This is in accordance with his special interest in the earthly life of Jesus. The miracles are signs of the fact that in him the age of salvation has been inaugurated. In them the divine epiphany takes place.

(d) THE JOHANNINE STORY OF THE MIRACULOUS FEEDING (6:1–15)

(i) The relationship between the Johannine and the synoptic tradition
John has recorded the story of the miraculous feeding in a version of his own. Certainly both within the narrative itself and also in the structure of the sixth chapter of his gospel he exhibits many points of contact, especially with Mark. Nevertheless a precise analysis reveals the fact that there is no direct literary dependence of the fourth evangelist upon the synoptics (Dodd, 196–222). The model from which he works is connected with them in terms of tradition history, but reflects a form of the story of the miraculous feeding which has attained a more advanced stage of development at the oral phase. Here, as so often elsewhere, we can discern in John a stage within the miracle tradition at which the actual element of the 'miraculous' has

been deliberately intensified. 'The miracles of the Johannine gospel are all "miraculous" in the highest degree, and, insofar as a comparison is possible, go beyond those recorded by the synoptics' (Smitmans, 274). The evangelist finds this intensification of the miracles already present in his source. But he does not press this development any further. Instead he arrests it at the stage at which he finds it and thereby rescues these stories from being corrupted and degenerating into mere wonder stories. He does this by giving them a consistently christological orientation. He condemns mere 'miracle' faith, and by the revelatory sayings which he attaches to them he interprets the miracles as signs. Miracle and interpretation belong together. Thus the story of the miraculous feeding too must be viewed in the context of ch 6 taken as a whole.

(ii) The miracle story as it existed in the Johannine model
The tendency to intensify the element of the 'miraculous' is clearly to be discerned in the story of the miraculous feeding taken over by the fourth evangelist. Whereas according to Mk 6:37 the disciples suppose that enough bread can be bought for two hundred denarii, according to Jn 6:7 this sum would not be enough 'for each one of them to get a little'. All natural means of assistance are utterly inadequate. He does not wait until the end of the story to tell us of the great number of individuals who were involved, but places this immediately after the minute quantity of provisions available, and thus brings out directly the contrast between them (Jn 6:9f; cf Lk 9:13f). Finally the effect of the miracle is emphasised by recording the reaction of those who were satisfied (the 'Greek chorus' conclusion), an element which is missing in the synoptics: they seek to make Jesus king (6:15).

The evangelist has had the story of the miraculous feeding made available to him in a version which is more strongly influenced by the typology of Moses and Elisha than the tradition known to the synoptics. How closely this version approximates to the story of the miraculous feeding by Elisha appears especially from the use of the term 'barley loaves' (6:9). In 6:14f the idea of the 'prophet like Moses' of the final age is clearly to be discerned.

(iii) The interpretation of the evangelist
The question of how the evangelist intends the story of the miraculous feeding to be taken can be answered only in connection with the discourse on the bread of life. Jn 6:26 turns our gaze on the 'sign' which is to be seen (cf the introductory reference to the sign which has already occurred in 6:2). Thus the question for the interpreter is what is meant by the *semeion*, sign, of the miracle. The full range of its significance is to be gathered from the revelatory discourse.

The evangelist takes the miraculous feeding not merely (as does his model) in the sense of a miracle performed by the eschatological prophet to strengthen belief in him. He employs the elements in 6:14f, which are precisely stamped with the Mosaic typology, in order to bring out the people's failure to understand, and he emphasises the contrast between Moses and Christ in the strongest terms: 'It was not Moses who gave you the bread from heaven; my Father gives you the true bread from heaven' (6:32). This characteristic contrast is to be explained by the confrontation between judaism and christianity as two distinct religions at the end of the first century (cf TWNT IV, 877).

The christological concentration
The initial point of interest is the purely natural gift of the bread. It is in this that the sign is contained. He who distributes the earthly bread, he, Jesus in person (*ego eimi*, I am), is 'the bread of life' (6:35). 'The bread bestowed upon men by him "shows" him himself as the bread of life which has come down from heaven' (Schnackenberg, ET 522). For this reason Jesus occupies the dominant position at the centre of the story of the

miraculous feeding. From the first to the last verse of this story all the lines of development lead to him: Jesus goes out; the people follow him (6:1f). Jesus goes up the mountain (6:3; the disciples receive only an incidental mention). Jesus lifts up his eyes and sees the people (6:5). There have already been three occurrences of the name 'Jesus' in the exposition following directly upon one another. The unpeaceful setting of Mark (cf 6:31, the coming and going) has been mellowed into a majestic picture: Jesus is 'the focal point of peace, from which all salvific activities proceed . . .' (Heising, 79). He is not swayed by the external circumstances or by any explicit request to intervene. He has neither spent the day up to a late hour in preaching or healing (Mk 6:35 par. According to Jn 6:16 the evening only comes on when the feeding is already long past), nor have the people already been with him for three days so that they are nearly starving (Mk 8:2 par). Jesus' actions are not conditioned by the situation. Rather they are imbued with a sovereign transcendence. He takes the initiative in the feeding (Jn 6:5; cf Mk 8:1 par. According to Mk 6:35f par it is the disciples who provide the initial stimulus). For his question to Philip is intended not so much to involve the disciples actively in what takes place as to bring to light their lack of understanding and their helplessness (Jn 6:7-9). They are reduced to bewilderment. Meanwhile Jesus demonstrates his transcendence of all human limitations. He needs no assistance. He knows what he will do (6:6). He directs that the people shall sit down (6:10), he pronounces the thanksgiving, he himself distributes the food (6:11—notice that this is not done by the disciples) he gives the disciples the task of gathering up the fragments that remain over (6:12f) finally by his sovereign act he withdraws from the clutches of the people (6:14f).

The new version of the story of the miraculous feeding in the fourth gospel is characterised by a christological concentration that is carried through quite consistently. Just as the bread itself points to Jesus, so the whole light of the miracle story falls upon him. It is christologically orientated through and through. 'But this christology is at the same time a soteriology in that it believes in the gift of Jesus, and believes in Jesus as gift' (Smitmans, 280). He who distributes bread (6:11) gives himself as bread for the life of the world (6:27ff, 51).

In virtue of this christological significance and the soteriological significance which is inseparably combined with it the miraculous feeding points us on to the eucharist (6:53–58). In this its fundamentally christological orientation is not abandoned but rather presupposed. It is made actual and relevant. For this reason it cannot be said that the feeding is 'not a eucharistic sign' but 'wholly and solely christocentric' in its orientation (Heising, 79). It is false from the outset to present these as mutually exclusive alternatives. The discourse on the bread of life reveals the feeding as a christological sign which finds its concretisation in the eucharist. Thus it is a eucharistic sign as well.

The lack of understanding with regard to the revealer.
Since the meaning of the miracle is not to be found within itself, but rather points on to Jesus, the question of whether we understand this meaning aright depends upon whether we 'see' this reference. We may call to mind the miracle itself, yet overlook its *semeion*, and thereby fail to arrive at the gift which it designates. Only to believers is this deeper meaning disclosed (6:68f; cf 6:36). The others do indeed verify the external fact of the feeding having taken place, but remain stuck fast at the procedures which can be verified by physical vision, and fail to recognise their true significance. Thus their acclamation (6:14f) stands revealed as a radical misunderstanding. Their gaze is fixed upon the earthly bread. They do not follow the direction of the sign. They have merely had enough to eat (6:26), and look to this alone for their salvation in other respects too (6:34), a salvation which is conceived of according to the ways and expectations of the world. Their short-sightedness is sternly

criticised and condemned (6:26f, 36). Jesus is not of the world (8:23), but comes from the Father (16:28). His cross stands as a judgment upon all 'this-worldly' expectations of salvation (12:23-33).

The proximity of Passover
The reference to Jesus as the bread of life is made against the background of his death. This is conveyed not merely by the all important verse of 6:51c and the eucharistic discourse attached to this (6:53-58), which already in the story of the miraculous feeding itself announces insistently: 'The Passover, the festival of the Jews was at hand' (6:4). 'This piece of information has not merely a chronological function. More than this, it has the effect of combining what Jesus is doing in the here and now with what was taking place at the Passover' (Schlatter, 164). The story of the miraculous feeding and the discourse on the bread of life are intrinsically associated with the Passover. Jesus becomes the bread of life in that he delivers himself up to death as the true paschal lamb.

Just as the reference to the Passover should not be taken in a purely chronological sense, so too the mention of the climbing of the mountain (6:3) which immediately precedes it must be something more than a mere geographical specification. It points to that 'exaltation' which is achieved on the cross. Jesus, the one exalted upon the cross, delivered over to death as the true paschal lamb, is the bread of life. 6:53-58 shows that it is against this background that we are intended to understand the eucharist.

III Concluding implications

1 The kerygmatic character of the miracle stories
The comparison we have made between different traditions of the same basic story as recorded in each of the four gospels, or even (cf the story of the miraculous feeding) between two dif-

MIRACLE STORIES: EXEGETICAL INVESTIGATION

ferent versions of that story recorded in one and the same gospel, yields conclusions which are significant and enlightening. It shows that the early christian community made no attempt to preserve the record of Jesus' deeds in a community archive, or to hand down the record of these to later generations in the form of records which were historically accurate and precise down to the last detail. The early christians are not interested in the past as such. The question that concerns them, rather, is the significance of the past for their faith in the present. The evangelists are far from being detached recorders, uninvolved in the facts they relate. Rather they are involved and committed witnesses. Their intention is not to reconstruct in the form of a biography certain extraordinary episodes, but to preach the claim which God has asserted in Jesus. So far as they are concerned his personal story has a relevance not as the memoir of a life, but rather as *kerygma*. They relate the miracle stories in such a way as to bring out who Jesus is, what God has done and continues to do in him for men, how he encounters them and what he summons them to.

In the miracle stories, therefore, we can discern a twofold interest. The focus of attention upon Jesus is combined with a further focus of attention upon the community. The changed situation in which that community finds itself at the time when a given evangelist writes is sketched in as the background to the personal history of Jesus himself. Or to put it the other way round: his personal history is viewed in the perspective of the living situation of the community at that time. This means that it is not regarded as something that belongs definitively to the past and that has now been concluded. Jesus of Nazareth is the living Lord of his community, present in that community until the end of the world (Mt 28:20). In relating his personal history on this earth the evangelists assert who he is in the present and what he does in the here and now. It is because he is believed in and experienced as the Christ that the tradition is alive and assumes traits that are contemporary, and it is for this reason also that, contrary to all doctrinal adherence to the letter, the tradition is interpreted with astonishing freedom and the writers themselves are astonishingly immune to any exaggerated preoccupation with historical factuality. This is not to say that their fresh approach to their task of relating the story of Jesus is an arbitrary one. In this approach they adhere firmly to the tradition throughout, but do attempt so to express the meaning of this tradition and so to bear witness to it that it 'has a place' in the altered situation of the community itself. Interpretation and tradition are mutually complementary and each is constitutive for the other.

The miracle stories do not merely belong to the gospel, they are the gospel. They bear witness to belief in Jesus Christ and are intended to summon men to this belief. Not only are the miracle stories composed in a general sense from the standpoint of faith, faith itself figures directly and explicitly as a topic at many points in them. From what the gospels tell us it can be gathered that the connection between miracle and faith is extemely complex. On the one hand the miracles appear (and in fact this is their predominant role) as an expression (sign) of faith, on the other hand they also figure as events which summon men to faith (cf the difference between the 'signs' and 'works' in John). In view of their structure and the intention underlying them they might justifiably be described as 'kerygmatic miracle stories'. Even though the application may vary, the tradition of the miracle stories in all the evangelists bears this character.

2 *The historical question*

It is no accident that the miracle stories are not primarily historical in their orientation. Nor can this fact adequately be explained by suggesting that there was a lack of reliable basic evidence. The real reason goes deeper than this. The miracles of Jesus are, in the last analysis, quite incapable of being handed down purely as historical facts. Any attempt at a precise and accurate record of the facts alone would never do justice to them, and would lead to a distortion of what really took place through an over-abstract approach. It could never hit upon what is precisely the decisive point: the claim of God which can only be apprehended and experienced in faith, that claim which is embodied in the event itself, and acquires fresh expression in the preaching of the witnesses involved in that event.

It would be impossibly superficial, therefore, to think of the tradition of the miracle stories as though there had originally been a historical record written from a completely detached and impartial standpoint, which had subsequently lost its precision and accuracy in the course of time through the constantly renewed attempts to make it relevant to the successive situations of the community and through the elaborations and embellishments which it would have undergone. There never was any such 'objective' record of the facts. 'Faith in Jesus Christ ... does not constitute merely a subsequent stage in the development of the tradition, but on the contrary is its very foundation and the *fons et origo* from which it developed and in terms of which alone it can be understood' (Bornkamm *et al*, ET 52).

This means that the historical question is subordinated to a wider and more all-embracing perspective. The questions of the kerygmatic significance of the miracle stories, their 'setting in life', their place and their function within any one of the gospels, these are (a point which has emerged in the course of our investigation) the questions that are primary. For the truth of a story of this kind is 'expressed obliquely by means of emphasis. It does not consist in the accuracy of its information with regard to historical facts and data. This truth does not consist in the fact that everything actually took place just as it has been set down. This would presuppose that it was written in order to guarantee the course of events as actually set forth, as factual to the individual (of our own age), and in order to make him happy by making a picture of the events available to him which agrees with the concept of history as a mere record of what has taken place' (Schlier 1964, 53). There is in fact no such presupposition. The miracle stories are not intended to bring men to 'believe' in certain extraordinary happenings, but rather to faith in Jesus Christ, which alone can make them blessed. This is the truth that they embody. The question 'what actually happened?' is one which was never raised in the process of composing these stories, and this way of formulating it is in fact typical of the 'new age'. As long as this question is put to them, therefore, they remain silent because it asks them too much (or too little). They will only yield their answer when they are asked for the truth that is actually in them. And this truth continues to be such even when it turns out that individual narrative motifs or even entire narratives derive from extra-biblical sources and have been transferred to Jesus in order to illustrate and to express figuratively who he is and how he encounters man. The authority that the truth carries does not depend upon the historical accuracy of a given story in which it is expressed.

Now this does not mean that the data supplied in the miracle stories are in all cases unhistorical. Nor is it in any sense being asserted that the attempt to recapture the historical facts is wholly irrelevant to faith. The early christian preaching does not emerge independently of the verifiable facts of Jesus' life. It is not intended 'to summon us to any kind of faith, but precisely to faith in *Jesus*' (Marxsen 1965, 57). Hence in this all-embracing understanding there is a justified interest in the question of whether, and to what extent, the miracle stories have a basis in the actual facts of his life, even if the truth of them does not stand or fall by our judgment of whether they are historically accurate in detail.

In any attempt at answering this question certain distinctions must be drawn. On the miracle stories treated of here this much must be said: that Jesus healed the sick cannot be contested as a matter of historical fact. The abundance of healing stories from an earlier age is 'absolutely inconceivable ... if healings of the sick were not achieved in reality "through" Jesus himself'. Those stories in particular have historical value which cannot be derived from the Hellenistic or Jewish sphere; for instance the miracle stories which are anti-Pharisaic in their orientation (the healings on the sabbath). With regard to the story of the storm on the lake there are, it is true, numerous parallels. But this does not of itself prove that the story is wholly unhistorical. It must have its basis in an event which took place on the lake in which the disciples in their distress actually experienced Jesus' help. Here, as in the healing story treated of above, a comparison between the synoptic gospels shows that the stories have not been rendered historically accurate down to the individual details they contain. In the case of the story of the miraculous feeding it is extremely difficult to break through the successive stages of literary adaptation to a historical nucleus. In this case we have to wait for the conclusions which further research has still to provide.

These statements are not dictated by the principle of 'economy' or even by the rationalist criticisms of the concept of miracle, but are prompted by our concern to make every effort to do justice to the manifold forms in which the tradition of the miracle stories has come down to us. We have to take into account the fact that 'for the early church the truth of the event of revelation is indeed bound up with the part it plays in the personal life of Jesus, but does not depend upon the historical accuracy or factuality of what is recorded' (Schlier 1964, 54). This latter element has a subordinate function. The claim of God which emerges in the miracle stories cannot be 'assured' or 'saved' in purely historical terms, nor does it have any need of this. It has its own certainty, which belongs to the personal dimension of faith, a certainty which, while it is not arrived at in total independence of the historical facts, is nevertheless not verifiable by them. The historical fact 'in itself' is ambiguous, and only begins to convey any message once one has taken up a definite attitude from which to interpret it. This is a phenomenon which is to be ascribed not to the distance in time between oneself and it, but is necessarily entailed by the contingent structure of the historical fact itself. One and the same objective situation, a 'driving out of demons', even though no-one calls it in question, can be regarded by some as the work of the devil (Mk 3:22), while others see it as a proof of God's power (Lk 11:20). The question of which decision one arrives at is not resolved by the brute fact itself, rather it falls within the sphere of belief or alternatively of disbelief. The fact, the 'driving out of demons', is that in which such a decision is, as it were, located. It is only to the eyes of the believer that it becomes a miracle. For he sees the finger of God (Lk 11:20) at work in the deeds of Jesus. The miracle stories of the gospels must be understood and preached from this standpoint.

5
PREACHING THE MIRACLE STORIES

I Basic considerations

Our exegetical consideration has shown that the phenomenon known as 'miracle' is not primarily treated of in the gospels as a subject in its own right, but is rather encountered in miracle stories. Hence the task of preaching the biblical message is not so much concerned with the question (which is one rather for systematic theology) of the possibility and nature of miracles 'in themselves'. Furthermore this preaching is not primarily referring back to some general 'theology of miracles', but has the duty of paying heed to the message of specific miracle stories within specific gospels, and of handing these on to its hearers. This presupposes that preparations have already been made to give these hearers the opportunity to understand the biblical message, and that obstacles have been removed which would otherwise have debarred them from access to it. In view of the contemporary situation with regard to preaching several points merit special attention in the four sections following.

1 The overthrow of the apologetic approach to miracles

The dubiousness of the apologetic approach to miracles
The preacher has to take into account the fact that the idea suggested to the minds of his hearers by the word 'miracle' is one of an extraordinary, inexplicable—indeed altogether strange event, and that not infrequently a certain element of the curious or the bizarre is regarded as characteristic of miracles. There is a widespread view that a given event can be accounted a miracle if it interrupts and, so to say, suspends, the system of the natural laws in force throughout the cosmos. This idea is nourished by the treatment of 'miracles' at the centres of pil-

grimage. This gives rise to the impression that miracles are capable of being measured by purely objective standards, and are able to be defined in medical terms (by commissions of doctors). It is regarded as a subject that is sufficient in itself, as an object of faith, though admittedly today it is more damaging than enriching to faith.

Theology and preaching must together bear the responsibility for the fact that we have gone so far astray in our understanding of miracles as to arrive at this unbiblical idea of them. In their controversy with the positivism of the new age they have allowed themselves to be drawn onto the positivists' own ground of argument, and have become imprisoned in the very system against which they are fighting. In the battle that they used to wage against one another positivists and apologetes both used to proceed from a common starting-point. This was the idea of a chain of natural causality which governed all earthly things. The point of controversy between them was whether it was possible for this chain of causality to be interrupted or broken by supernatural forces. The positivists rejected any such possibility, while apologists regarded it as given in the omnipotence of God, and held that this possibility had been actualised in the miracles. They regarded the actual interrupting or going beyond the natural laws as the specifically miraculous element, and considered that in such acts they had at their disposal a means of proving by objective evidence that God had in fact intervened, a means, furthermore, of authenticating revelation and excluding all reasonable doubt of its reality. The point in question is not 'the how and what of the miracle, for it can assume many forms and come to exist in many different ways. The point to concentrate on, rather, is that one factor which is common to all miracles, namely that they go beyond anything that can be explained in terms of natural causality. They must have the property of *transcending the physical order*, the distinctive quality of the miraculous ... All miracles are arguments in support of openly recognising the supernatural' (Lang, 120f).

Obviously such arguments depend for their validity on the prior assumption that everything in the world is governed by a system of natural causality. 'If the world and its contents are not governed by certain definite laws then there can be no exceptions to these laws, in other words no miracles' (Lang, 118).

Any attempt to explain miracles in this way cannot appeal to the gospels for support. On the contrary, against their background it stands revealed as misconceived. Furthermore, even from the point of view of the purely natural sciences it proceeds from ideas which have been rendered obsolete.

(i) The kerygmatic character of the miracle stories shows that the miracles belong to the dimension of personal decision in which they have the function of signs with a message of their own to convey. The evangelists do not intend to prove that certain natural laws have been suspended or interrupted (this way of posing the question is wholly alien to their basic outlook). Rather they are bearing witness to the fact that in the events of Jesus' life men have actually 'seen' God at work, and have encountered him there. Nor can it be said that the first way of viewing miracles derives from the second (the biblical one). On the contrary it is radically different in kind, unbiblical. This point must now be explained in greater detail.

With regard to the two kinds of human experience, those of personal encounter on the one hand and of the empiricism involved in the natural sciences on the other, it has to be recognised that the first exists on a radically different level from the second. The first cannot be calculated in physical terms, but rather achieves its reality in the dimension of freedom. It is not to be thought of as a synthesis of various apprehensible facts, nor even as that which we can move on to when we have achieved such a synthesis. Rather it constitutes a dimension in human cognition which is *sui generis*, so that we cannot pass into it merely by projecting our existing mode of cognition, so to say, forwards without interrupting or radically changing it. The observations of natural science are always confined to the physical processes themselves, and it reaches its limits once it has arrived at the physical causes of these processes. If in making these observations the categories at the disposal of the natural scientist fail to fit in particular cases (cf the idea of 'interrupting the laws of nature' in the terminology of apologetics) then it may be that the natural scientist is reduced to a temporary embarrassment and driven to revise his categories. But in no sense is he *eo ipso* affected at the existential level by this, or—perhaps through having recourse to the idea of 'physical transcendence' (see above)—brought face to face with the question of God. To maintain this would constitute a quite inadmissible *metabasis eis allo genos*. There is no no point of transition (in the form of a proof) from the physical to the personal level such that under certain circumstances we are compelled to make this transition. In the first-named dimension the appropriate activity for the human mind is to demonstrate, to prove by argument. In the second it is to acknowledge. According to the witness of scripture the dimension in which the miracle becomes a living force is not that of the observations of the natural sciences but that of personal encounter. If it is excluded from this dimension then it ceases to perform its function as a sign that conveys a message, is reduced to the level of a mere piece of wonderworking and becomes dead.

(ii) This is in no sense to surrender to subjectivism. Anyone who raises such an objection against these observations shows thereby that he has ascribed an absolute value to the empiricism of natural science and raised it to the level of being the sole standard and measure of every kind of valid apprehension of reality, refusing to recognise that there are more elemental, more all-embracing and more profound possibilities of experiencing reality, which are no less valid and legitimate. Apologetics has fallen into the snare of this restricted outlook, and from fear of being accused of subjectivism, has attempted to provide support for faith by means of 'objective facts' which are external to it. In this attempt it has failed to attain its goal.

Admittedly this does not apply only to apologetics. R. Bultmann too (GUV I, 1952, 214–17) remains entrapped in the rigidly defined objectivist concept of the world evolved in the previous century, and allows himself to be guided by this in treating of the question of miracles. The respective movements of apologetics and radical criticism confront one another on the common ground of an idea of the world that is antiquated (cf Schwarz, 34–54).

In the last analysis the certainty to be attained in faith—and this is true of certainty in the personal dimension in general—is not to be achieved by means of external supports, for instance by presenting some particularly impressive fact (a piece of wonderworking). 'Personal encounter is something that is immediate and contained within the limits of its own specific category of experience. In the very mode of existence that is intrinsic to it it is not susceptible of being evaluated from the basis of dimensions which are external to its own . . . For what takes place here proceeds in the light of a certainty that is intrinsic to itself' (Welte, 341). It is no less certain than the certainty of mathematics, but it is different in kind. Within this certainty there are degrees, and to him who undergoes this personal encounter these are living and real. But they are proper to this particular kind of certainty, and meaningful only in terms of it.

The attempt to give certainty to faith by adducing 'objective' criteria external to itself has the effect of degrading the miracle to a phenomenon which is apprehensible in terms of the natural sciences (the paradoxical hypothesis of a 'physical transcendence'). 'A kind of irrationalist rationalism develops in which the degree of absurdity in a miracle story becomes the measure of its religious value. The more impossible, the more revelatory' (Tillich, ET 128). Again if the miracle is regarded as belonging to the field of investigation of the natural sciences, then it would have to be accorded the kind of recognition that is appropriate to a physical finding. Its real nature would be distorted and it would become a factor in a process of scientific testing. God would be assigned a position at the end of a syllogistic argument. The decision of faith would be done away with. Unbelief would be pronounced stupidity (a conclusion which is not infrequently drawn in practice).

The rejection of the demand for a sign in Mt 12:39 par stands as a condemnation of all such speculations. The faith which Jesus demands is neither demonstrable nor compellable. Certainly external events are capable of bringing the individual to the point of faith, bringing him face to face with the question of God, and impelling him to the decision of faith. But they do not do away with the necessity for this decision. On the contrary they summon the individual to commit himself to it. They both are and should be understood 'as a question which cannot be solved by any answer that we can provide, as an encounter which one experiences indeed, but which one cannot simply verify or perhaps even evaluate' (Käsemann, 228). The construction of an 'objective' proof through miracles is a contradiction in itself (Tillich, ET 130). The function of miracles is to act as signs which render that which is signified not apprehensible but worthy of belief. The fact that they remain unresolved and 'open', and are not susceptible of any scientific methods of investigation at our disposal, is an expression not of any weakness or inadequacy in them, but rather of the fact that they belong to this special and personal dimension.

(iii) The illegitimate attempt to transfer the miracle to the sphere of the natural sciences brings its own requital. It is only to outward appearances that faith seems to be set on a solid foundation by these means. Natural science understands the natural laws as a working hypothesis. It ascribes an empirical and statistical value to them, and regards them as in principle able to be suspended. In other words it does not regard them as metaphysical entities (hence it is illegitimate to conclude, from the fact that natural science has no explanation to offer for a given phenomenon, that the phenomenon belongs to the metaphysical dimension, though this conclusion is not infrequently drawn in apologetics). The category of phenomena for which explanations are found is constantly being expanded. 'Miracle faith' finds itself constantly in the position of having to retreat before the advances of natural knowledge, and once a 'natural' explanation has been found for the supposed miracle the 'faith' which it was meant to support falls with it. Crises of faith not infrequently have their origin in the fact that assurances and supports are sought for and offered in the purely natural sphere which are incapable of giving any real support.

(iv) The natural science of modern times has shown that the static determinism of classical physics is inadequate. Just as the conception of the world in terms of mechanical causality has been rendered obsolete, so too has the apologetics which is dependent upon this conception.

Miracles as signs through which personal communication is achieved
Theologians have recognised that it is necessary for their researches to be rooted more firmly and more closely in sacred scripture, and to the extent that they have achieved this the definition of the miracle put forward by apologetics, namely 'the supernatural interruption of the natural laws' has been left grasping at a void. It is only gradually and with hesitation that the insights offered by theology are beginning to have their effect upon preaching. Preachers and congregations alike are still to a large extent held captive by the misconceived idea of miracles that was evolved by apologetics or, in some cases, their attitude towards miracles has become one of bewilderment and scepticism, in view of the fact that what seemed to be the unshakeable bastions are tottering. It is all the more important, therefore, to create the conditions in which the message of the miracles can be understood.

Revelation is addressed to men. It never (not even incipiently or temporarily) takes place in the sphere of pure nature. There is no sphere prior to, concomitant with, or apart from faith from which we can submit it to any kind of 'objective' testing and so judge it. Existentially speaking the sole possibility, apart from belief, is the decision to disbelieve. Any appeal to a neutral arbitrator is ruled out for believer and unbeliever alike.

The kerygmatic character of the miracle stories makes it clear that the miracle is being taken not as a demonstration of God's omnipotence in the realm of nature, but as a sign at the level of personal encounter. It is not primarily a physical event which is only in a secondary and derived (a more or less accidental) sense a sign as well. On the contrary, its whole existence as miracle consists in its being a sign. It is not a proof which makes a given reality available to us, but a sign that summons, which touches man at that point where he finds himself spoken to by God over the meaning of his existence, namely his salvation, and where he has freely to decide whether he will respond to God with belief or refuse him in unbelief.

In explaining the nature of miracle, the actual structure of personal encounter might be made to serve as a kind of analogue, and thereby not only bring us to a better understanding of the miracle in itself, but also help to indicate what we mean by man's openness to the experience of it. Personal encounter, then, is not to be thought of as the outcome of purely physiological factors, or even as something that we arrive at once we have transcended these factors. 'On the contrary, in achieving personal encounter we are, right from the outset, moving directly and immediately in a different sphere altogether, without availing ourselves of any means of ascending to it external to this sphere itself. Right from the outset we are regarding not the physiology of a seeing eye, but rather a man who regards us. We are immediately faced with the "thou", and we do not understand the "thou" from the vision we have of him, but rather understand the vision from the "thou"' (Welte, 340f). The person as a whole is immediately involved in the encounter. It is not initially there as an amalgam of particular apprehensible elements (eyes, mouth etc) which then project us further as part of one and the same cognitive process into the personal dimension. The person exists from the outset in his free and open personality. He cannot be deduced or derived from anything else, nor is he ours to manipulate or control.

Certainly the dimension of the factual has a significance of its own, and an indispensable part to play in personal encounter. For although the person exists directly and is not constructed from more rudimentary components, nevertheless he does not exist purely in the personal dimension, but is always immersed in the realm of the factual and material, never achieving total independence of this. Again it is not only in language that the person imparts himself to others. He also avails himself of material things as an expression of the fact that what he says is worthy of belief, and as signs by which to communicate with others (gifts). Signs are material things of this kind, not 'in themselves' or taken in isolation from the personal encounter, but only so long as, and to the extent that, they retain this personal reference.

On this basis miracles are to be thought of as signs of personal encounter between God and man. They too have existence in their 'sign' nature only so long as, and to the extent that, they remain within the dimension of the living (and life-giving) communication of faith. It is in faith (not as external to it) that they have their indispensable relevance. They show that God is addressing us at the physical level of our being (how should he address us otherwise than in this?), and that too in such a manner that he not only says that he loves us and is encountering us in the word that is an event, but also causes the Word to become flesh, and thereby makes the visible body—not merely words—the vehicle of his love and of the claim which his revealed truth represents for us. He has not merely spoken in order that we may 'hear'; he has made himself known to us in visible form in order that we may 'see'. Admittedly 'hearing' and 'seeing' are possible only in faith, never in isolation from it. But it is precisely in faith that 'seeing' as well is possible, and what the miracle stories tell us is that the encounter of God with man involves 'not merely our reason or interior spirit, but our whole existence as well in all its dimensions, including that of the physical. Furthermore, because the physical level of our being has the effect of uniting us to the world, this encounter of God with man also involves our relationship to the world itself' (Käsemann, 229).

2 Overcoming the limited understanding of truth established by history
That evaluation of the miracle stories which is primarily historical in its approach is in conformity with the interpretation of miracles as 'the supernatural breaking in upon the laws of nature'. This initial misunderstanding leads on to the second and subsequent one. Both are the outcome of a positivist approach. If we set out to establish with the precision of the natural scientist that the laws of causality have been broken or interrupted at a particular point, then this method of proof stands or falls by the historical exactitude of the stories themselves. Now since this is becoming increasingly uncertain, the 'miracle faith' which is based upon it is drawn down into ruin with it when it finally falls. In the common understanding of what faith means, when scepticism is engendered with regard to the historicity of the miracle stories it leads to scepticism with regard to the possibility of miracles in general, and finally to a radical scepticism with regard to faith itself.

The historical question has already been treated of *in extenso* (see above pp 156ff). The preacher has to bear in mind that the present-day situation of preaching is conditioned by the fact that so far as the categories of human knowledge are concerned man's conception of the world is dominated by the outlook of natural science. To a large extent the attitude of mind in one's listeners is such that they are only willing to accept something as true if it can be verified historically or empirically. Truth is restricted to the correctness of an observation. Theology and preaching are also influenced by this outlook to the extent that in these areas too this same positivist conception of truth has come to predominate.

This arbitrary restriction must be overcome. It must be pointed out that truth has deeper levels of significance than that of mere factual accuracy. Thus it is obvious to every sensible person that the value and truth of a picture are not to be measured by the criterion of how far it reproduces its subject with photographic exactitude. It goes beyond the level of mere external conformity and is projected into the dimension of personal communication. Similarly the truth of sacred scripture is not a purely factual entity, but a personal event: God speaking to us in Jesus Christ as expressed in the form of preaching.

One of the tasks of preaching is to prepare the way for this understanding. It is only in the light of it that the miracle stories can begin to speak to us, only so can the truth that is in them be brought to light. All of them bear witness to *that* miracle that is the presence of God in Jesus. They summon us to the encounter with him. And it is precisely this that is also the aim of preaching. It has to bring the hearers to Jesus, to belief in him, not to belief in wonderworking, in the last analysis not even to belief in the miracle itself, but to belief in Jesus, in that Jesus who in word and deed alike has borne witness to the fact that he is the Christ. Obstacles which bar the way to him must be removed. The preacher fails in his fundamental aim if he strengthens the obstacles that already exist, or places fresh ones in the path. He can do this either by thoughtlessly repeating outworn ideas which are conditioned by a particular conception of the world (for instance the ideas of historical positivism), or by confronting his hearers with the findings of historical criticism without any introduction or any aids to their understanding, so that the problems which are raised by historical criticism finally become stones of stumbling for them. Both of these approaches are equally damaging in their effects. In both cases he is provoking an immediate reaction of shock and unease, and at the same time diverting attention from the true cause of scandal. His task is neither to disseminate any specific conception of the world, nor to induce his hearers to decide upon questions of historical criticism. His task, rather, is to bring them to the decision of faith.

3 Inadmissible attempts at 'playing down' the miracle stories

A factor which cannot be overlooked is that as a result of gross misconceptions on the part of congregations and preachers alike the miracle stories have, to a considerable extent, become a problem for modern man. Nevertheless he does not solve this problem by evading it.

The rationalist explanation

In order to 'save' the miracle stories from total rejection on the part of thinkers whose ideas are orientated in the direction of natural science it is not infrequently attempted to explain them in purely 'natural' terms. For instance we may point to the interplay and mutual influence of soul upon body and vice versa, to the phenomenon of psychosomatic sickness and its cure, and we may seek to regard the miracles of Jesus in the light of this. It must not be denied that comparisons of this kind viewed purely from the medical point of view can, in certain cases, be justified to some extent. Nevertheless it is manifest that the underlying approach here is identical with that involved in attempts at explaining the miracles which point to an interruption of the natural laws. The only difference is that in the case of these latter comparisons they are devised at the cost of much embarrassment in order to remain within the limits of the 'natural', and so to avoid giving any offence.

In reply to interpretations of this kind it is hardly enough to draw a distinction between the so-called 'relative' miracles and the 'absolute' ones, and to say that we take our stand upon these latter alone and put them forward as our ultimate line of defence in this discussion. Such a line of argument likewise remains stuck fast at the level of applying empirical criteria to the miracles. On the one hand it leads to the conclusion that according to the stage which contemporary science has arrived at, and on the basis of its judgment, a whole section of the miracle stories has been rendered out of date. On the other hand it proceeds from the false position that within the sphere of our contingent world there is a suprahistorical standpoint such that from it it is possible to divide miracles into 'relative' and 'absolute' ones. So far as the material aspect of the miracle (the material nature of the sign) is concerned, this is always relative in any case. The concept of the absolute can be applied only to the message which God addresses to us, and which is freely expressed in the contingent events of this world (including the so-called 'relative miracles').

The 'spiritualising' falsification
The 'spiritualising' interpretation of the miracle stories is greatly favoured. The stories are 'spiritualised' and taken as an image of developments within the interior spirit: the healing of the blind is regarded as a liberation from spiritual blindness, the healing of leprosy as forgiveness of sins, the miraculous feeding as spiritual nourishment etc. The action of God is dissolved into a process which takes place exclusively in the private sphere of the spirit. This is a subject on which 'the hearer can successfully be addressed, because he . . . has long since had the inclination to withdraw from the physical side of his nature and from the creaturely world, and to confine his thoughts to the purely spiritual level and his religious experience purely to the realm of the interior spirit. By this means he avoids any conflict with scientific ideas' (Frör, 326). The division of man into body and soul is alien to sacred scripture, which envisages the whole man and thinks of him as an unity. It is precisely the miracle stories which emphasise that God addresses man not exclusively in the sphere of his interior spirit, but in his existence as a physical being too. Certainly in these miracle stories there is something more than merely the description of processes which are wholly

organic in character. But it is equally true that they are concerned with something more than merely the spirit. They are concerned with the salvation of the whole man.

This state of affairs, which our exegetical investigation into the miracle stories had already led us to recognise (see above p 142f), is confirmed by various sayings contained in the *Logia* tradition which refer to deeds of power performed by Jesus. In these the healings are taken as eschatological signs (Mt 11:2-6; Lk 7:18-23). They show that the promised messianic age of salvation has been inaugurated. They are not merely some kind of preliminary signs of its approach, but rather expressions of the fact that the kingdom of God is actually present. This is asserted above all in connection with the driving out of devils: 'If it is by the finger of God that I cast out demons then the kingdom of God has come upon you' (Lk 11:20; Mt 12:28). Jesus breaks the kingdom of Satan and inaugurates the kingdom of God. The power of Satan is in the act of 'falling' (Lk 10:18). He is forced to yield to one who is 'stronger' than he (Lk 11:22).

This connection between the healings and drivings out of demons on the one hand, and the setting up of the kingdom of God on the other, which is attested chiefly in the *Logia* tradition, should serve as a warning to us against any kind of 'spiritualising' tendencies. What Jesus' works of power are concerned with (and this applies to his preaching of the word as well) is not developments which take place in the private sphere of the soul, but rather the breaking in of the kingdom of God upon the world. The preacher's task is not to render the miracle stories plausible to his hearers, but to deliver the *kerygma* they contain unattenuated and undiminished. It is erroneous to suppose that the gospel is easier to preach if one tacitly passes over the miracle stories or 'plays them down'. In his word (provided there is no intention of 'playing down' this element as well) Jesus makes the same claim as is also asserted in his acts: that in him God is actively intervening in the life of man and in the world. There is no way of making the decision of faith any 'easier'.

4 Adhering to the real facts in preaching on the miracle stories
While it is of prime importance to create the conditions for an understanding of the miracle stories that does justice to them as real facts, and to warn one's hearers against misunderstandings of them, it is also vital that it is the message itself that is expressed. The exegetical investigation has cleared the ground for this.

From this point of view the miracle stories do not constitute so many separate compartments existing side by side, but cut off from one another so that it was only by a process of adding certain specific events that they were welded into a whole, and a miraculous history of the life of Jesus emerged. On the contrary, each individual story expresses in its own distinctive manner the whole event of Christ. In accordance with this, preaching has to give expression to the claim of Christ which is indivisible precisely as attested in the miracle stories. Otherwise the miracle stories will be reduced to a list of strange 'wonderworking' stories.

Each of these stories reflects the witness of the one Lord Jesus Christ in its own distinctive way, and thus this witness appears in a fresh form in each individual story. Each story has to be enquired into in its own right with a view to establishing its specific *kerygma*. In this the general context of the particular gospel involved has to be borne in mind. As the exegetical enquiry has shown, the place a particular story occupies in the gospel is vitally important for our understanding of it (see above p 130f). The preacher must not confine himself to the question of the special message of a given pericope. It is his task to find new words—in the new situation—in which to express this message.

II Treatment of individual pericopes

We shall examine the current catholic sermon literature to determine how far it does give expression to the actual message of the miracle stories, and we shall attempt to make suggestions for a kind of preaching that is in conformity with the real content of this message. For this purpose we have selected from the tradition of the three stories treated of above (in the exegetical section) those four pericopes in particular which were read during mass in the pre-1969 arrangement of sections of scripture in the Roman liturgy, with the original place of use in brackets.

The story of the healing of the paralytic (Mt 9:1–8).
(18th Sunday after Pentecost)
The story of the calming of the storm (Mt 8:23–27).
(4th Sunday after the Epiphany)
The story of the feeding of the four thousand (Mk 8:1–9).
(6th Sunday after Pentecost)
The story of the feeding of the five thousand (Jn 6:1–15).
(4th Sunday in Lent)

As before, a list of the present position of all the passages discussed exegetically is found below, in Appendix 1.

1 The story of the healing of the paralytic

(a) ON THE SERMON LITERATURE

The story of the healing of the paralytic in the tradition of Matthew was originally the gospel for the eighteenth Sunday after Pentecost. In addition to repeating the story with amplifications of their own, preachers show a special preoccupation with the connection between sin and sickness, the relationship between spiritual and physical healing, the miracle and confession. In all this the contact they retain with the pericope itself is for the most part only superficial.

The re-telling of the story with embellishments

Many composers of sermons display a great interest in the previous history of the paralytic, and thereby are carried far beyond the limits of the actual story as it exists. 'What efforts the sick man had already made to try everything possible! What cures he had tried, what pills and mixtures he had taken, and yet nothing had helped in the least!' 'Perhaps he had paid out a fortune to the doctors—all in vain!' 'He suffers still more from the wretchedness that is within him.' 'Do we not discern the drama of a misspent life in his background . . . ? Formerly he was anything but one of the elect . . . Who knows what illness lies concealed under the popular diagnosis "paralysed"? Perhaps it was the kind of paralysis that was a consequence of the sins of his youth. No wonder that he felt anxious about his meeting with Jesus.' 'Perhaps he put up a resistance when his companions laid hold of him in order to bring him to Jesus.' It is a 'difficult journey for him, and sometimes he has to grit his teeth with pain. Now he is lying before Jesus, filled with a deep excitement . . .'; '. . . the gaze that he directs towards the Lord is a deep, earnest and longing one'. 'A dark cloud of human misery hangs over the gloomy interior of the typical near Eastern house . . .'. The people 'are crowding in thickly. They are almost bursting with curiosity. Their eyes are really popping out of their heads.' 'The Lord takes in the situation at a glance.' 'For all his seriousness, he wears a gentle smile on his lips.' 'How penetrating and transforming the dialogue must have been that would have taken place then between the Master and the sick man! What sort of sins did the Lord see in the heart of the paralysed man? What "insight" the paralysed man himself must have gained into his own sins, there before the eyes of the Lord . . . How he must have felt their full gravity and utter hatefulness and wrongness!'

In the examples cited the indeterminate expressions 'perhaps', 'may', and 'who knows?' (which are all too easily multiplied) plainly betray the fact that here fantasy has taken control over the text and suppressed its real message. The urge to indulge in fables runs directly counter to the real tendency of this story. Our exegetical examination has shown that Matthew deliberately dispenses with many of the purely narrative details contained in his Marcan model in order to focus the story as a whole consistently upon the central question of the authority to forgive sins. His intention is totally frustrated by these preachers. They go far beyond Mark and Luke in devising a whole flood of new motifs which change the shape of the story, and it is these that are now accorded a dominant position in the forefront of it. And to this extent the kerygma of the story is pushed into the background and, in the last analysis, never expressed at all. The gospel is replaced by a story which has only a few superficial descriptive details in common with it, but which, basically speaking, goes a way of its own and pursues a goal of its own (the description of an episode in vivid hues). It is degraded to the level of a springboard for the preacher's own ideas.

This becomes apparent mainly in the fact that instead of Jesus the paralysed man becomes the focal point of interest. The kerygmatic story of the forgiveness of sins upon earth is turned into a kind of medical history—without any foundation in fact. For the past history of the sick man is not to be reconstructed by vague speculations. On this topic the text itself is silent. It shows astonishingly little interest in the paralysed man, and hardly tells us anything about him, nothing of his thoughts, words or deeds, simply that at the word of the Lord he stood up and went to his house (Mt 9:7). It is not he personally that is the point of this story, but rather the authority of Jesus and of the christian community to forgive sins.

The connection between sickness and sin
In this interest in the previous history of the paralysed man we have already had occasion to perceive that tendency, which is so frequently to be met with in sermons, of connecting sickness with sin. 'In this Sunday's gospel two factors in particular are strikingly evident: the sickness of an individual and his sins. Sickness and sin! This is a theme which has long been of great

concern to men.' The manner in which it is treated of varies considerably. 'It may be that the sequence of the two healings ... is conditioned by the fact that the sickness of soul, the sin, is connected with the sickness of the body, the palsy, as its deeper and more underlying cause.' 'Today we know very well that increasing physical paralysis can be due to the pressure of some inner spiritual burden.' Even the paralysed man knows 'that there is an intrinsic connection between his own paralysis and the sickness of his soul. He is heavily burdened with a bad conscience. For it is his own fault that he is a poor cripple.' If he had 'kept God's commandments and so avoided sin Christ the Lord would not need to perform the first miracle of healing ... And in consequence of this probably not the second either ... For if the man who was healed had avoided sin, the sickness of the soul, he would probably also have escaped from the evils of physical sickness.' 'The saying of the sage of the old testament continues to be valid in many cases even today: "He who sins in the eyes of his creator falls into the hands of the doctor".'

Certainly in observations of this kind it is not always asserted in so many words that there is an underlying connection between sin and sickness. Nevertheless this is what is intended. Against this, on the other hand, we are told with refreshing clarity: 'From the fact that an individual is sick I cannot draw any conclusions with regard to his personal guilt.' Nevertheless it is maintained that there is a connection between sin and sickness: 'Probably it would be unjust and exaggerated to seek straightway for some personal sin, some spiritual wound underlying this state of sickness ... But yet at the deepest roots of every kind of sickness lurks that sin of Adam which has corrupted our human nature.'

This is not the place to enter into the complex problem of sin and sickness. In our present context sin is understood not as a moral betrayal which is punished by sickness. It affects the entire existence of man in his relationship with God. The mission of Jesus is characterised in all its aspects by the fact that he redeems his people from their sins (Mt 1:21). On this basis the forgiveness of sin signifies not merely the washing away of some moral stain, but the building up of the new people of God as an eschatological deed.

Our exegetical investigation has led us to conclude that in the story under examination no causal connection is stated to exist between the sin of the paralytic and his sickness. All attempts at constructing such a connection represent departures from the text. This contains no mention whatever of any particular personal sins or feelings of guilt on the part of the sick man. His healing does not follow automatically from the forgiveness, but constitutes a separate act in its own right in the episode as a whole, which follows upon the separate word spoken by Jesus. (A further point is that apart from this instance there is hardly any mention of sins and their forgiveness in the context of the healings.) Above all we should pay due heed to the following factor: In the story being treated of here the central point of concern is not the actual forgiveness of sins in itself at all, but rather how it can be shown that the exercise of this is legitimate. It is intended to be confirmed by the healing.

The rigid pattern of retribution according to which sickness and suffering are taken to be punishments for personal transgressions cannot claim Jesus' authority in its support. He has firmly rejected any such legalistic approach to the problem, which was in fact a decisive factor in the teaching of the judaism of his time (cf Lk 13:1–5; Jn 9). His own approach is diametrically opposed to all attempts to conclude that an individual is particularly sinful from the fact that he is suffering.

Healing of the soul and of the body
A theme that runs through almost all sermons on the story of the healing of the paralytic with a monotony that is alarming is that of the primacy of the soul by comparison with the body. 'Jesus is first a doctor of the soul, and this is his prime concern.' He heals 'the wounds of the soul first before he heals the sick-

ness of the body'. The reason for this is not far to seek. It is quite simply 'that sicknesses of the soul are worse than sicknesses of the body'. This in turn is based upon the astounding premiss that the body is merely a kind of vehicle for the soul. 'In this shell we journey through life until at some point and in some way we have to come to a halt at the limits of the way of life.' Once forgiveness of sin has been attained to '... everything is finished. The sick man has been made whole in his innermost soul. Now he can die ... The kingdom of heaven is standing open. O die thou happy man! Die as quickly as thou canst, die!' 'What is of concern to Jesus Christ is always the soul of the man ... He regards the body as simply the curtain. This he pushes aside ...'. The healing is deprived of its weight: 'Pain and suffering and even incurable sickness are only on the surface. Painful though they are they are superficial.' 'Whether a man is healthy or sick is irrelevant.' 'Oh yes, if afterwards Jesus had not healed the body the sick man would still have been consoled, for his soul was indeed already healed. Then he would joyfully have endured the pains of his body. For it is quite certain: Once they had let him down from the roof, when he lay before Jesus, when he looked into the pure and holy countenance of the saviour then he no longer felt any pain in his body. Only the pain in his soul still troubled him then.'

Finally the pericope is turned into a moral tale designed to serve as an example. Jesus' intention, so we are told, was to point out to the man 'the correct order of values in the relationship between body and soul' and to charge him 'to care for the world within him'. 'First comes health of soul ... Then comes the healing of the body ... First comes Sunday and holy mass, then comes the excursion, the journey to the lake or into the woods ... First, therefore, church, then the inn or the recreation room.'

It is no part of our present task to throw light upon all aspects of these quotations, significant though they are. They serve to show the corrupting and distorting effects upon the interpretation of scripture of that dualism which seems to be indestructible and which is hostile to the physical. They show, furthermore, how right into our own days the shadow of this great misconception hangs over the proclamation of the christian message.

There is no doubt that the centre of the story is taken up with the question of the forgiveness of sins, and in particular with the authentication of this. By comparison with this the healing of the paralytic (the miracle story) is of secondary significance. Matthew precisely—this is a point which was brought out in our exegetical investigation—has been consistent in making it subordinate to the main theme. But this fact should not lead us to conclusions which are false. However illegitimate it is to deduce a specific conception of the body/soul relationship from the juxtaposition of the two narrative units, it is no less illegitimate to deduce from the fact that the forgiveness of sins takes priority that the soul has priority over the body. Attention has already been drawn to the fact that the dualism of soul and body is quite alien to biblical thought. The bible does not recognise the duality constituted by two substances of unequal value. The division takes place in a different dimension, in the personal and historical decision between salvation and perdition. This is not in any sense concerned exclusively with the salvation of the soul, or with caring for the 'world that is within', but with man as one, undivided and indivisible. Just as sin does not represent a spiritual phenomenon, while illness represents a physical one, but rather both affect man as a whole, so in the same way the effects of forgiveness and healing respectively do not bear upon either soul or body taken in isolation, but upon man. The message of his salvation is addressed to him as a concrete whole in the totality of his physical existence. The healing story emphasises this. For this reason it is an utter misconception of what forgiveness means here to deduce from it the conclusion that the soul should make haste to rid itself of the body (see above, 'O die thou happy man! Die as quickly as thou canst...'). The point of this story is precisely the need for forgiveness to be made actual in the world, 'on earth' (Mt 9:6).

These considerations apart, a further objection to the sermon literature we have quoted is that it represents a complete departure from the real theme of the story.

The miracle of healing
(i) 'Once more Christ stands before us today as the miracle-worker round whom the crowds throng, as the doctor and helper who delivers from need. Once more he stands before us as the warm-hearted friend of the sick and the crippled, as the bringer of happiness and blessing in distress of body and soul. Once more it is the Christ whose nature radiates kindness, the Christ with the burning eyes, with the enchanting smile, with the words that transform our lives, with the warmth of heart.' 'It has always been like this. The waiting-room of a famous doctor is constantly crowded... It was just the same in the life of our Lord and saviour. Throughout the whole land he had the reputation of being a mighty wonder-worker and a kind doctor endowed with miraculous powers.' 'There was unreserved confidence in his power to work miracles and his kindness. He had already proved himself magnificently to be the saviour of the sick.' His 'hands were overflowing with miracles of this kind'. 'He is the master of the impossible.' 'With the utmost ease Jesus commands the man sick of the palsy...'. He deals with the laws of nature 'as only God can deal with them and control them'. All in all, a most unfortunate line of argument.

(ii) The miracles of Christ do not cease. 'His divine power works miracle upon miracle, in spite of all those who deny them, at Lourdes and Fatima. We can seek out those who have been healed in all the countries of Europe. We can read descriptions of their often terrible sicknesses and their miraculous healing in medical records, and study x-ray photographs of them.' 'An international association of doctors tests and studies the miraculous healings. More than half of these are not christians at all. Many are doubters to the core, full of hatred against God and the church.' 'Let them only doubt and search desperately to scrape together counter-proofs against them! There are, on average, fifteen cures every year, such that even the most obstinate disbeliever in them can no longer find even the semblance of a way out.' 'What specialist in the study of bacilli is there who can explain why it is that the dirty evil-smelling water of the baths at Lourdes has never infected a single individual throughout ninety years, while at the same time this same water has probably healed more than a hundred in every year. No, he who believes in the church of Rome has no need to deny the shrines where miracles of divine healing take place.'

As against this view it is often openly and plainly stated in a sermon that the miracles are there 'not for their own sake but ... in order to awaken in us faith in Jesus and his message ... They are not there in order to satisfy the desire for extraordinary things entertained by certain devout christians. To suppose this would simply be a misunderstanding of the nature of the miracles which would lead to questionable and dangerous consequences.'

On (i): If Jesus is described as a doctor endowed with miraculous powers then the impression is given to the hearers that he is to be assigned to the category of miracle doctors. The healings are thereby deprived of their character as eschatological signs. They are regarded as medical phenomena and degraded to the level of mere wonder-working. Magical conceptions are disseminated. We have already explicitly drawn attention to the fact that any interpretation of the miracles that suggests this kind of wonder-working is in contradiction to the witness of the gospels themselves, and just as vigorously to be rejected as that other opinion according to which the miracle was intended to demonstrate that Jesus is endowed with a plenitude of divine power and able to manipulate and control the laws of nature at will. The healing of the paralytic is no arbitrary demonstration of the omnipotence of God, but a sign that directs the attention of the bystanders to Jesus himself and his authority to forgive sins. It is a question not of believing in miracles but of believing in Jesus.

On (ii): It is inadmissible to place the 'miracles' of Lourdes and Fatima on the same level as the miracles of Jesus. To adduce commissions of doctors, specialists in the study of bacilli and x-ray photographs as arguments plainly involves the danger of attempting to make the department of medicine responsible for answering the question of miracles. Not a few preachers do incur this danger.

The authority to forgive sins
(i) Not a few sermons are concerned with the question of justifying the forgiveness of sins. By his word and 'by the miracle which follows upon it Jesus intends to show that as Son of God he has the power to remit sins'. This power is, for the most part, taken in the sense of a 'power in the sphere of the soul and spirit', and is concretised in the sacrament of penance. The confessional is 'a "first-aid post" for those of all ages who are sick of soul'. 'Shortly before Christ quitted this world he handed over his great authority to men. These are the priests. They can exercise this authority in the name of Jesus, for behind the priest stands Christ.' 'God has handed over jurisdiction over the grace of forgiveness here upon earth not only to his own Son (Jn 5:22), but to innumerable priests as well. The grace of divine forgiveness here upon earth is laid in the hands of the priest. "Go, show yourself to the priests" (Lk 17:14).' The quotation is of course used in a nonsensical way. The same author goes on, later in the sermon: 'this God has given his priests the power to alter realities suddenly at a mere word, to transform them and to substitute the divine for the creaturely ... God has given the priest the power of command over his own presence. He himself pays heed to the word that transforms.' Any comment on this quotation would be superfluous.

That Jesus should have forgiven sins is already much in itself. 'But that men should do this (in virtue of a general authorisation)—this is still more. God's power in his priests! The priests, ministers of the divine omnipotence upon earth!' Against this we are told in another sermon: 'God alone forgives sins. The church and the priests are only God's instruments, and this authority has been given to men not in order that they may have power and authority to exercise, not that they may thereby make themselves great or give themselves airs, not that they may tyrannise with it over others. On the contrary, it is intended to bring home to all men the kindness and benevolence of God to humanity.' For the most part the forgiveness of sins is restricted to confession: 'There is only one way by which we can come to this: the way marked out by Christ when in the evening of Easter he bequeathed to his church the authority to forgive sins in such a way that they counted as forgiven in God's eyes . . .'. There is seldom any reference to other possibilities of forgiveness, whether sacramental or extra-sacramental.

(ii) The connection between the forgiveness of sins and healing in the story we are here considering gives occasion to many composers of sermons to ascribe the power to heal physical ailments to confession. It is 'the greatest benefit which can befall a man. Even the medical profession is coming to recognise its spiritual value more and more. Even the protestant church admits that auricular confession and the words of absolution should never have been done away with.' 'The consciousness of "standing well with" God makes a man joyful . . . A new joy in his work evinces itself. It seems to him that he could pluck up trees . . . The motions of the heart and nervous system in particular experience a strong and healing influence deriving from this grace.' '. . . It would be of great benefit for a "blessed" and peaceful sleep if the men of today were more diligent in going to confession. And the doctors too would not be so overworked . . .'. 'It is not wholly wrong to say that for every new confessional that is built a cell in a mental hospital could be

PREACHING THE MIRACLE STORIES

closed. At any rate the confessional is the sole refuge for those who are not wholly healthy in their souls, and all too easily become a prey to psychopathic conditions, especially in the religious sphere.' In some cases the fear of psycho-therapy becoming a rival is plainly to be discerned: 'The priest can say something that not even the best doctor, or even the best psychiatrist can say: "Your sins are forgiven you". Hence it is not surprising that still more people wait at the door of the confessional than in the psychiatrist's waiting-room. Here people do not merely receive advice and consolation, here they are actually helped.' 'Medicine can never be made a substitute for morality. That is the lesson which the Lord wants to teach us in this healing of the man sick of the palsy.'

On (i): The fact that the question of the authority to forgive sins is more frequently made a topic in sermons is to be welcomed. It is the subject of the pericope under consideration. Sermons which fail to recognise this miss the point of the story altogether. Our exegetical investigation has shown that Matthew in particular develops this point of Jesus' authority to forgive sins more than the other evangelists, and regards it as having become a real and living factor in the life of the christian community. For this reason it is legitimate to relate this authority to the sacrament of penance as one concrete form of forgiveness as practised in the church. The manner in which this is done, however, represents to a large extent a departure from the text. Here the primary and all-important point is the forgiveness which Jesus bestows. Certainly clear expression is also given to the fact that God has 'given such power to men' (Mt 9:8). Nevertheless this saying must be viewed in the context of the gospel as a whole. If we adhere to Matthew's meaning it is impossible to say that Jesus has quitted the world and has nominated priests to have and to exercise a general authority during the time of his absence. As the exalted Lord he is constantly present in the church: 'I am with you always to the end of the world' (Mt 28:20). This is the promise by which the community lives. Jesus *is* forgiveness in person (1:21). Forgiveness as practised in the community is to be understood simply as an 'actualisation' of his authority in the present. Any attempt at asserting such authority independently of him is thereby cut off from its roots and reduced to the powerlessness of relying on one's own power.

With regard to Mt 9:1–8 the idea that the forgiveness of sins should be restricted exclusively to the sacrament of penance as conferred by the priests represents a one-sided and prejudiced interpretation. Certainly the thought in this pericope is close to that in the saying concerning the power of the keys (16:19; 18:18). Nevertheless its message should not, on that account, be confined to the idea of an official authorisation. It has an application to the sacramental forgiveness of sins, but is in no sense restricted to this. The phrase 'to men' (9:8) does not refer exclusively to specific officials. In the church which Matthew knew there were various degrees in the practice of the sacrament of penance, as well as numerous forms of extra-sacramental forgiveness (cf eg 3:23–25, and especially 18:15–18). 'A great contribution could undoubtedly be made to the task of bringing the practice of penance to life if the communities in the church were made more vividly aware that the forms forgiveness can take are manifold and varied in this way' (Trilling 1960, 51). The word of forgiveness that liberates man must not be fettered by being forcibly restricted to confession.

On (ii): it is erroneous to attempt to bring out the significance of the sacrament of penance by referring to the various curative effects which it is alleged to be capable of producing at the physical level. Not only does this line of argument savour unpleasantly of cheapness and lack of reverence (it is suggestive of an advertisement for a closing sale) but also, over and above this, it gives the impression that confession is a kind of psychotherapy. 'We do not want to be psycho-therapists in the confessional. This is not our job, and would merely be silly charlatanism' (Rahner 1956ff, ET III 205). Certainly we should 'know when to regard a penitent as a patient for a psycho-therapist and send him to one'.

Any rejection of psycho-therapy in principle, or any radical scepticism with regard to it, betrays a deficient insight and a fear of competition. Certainly there is no substitute for the service provided by the priests. Nevertheless the doctor too has his own indispensable function. In many cases what was said above applies to him rather than to the priest: 'Here it is not merely advice and consolation that is given, but actual help' (see above). Instead of unrealistically erecting his own department into something that is absolute and all-sufficient, each of these functionaries must recognise the competence of the other in his own different sphere. In this it should be noticed that priest and doctor, for all the differences between their respective tasks and responsibilities, nevertheless do have points of contact with each other, and should refer to each other in the nature of their work.

(b) SUGGESTIONS FOR PREACHING ON MT 9:1-8

The sermon should be developed from the central point of the story. The point upon which the spirits are divided is this: has Jesus and, further, has the church the authority to forgive sins upon earth? Or does his, or alternatively the church's exercise of this authority constitute a blasphemy against God? The answer supplied by the biblical text is unequivocal: Jesus has authority to forgive sins upon earth.

The authority of Jesus to forgive sins
The forgiveness points back to the sins that are in need of forgiveness. Just as we cannot speak of the resurrection without having first taken cognisance of the fact that man is marked out for death, so we cannot speak of forgiveness without recognising that he is a sinner. In this context sin signifies not primarily a moral failure, but the state of man as bereft of the hope of salva-

tion. This is ultimately rooted in the fact that he hopes for salvation from himself, and thereby withdraws himself from God. Jesus is he 'who redeems his people from their sins' (Mt 1:21). As the eschatological bringer of salvation he constitutes his people for himself by delivering them from their sins. Forgiveness 'is the word that is basic for the kingdom of God and his dominion. It is the constitutive law of that kingdom' (Iwand, 465).

Within the synoptic tradition as a whole the story of the healing of the paralytic is the prototype example of Jesus' authority to forgive sins. Jesus anticipates the last judgment. In his action the *eschaton* breaks in upon the world, the promised age of God's great reconciliation with men. It is no longer an event that is remote, other-worldly, present only in hope. Instead it has actually come upon the earth in him (Mt 9:6). It takes place in the midst of our world before the eyes and ears of men, in men's sight and on their behalf. In Jesus God is actually bringing about forgiveness and salvation 'today' (cf Lk 5:26), in the here and now. It is his immediate closeness that consoles and encourages the sinner (Mt 9:2), but at the same time it also provokes scandal for all those who are only willing to have God and reconciliation in heaven, not 'upon earth' (9:6). He encounters man with such immediacy that he finds himself faced with the decision inescapably in the here and now. The estimation of the bystanders ('blasphemer' or 'Son of man') corresponds to the division between those who are acquitted and those who are condemned.

The healing is a sign of the age of salvation. Jesus manifests himself as the messiah of the final age. His miracles serve to show that the dominion of God has been inaugurated (cf Mt 11:5; 12:28), that the time has already arrived in which the forgiveness of sins can take place. That which follows from forgiveness and healing is not to be taken as a way of proving their reality conclusively, as though forgiveness could be demonstrated. It is only to be experienced in faith (cf 9:2). The miracle serves to underline the authority of Jesus before the eyes of the bystanders (those whose eyes are opened, those who 'see'). Not only does he pronounce forgiveness, he actually causes it. His word is not empty, it takes effect. He heals the whole man in his physical existence radically and throughout his entire being. He liberates him for a new task in the world, the task of contributing to the new creation.

The authority of the church to forgive sins
The church does not arrogate power to herself in any spirit of self-glorification or of her own power. Rather she pronounces forgiveness in the authority of the Lord present within her. Those who are already reconciled with God in Christ have the task of contributing to the reconciliation of others (cf 2 Cor 5:18).

In the light of Mt 9:1–8 we have the following observations to make with regard to the present-day practice of penance in the church:

(i) The forgiveness of sins is a gift of the age of salvation bestowed together with Christ, and possible only by reference to him.

(ii) It is no mechanical process (confessional automatism), but a personal event taking place in the sphere of faith ('When Jesus saw their faith . . .' 9:2).

(iii) The representative function of the believers themselves is important.

(iv) The forgiveness of sins is not necessarily restricted to sacramental absolution. In this connection attention should be drawn in particular to preaching itself as one of a whole range of possibilities of extra-sacramental forgiveness: the word of God not only *speaks of* forgiveness. Where it is heard in faith it actually *effects* forgiveness (cf 'the word of the gospel blots out our sins').

2 *The story of the calming of the storm*

(a) ON THE SERMON LITERATURE
The story of the calming of the storm in Matthew's version was prescribed for liturgical reading on the fourth Sunday after Epiphany. The sermon literature concentrates its efforts mainly upon giving the story a lively tone by embellishing it with vivid descriptions and emphasising its miraculous character. In many cases the stormy journey is applied to the life of the individual christian, less frequently to that of the church.

Embellishment of the text
'Many preachers—perhaps they are already too many for the hearers—have already striven to make themselves masters of the scene of today's gospel in their words.' In order that the power of the storm may really have its full effect an imaginary picture is first drawn in vivid colours. This is 'the lovely picture, full of the atmosphere of evening and tranquil peace'. 'The brilliance of the evening held all the senses captive. The sun was still touching the peaks around the shore with glowing points of light, and dipping the nearby mountains in a radiant stream of gold. The lake breathed an atmosphere of quiet and the cool refreshing breeze from it flowed over the boat. All the noise and bustle of the busy day fell silent . . . Only the little waves lapped about the boat.' 'A wind so weak as hardly to be noticeable softly ruffled the wide expanse of water . . ., then the first veils of night drifted down over the lake. Jesus the Master, tired from his day's work, had sought out a little place of rest for himself, and had soon fallen into a gentle sleep.'

'But soon the captivating scene changes. Very soon this peaceful picture becomes the stage of a life-and-death struggle. The waves tower up as high as houses, and the menacing roar of the abyss fills its whole expanse.' 'We cannot picture to ourselves what a storm at sea on the lake of Genesareth was like quite so simply as perhaps the brief homely account in Matthew may have led us to suppose. In fact this must have been an unleashing of the elements . . .'. 'A fierce hurricane sweeps down over the lake. The waves rise high and toss the little ship from the crest of the waves to the trough below in a raging tumult.' '. . . Could anyone blame Peter at that moment if he muttered somewhat angrily between his teeth: "Now we are really in for it!".' 'And Peter commanded quickly: "Every man to the helm! Otherwise we shall be wrecked." Then it really began . . .'. 'The arms of twelve men are struggling for their lives with the forces of nature. The sweat runs down over their sunburned faces. But the storm rages on relentlessly. The waves keep coming ever more menacingly. The weary hands let the tiller fall. The hot sweat of fear is changed into the cold sweat of death. They are helpless and lost. The watery grave of the waves is already gaping on the sea bed.' 'Death as seamen know him stands grimacing at the now useless helm, and see! At his feet the saviour still sleeps peacefully on and never hears the terrible storm of wind or the beating of the waves.' 'But when the mast breaks and goes overboard, and they can no longer hold the tiller, the ship runs out of control and begins to sink. Then they awaken him . . .'. 'He looks at them with a kind smile on his lips, then simply says to them: "Why are you so afraid?". Then in a stronger voice he cries out the words of his omnipotence into the fury of the howling storm . . .'. 'A splendid picture! Raging storm, heaving sea, an inferno of natural forces, a boat dancing about on the waves, terrified men hovering on the brink of death, the mastery and majesty of the Lord . . .! Who would not be stirred at such a picture on this present morning?' 'Night vanishes. The hurricane subsides. The sun smiles from a clear sky and the little ship completes its journey in peace to the friendly and welcoming shore, and all are saved in the mighty protection of God.'

Undoubtedly the preachers do succeed 'in making themselves master of the scene of today's gospel in their words'. Their own ideas dominate the text so that its *kerygma* is no longer expressed. The motive which inspires such flourishes is clear and unequivocal: the storm scene must be depicted in vivid colours before the eyes of the congregation in order to grip their attention. Let us leave aside the question of whether in fact this object is achieved through the picture which has been presented. Whatever conclusion we come to, this is not in conformity with the text. Matthew deliberately dispenses with illustrative details and edifying overtones. His story is consistently theological in its presentation. It is not intended in any sense simply to describe what once took place during a storm on the lake. His intention is to make clear to his community by means of an example the full significance of what discipleship means. To a large extent preachers fail to recognise this. His presentation is regarded as an account of the facts which is unfortunately all too colourless, and therefore is in need of filling out with detail: 'We cannot picture to ourselves what a storm on the lake of Genesareth was like quite so simply as ... Matthew may have led us to suppose' (see above). Thus the biblical narrative is replaced by a narrative of the preacher's own, one which simply uses the individual motifs which go to make up the biblical story as so much material with which to achieve its own aims. The preacher's story represents a departure from the text before him. It does not follow the direction which the text prescribes, but rather turns aside from it.

The miracle
'We live in a world of superlatives ... Even theology and the catechism are full of superlatives ... God is a being of still more potent superlatives ... Now in today's gospel we experience one of the superlatives of God expressed not merely in written words on paper but as a reality.' We see 'an impressive nature miracle. The Lord does not actually appear as the author of the weather, but he does intervene to correct it.' 'Then all at once the incomprehensible happened ... The Son of Man who,

only a moment before, was sleeping apparently so weak and helpless in the storm-buffeted boat, who seemed to be subject to the laws of nature like all the rest, suddenly showed that he was above all things, even over all the law and all the forces of nature.' 'He breaks through the majestic immovability of the natural law.' He is 'sleeping more deeply than death and hell. The apostles have actually experienced it.' The word of power uttered by the Lord achieves in the twinkling of an eye what all that toil has been unable to accomplish. Certainly 'a powerful man such as the President of the United States can give orders that forthwith a hundred ships are to travel across the ocean at great speed. But he cannot command that the wind shall stop blowing or that the waves must smooth themselves out. This is something that only he who is Lord over nature can do . . .'. By doing so he intends 'to show that he is indeed the Son of God'. 'We do not know how often the Almighty performs miracles. Certainly he has performed very many . . . But it is also certain that he does not perform them so often as was believed in earlier ages, which tended on the whole to claim that God had intervened miraculously in cases in which we, in the light of our more advanced knowledge, see only the effect of natural forces.' Exegesis has shown that what the evangelists, and Matthew above all, are concerned with is neither to demonstrate Jesus' power over the elements of nature, nor to provide a proof of his divine sonship. The interpretation which appears in the examples we have quoted is unbiblical. 'All at once', 'in the twinkling of an eye', Jesus becomes 'a being endowed with still more potent superlatives', a magician in the realm of nature who can do all things and is even more powerful than the President of the United States. The miracle degenerates into a mere piece of wonder-working. It is defined in terms of the categories of natural science (suspension of the laws of nature) and it is consistent with this that it should be 'the more advanced state of our knowledge' that should decide what is or is not to be accounted a miracle today. Faith is made subject to the judgment of natural science, and thereby in the last analysis made to surrender to it.

The 'ship of life'
(i) The story of the calming of the storm is frequently interpreted as an image of the life of the individual man with its vicissitudes. The believer 'knows that even the silent Genesareth of the heart, which at times can lie as calm as a lake and reflect the heavens with great joy, may suddenly be thrown into a raging foaming uproar by unsuspected storms...'. 'The ship of the disciples in the storm on the lake is an image of the individual christian soul in times of distress and affliction', an 'image of the soul when it is lonely and apparently abandoned by God'. 'From the first hour of our earthly life right up to the last we live in a ship with which, for better or for worse, our fortunes are bound up—the ship of our own body. The journey of our life was quiet and tranquil when it began ... No clouds troubled the heavens of our happy childhood ... Then all at once, unexpectedly, unlooked for, unforeseen, the barometer stood at "stormy".... Perhaps we were forced to discover soon enough that the ship of our life, precisely our own body, was not equal to such storms, that it became leaky and rotten, sick and weak. Moreover there are storms which no-one notices anything of, which rage secretly and silently, and yet these are, perhaps, still more harmful in their effects than all the others. They are the storms of the soul ... Even a soul that is completely pure and loves God can undergo the direst spiritual struggles and conflicts.'

(ii) For the voyage in the 'barque of life' the most varied counsels, maxims for life and rules are put forward, and the support of the gospel is invoked for all these. 'Storms have a meaning. They make us restless. They wake us up...'. 'Yet how quickly human nature, with its inclination to comfort, grows about itself a shell of pleasant living conditions, and takes refuge in a state of well-being that consists in effortless enjoyment... "There is nothing harder for man to bear than a series of good days."' 'Of course God might have saved us from all danger right from the outset... In fact he might have set us in heaven straight away instead of in this perilous world. But it is precisely his will that we shall be able to prove ourselves, that we ourselves shall be able to show what we are worth.' 'It is only in time of storm that what is in man is brought to light.' God will 'draw out the whole strength of faith from our hearts in time of peril'. Thus even the fact that he is asleep is 'no accident, but a method, though admittedly a risky method'.

In the storm 'it is important to struggle with every conceivable resource and power of one's own in order to escape from the danger. God helps those who help themselves... This ancient proverb contains a deep truth within itself.' Against this, on the other hand, the following is put forward as 'the first and important lesson of the storm': 'Do not trust in your own power... The first blessing of the storm is the knowledge of the inadequacy of our own strength.' It is 'only through the most severe disasters and through the most bitter experiences that we arrive at the conviction: We need a God who can help'. 'Human strength achieves little... United with God we arrive at the goal... We must cry to Jesus. Then everything is only half as dangerous. We must call Jesus to our aid. Then the worst of the evils is overcome in a twinkling. We can do this, in fact, because he is the saviour and because he is God. It is as simple as that.' 'What can happen if God is with us, and what can befall a christian who believes in the promise of the Lord? Even physical death itself could only bring him victory. Has not eternal bliss been promised to him?' We know indeed that the Lord 'will save us from the death that puts an end to our temporal lives and will carry us across to the shores of eternity and to the islands of the blessed'. Therefore 'patience is commanded us in this present hour'. 'It is certainly not an article of faith, but it probably is a good practical application for our devotion if I say that Jesus' slumbers in the midst of the raging of the storm can teach us a lesson. Perhaps it is quite simply and plainly the lesson that we men too must not forget the necessity of sleep amid all the tempests of our lives.'

On (i): Exegesis confirms the fact that the story of the calming of the storm as presented by Matthew is paradigmatic in character. But it points in a quite different direction from that indicated by the sermon literature presented here. In the case of this latter it is a feeling for the 'new age' ideal of devotion, 'God and the soul', which directs the interest towards the fate of the 'individual christian soul' which is journeying in the ship of life, the 'body', to the 'islands of the blessed', and in the course of so doing falls into distress by reason of the reverses which life has to offer. Distress and deliverance are interpreted in individualistic terms. Against this what Matthew intends to say is that in the course of following the way of discipleship of Jesus which all have in common (not only, therefore, when the circumstances of life are hostile) the church is assailed and then delivered by her Lord.

On (ii): In the sermons emphasis is rightly laid upon the importance of proving one's self and having trust. Nevertheless the fact that the story of the calming of the storm has this paradigmatic character should not lead us to set up laws according to which everything has to evolve in this way, or to offer blueprints for man to act upon. 'Nothing is more dangerous than for the issues of faith's temptation and faith's victory to be reduced to mere commonplaces', and degraded to the level of stereotyped expressions of worldly wisdom. The preacher is placing a false interpretation upon the story if he constructs a popular system from it and makes even the sleep of Jesus a 'method'. The real intention underlying this story is precisely to give expression to the fact that the way of discipleship cannot be calculated or foreseen, and the actions and attitude of Jesus cannot always be comprehended. The journey turns out to be precisely not as 'man' expects it to be. Faith involves risks and hazards. To make Jesus a factor in human calculations is to contradict the witness of scripture. Furthermore it not infrequently happens that in the minds of the hearers he is reduced to the level of a helper in distress who is at their disposal in critical situations, and whom we can 'use' at will. The preacher should strive to eliminate this unchristian attitude. At any rate he should not provide fresh fuel for it.

The church as the 'barque of Peter'
'From time immemorial the fathers and doctors of the church have regarded the boat of the disciples in the storm on the lake as an image of the church in the storm of the age.' She is 'on the way to harbour, but has not yet arrived at her goal. Rather she is constantly exposed to denial, persecution, error, hostility and attack, constantly called, in the midst of her helplessness, the breakers that threaten her and the weakness of her human members, to cry to the Lord in her distress.' 'He who decides to follow Christ does not have a quieter or easier life. Quite the contrary!' Many preachers point less to the dangers involved than to the security which the church guarantees. 'In the last analysis there is only one power which can rescue man from his distress and restore him to health.' 'The true and the only passenger ship willed by God, which, according to the will of Christ, is intended to carry all men to their final goal, is the catholic church. She is the ark of the souls of all men.' 'The church survives every storm. Bismarck, the Hohenzollerns, the Prussian state and even the "Third Reich" did not take a thousand years to fall into utter ruins in order that the church might enjoy her freedom anew.' 'Storms from the East started by Bolshevik inhumanity fall upon us to rip to shreds the sail of peace that is spread aloft over the world, and to make shipwreck of the voyage of good will by the destructive force of godlessness. In the midst of all this stands the church.' 'The church cannot be reproached with having wavered even on a single occasion in the course of her long history in her faith and loyalty to Christ . . . All other considerations pale into insignificance

beside this fact.' 'Our task: Let us range ourselves, with a deep sense of duty, behind those who support and defend the church, and acknowledge her truth.' The saying holds good for these present times too: 'It is good to dwell under the staff of episcopal authority' or 'It is good to live in the barque of Peter'. The church 'is meant to be a place of rest amid the storms of life. In all ages she has succeeded in drawing in a rich haul of immortal souls, and so it will remain.'

Matthew himself is the first preacher who has applied the story of the calming of the storm to the church. This interpretation, therefore, is not merely possible, but is already present in the text itself. To this extent we may whole-heartedly agree with the sermon literature which we have been considering.

Unfortunately it is only rarely that preachers adhere to the image presented by the story itself and the statements it contains which are of such significance for our understanding of the church. Other images are tacitly allowed to dominate our awareness: the rock amid the breakers and the house that is all glorious, built from eternal stones that stand firm and do not totter, guaranteeing a 'place of rest' and providing a place where one may 'live a good life'. Quite apart from the fact that this represents a falsification of the church's history (cf the assertion that she has never 'wavered in the course of her history') it also distorts the intention underlying the text itself. This points precisely to the fact that the church does not stand immovable, but is 'in a state of flux', that she is a centre 'not of rest', but of assaults and dangers. She does not carry with her any talisman such as can guarantee a good life. She is exposed to the attacks of hostile forces. This is true not in any sense in spite of the fact that Jesus is in the ship, but precisely because it is he himself and his followers that are the point at issue.

(b) SUGGESTIONS FOR PREACHING ON THE STORY OF THE CALMING OF THE STORM (MT 8:23–27)

The message of the story of the calming of the storm in Matthew acquires a special significance in the contemporary situation. The image of the ship in the midst of the storm serves to underline the dynamic initiative embodied in the second Vatican Council's *Constitution on the Church*. This image gives us an understanding of the developments taking place within the church at the present moment, which cause not a few christian misgivings: to their eyes it seems as though immovable bastions have been thrown into 'a state of flux'.

The church as rock and as barque

We quite commonly find the idea of the church as a house that has been firmly 'compacted' together. Matthew knows of a similar image: the church as built on the rock (16:18). At the same time, however, he also knows (and in this he differs from many christians of the present day) of a different image which seems to be in contradiction to the first: the church as a ship in the midst of a storm at sea. Now all at once she is no longer standing there immovably as a rock in the midst of the breakers. She has been abandoned to the floods. She is 'drifting helplessly in them'. As she makes her journey she finds herself menaced and assailed.

None of these images can be accorded an absolute value (though in the past the image of the rock was thought of in this way). The nature of the church cannot adequately be expressed in any one particular image. All we can do is to build up some kind of composite picture by combining several different images which are often dialectically opposed to one another. 'Natural science presents us moderns with a remarkable analogy for such a process of combining images: it tells us that we can only understand what light is by allowing the two images of corpuscles and waves to complement one another. So far as the investigator is concerned these two images cannot be reduced to a single common denominator, yet at the same time they do reveal to him two contrary aspects of light, so that by holding both together he can ultimately attempt to grasp the mystery proper to light itself' (Ratzinger, 9).

The profound degree of commitment involved in discipleship
What does Jesus promise to those who become his followers? Does he guarantee that they shall have a trouble-free journey? It might be thought, 'If he is with us then nothing untoward can happen'. This expectation turns out to be a delusion. Jesus is the Son of Man who has nowhere to lay his head (Mt 8:20). His journey ends on the cross. His community will have to share in the state of defencelessness and the cross of their Lord. The community has been taken with him on his journey. He steps into the boat first and the disciples follow (8:23). In the storm it is precisely Jesus who is the central point of concern. Still more dangerous than the onslaught of the demonic powers is the scandal which Jesus himself arouses: he sleeps as if all this was of no concern to him.

The disciples are not equal to this twofold assault. In moments of crisis their faith ought to become stronger. Instead of this it is swept away by the storm. It is made clear that even they, the disciples (the christian community) are not sure of their faith absolutely and in all circumstances. They are hovering on the brink of doubt. Discipleship leads them into situations which are totally unforeseen and incalculable. There is a great danger that they will remain stuck halfway through their journey. Their faith has to prove itself in a decision against unbelief which is constantly renewed. Unbelief is not a factor that exists only outside the confines of the church. It is also a problem for the church's interior life: 'I believe! Help my unbelief!' (Mk 9:24).

The glories of discipleship
In their state of doubt the disciples do not feel that they are thrown back upon themselves. They do not in any sense cling to one another, nor do they bow, deprived of their own glory, to

the dominion of the forces of nature. Instead they turn to their Lord. He holds them even as they fall, and overcomes the paucity of their faith. His word of power brings about the great transformation from 'a mighty storm' to 'a mighty calm'. This arouses astonishment and questioning even among 'those men' who do not yet belong to the community.

The church of Christ is on the way, 'voyaging'. She must not imagine that she is sure of attaining her goal. Precisely because she is following her Lord she falls into afflictions. But she follows the Lord who picks her up when she has fallen and sets her right, the Lord who makes effective the dominion of God, and thereby bestows a new kind of protection (the eschatological peace, the 'great calm'). The depths of personal commitment and the glory of discipleship! This is the theme for preaching on the story of the calming of the storm in Matthew.

3 *The story of the miraculous feeding*

(a) THE SERMON LITERATURE

Two versions of the miraculous feeding were former Sunday gospels, and thus the theme of sermons in the published collections. The Johannine version provided the gospel for the fourth Sunday in Lent, while the second of the two Marcan accounts (8:1–9) constituted that of the sixth Sunday after Pentecost.

Though each of these passages brings out different aspects in the story, and has a distinct message of its own to convey, the sermons preached on them hardly allow for this at all, and are virtually indistinguishable from one another in terms of content. Even though—in defiance of all the findings of exegesis—they still persist in taking the story as referring to two separate miracles, their treatment of it is still one of monotonous uniformity. Attention is so wholly concentrated on the 'multiplication of loaves as an objective fact' that the specifically kerygmatic factors in the presentation of the story are overlooked. The following quotation is characteristic of the basic attitude and outlook which preachers generally adopt: 'Since it is, basically speaking, the same episode that is being described in both the Johannine and the synoptic accounts, the only specific differences which we can find in their respective messages will derive from the positions assigned to each version in the church's year.' But even the influence of the church's year must not be exaggerated here. All too often all that it amounted to is that whereas sermons for the sixth Sunday after Pentecost contained general exhortations to go to holy communion, those for the fourth Sunday in Lent contained reminders of the importance of 'fulfilling one's Easter duty of receiving communion'.

Since we can discern no essential differences between the two groups of sermons arising from the actual texts preached upon, we can combine the sermon literature for both Sundays in a single overall presentation. Similarly, the approach of the preachers concerned to questions involving biblical criticism is not determined by the special turns of phrase used by the particular evangelist concerned, for in the available sermon literature no particular cognisance is taken of these. Rather their approach is determined by the overall kerygmatic orientation which all the stories of the miraculous feeding have in common. By contrast with this, in our 'suggestions for preaching' we shall attempt to do justice to the special interest of each individual pericope.

Not infrequently the composers of these sermons content themselves simply with a restatement of the events recorded in the gospel narrative embellished with descriptive detail, devoting special attention as they do this to the actual miracle itself. They attempt to impart relevance and 'actuality' to the narratives by relating them to the eucharist (and more specifically to the reception of communion), and by relating them also to the 'miracle' of nature renewed each year of crops coming to harvest (this is especially true of sermons preached during the summer season on the sixth Sunday after Pentecost). At the same time they try to urge their hearers to observe with due reverence the practice of saying grace before and after meals.

The story itself retold in the preacher's words
'Today's gospel is probably the most popular and the most relevant to our own times.' 'Does it not paint an awe-inspiring —indeed a colossal—picture . . .', 'a drama truly on the grand scale crammed with dramatic tension?'. 'An atmosphere as it were of the freshness of spring and the scent of flowers hangs over the blessed scene.' 'Grass and flowers are flourishing everywhere under the spell of the spring sunshine. This is where we find Jesus.' 'And countless thousands follow him. It is as though the lake were overflowing with a human flood bursting into the countryside, wave after wave of men surging up the slope on which he sits.' 'The widest possible diversity is to be found among them, every variety of character, class and level of education being represented, and they have all the shortcomings which human limitations entail.' 'Who knows how many idlers, sceptics, hangers-on and sensation-seekers were among them! ... Who knows what may be done afterwards under cover of night.' 'They have their faults in plenty. But for all this at the present moment they come full of eagerness. This Jesus has struck a chord which reverberates in their innermost hearts.' 'It is so beautiful when he speaks of the lilies which bloom round about, of the birds of the air which add their chorus of "joyfully praise the Lord". It sounds like a fairy-tale and yet it is sober truth when Jesus depicts the joys of heaven.' 'So deep was the impression which the words and personality of Jesus made upon them that they even forgot to eat until their stomachs rumbled too loudly to be ignored and would not brook any further neglect of their needs.' Then 'from the soul of Jesus a cry was wrung which gives us a deep insight into the solicitude of his divine heart: "I have compassion upon the people"'. 'However high the spirit of Jesus may soar he can not be indifferent to the hunger of these masses.'

'Christian men, only picture to yourselves the attitude of the saviour standing there! ...'. 'It is not enough here simply to listen to the words. We must keep a vivid picture of the Lord before our eyes as with deep reverence he takes the bread into his hands ... It seems, then, that it was a special trait of the Lord's to take bread in his hands in this way and to say grace over it.' 'For only see what is happening! Do our eyes deceive us or is it all a dream? Jesus reaches into the little basket which a boy holds out to him, takes from it the seven loaves (strictly speaking they were only rolls) one after the other ... And then something astounding and unheard of happens: in the ordinary course of events we would expect the bread to become less and less as it was handed out. Here the opposite takes place. It becomes more and more.' 'From the hands of the Lord flowed a superabundance of bread.' 'In his adoring hands he holds bread enough for thousands.' 'And the disciples go to and fro through the long ranks intent upon their task, distributing bread to each one ... Far from being a mere snack, it was a full meal, so that after it nobody could complain that he had not had enough.' Certainly it 'tasted good to them, quite spart from the fact that for all that the fragments of bread made such a simple meal it really was good as well. Never before had they been catered for in so cheap and practical a way.'

Exegesis has shown that when we examine the various tradition strata in which the story of the miraculous feeding has been handed down it cannot be taken as literal historical fact. This story sketches a picture for us in broad outline. The details remain vague. The form of the picture is determined by certain specific theological considerations, and it must not, therefore, be viewed as though it were a photographic reproduction. It is intended not so much to depict that which is apprehensible to us, but rather to point to that which is mysterious. To attempt to enquire into the exact manner in which the miraculous feeding took place shows a failure to understand the true purpose of the story. If in spite of this we insist on taking this approach, and try to fill in the details from our own 'imagination' it becomes distorted in the same way that an expressionist painting becomes distorted when we seek to interpret it, or even 'touch it up' according to the categories of realism or photographic exactitude.

To a large extent the sermons we have quoted fail to recognise the real character of the story of the miraculous feeding as a narrative that is essentially kerygmatic in quality. They attempt to retouch the picture, and in doing so introduce elements which are wholly alien to it and which distort it. It becomes 'edifying', 'captivating', 'imposing', 'magnificent'. In short it is brought into line with the portraits of Jesus of Nazareth characteristic of repository art. The advice of the preachers is revealing when they suggest that here we should 'not merely listen to the words', but 'picture to ourselves' the attitude of the saviour and imagine 'his special way of taking bread into his hands'. In the same way we are told that 'the bread flowed from the hands of the Lord'. In place of the simple restrained language of the synoptic evangelists themselves, which has a direct and unmistakable reference to the last supper, we are confronted with a tale of magic that is over-elaborate and grotesque, a wonder-working show.

These criticisms are not intended to rule out every element of the visual in the story. The story itself is, in fact, presented in visual terms. But at the same time it remains true that we shall only be able to present it afresh and to enter into its real meaning when we confine ourselves to listening 'simply to the actual words' of the gospel text, and banish all other preconceptions from our minds. If we want visual representations of the story of the miraculous feeding to serve as preparations for our sermons then the illustrations to be found in mediaeval books provide numerous examples.

The miracle
It has already been shown in the foregoing section that when

embellishments are introduced intended to depict how the miracle was performed in defiance of the actual text, these have the effect of mutilating this story of the miraculous feeding. The same danger is entailed by that false understanding of the miraculous which underlies so many sermons.

'In today's gospel the Lord provides a miraculous answer . . . to the question of how the body is to be nourished and our physical needs are to be fulfilled.' 'Thus he bends himself to the task of . . . doing away with social need for all ages.' He 'sought to come to the aid of the hungry even when it needed a miracle to do so'. 'To satisfy the needs of five thousand people is no small task. According to the standards which we of today would consider normal it would take a good many waggon loads of food to achieve this.' 'This in itself is almost beyond belief . . . to make so much out of seven loaves!' With 'a simplicity that is superb and an effortlessness that is wonderful', 'without a single audible word, Christ used the blessing of his hands to multiply the small portions brought to him by his disciples'. Thus there is suddenly bread there 'which a few moments ago did not exist upon this earth'. 'Thousands beheld it quite clearly in the bright light of the sun . . . No, it was no deception, no magical trick but a miracle, a genuine miracle, something only to be explained in terms of the divine power which Jesus possessed in himself. He is the all-powerful Lord of nature . . . His miracles give proof of it.' 'The Lord of nature stands above the laws of nature.' 'No mortal man would have been able to do such a thing—to satisfy these innumerable masses of hungry people with a few words. All . . . soon sensed that he was something more than an ordinary man.' 'In the light of the miracle Jesus stands before us as the Lord to whom all is obedient, even bread and all worldly things.' 'He always rewards those who have time for him. For these he performs every kind of miracle.'

The thought pattern underlying such interpretations is transparent: what Jesus does goes beyond human powers and the laws of nature. This is something that can only be explained by the fact that more than earthly powers are at work in him, and this is a proof of his Godhead. To seek to prove the divinity of Christ in this way is to turn the eschatological sign of the feeding and the actual meal into a demonstration of the divine omnipotence: Jesus can do whatever he wills, even to the point of creating 'waggon-loads of food' in an instant. But this is to bring his activity close to the realm of magic. He becomes a kind of magician who from time to time 'allows a miracle to be demanded of him'. In such statements as these the focus of interest is upon the extraordinary 'multiplication of the bread', a factor which—and this is a point which should make us pause and consider—goes altogether unmentioned in the actual story. The message which this is intended to proclaim is that Jesus shares a meal with men and is united to them in the sign of the bread. But those who present the story in a purely material way completely lose sight of this personal dimension. For such presentations separate the gift from the giver. In place of the witness which the story is intended to bear proofs are adduced which are intended to support our faith in miracles.

'*The bread of the Spirit*'
The tendency to play down earthly, and in particular material, realities runs through the sermon literature like a scarlet thread. Thus for many authors the content of this story of the miraculous feeding consists in a 'unique miracle' precisely because it is concerned with bread of a purely earthly kind. For this reason they point us on beyond this to the 'bread which we need for our souls'. 'Christ is well aware that he has not been sent to preserve them (men) from hunger, or to care for them by bringing them bread. His mission is to save their souls and to tell them the truths of which they stand in such vital need concerning God and eternal life. He caters for the other need only incidentally and by way of exception because he has compassion upon them.' 'His mission was . . . a spiritual one, and all

transient and material things are wholly peripheral to the vision he has before his eyes.'

The findings of exegesis have shown that in all the traditions of the miraculous feeding which have come down to us the story has a deeper significance than the description of a purely physical feeding. To that extent we must agree with the preachers. Yet when they introduce the idea of the 'bread of souls' they are going beyond the gospel text. This idea is not merely unbiblical but actually runs counter to the meaning of the story of the miraculous feeding precisely in its spiritualising tendencies.

The thought of the disciples in the crisis is: 'Send them away in order that they ... may buy something to eat' (Mk 6:36 par). Jesus does not fall in with this suggestion. He is still there to help the people, therefore, even when the sermon is over and the hunger begins. Union with him is something that affects the whole man. 'It is important to point out to the congregation how often we find mention not only in the old testament but in the new testament as well of eating and drinking ... and that not as something introduced as an aside, but as something that belongs integrally to the kingdom of God. The area of life which we regard as profane is not, so far as the new testament is concerned, merely profane and nothing more. That which we regard as pertaining to the 'material' sphere is, so far as the biblical message is concerned, not merely set in opposition to the 'spiritual' and nothing more.

How the story of the miraculous feeding is related to the eucharist

In order to give relevance and 'actuality' to the story of the miraculous feeding various approaches are adopted. Most frequently we find it related to the celebration of mass, and in particular to receiving communion.

'Do not say "That was long ago", for this miracle is re-enacted anew a thousand times over before your questioning eyes! See the small white host which the priest holds up before you . . .' 'On 40,000 altars this daily bread of the holy eucharist is bestowed upon us as the food of our souls. As though Jesus wanted to extend the effects of his miracle of the multiplication of loaves to all ages, he sends his consecrated disciples out with full ciboriums to those who are lying hungry.' 'That very moment at holy mass when the priest bows down at the consecration and pronounces the words of consecration of Jesus himself, in that moment something is suddenly present in our midst (in the form of bread) which comes not from this earth but from the innermost depths of God himself . . . true manna rained down upon us which is descending at every moment of time somewhere or other upon this earth . . .'. '"Gather up the fragments that are left over!" This is an image of the holy eucharist, the re-enactment of the miracle of the loaves. Here it is the fragments left over from holy mass which are gathered up in order that we may be fed upon them . . . The holy mass is celebrated every day to the accompaniment of millions of communions.' This 'bread is easier to "provide" than to distribute . . ., it is present in greater quantity than can be consumed.' For this reason 'the provisions which God has made to answer the world's hunger for salvation and redemption will never be exhausted'. 'The "larder" where the holy eucharist is stored will never be empty. Truly Christ is the richest of gifts. Of him we can say: "Truly he has the answer to our needs . . .".'

The supernatural 'food' 'must be a special kind of bread'. 'With this bread we absorb into ourselves the life of God himself, the glory and holiness of God, the peace and blessedness of God . . .'. We are 'in close bodily contact with him for a whole quarter of an hour . . .'. 'What wonderful effects this bread of the eucharist has upon the body and soul of man.' It offers 'security against misfortune'. Taken in connection with the sacrament of penance it offers an '"after care" to him who has recovered from his spiritual sickness . . .'. 'Communion provides a radical solution to all the difficulties of modern times. It sets us free from that state of being at odds with ourselves which isolates us from others; it removes from us the elemental anxiety of life and does away with the harmful effects of rootlessness.'

'For this reason we joyfully choose to take upon ourselves the "hunger cure" or "fasting cure" entailed in our reception of the sacrament.' 'It is much easier to prevent malnutrition of the soul . . . than that of the body. God has made it so easy for us. Here we do not need to initiate any collective action against hunger. We do not need to beg from others. On the contrary the table is always laid and ready.' Thus in accordance with the aphorism 'bread is there to be eaten' we are exhorted to receive communion frequently, above all at Paschal time. 'May I ask you: have you all already attended to your Easter duty of receiving holy communion? Have you already caused the eternal sources of life which come to you from your saviour to spring up in your souls like brooks in the springtime with their banks blooming with the flowers of true joy?'

All the gospels establish a connection between the story of the miraculous feeding and the last supper. The reference to the eucharist is therefore to be found in the pericope itself, and is appropriate above all in cases in which this pericope is read as the gospel for the mass of the day. To this extent we can unreservedly fall in with the preachers whom we have quoted. But the parting of the ways comes in their interpretation of the eucharist. The story of the miraculous feeding testifies that with Jesus the time of salvation and the kingdom of God has been ushered in. He gathers men together to form the new people of God and unites them by partaking of a meal with them. This sharing of a meal is an expression of the fact that the closest possible contact with God has been achieved. It is far from being simply a question of people being fed and satisfied. What is in question here is the proximity of God revealed in the meal. It is the gift of God in person which Jesus bestows in the symbolism of the bread. The story of the miraculous feeding is too strongly focused upon Christ to allow us to separate the meal from the giver. The bread is transparent; in and through and beyond it we see Christ. What he gives with the bread is something quite unique—nothing else than himself in person, as John above all insists ('I am the bread of life' 6:35). The bread can only be 'eaten' in faith.

This story, then, is to be interpreted against the background of a wider understanding of the eucharist of which this is only the starting-point. In comparison with this the quotations from sermons which we have given display notable limitations of vision. They proceed not from the dynamic ideas of the bible but from conceptions which are static (ontological). They take the loaves and fishes in isolation and in themselves as a supernatural 'food', a 'reserve supply of bread' and a 'precaution', as so much 'provisions' which are laid up in the 'larder'. If the communion of the faithful is taken as a distribution of the 'fragments left over' 'which have fallen from the table of holy mass' (in other words as a kind of 'by-product'), then this is tantamount to saying that the mass is essentially and in the last analysis the business of the priest. All others obtain from it only that precisely which is a by-product of it.

On this understanding of the eucharist the constant exhortation to frequent reception of communion (as the victory that comes at the end of the 'hunger-cure') induces an attitude of sacramentalism in the hearers. In the same way the exaggerated and inadmissible concentration on the words of consecration ('then something is suddenly present...') borders on the magical. In their undue narrowness these ideas go hand in hand with the false understanding of miracles set forth above. In both cases the personal dimension is suppressed in favour of material categories of thought.

The sermon literature enables us to recognise how tenacious of life certain one-sided ideas of the eucharist are, ideas which lead to an exaggerated sacramentalism. They linger on in spite of recent developments in theology, in spite of the liturgical movement and the liturgical constitution of the second Vatican

Council, and still continue to have their damaging effect upon preaching right up to the present moment. In listening to the message of the story of the miraculous feeding they can be set aside.

The connection between the story of the miraculous feeding and harvest time

Many authors of written sermons attempt—especially in sermons for the sixth Sunday after Pentecost—to 'actualise' the story of the miraculous feeding by drawing a parallel between it and harvest time.

'Certainly it is not without a wise purpose of her own that the church causes the story of the second miraculous multiplication of loaves to be read before harvest time.' 'Those who consider the matter more deeply will recognise that God has been performing a similar miracle year after year right from the dawn of humanity down to the present day, and that he will continue to perform it to the end of time.' 'Now, when you walk through the fields, it is just as though Christ were invisibly stretching out his hands over them in blessing. And beneath his kind hands the seed begins to germinate and to grow, and from a single seed a whole ear develops with fifty, sixty or seventy seeds. Thus in a miraculous way God multiplies the bread in the soil.' 'It is not in a single moment but in three or four months that the miracle so familiar to us comes to completion.' 'The arm of the Lord is not shortened. His earth is still fruitful. The power of the seed to germinate still persists. Normally speaking he still continues to give rain and sunshine in their due season.' 'Ah so many are so terribly remote from the fragrant cornfields! . . . Today let us follow Jesus through the midst of the cornfields . . . Let us contemplate the works of our heavenly Father who provides us with bread.'

The interpretation set forth above can in fact claim the support of Augustine in some degree (*Tract in Johann* xxiv). Nevertheless it does represent a departure from the gospel text. The episode spoken of in the text is one which precisely does not take place everywhere 'year after year' so that a whole series of such events can be seen extending from the 'dawn of humanity... to the end of time'. It is intended to bear witness to the fact that with Jesus a new age has been ushered in and a new state of affairs has been created, one which has not been in being all along, one to which the world cannot give rise of its own resources. The sermons quoted confine their attention once more to the bread and its 'multiplication', taking this in isolation. And they seek to point to a similar phenomenon in the present as an analogy to this, whereas the story of the miraculous feeding is intended to draw our attention to Jesus. It proclaims that in him alone God has drawn near to men once and for all, so near that he shares a meal with them.

Saying grace and adopting an attitude of reverence before meals
Many authors of written sermons draw from the story of the miraculous feeding the moral that we should regard our food as a gift of God and say grace before meals.

(i) 'But notice how the Lord said "Gather the fragments that remain over into baskets"...! Jesus had such reverence for food as God's gift. And we?' 'Do we have an attitude of true reverence, regarding our meals as a gift of God? It ill becomes any of us to omit saying an earnest prayer over our daily bread.' 'If you fail to recollect yourselves before meals then you are treating God himself disrespectfully.' 'We eat to the honour of God, but not too much! The danger of over-eating is perhaps the greatest.' 'Have an attitude of reverence at mealtimes, for the food you eat is a gift from heaven. Keep an attitude of respect over your meals, the reward of labour. Pay due heed to your bread, the staff of your life.'

The following quotation may be taken as characteristic of the approach adopted in this line of interpretation: 'Listen to the talk all about you. What is the chief topic of conversation? The weather and "dear" money. Today Jesus himself is preoccupied with bread and the buying of it. Philip presents an accurate balance-sheet. Therefore we shall take as the subject of our sermon "dear" money.'

(ii) On the subject of grace at meals we are told: 'Bread (Brot) rhymes with God (Gott)! Bread comes from God; there is a connection between bread and God! . . . God wills to be the Father who gives us our daily bread. Therefore we must call upon him when we stand at our tables.' Through the miracle of the loaves Jesus has 'set us all an example of the importance of saying grace'. It is 'a custom deeply implanted in the religious practice of human cultures everywhere and at all times. When modern man dispenses with grace before and after meals he is being false to the religious instincts of humanity as such! . . . Are we willing, therefore, to incur the same responsibility, to share in the guilt of this betrayal which is characteristic of modern atheism, the guilt of this barren secularisation and desecration of life? Do we really want to be "worse than the pagans"? One thing alone will save us from this, a loyal adherence to the practice of saying grace!'

The importance of maintaining a right attitude towards food and of the saying of grace should not be called in question. As occasion offers the preacher can remind his hearers of this anew; but in doing so he must guard against statements that are too extravagant to be taken seriously.

In the present context, however, it must be emphasised that the story of the miraculous feeding provides no basis for exhortations of this kind. The gathering up of the fragments left over is not a sign of the importance of a right and reverent attitude towards our daily bread. Rather it is intended to indicate the abundance of the food which has been distributed and serves to point to the significance of the feeding as an eschatological banquet. The thanksgiving pronounced by Jesus is to be taken not as an example of the importance of saying grace, but as pointing us on to the last supper.

These quotations enable us to realise the lengths to which

preachers often go in following their own caprice in their interpretations. They fasten arbitrarily on certain individual key words which they take out of context, forcing them to fit into a preconceived pattern constructed according to their own personal views ('dear money', '*Brot* rhymes with *Gott*'), and in doing this they do violence to the meaning of the scriptures.

(b) SUGGESTIONS FOR PREACHING ON THE STORY OF THE MIRACULOUS FEEDING

Our exegetical examination has shown that the various traditions of the story of the miraculous feeding differ one from another in the underlying kerygmatic message which each seeks to convey. This applies not merely to the Johannine tradition as compared with that of the synoptics. Within the synoptics themselves also differences can be discerned in their mode of presentation. In fact not only do the individual evangelists differ from each other, but also the different tradition strata within one and the same gospel show similar variations of expression. In preaching on the gospel the preacher has to take each single one of these variations into account. None of them must be ignored or glossed over. His task is not to speak in quite general terms about the 'multiplication of loaves' (as in the sermon literature summarised above) but to expound one particular account of the miraculous feeding as set forth in the concrete in one particular gospel. The *differentia specifica* therefore which the preacher has to take into account arise not initially, and not primarily from the particular place assigned to that gospel passage in the church's year (though we do not deny that this too may be allowed to play its part in the total message of the sermon), but from the part and function which the given passage has in the specific gospel to which it belongs.

(i) *John 6: 1–15*

As it stand this pericope is a torso. If it is taken in isolation this story of the miraculous feeding will lead to misunderstandings (and this is precisely the opinion of the evangelist also: it leads to the idea that Jesus is the king who gives bread to his people). The key to the meaning of this story is supplied by the discourse on revelation which follows it. This constitutes the apostolic preaching, which interprets the miracle story, and every sermon should derive its orientation from this. The key points in this discourse, therefore, should be read in conjunction with the prescribed pericope, or at any rate they should be included as an integral part of the church's message. The story of the miraculous feeding itself demands this treatment. In the mind of the evangelist it is to be taken only as a prelude to the actual preaching.

Jesus as the bestower of the bread
Hunger leads to death. Bread signifies life. When he gives bread to men Jesus is revealing himself as source of life. He knows what their needs are even before they themselves have adverted to it. He himself as host gives these gifts to his guests. They do not have any resources of their own from which to supply this bread. They cannot cater for their needs by their own resources —even the disciples do not know whence they can obtain bread (Jn 6:5-9). It is Jesus who distributes it (just as he alone is the source of living water cf Jn 4:7, 37f). It is he who takes the initiative. The people merely receive the bread from his hands.

The basic misconception
Those who have been fed and satisfied discern the gift indeed but not the giver. They want some *thing* and fail to realise that it is *he* who stands before them. He is of interest to them only to the extent that he has 'something to offer them', to the extent that he satisfies their hunger (6:26). They want to receive him as a kind of means of nourishment for the furtherance of what they themselves expect of life. They take the bread which he gives them 'as though it were bread from the baker'.

This misconception is as alive today as it was then. How often is the christian faith understood and presented as a 'something', as an instrument which serves our own purposes and ideas, as an object for consumption for the enrichment of our 'interior lives', for the satisfaction of our 'religious feelings'. The sermon should lay bare this misconception for what it is.

'I am the bread of life' (6:35)

Jesus does not bestow something; he bestows himself. Through and beyond the bread we see himself. The gift points us on to the giver. In the last analysis men can not live by any kind of nourishment, but only by him: 'I am the bread of life'. In the gift of the bread he gives them his own self. In his own person he is God's answer to the elemental question which their very existence raises. God has made his (Jesus') 'I' the cornerstone of life itself. In him he is present for and to men, and that too—despite all that the docetists may allege—present to them in their full human nature: in the flesh. 'The bread . . . is my flesh for the life of the world' (6:51).

For Jesus to become the bread of life means something more than a mere going beyond the ordinary processes of nature (this expectation is explicitly rejected, cf 6:14f). Rather it means that he delivers himself up to death as the true paschal lamb (cf 6:4, 51). His gift is consummated in the delivering up of his own self. The cross and resurrection are the means through which he bestows life upon the world. By falling into the earth and dying the grain of wheat bears much fruit (12:24).

The eucharist

Jesus' gift of himself as bread of life acquires concrete form in the eucharist. The process by which his self-bestowal is achieved is not confined merely to the realm of ideas: 'He who eats my flesh and drinks my blood has eternal life' (6:54). This assertion is rightly to be understood only against the background of what has gone before; the preacher, therefore, must not be entrapped in a 'eucharistic fixation', and fasten upon the eucharistic part of the discourse on the bread of life without taking the part that has led up to it into account. It is not 'something' that the people are offered to eat; 'he' offers his own self. The sharing is achieved in the dimension of the personal. But it signifies that we make contact with him who has come to us in the flesh, and therefore needs to be expressed in the visible form of sacramental eating. Certainly the eating of the flesh is only meaningful in terms of a spiritual eating—in faith. But it is an eating of the flesh nonetheless.

This approach does away with a twofold misunderstanding of the significance of the eucharist: against the docetists it is emphasised that God's word has become flesh and that faith in Jesus achieves its ultimate concretisation in an act of physical eating, in partaking of the sacramental meal. Against the tendency of others to interpret the eucharist as a sort of magical materialisation (the misconception of a sacramentalism that fails to look beyond itself) it is particularly insisted that this sacramental eating can only take place in the context of the personal and spiritual communication of faith.

(ii) Mk 8:1–9
Two main lines of approach are open to us in our homiletic adaptation of this pericope. The preacher may concentrate upon the actual feeding and interpret it as an eschatological sign: Jesus liberates men from the power of hunger. In him, in his action, the new aeon is ushered in. Admittedly the preacher must not forget to point out the implications arising from this for the people he is addressing: the Lord whom they are committed to follow is one whose activity is not confined merely to taking to himself those souls who find the world too much for them and seek refuge from it. Rather he is a Lord who wills to impose his dominion in the everyday life of the world, one who 'in the bread that he breaks gives nothing less than his own self'.

But there is another course open to the preacher. He can

allow himself to be guided by elements in the text itself which connect this episode with the last supper. In the primitive christian community the story of the miraculous feeding was laid under contribution in a catechesis concerning the significance of the last supper. The fact that even apart from this the story is in fact read in the context of a eucharistic celebration makes it natural for us to lay special emphasis on this element in it, and to draw out the implications which are to be found in the text itself for our understanding of the eucharist. We shall opt for this second line of approach.

Jesus shares a meal with mankind
Jesus proclaims the inauguration of the kingdom of God. That which he announces he himself accomplishes in his own life. His message achieves concretisation in the meal that he shares with others, which ever since has been a symbol of the closest possible union with God, and a figure of the joy of the messianic age. Jesus sits down to table with mankind, not only with his disciples and other edifying people, but with publicans and sinners as well, with those who are looked down upon in a religious and social sense: 'He eats with the publicans and sinners' (Mk 2:16). He breaks down the barriers of pharisaic exclusivism and communicates with all who have need of him. He does not merely tell us that God is near to all men and that he invites them into his kingdom and to his table. He makes it real. In doing this he anticipates the sharing of the eschatological banquet in the kingdom of God. No-one's need will go unanswered. The story of the miraculous feeding belongs to the context of this event. It bears witness to the fact that the time of salvation has been ushered in. In Jesus God has drawn near to men and shares a meal with them. It is not merely a few exceptional individuals who are invited to his table but all the people without exception. The compassion he feels for the hungry takes the form of giving them the bread they need for every day (not merely 'spiritual' bread). 'We see, therefore,

that he wills to preach the word of the kingdom of God and yet at the same time not to overlook the needs of everyday life. The kingdom of God—yes! But here it becomes apparent how this is to be understood: in condescending to their needs, serving them, giving himself to them, in the breaking of bread, in the cross' (Keuck, DW 2, 94).

The connection with the eucharist
There is a direct connection between the miraculous feeding and the last supper. Here Jesus gathers his disciples—his people—in order to feed them once more in view of his approaching death. He looks back over the earlier meals which he has shared with them (cf 14:25). Now they are at an end and are to be replaced by a new one. Through and beyond the cross and resurrection Jesus creates the possibility of a new kind of sharing, a new communion in eating and drinking.

From the story of the miraculous feeding important conclusions are to be drawn for our understanding of the eucharist. To celebrate the eucharist does not mean that the individual receives a sacrament, but rather that Christ gathers the people of God and shares a meal with them, and that he renews their covenant with God. For this reason it should not be the objective process by which this is achieved (transsubstantiation) which constitutes the dominant feature in our understanding of the eucharist, but rather the sharing of the meal as a personal event which is intended to be maintained in the daily practice of the breaking of bread. This kind of sharing is not self-sufficient but leads, of its very nature, to something beyond itself. It leads us in a spirit of thanksgiving (*eucharistesas* 8:6; cf 6:41 par) through Christ to the Father.

Two aspects, therefore, are to be distinguished in the celebration of the eucharist: communication with the people of God and thanksgiving (the horizontal and vertical dimensions). It is because men achieve union with one another in Christ that their glorification of the Father is achieved through him.

'And he sent them away' (8:9)
The sharing of the meal is a transient and provisional event. It takes place on the way, achieves reality in a constant state of departure. Its final and definitive form has still to be achieved. It is something that we wait for. The celebration of the eucharist is not simply a further projection of the meal with the historical Jesus in the past. It is at the same time a sign and a foretaste of the eschatological banquet which is to come (cf 14:25). In the meal of which we partake in the present the memory of that which has already been bestowed in the past (*anamnesis, memoria*) is combined with an orientation towards that which is to come.

6
THE INFANCY NARRATIVES: EXEGETICAL INVESTIGATION

I Introduction

1 The infancy narratives in the context of the apostolic preaching
Matthew and Luke differ from Mark and John in that their accounts of Jesus' public ministry are preceded by stories of his birth and childhood which serve as prologues or introductions to their respective gospels. These infancy narratives belong to a later stage in the gospel tradition (cf Dibelius [4]1961, 119–28). Insofar as we can draw any conclusions from the writings of the new testament it seems clear that the earliest christian preaching did not concern itself with the beginnings of Jesus' life, but concentrated rather upon the cross and resurrection of the Lord. It was not until faith in Jesus as the Christ and the Son of God grew firmer in the light of the Easter events that the content of the preaching was expanded so as to include an account of his earthly life prior to the crucifixion. In this process interest was focused initially and primarily—so much can be gathered from the tradition strata of the gospels—upon the works of his public ministry. The disciples were in a position to draw upon their own personal experience to bear witness to what took place 'during all the time that the Lord Jesus went in and out among us, beginning from the baptism of John until the day when he was taken up from us . . .' (Ac 1:21ff). With regard to the beginnings of his life, on the contrary, they had no personal experience and, so far as can be gathered from the gospels themselves, Jesus did not adduce the miraculous events of his birth and childhood in order to authenticate his mission.

It is not until a later stage in the development of the apostolic preaching that we find references to the origin, birth and childhood of Jesus. These are not prompted by interests of a biographical kind. 'It was no part of the evangelists' intention to collect private reminiscences from the circles which had personal acquaintance with Jesus. Their aim, rather, was to proclaim the saving deed of God as made manifest in Christ' (Schierse, BiLe I 219). They testify that Jesus was what he subsequently proved himself to be right from the very outset. From the standpoint of the Easter event they point back to the origins of his life. That underlying significance which they had already come to realise in their crucified and risen Lord they finally recognise as applying to the circumstances of his conception and birth as well. From the first moment of his life onwards he is the messiah who brings salvation and redemption. In him God is at work.

2 The literary form of the infancy narratives
In order to arrive at an objectively accurate interpretation of passages in the bible it is necessary to determine as precisely as possible their exact literary form. This applies in a special degree to the infancy narratives. They occupy a quite special place in the gospel tradition, not merely in respect of the particular details of the narrative, but in the overall manner of their presentation as well.

Up to the present scholars have disagreed sharply in the various answers which they have proposed to the question of the literary *genre* of these narratives. Conservative exegesis has shown itself anxiously preoccupied to defend the value of the infancy narratives as historical records, and has not infrequently claimed them as records of historical fact and as such a basis for faith. Against this the historical researches of the higher criticism have characterised them as 'edifying legends', to a large extent denied that they have any historical value, and interpreted them as records of the development of early christian devotion. The dilemma is well known. So long as these passages are investigated and evaluated primarily or even exclusively in terms of their historicity no objectively accurate interpretation of them is possible. They cannot be forced into the confines of our modern understanding of history. Those who view them from the point of view of history writing and take them as reliable records in this sense will find themselves inextricably entangled in contradictions and irreconcilabilities between the various statements they contain. On the other hand even though the designation 'legend' does not necessarily exclude information of a genuinely historical nature, still this concept too fails to express the distinctive character of the narratives in question.

In recent times a fresh approach to the interpretation of the infancy narratives has been devised, one which bypasses the stalemate represented by the alternative 'either historical record or edifying legend', and which makes it possible to arrive at an estimate which really does justice to the literary form of these narratives. In this approach it is recognised from the outset that motifs drawn from the history of the patriarchs of Israel have left a deep impress upon these narratives (cf Laurentin, *passim*), and influenced the manner of their presentation in a striking degree. Not only are there constant references back to the old testament in the form of explicit citations, but also use is made of a special literary form evolved in Jewish tradition. These stories approximate to the rabbinical forms of tradition known as *midrash* and *haggadah*. Over and above this the *genres* of typology, prophecy and apocalyptic have had an influence upon the formation of particular parts of the narratives. These various elements enable us to recognise in general that the infancy narratives are primarily kerygmatic in their orientation.

3 The relationship between the infancy narratives

A comparison of the Lucan infancy narrative with that of Matthew reveals notable points of divergence between them (cf Schmid [4]1960, 88–90). It is true that in the theologically significant statements of the virgin birth and the Davidic descent of Jesus they corroborate one another. But even here the two lines of tradition are independent. This applies even to the tradition of the birth of Jesus. For though Matthew presupposes this (2:1), he does not actually describe it. There are very marked differences in the final outcome of the events as presented by each evangelist (cf eg Lk 2:39 with the sequence of events presupposed in Mt 2). It seems that neither evangelist knew of the other's presentation and, moreover, that with few exceptions the data available to one were unknown to the other. In their narratives we encounter special traditions which manifestly do not belong to the stock of traditions underlying the synoptic gospels and do not go back to a common source. Matthew and Luke have, each in his own way, made them serve the special interests of their respective gospels. The realisation of this should warn us against attempting to harmonise the two accounts. Each of the narratives goes its own way, and they do not admit of the sort of comparisons which are appropriate elsewhere in synoptic studies. The infancy narrative of one evangelist cannot be explained by reference to the vision of the other. Each is conceived independently of the other. Each must be interpreted in its own right and, moreover, in the context of the gospel to which it belongs.

II Interpretation of selected narratives

1 The Lucan infancy narrative

(a) SPECIAL FEATURES AND CONNECTING LINES IN THE LUCAN INFANCY NARRATIVE

When compared with Matthew's infancy narrative that of Luke is seen to be the more comprehensive. It is cast in a consciously contrived pattern and rounded off with a formal conclusion. At first sight the individual sections of narrative seem to have been carefully constructed so that one leads on to the other, and the whole appears to represent the unified work of a single author. On closer examination, however, the unevenness of the narrative at a number of points is unmistakable. In the first chapter the infancy story of the Baptist (which we shall not consider in detail here) originally conceived of as a unity, has clearly been interrupted by the prophetic announcement of the birth of Jesus (1:26–38) and the attached story of Mary's visit to Elizabeth (1:39–56). The narrative 'joins' appear at the beginning (1:26) and especially at the end of the insertion: vv 56, 57 of ch 1 are juxtaposed without any connection between them, while in vv 57–80 the story of the Baptist is continued without taking any cognisance of the narrative elements immediately preceding it in vv 26–56. On the other hand, however, certain connecting links with the story of the Baptist do seem to have been inserted into these narrative sections, namely the time reference (added by Luke himself) in 1:26, the reference to Elizabeth in 1:36, and especially the meeting beween the two mothers-to-be in 1:39–56.

With regard to the second chapter there is no direct connection between this and either the infancy narrative of John or the annunciation narrative. It is simply juxtaposed to the first chapter without any intrinsic connection, and carries its own independent interpretation without reference to it. Although Joseph and Mary have already been presented to us in 1:26f, they are introduced in 2:4 as though for the first time. The narrative elements in Lk1–2 derive from different sources, and have only been blended together in the course of a long traditio-historical development. The story of the Baptist constitutes an independent unity in its own right. It has been developed earlier than, and independently of, the infancy narrative of Jesus. The thought here is Palestinian Jewish, and it has been worked out in dependence upon motifs drawn from the old testament. The Semitic language (whether Hebrew or Aramaic is difficult to decide, cf Laurentin, 12f) in which it was originally composed has subsequently (though still before the composition of the third gospel, as the uneven style indicates) been translated into Greek. We may conclude that it derives from Jewish christian circles.

Several different and independent narrative elements have been combined to form the infancy narrative of Jesus. A factor which is common to them all, however, is the fact that their thought is coloured by Jewish ideas and rooted in the conceptual world of the old testament. In their original form they are of Jewish christian origin, and as they now stand they plainly evince Hellenistic influences. But it is plainly false to say that their standpoint is exclusively either pre-christian or Hellenistic, as has often been maintained.

However complex the development of tradition in the first two chapters of Luke's gospel may appear to us, and however many different levels of tradition it may seem to contain, it is unmistakable that the various traditions have been co-ordinated according to a single predetermined principle. The narrative elements of the annunciation, birth, circumcision and naming of the Baptist are followed by corresponding narrative elements in the story of Jesus, and that too in such a way that each element in the first story is paralleled by a corresponding, though more important, element in the second. Thus the story of Jesus is made to stand out as supremely significant, and overshadows that of the Baptist. All that John is Jesus is too, but at the same time he is also incomparably more. 'Plainly, therefore, it is only on account of Jesus that the story of John has been included here' (Schürmann, BiKi 21, 107). From this it may be concluded that certain kerygmatic viewpoints have exercised a decisive influence upon the Lucan infancy narratives even in their very structure. The redactor consciously seeks to bring out the relationship between the Baptist and Jesus. They are ordered one to another and cannot be played off against each other as though they were rivals. Pride of place belongs to Jesus and not, as the Baptist sectarians pretend, to John.

Although in his infancy narratives Luke is more dependent

upon a pre-existing stock of tradition than he is in the rest of his gospel, still he has imposed his own characteristic stamp even upon this. These narratives are not foreign bodies in the gospel as a whole, but fit into it and impose their own stamp upon it. They are to be viewed in the total context of the Lucan writings, and cannot just be set aside, as for instance Conzelmann does (for criticism see Oliver, 202–26).

(b) THE ANNUNCIATION OF THE BIRTH OF JESUS (LK 1:26–38)

(i) Structure of the narrative
We have seen that the characteristic principle of the Lucan infancy narrative is that of 'heightened parallelism'. This appears particularly clearly in the annunciation stories. For this reason a fuller exposition of this principle must be given at this point, precisely in its significance for our interpretation.

The pattern of the annunciation stories
Annunciation stories in the broader sense, that is not restricted solely to promises of future births, are already known to us from the old testament (cf eg Gen 17:15–22; Jg 6:11–24). This particular type of tradition has developed a fixed literary form of its own which is also to be met with in the new testament and above all here, in the Lucan writings. It is this form which underlies the story of the annunciation of John's birth, and also the parallel story of the annunciation of Jesus' birth which corresponds to it in form. In both cases the scene displays the same structure: the angel appears (1:11, cf 1:26–28); the human party is disquieted (1:12, cf 1:29); the angel soothes them (1:13, cf 1:30), promises that the child will be born, tells them what name it is to bear (1:13ff, cf 1:31), and indicates the part it is destined to play in salvation history (1:15–17, cf 1:32ff). The human party then asks how the promise will be brought to reality (1:18, cf 1:34) and obtains a sign (1:20, cf 1:38).

INFANCY NARRATIVES: EXEGETICAL INVESTIGATION

The common structure which unites both stories gives the author the opportunity to bring out the significance of Jesus all the more impressively in that each of these elements in the story of Jesus surpasses in importance the parallel elements in the story of John.

Heightened parallelism
In announcing the birth of John the angel Gabriel addresses himself to his father, Zechariah. In announcing that of Jesus he addresses himself to Mary. Zechariah and Elizabeth are just before God and blameless in their observance of the commandments (1:6). They are situated still wholly within the framework of the Mosaic law. The place in which the birth of their son is announced is the temple. Mary is she who has been favoured with grace (1:28). She is just before God, not in virtue of her position or her actions, and Jesus is not bestowed upon her in answer to her prayer (cf 1:13). All the initiative comes from God. He calls this unknown young woman from the quite unimportant village of Nazareth. 'Here appears an example of God's election which breaks through all that Jewish minds and imaginations could conceive of as possible' (Grundmann ²1964, 55).

A new age begins. John 'will be great before the Lord' (1:15). Jesus is great absolutely and without restriction (1:32). John is a prophet of the Most High (1:76). Jesus is the Son of the Most High (1:32). John is filled with the Holy Spirit from his mother's womb (1:15). Jesus is conceived by the power of the Holy Spirit (1:35). In the story of John the effect of God's action is simply to remove the barrenness of Elizabeth. In the story of Jesus his creative power takes over the part played by the husband in human generation. With this reference to the conception of Jesus performed by the power of the Spirit—the central point of the narrative (cf Dibelius 1953, 16)—the statements in the second part, heightened by comparison with the corresponding statements of the first, achieve their climax.

Jesus has his origin directly and immediately in God. Faith alone can accept this mystery. There is a significant contrast between the assent uttered by Mary to God's action upon her on the one hand, and the dumbness of Zechariah on the other.

(ii) The elements in the annunciation story of Luke 1:26–38 against the background of the old testament

Certain motifs which are of central importance in the old testament have had a decisive influence upon this story, so that it can only rightly be understood against this background. This applies to the very first word of the angel's message: *chaire* is not in any sense a mere conventional formula of greeting but a summons to rejoice—this is the word with which the prophets introduce the joyful tidings to Israel that Yahweh is taking up his world dominion in her midst (Zeph 3:14; Zech 9:9; Joel 2:21, 23). Now Mary becomes the recipient of this messianic cry of joy. She is addressed not as a private individual, but as the representative of God's people, as the antitype of the 'daughter of Zion' (Zeph 3:14). In her Israel experiences the saving presence of God.

'The Lord is with you' (1:28). These are the terms in which the angel addresses her. His message sets Mary in the line of those great figures of the old covenant whom God called to lead and to deliver his people: Isaac (Gen 26:3), Jacob (Gen 28:15), Moses (Ex 3:12), Joshua (Jos 1:5), Gideon (Jg 6:12, 16) and above all David (1 Sam 12; 2 Sam 5:10; 7:3, 9). All of them have received the same form of address. Most of all it belongs to the context of Yahweh's covenant with David the king (2 Sam 7; 23:5). Israel's messianic expectations have been sustained by the promise of this everlasting covenant. In the message addressed to Mary it reaches its goal. The messiah, the anointed one of God, is the fulfilment of the promise.

Lk 1:31 serves to underline this connection. This verse plainly echoes the Septuagint version of Is 7:14, and 'actualises' the promise of Emmanuel, one of the central passages in the covenant tradition of the old testament. In the words spoken to Mary by the angel 'God with us' becomes a present fact.

Already even in this annunciation of Jesus his significance is revealed. The title 'Son of the Most High' (1:32) designates him as messiah (cf Dibelius 1953, 15). And when it is said that he is to sit upon the throne of David as king forever over the house of Jacob (1:32ff) this serves to emphasise this dignity of his. In him Nathan's oracle to David (2 Sam 7:12-16) finds its fulfilment. Jesus is the enduring upholder of the eternal dominion promised in that oracle (cf Is 9:6). It is a dominion that is no longer confined merely to the old Israel. Now it includes the new people of God, the church (Conzelmann, ET 145-49).

The angel's prophecy reveals the fact that Jesus is the messiah right from the outset. The miraculous manner of his conception is in accordance with this dignity which belongs to him. The question which Mary puts (1:34) has the effect of making this the focal point of interest. This question must neither be understood as an indication that Mary has taken a vow of virginity nor interpreted in a psychological sense as an expression of bewilderment and surprise. As the evangelist uses it it has a stylistic function, drawing the reader's attention to a point of central importance and serving 'as a pointer to a fuller understanding of the angel's message'. It is no part of Luke's intention to describe Mary's interior feelings. He wishes, rather, to focus our gaze upon the central point of the story.

1:35 contains the climactic statement of the messiahship of Jesus. The Holy Spirit will come upon Mary. This is the 'spirit of the Lord', the directing force of God at the creation (Gen 1:2) and in the history of his people. Israel's leaders were possessed by this spirit: Moses (Num 11:25); Gideon (Jg 6:34), Samson (Jg 13:25), Saul (1 Sam 10:6f) and David (1 Sam 16:13f). It supports the kings and achieves its effects supremely in the messianic age (Ezek 36:25-27; Joel 3:1-5) and in the person of the messiah (Is 11:2). This divine *dynamis* (power) comes upon Mary and overshadows her. The term 'overshadow' is a reference to Ex 40:35. As the cloud overshadowed the tent of meeting, a visible sign of the presence of God, so the power of God overshadows Mary. 'Power of the Most High' is, for Luke, identical with 'Holy Spirit' (cf Sahlin, 123, Grundmann 1964, 58, Oliver, 224f). The Spirit is central to Luke's theology. It constitutes the life-giving initiative through which the angel's message is brought to its fulfilment. Jesus is not merely in some sense chosen and called by the Spirit of God, he is actually conceived by its power. He is unlike the leaders and prophets of Israel in that in his case the Spirit is not sent down upon him *ab externo* as a gift. It is present in his very origins. So deeply and integrally does it belong to the very essence of his life that it actually provides the basis for his existence. It is through him that the Spirit penetrates into the world and inaugurates the messianic age of salvation. The same Spirit which is present at the outset of the creation (Gen 1:2) brings about this new beginning, this new creation also. It is possible that the background to Lk 1:35 is to be found in Gen 1:2 (TWNT V, 834). Here God initiates a new act of creation. Jesus is the new creation of God in the eschatological age. The 'Adam/Christ' typology in Lk 3:23–38 shows that this idea is not wholly foreign to the evangelists's mind.

Jesus the messiah has his origin in the creative power of God. There is a manifest difference between this story and the Hellenistic stories of the birth of divine sons in that here the Spirit is not united to Mary in any sense in a kind of divine marriage. The action of the Spirit is not meant to be understood as taking effect at the biological level upon the body of Mary, as though a physical seed were implanted in her with the result that Jesus was in some sense half divine and half human. 'The fact of the conception by the divine power is the primary and essential point. The actual manner in which this is achieved remains a mystery, and as a mystery it is intended to endure' (M. Dibelius 1953, 20). How questionable it is to treat the material on the biological plane is illustrated in the apocryphal Protevangel of James: 'Salome said: "As the Lord my God lives, if I do not put (forward) my finger and test her condition I will not believe that a virgin has brought forth". And the midwife went in and said to Mary, "Make yourself ready, for there is no small contention concerning you". And Salome put (forward) her finger' (Hennecke, 385). A distinguishing feature of the apocrypha both early and late is that they have an exact knowledge of, and purport to describe everything that took place, and wholly to resolve the mystery.

Luke's statements are intended to be understood in a kerygmatic, and not in a physiological sense. The reality to which they refer is not the union of the Spirit with Mary. In fact they are not concerned with Mary at all in any primary or essential sense, but with Jesus and with the proclamation of his messiahship. Jesus depends upon the Spirit of God for his very existence. So radically is this the case that right from the first moment (even while he is still in the womb of the Virgin Mary) it is the Spirit which upholds him in being. He is 'God with us' in a sense so absolute as to exclude any intermediate cause of his coming into being. What is being asserted in the symbolic language of this passage is that the physical level of his being too is the outcome of a direct and immediate act of creation on God's part. The virgin birth is being made to serve as a signpost in saving history that points us on to the true message and meaning of Christ.

Summoned into existence by the Holy Spirit, Jesus is holy and called 'Son of God' (35b). As used here this title is intended not so much as a static definition of the nature of the messiah but rather as a dynamic statement of his function. Jesus lays open the way to salvation. That which he is solemnly proclaimed to be at his baptism (3:22), that he is right from the first moment of his existence—the Son of God.

To the event which befalls her (1:38) in the angel's words, and which causes her to become the mother of the messiah,

Mary utters her assent. Her response is faith, and therefore she will be called blessed (1:45). 'It is Mary, therefore, who stands here in the "centre of time". Certainly she stands there because she is the mother of Jesus. But according to v 45 she also stands there because she has believed, and by her belief the purely external pattern of the centre of time has been broken through' (Dinkler, 219). In the claim that is made upon her and in the response that she makes to this claim she is the representative of the people of God. 'What is said by her and to her applies to the entire church, and to each individual who is summoned by God in faith' (Schierse, 220).

It is because old testament traditions are made actual in it that the annunciation narrative is made to convey statements which are significant in a kerygmatic sense. These statements are primarily christological in their orientation, and an expression of the specifically Lucan christology. The saving history of Jesus the messiah begins with his conception in the womb of the Virgin Mary. Right from the very origins his life has a messianic quality. In him the promises of Yahweh's covenant and the promises made to the house of David come to their fulfilment. He is 'God with us' in so absolute and exclusive a sense that right from the outset his existence is due to the Holy Spirit. As their representative Mary commits herself on behalf of the people of God to the event of salvation.

(c) THE BIRTH OF JESUS (LK 2:1–20)

The account of Jesus' birth (Lk 2:1–20) initiates a fresh stage in the Lucan infancy narrative. It originally belonged to an independent tradition, and has no direct connection with what has gone before. Joseph and Mary are introduced anew, and we are told where they live and also the place with which they are associated as a matter of tribal origin (2:4ff). This information is given 'as though nothing had been said about them up to this point' (Dibelius 1953, 9). Nevertheless the redactor has made this account fit in with his overall conception: in his scheme of heightened parallelism it follows upon the story of the Baptist to which it corresponds. The fact that the birth of Jesus has a deeper significance appears above all in the fact that it is proclaimed by angels. Furthermore, whereas the birth of the Baptist is aimed merely at playing a part in the history of Judah (1:5), the birth of Jesus affects the whole inhabited world, the cosmos. The name of Augustus (2:1) carries us far beyond the limited horizon of Palestine, and serves to indicate what Luke seeks to express in this detailed introduction which he supplies: what he is primarily concerned with here is neither the exact date at which these events took place, nor a more detailed description of contemporary events (Augustus, Quirinius, the census). His intention is, rather, to assign the birth of Jesus to its place in world history (contrast Mt 2:1, and the way in which Luke traces back the ancestry of Jesus to Adam, 3:38, not merely Abraham, Mt 1:1). Here, at the beginning of Jesus' mission to the world, our gaze is already directed to Rome, the capital of the world, towards which the mission of the church is subsequently to be orientated (Ac 28:15–31).

Bethlehem, place of the promise
The angel's message was: 'The Lord God will give to him the throne of David his father' (1:32). Thus the way followed by Joseph and Mary leads from Nazareth to the 'city of David which is called Bethlehem' (2:4), and it is explicitly insisted upon that it was 'while they were there' that Mary gave birth to Jesus (2:6). This event brings ancient promises to their fulfilment (cf Mic 5:1) and that too in circumstances almost wholly conditioned by secular events. The episode of the census belongs to secular history, yet it is used to ensure that saving history achieves its goal. Jesus' messiahship is indicated not only by the fact that Bethlehem was the scene of his birth. The circumstances in which he comes into the world likewise serve as pointers to it. Shepherds are nearby (2:8), the class from the ranks of which David his ancestor was once called (cf 1 Sam

16:1–13). Certain promises are associated with a 'tower of the flock': 'And you, O tower of the flock, hill of the daughter of Zion, to you it shall come and return, the former dominion, the kingdom of the daughter of Jerusalem' (Mic 4:8; cf Gen 35: 21). Later Jewish tradition connected this promise with the 'tower of the flock' of Bethlehem, and expected the birth of the messiah to take place there (cf Targ Ps-Jon on Gen 35:21). Now this expectation is fulfilled.

The child in the manger

The birth itself is recorded in concise and factual terms (Lk 2:6ff) without any kind of mythical elaborations, almost laconically indeed, as though it were an everyday affair that was being related. No angel guards the manger, no supernatural voice utters its message. Mary wraps up her first-born child just as every mother does. 'This, therefore, is a real child, not a prodigy' (Grundmann ²1964, 80). Jesus is human in a fully physical sense. In the whole episode the one striking point is this: the new-born child is laid in a manger. This extraordinary procedure, the reason for which is the lack of room in the inn, is intended to serve as a sign to the shepherds. It is a special kind of sign. He has already been proclaimed as messiah, although in a restrained and muted manner, by reference back to the old testament promises. Now this same messiah is lying as a child in a trough for feeding animals. At first there seems to be no explanation for this enigmatic and paradoxical sign. It is intended not so much 'to explain the mystery of the child as to pose it as a question. Whatever can a child found under these circumstances be destined to become? That is, so to say, an open question' (Schürmann, LUM 39, 30).

The indications supplied by the prophets do not, in the last analysis, provide any answer to this question. Much less is the mystery of the child revealed to the individuals actually taking part in the episode by any kind of miraculous signs with which they are favoured. The birth itself tells us nothing about the significance of him who is born. Not even his parents would have recognised it of their own resources. This mystery would have 'remained unnoticed if heaven itself had not spoken' (Fuchs, 433). God proclaims through his messengers the meaning of what is taking place.

The message proclaimed by the angels
The prophets of the old testament throw an initial light upon the child in the manger. But ultimately the mystery of him is illumined by the radiance which comes from the 'glory of the Lord' (2:9). This mystery is not presented in such a way as to instruct or inform the bystanders, but rather powerfully proclaimed. 'In the Spirit God has bestowed truth upon the apostolic church in the form of his revealed word and the light of grace with which he illumines the event of Christ's coming. He has done this in order to disclose the mystery of his Son in revelation, and to enable believers to understand it. And this truth seems, as it were, caught up in the light which, together with the message proclaimed by the angels . . . falls upon the shepherds' (Schürmann, LUM 34). The entire narrative is drawn to this point as its climax. The angel first proclaims 'a great joy' (2:10), the great joy, that is, of the time of salvation, which is announced together with the proclamation of the messiah (1:28), is ushered in in his birth, and radiates from him right up to his ascension (24:52). It is a joy which is then prolonged in the preaching of the apostles (9:6 and Acts *passim*), a joy in which the shepherds and 'all the people' share. 'All people' is a phrase originally applied to Israel, but here Luke must already have the christian community in view. The promised salvation is present. In Jesus it has become a reality of 'today' (2:11). He is the deliverer and, moreover, not merely one among the many deliverers of his people (Jg 3:9, 15), but the messiah and Lord who comes from the city of David. 'So far from representing an "idyllic" scene, this revelation contains within it something of the harshness of a paradox: it is the eschatological salvation

from God which has entered the world with the "new-born baby in the manger"' (Schürmann, LUM 39, 34).

The message of the angel is prolonged in the hymn of the heavenly host (2:13ff). Their hymn is a 'messianic acclamation'. It proclaims what is now taking place in the birth of the messiah: 'Glory to God in the highest, and on earth peace...' (2:14). The hymn is taken up by the people at the entry of Jesus into Jerusalem (Lk 19:38). In Jesus the glory of God and peace upon earth are drawn into a unity. He unites heaven and earth. With him the glory of God breaks in upon the world and brings salvation to men. They owe this not to their own good will, but to the graciousness of God and to his free choice. The expression 'Men of (God's) good will' is 'to be taken neither as applying to the Jews in particular nor in a universalist sense without any roots in salvation history. It is intended to have an eschatological application to the chosen people of God's salvation' (TWNT II, 748). God's *eudokia* (favour) allows men to share his *doxa* (glory).

Witnesses to the message
The shepherds show themselves to be men of God's favour. They accept the truth of what has taken place and themselves become witnesses to the message which has been imparted to them (2:15–20). Luke uses the word *rhema*, here and often, since it signifies 'word' and 'event'. God's word does not remain ineffective (Lk 1:37). It takes place. It is there palpably and in physical form. For this reason not only hearing but seeing too has a significant part to play (2:15, 17, 20, 26, 30). They acquaint the parents with the mystery of their own child. On their return to their own avocation they continue the mission of the angels: they give tidings of the glory of God and praise him. The message they proclaim is the preaching of the early christian community: all are astonished at what they are told (2:18). So far as the gospel is concerned we do not follow the shepherds any further along their path. They have fulfilled

their mission. They direct our gaze beyond themselves to Mary. They reveal to her, in the first instance (2:16) that in the birth of her child God is fulfilling his promises. Here, as in the other stories included in the infancy narrative, she figures especially prominently. She keeps the individual episodes in her heart and relates them to one another (2:19). Her faith reveals to her the underlying coherence of what is taking place. She is the type of the community which hears and believes.

(d) THE PROPHETIC WITNESS OF THE PRESENTATION IN THE TEMPLE (LK 2:21-40)

The introductory verse (2:21) serves not merely to establish the connection with the annunciation and birth of Jesus, but at the same time to refer back to the corresponding pericope in the story of John (1:59-80). In spite of this artificial redactional 'join', it is unmistakable that the tradition now embodied in Lk 2:21-40 was originally independent. 'The astonishment of his parents (v 33) gives the impression that this story contains the first prophetic declaration concerning the child that has been bestowed upon them, and that it was once independent both of the annunciation story and of the story of Jesus' birth' (Grundmann ²1964, 88).

Heightened parallelism

Here again the parallelism of the two narrative sections clearly brings out the greater significance attached to Jesus. In both cases the naming of the children, as distinct from their circumcision, is particularly emphasised. Both children receive their names from God. Both are the subject of hymns of praise: John is praised by his father Zechariah (1:67-69) while Jesus is praised by the aged Simeon (2:29-32) who—and this point is repeated three times over for the sake of emphasis—is filled with the Holy Spirit. The message of his hymn goes beyond that of Zechariah in the following points:

(i) In place of the future tense of promise ('You will . . .' 1:76) it has the *nun* (now) of fulfilment.

(ii) Jesus brings salvation not only to Israel but 'to all peoples'. He is the light that dispels the darkness enveloping the peoples (1:78ff).

(iii) Whereas the salutation of John takes place in the house of his parents, that of Jesus is composed to celebrate the public manifestation of his messiahship in the temple at Jerusalem when the days of purification are fulfilled. 'The story of John began in the temple and led to the wilderness (1:80). That of Jesus began at Nazareth and led to the temple.' Jerusalem and the temple play an important part in the theology of Luke. The importance of the temple comes out above all in the infancy narrative to his gospel. This narrative begins in the temple (1:5). It records how Jesus is brought there soon after his birth (2:22–24) and receives prophetic greetings there (2:25–38), and it ends with his first appearance there (2:40–52). But the temple is also accorded its due importance in the wider development of the gospel as a whole. It is here that the devil is definitively rejected (4:9–13), here that the entry into the holy city reaches its goal (19:28–48). By taking possession of the temple and teaching there daily (19:45–48) Jesus fulfils that destiny which began with his presentation and his initial appearance there at twelve years old, cf Laurentin, 103f, H. Conzelmann, ET 75–79.

The prophetic witness

As a member of the Israelite people Jesus is 'subject to the law' (Gal 4:4). No special provisions are made governing the treatment of the child by his parents. They act 'in conformity with what is written in the law of the Lord' (Lk 2:23; cf 2:22, 24). The story first relates how they fulfil the prescriptions contained in Lv 12, but then goes on from this to its climax, the prophetic words of Simeon and the canticle of Anna (2:29–38). Both are presented as figures who are faithful and devout in their observance of the law of conformity with the ideal of old testament devotion, and who look for the salvation which the messiah is to bring. The revelation of what he really is goes beyond their

INFANCY NARRATIVES: EXEGETICAL INVESTIGATION

expectations, for with Jesus something more than the hoped-for 'consolation of Israel' (2:25) has come. The messiah who has appeared in the temple of Israel is—this is the witness of Simeon when he is filled with the Holy Spirit—'a light for the enlightening of the Gentiles' (2:32). The proclamation of a salvation that is universal here echoes Is 52:10; 42:6; 49:6. It is a central theme in Lucan theology, cf Oliver, 221f. Through this messiah Israel is confronted with a decision. Those who stand now are destined to fall, while those who are fallen are to stand (2:34). The claims he makes provoke a contradiction which is to affect Mary too (2:35).

No specific message is placed upon the lips of Anna the prophetess. She praises God for the salvation which has been received and, like the shepherds, proclaims it to those who are looking for it (2:38).

The shepherds tending their flocks outside had no expectation of the proclamation of the messiah, and were astonished when it came. Simeon and Anna, having spent their whole lives in devotion to the law, were looking for it. Both witnesses are set side by side, and both are valid (Dinkler, 222). God is not circumscribed in the ways in which he chooses to bring his salvation.

(e) JESUS IN THE TEMPLE AT TWELVE YEARS OLD (LK 2:41–52)
This story, originally complete and independent in itself, is the only one which has been handed down to us concerning the boyhood of Jesus. Once more his parents at first do not dream that something extraordinary could be taking place in their Son. What we have been told of him in the earlier stories seems to be totally unfamiliar to them. This section of text has no counterpart in the story of John. It may be concluded, then, that at this point the story of Jesus goes beyond it. There can be no parallel to an episode in which Jesus reveals himself as the Son of God.

A twofold connecting link is to be found at the beginning and end of the story of Jesus at twelve years old. 2:39 corresponds to 2:51. Both speak of returning from the visit to the temple. The second point of connection is still more important. It is the correspondence between vv 40 and 52, the verses with which the pericope begins and ends. These verses plainly refer back to 1 Sam 2:21, 26 and, furthermore, an antique style of writing is discernible in them. Admittedly there is a noticeable interruption in the biographical development of the story at the point where the description of the extraordinary physical and spiritual growth of its hero has been inserted: the emphasis is laid upon his spiritual development, and upon the divine *charis*, grace, with which he is endowed. In addition to these his wisdom is mentioned in vv 40 and 52. For our understanding of the story as a whole this point is especially significant.

Certain striking connecting links can be discerned between Jesus' first journey to Jerusalem and his last. In both cases he is found again after three days (it is 'no accident' that this period has been included (cf 2:46 with 24:7, 21, 46). As in that passage so also here no other explanation is assigned for the fact that he is 'lost' than that it 'must' be so according to the will of the Father (2:49; 24:7, 26, 44) an explanation which here, as in that passage, meets with incomprehension (2:50; 9:45; 18:34; 24:25). Is it the evangelist's intention already here, where he is describing Jesus' first journey to the Passover, to foretell his final journey thither, when he will himself become the fulfilment of the Passover?

The motif of wisdom
The key word 'wisdom' occurs in the opening and closing verses. What precisely this wisdom consists in is illustrated more fully in the intervening section of narrative. In anticipation of the works of his public ministry (cf Lk 11:31) Jesus is regarded as endowed with wisdom even in his youth. In listening, asking questions and giving answers he reveals a degree of insight so unprecedented that those present are beside themselves with

astonishment (2:46f). The wisdom which he possesses in such unique degree is not the wisdom of the Hellenistic philosophers. His insight is directed towards the word of God and the revelation of his will as contained in the scriptures.

The Son of a divine Father
The motif of wisdom is connected with, and made subordinate to the idea of divine Sonship. The truth that Jesus is the Son of God occupies a central and dominant position in the message of Lk 2:40–52.

The first word that Jesus utters is spoken in the temple (2:49), and in it he calls God his Father. This appellation does not merely reflect the linguistic usage current at that time among Jewish children, who were taught to call God their Father. Rather it marks Jesus off as having a unique messianic vocation (cf TWNT v, 988f). This passage should not be interpreted as a historical statement concerning the messianic consciousness gradually developing in the boy. Luke bears witness to the belief in his own community in Jesus who is the Christ. In the light of this faith the first appearance of Jesus in the temple appears pre-eminently as an act fraught with messianic significance, his first words as messianic words. Right from the very outset—this is what the verse bears witness to—he stands in a unique relationship to God.

This means that he transcends human ties and human understanding. In the last analysis his mother has no rights over him. She cannot shape the course of his life. He belongs not to her but to God. He must be where his divine Father is. The term *dei* (must) is used initially and primarily in passages assigning the reasons for the passion. By extension from this it comes to be applied to the entire life of Jesus, and serves to bring out its character as saving event planned by God to take place in this way. From beginning to end Jesus is subject to God's will. Thus a certain distance is interposed between parents and child. They do not understand their own son (2:50). They have sought him sorrowing (2:48), and now that they find him they feel the pain of his mysterious answer still more deeply. The visionary message uttered by Simeon becomes a reality. But still Mary submits to the call of God, which reaches her in her own son. She keeps his word in her heart (2:51). Her greatness lies in her faith.

Behind the parents, all uncomprehending of their own son, stands the christian community. This too does not understand the claims that Jesus makes upon it. It needs to be reminded again and again that Jesus must be about his Father's business (2:49). Only the believer can accept and keep this word that comes to him in the message of his faith. To him the claims of Jesus, which go beyond all merely human understanding, are made known.

After his public appearance in the temple Jesus returns with his parents to Nazareth to resume his former obscurity. The great theme of his life has been defined: he is the Christ.

(f) CONCLUSION

By incorporating the infancy narrative into his gospel Luke projects 'the saving history of Jesus Christ the *Kyrios* back to his very birth' (Schlier 1964, 17), indeed back to his very conception. Right from the first instant of his existence and origin he is the messiah. 'For Luke there was never any time at which Jesus was not the Son of God, even though the history of this Sonship does not properly begin until the moment of his baptism when it is proclaimed. The process by which this human figure is made to function as Son of God and messiah and his actual generation are one and the same act of the Holy Spirit and of the power of the Most High' (Voss, 173). The individual stories which go to make up the infancy narrative constitute so many signposts pointing to the messiahship of Jesus, and already indicate in anticipation what his mission is to be. The seeds of this mission are already present right at the outset.

There is a symmetrical correspondence between the infancy

narrative and the story of the baptism. At his baptism Jesus is anointed with the same Holy Spirit (3:22; cf 4:18) to whom he already owes his existence (1:35). Although these two statements may seem to be in competition with one another, one should not feel compelled to opt for the second rather than the first in such a way as to accord all the value to the anointing with the Spirit at baptism. In his infancy narrative it is in fact precisely Luke's intention to show that Jesus was the messiah right from the beginning. Thus for his thought as a whole the infancy narrative is of the highest significance because in it the saving history of Jesus the messiah is projected back right to his very conception. The fact that the conception through the Spirit is thus set side by side with the baptism does not imply any difficulty or rivalry between the two for Luke. 'The essential thought here is not in fact concerned to explain the progressive emergence of a "wonderman". Rather both narratives are intended to proclaim the uniqueness of Jesus as an already accepted truth of faith. The narratives achieve this by showing us God's direct action upon Jesus at certain decisive points, and thereby conveying to us that in him God himself is at work' (TWNT VI, 398). Both accounts are linked together and made to complement one another by the evangelist by means of the central idea of the *pneuma hagion* (Holy Spirit). The 'baptism narrative prevents us from misunderstanding the account of the conception through the Spirit by taking this to imply that Jesus was equipped with a physical nature that was not of this earth and not really human ... Conversely Lk 1:35 prevents us from misunderstanding the baptism narrative in an "adoptionist" sense by supposing that Jesus was originally a pious man who was only chosen to become Son of God at a later stage in his development' (Flender, 123).

Even though the evangelist has loosely connected the stories together they are still not to be taken as elements in a single integral story, or even as so many stages in the development of a human idea. They are incompatible with a biographical presentation. 'It is plainly evident that they are not so much co-ordinated to one another as set side by side with one another without any real connection' (Schierse, 220). Even though the messiahship of Jesus has been unequivocally stated in the annunciation scene, the stories which follow return again and again to the starting-point. No-one perceives the mystery of the child. Even his parents do not recognise it. No-one discovers it of their own resources. Each time it has to be revealed anew and proclaimed: through the messengers of God (2:10–14), through prophetic oracles (2:29–32) and finally through Jesus' own avowal (2:49). Each separate story begins, so to say, afresh from the starting-point, and states afresh the message of who Jesus is and what God designs for him. Each story is in itself a proclaiming of the message, contains within itself the gospel.

In the background of the personages whom we encounter in these stories stand the hearers to whom the evangelist proclaims over and over again the mystery of Christ.

2 The infancy narrative of Matthew

(a) THE SPECIAL CHARACTER OF MATTHEW'S INFANCY NARRATIVE AS COMPARED WITH THAT OF LUKE

Matthew too introduces his gospel with a history of the antecedents. Like Luke his intention in doing this is to convey that even the very beginnings of Jesus' life correspond to old testament expectations and show him to be the messiah. But in their respective methods of conveying this each of the evangelists goes his own way. Whereas Luke brings out the underlying significance of Jesus first and foremost by the parallelism he institutes between the narratives of the Baptist and Jesus respectively, Matthew omits all mention of John, states his thesis straight away by introducing in the very first verse the avowal that Jesus is the Christ, and concentrates exclusively upon this. Biographical data hardly interest him at all. In comparison with Luke his presentation is doctrinal and restricted to bare essentials. The only episode recounted in any detail is the adoration of the magi (Mt 2:1–12). The remaining pericopes are laconic in their mode of presentation and theological in interest.

Both evangelists attempt to bring out the connection between promise and fulfilment, each in his own way. Whereas in the Lucan infancy narrative the old testament citations are blended into the stories themselves, Matthew emphasises them by introducing them in each scene by means of explicit quotation formulae in order to provide a clearly expressed record of the fact that in them the scriptures are fulfilled. Here in the infancy narrative, as throughout his entire gospel, he has a special interest to demonstrate the messiahship of Jesus on the basis of the old testament because of his controversy with the Jews.

Matthew's history of the antecedents comprises two distinct units of narrative. These coincide with the existing division of chapters. In terms of subject matter the point of convergence between them is to be found in 1:21.

(b) THE GENEALOGY OF JESUS AND HIS BIRTH (MT 1)

At first sight the stereotyped list of names seems totally devoid of kerygmatic relevance. For all this, however, certain considerations should warn us not to regard it as a record which has no further interest beyond the purely historical one and against setting it aside from our considerations on these grounds. Already in the old testament great significance is attached to genealogies. Moreover both Matthew and Luke independently of one another include a family tree of Jesus in their gospels, and thereby show us that they regard this as an element of vital importance in those gospels. It is quite evident that their primary preoccupation is not to produce a table of ancestry which is historically exact. Here and there they skip generations. Their intention is not to set forth a complete record without any omissions, but to preach Christ even in so monotonous a mode of expression as a genealogy represents. For this reason the family tree of Mt 1 must be examined in terms not so much of its historical exactitude as of its kerygmatic content.

The theme: Jesus Christ
Matthew begins with a thematic statement of his purpose (1:1). His subject is Christ and his history insofar as this affects us. Jesus is in no sense an idea, a mythological being. He belongs to human history. He has his own place in the long sequence of generations that go to make up a family and a people. He comes from the royal house of David, the recipients of Yahweh's promise (cf 2 Sam 7:12–16) and he is a descendant of Abraham the patriarch of Israel, which enables us already to glimpse that the new people of God comes from all nations. Both of these factors serve to indicate the nature of his mission: Jesus is the messiah of Israel. The difference in orientation of the two genealogies of Jesus becomes apparent at this point. Matthew assigns Jesus a place in the history of Israel, where the special emphasis on his descent from Abraham already points on to the new people of God. Luke traces the line of ancestors back to Adam, and brings the history of Jesus into line with the history of the world. (On the 'Adam/Christ' typology in the Lucan genealogy cf TWNT I, 141.)

How the genealogy is divided
The chain of ancestors is divided in a manner that is significant. Abraham marks its point of departure, David its highest point, the Babylonian captivity its lowest. The mention of Jesus represents the goal towards which all these heights and depths lead. By singling out the three climactic points in the genealogy mentioned above the author has divided the whole into three main epochs, each containing fourteen generations. As v 17, the verse immediately following the conclusion of the genealogy, shows, this rigid schematisation is deliberate and intended by Matthew himself. The genealogy does not fall into this pattern naturally or *sua sponte*. In accordance with the current conven-

tion of composing 'genealogies' the evangelist has felt free to omit generations. Only by doing this has he been able to arrive at his artificial division into periods. His purpose in doing this is to convey to us that it was not mere chance or caprice that caused this family tree to develop in the way that it has, but rather the providence of God. Ultimately speaking when God called Abraham, chose David to be king, and led back the people from Babylon, he already had Christ in view. The whole history of Israel presses on in its three great stages of fourteen generations each towards Christ as its goal. He came into the world—this is what the schematic numbering is intended to convey—'when the time was fulfilled' (Gal 4:4).

The genealogy is not of itself sufficient to designate Jesus as a figure of special dignity and significance in saving history. His descent from Abraham and David is certainly not unique. This is something which he has in common with his forebears. What sets him above them is the special position assigned to him in the total succession. Jesus is born in the hour of eschatological destiny, at the end of the period covered by the third group of generations. He who knows how to read the history of Israel recognises from this that Jesus is the messiah.

The manner in which the name of Jesus is introduced in the genealogy
The actual form in which Jesus is introduced into the family of Abraham and David also serves to throw clearly into relief the uniqueness of his position in it. If the rhythmic pattern which runs through the whole passage had been maintained at this point it would have read: 'Joseph begot Jesus'. But Joseph only figures here as 'the husband of Mary from whom Jesus was born'. The formula used throughout the genealogy, therefore, is not applied to Jesus. He stands outside the normal process by which generations come to be, and yet he is the Son of David and of Abraham. The evangelist explains the connection in a special excursus (1:18–25) on the information supplied in v 16.

Joseph's status is not that of the physical father of Jesus. He is generated by the Holy Spirit (1:18–20) from the Virgin Mary. Nevertheless he does belong to the race of David. For Joseph—explicitly presented as a 'son of David'—is directed by an angel to take Mary as his wife and to give the name ordained by God to her son. It is because he complies with this command that Jesus is juridically recognised as his son and incorporated into the tribe of David. In his providence God has wonderfully provided for this and ratified him as messiah.

The message of Mt 1 is that Jesus is the messiah whom Israel awaits. His physical descent supplies the necessary proof of this. He belongs to the race of Abraham and David, the recipients of God's promise. He is assigned a place in the genealogy which is eschatologically significant and is incorporated into it in a miraculous manner.

The function of the messiah
Matthew does not content himself merely with pointing out the messiahship of Jesus. Already in ch 1 he indicates what the destiny of the messiah is to be be, and then goes on to state this explicitly in ch 2. The very name assigned to him serves to indicate this destiny. Jesus 'will save his people from their sins' (1:21). He is the eschatological bringer of salvation who creates himself a new people by redeeming them from their sins. His work is no longer confined to a particular nation, but—the fact that his genealogy is traced back to Abraham is in itself an indication of this—is aimed at all peoples. Jesus is the founder of the new people of God, and is hailed by that people as 'God with us' (1:23).

(c) THE CHILDHOOD OF JESUS (MT 2)
The material treated in ch 2, though conceived of as a unity, is divided into four scenes. The expedition of the magi (2:1–12) is followed by the flight into Egypt (2:13–15), the massacre of the innocents at Bethlehem (2:16–18) and the return to Nazareth where the family establish themselves (2:19–23).

The focal point of each scene is a proof from scripture. The place names contained in the citations can hardly be thought to provide the key to the interpretation of the entire story. For instance it is not Matthew's intention merely to explain 'why Jesus is called Jesus of Nazareth even though he was born in Bethlehem'. Certainly the question of Jesus' place of origin has had some influence on the development of the author's ideas. But over and above this the evangelist has certain kerygmatic aims to pursue and these are more essential to him.

His central preoccupation is one which corresponds to the argument of his gospel as a whole, and in particular to that of his infancy narrative, namely to explain the messiahship of Jesus and more specifically his precise function as messiah. This is why instead of making a purely biographical presentation of the story of Jesus he establishes connections between it and the central personages and events of Israelite history, and interprets it against this background. His purpose is to disclose the inner meaning of Jesus, and to stimulate belief in him. For this purpose he invokes the midrashic developments of the stories of Jacob and Moses, which were part of the stock of Jewish tradition, and regards these as fulfilled in Jesus.

The story of the magi

The events which Matthew narrates in ch 2 are initiated by the arrival of the magi in Jerusalem. '*Magos* here designates the possessor of special (esoteric) knowledge, especially with regard to the possibility of discerning the significance of the star's course and the factors in world history corresponding to it' (TWNT IV, 362). For these men from the East a special star has arisen, the star of the new-born king of Judah. The question of the precise origin of the 'star' motif remains open, but its function in the story is, nevertheless, unmistakable. The star is understood as a sign from God which inspires the magi to set out on their journey. They journey from the East to the capital of Israel in order to do homage to the king there (2:1ff).

Which king? Surely if it had merely been one of the many Jewish kings they would hardly have seen 'his star' and set out on a journey. They are not prompted by political expectations. Their journey to Jerusalem is taken as a sign of the fulfilment of that old testament prophecy which promises that at the end of days kings and peoples from the four corners of the earth will come in streams to Jerusalem in order to adore God and bestow their presents upon him there (Is 2:2ff; 60:1–6; Ps 72:10f). The 'end of the days' has been ushered in. The 'new-born king of the Jews' is the messiah.

Only one question interests the magi: 'Where is the new-born king of the Jews?' (2:2). 'His star' has been the occasion of their journey, and now they look questioningly to Jerusalem. A cosmic sign has led them close to the messiah. Now they expect the guardians of the word of God to tell them exactly where they can find him.

Their alarming news and the disturbing message they bring affect the king and the city (2:3–6). There can be no mistaking their reaction. Instead of joyful surprise all together are shaken with fear. 'The whole of Jerusalem' (2:3) has achieved an unexpected degree of solidarity. There was constant opposition between the king and the Sanhedrin and, furthermore, Herod had no authority whatever to convene the Sanhedrin. The narrator ignores these factors in the historical background. What he seeks to express is that 'the whole of Jerusalem' rejected the messiah from the very beginning. When their hated tyrant is so disturbed all are affected, all realise what is at stake. Herod has straightway grasped the true implications of the question which the magi ask: it concerns the messiah (2:4). The decision goes unambiguously against him—this is what the evangelist means to say—right from the first moment of his coming. Probably the experts in scripture and representatives of Israel supply the right answer to the question of where the messiah is to be born straight away. Indeed their knowledge goes far beyond merely providing the answer to Herod's question. They already know precisely what the significance is of the messiah born in Bethlehem: he is the 'prince who will shepherd my people Israel' (2:6) promised in scripture. He is the leader of the people of God in the final age. All this they know, and they point out the way to him to the magi yet they themselves do not go to him. Whereas Gentiles do homage to the child the king of the Jews seeks to kill him. The messiah comes to shepherd his people and the people refuse to accept him. And so the way leads on beyond Jerusalem. Henceforward it is no longer the holy city that constitutes a central point of salvation, but the new-born messiah at Bethlehem. It is here that the adoration of the peoples promised to Jerusalem (2:11) is enacted.

Side by side with the mystery of the divine vocation of Israel stands the 'mystery of her disobedience and her rebellion against this her God' (Schlier 1966, 175). Just as in the minds of the biblical authors election is something that affects not merely individual Jews in some sense but Israel as a whole, so this denial is the responsibility not of a minority of individual Jews who participated directly in the circumstances of Jesus' death. It involves Israel herself as the chosen people. In Jesus the God of Israel has 'achieved a physical confrontation with his people, and so, at this point in history, the decision of this people in response to the final and definitive command of God was made, and made manifest the mystery of their sins. With regard to the new testament this reading of history in it may not be suppressed or distorted. It must not be suppressed or distorted, otherwise one is suppressing and distorting either the uniqueness of the person and the event of Jesus Christ, or the uniqueness of this people, Israel, upon which God has bestowed the grace of his own nearness as he has not bestowed it upon other peoples' (Schlier 1966, 175f). Matthew on the one hand emphasises the election of Israel, while on the other he throws sharply into relief Israel's own denial.

In the footprints of the fathers
Joseph receives a directive from God to flee to Egypt with the child and his mother (2:13–15). 'With this the history of the messiah is guided into those channels which were marked out for it long before by the history of the patriarchs and the people . . .' (Lohmeyer–Schmauch, 28). Just as Israel (Jacob) travelled the way to Egypt and was brought back from there to Canaan, so now the same experience befalls Jesus. He comes to Egypt in order to set out from there upon the exodus which leads him to his own homeland. And just as the life of Israel then was imperilled by plots to annihilate it, so it is with Jesus now (2:16–18). The massacre of the innocents at Bethlehem contains an echo of the 'Jacob-Israel' midrash, and also of the history of Moses. In Jesus' fate the history of Israel is reflected and brought to its consummation. Even the massacre of the innocents cannot frustrate the promises of God.

The homecoming of Jesus from Egypt takes place in two stages (2:19–23). Initially—and this corresponds to the exodus of the people of God in the old testament—the goal of the journey is 'the land of Israel'. Afterwards, in accordance with the ancient message of the prophets, there follows a further migration to Nazareth, and it is this that explains his appellation, 'Jesus of Nazareth'.

Matthew too shows that the way followed by Jesus right from the very outset is one that was already marked out in scripture, and one that confirms his messiahship. It is through him that the promises of the old covenant have been brought to their fulfilment. In journeying to Egypt and thence returning in a personal exodus of his own he travels the way which Israel travelled before him. He is the new Jacob, the new Moses. In him the history of Israel attains its fulfilment. He is the founder and leader of the eschatological people of God. Already, even in his infancy, the fate that awaits him in the future can be discerned. While the representatives of Israel decide against him, and while the cross already casts its shadow before, the representatives of the Gentiles draw near to him.

III Concluding implications

1 The kerygmatic structure of the infancy narratives
By opening up the question of Jesus' provenance the infancy narratives provide the answer to the further questions of who he is and what he signifies for the salvation of men. Right from the first moment he is the Christ, that same Christ whom he has proved himself to be through his cross and resurrection. The light that shines out from the end of his life falls upon the beginnings of it as well.

However much the individual stories may differ from one another in particular points of detail, and however impossible it may be to reduce them to harmony in terms of sheer historical fact, they do coincide in being orientated towards a common goal. 'What holds all these passages together in the deepest possible unity is the fact that they embody the witness of the post-Easter community to the messianic status of the risen Christ' (Frör, 283). These are no mere records of episodes in the private family life of Jesus. These events affect the entire world (Lk 2:1) and all its ages. Their relevance reaches back to the very origins of the chosen people (Mt 1:1ff) and of mankind (Lk 3:38), and forwards into a future without end (Lk 1:33).

The apostolic preaching, therefore, in contemplating and interpreting the origins of Jesus' life, has done so not merely in the light of his resurrection, but also with retrospective reference to events which are central to the history of Israel. They link the beginning with the end, and thereby underline the continuity of God's action in history. What he initiated with the patriarchs, that he has consummated in Jesus. This is the witness they bear. Jesus is the fulfilment of the promises of the old covenant.

The underlying kerygmatic purpose which the authors of the infancy narratives have set themselves has influenced even the literary structure of those narratives. The patterns in which promise and fulfilment are made to correspond, the patterns of 'heightened parallelism' (Lk 1–2) and the artificial structures which have been imposed upon the annunciation stories (Lk 1: 26–38) and the genealogy (Mt 1) all serve to show as clearly as possible that the author's central preoccupation here is not to produce a biographical reconstruction of the childhood of Jesus, but to proclaim the deeper truth embodied in it.

2 *The historical question*

In treating of the question of how far the infancy narratives can be held to relate actual historical facts we must bear in mind the further question of how its literary genre should be defined. It has been shown that these narratives are not to be taken as historical records, for they have been constructed according to certain definite and predetermined literary patterns and approximate to the forms customary in Jewish tradition known as *midrash* and *haggadah*. In these forms of tradition the writer attaches his ideas as closely as possible to passages from the old testament which he attempts to make relevant and actual by placing either an edifying or a doctrinal interpretation upon them. The stories in the infancy narratives are far more kerygmatic than biographical in their focus of interest. They are intended to attest the significance of Jesus for salvation. Anyone, therefore, who reads them 'as a historian in order to satisfy his scientific curiosity, even if he does this with the most pious of intentions . . . has missed their essential point' (Schierse, 221). He will become inextricably involved in contradictions which are only capable of solution when the kerygmatic origin of these stories is adverted to. Elements which could not fail to strike one as out of place, inappropriate and improbable in an account written from a strictly historical point of view are not *ipso facto* to be judged by the same standards in a *midrash*. The reason is that precisely in this *genre* it is not primarily, or at any rate not only the concrete historical details that are of concern, but rather the expounding of a particular aspect of saving history. In fact the story derives its meaning and its relevance precisely not—or at any rate not primarily—from its historical aspects, but rather from the special kerygmatic aspect proper to it.

To say that the infancy narratives approximate to the genre of *midrash* is not to assert that they are devoid of any historical value. For they can by no means simply be identified with *midrash* without any distinction. They display elements of *midrash* and are midrashic in their general presentation. In any case *midrash* too is not incompatible with a nucleus of historical fact.

The passages in the Lucan and Matthaean infancy narratives which are kerygmatically structured are neither pure creations of their authors, nor are they simply woven from strands of old testament tradition. These stories are inspired by specific events and record objective data from the history of Jesus. They are initially based upon the universal human experiences of conception, gestation and birth, incorporation into a specific family, circumcision and naming. The historical data independently recorded in the respective witnesses of Matthew and Luke supply, at any rate in outline, an objective history of how these general stages in human development took place in the case of Jesus: the fact that Mary gave birth to him (Lk 1:26-38; 2:5-7; Mt 1:18-25), the espousal of Mary with Joseph (Lk 1:27; 2:5; Mt 1:18-20), the fact that he belonged to the tribe of David (Lk 1:27; 2:4; Mt 1:16, 20), the fact that their home was at Nazareth (Lk 1:26; 2:4, 39, 51; Mt 2:23) and that Bethlehem was the place where Jesus was born (Lk 2:4, 11; Mt 2:1-12). A further point which both evangelists agree in asserting is that the conception of Jesus was caused by the Spirit (Lk 1:35; Mt 1:18).

From the historical point of view this still leaves many questions unanswered with regard to the objective course of events.

'Precisely with regard to the infancy narratives it would be quite out of place and over-dogmatic to pretend that we could provide, with any degree of certainty, the sort of confirmation of the events described which would meet the standards of modern scientific history' (Trilling 1966, 81). An over-dogmatic or over-confident approach of this kind can prove an obstacle to a right understanding of the message of the passages involved just as much as the kind of exegesis which sets aside the stories from the outset as historically irrelevant. Scholarly research must 'be allowed time to answer those questions which are raised by an exaggerated and one-sided preoccupation with the chronological and historically factual aspects. Faith is not discredited if it allows certain still unexplained questions to remain open' (Schürmann, BiKi 111).

At any rate for the time being our concern should not be to reconstruct the course of events anew in such a way as deliberately to omit all those elements (angels, the star etc) which modern readers find 'putting off'. Such attempts are still subject to the limitations of an over-rationalistic approach. They are designed to 'save' the narratives by 'giving them a helpful push' along lines which are foreign to the true intention of their authors. This does no service to the task of preaching the gospel message. On the contrary it raises fresh difficulties for this. The preacher now has to explain the differences between the development of the biblical story and the new hypothesis which seeks to explain the 'real' course of events. And in all this the preacher wholly fails to express what the evangelists intend to convey. Now this is precisely the preacher's task: to listen to their message concerning Jesus, and to proclaim *this* message anew.

7
PREACHING THE CHRISTMAS STORIES

I Basic considerations

The christian faith finds its starting-point in the cross and resurrection of Christ. The confession of faith in the Easter event provides the foundation and the central point of the apostolic preaching even—as has been shown—in the stories of Jesus' birth and childhood. These are not presented as private or self-contained memoirs of the holy family. They point us on to Easter, and that too not merely in the sense that there is a necessary connection between the beginning of any course that is mapped out and its end, or that the self-abnegation of the cross is already visible in the poverty of the manger. The connection is absolutely fundamental. The infancy narratives are to be understood only in the perspective of Easter. In the manner of its development the proclaimed message does not merely follow the 'natural' course of events, so to say, from Christmas to Easter. It may be that the converse is true, that it is only because of what Easter means that the origins of Jesus' life have been accorded a place in the total message. The fact that as a matter of liturgical history the celebration of the birth of Christ can only be understood in the light of the celebration of Easter is in accordance with the interrelationship between the relevant texts in the bible itself (cf H. Rahner, ET 89–176).

1 The structure of the preaching of Christmas as conditioned by the message of Easter
It is in the perspective of Easter that that dimension opens up in which the message of Christmas has its origins and from

which it still derives its force as vital and relevant for today. It does this in the following ways:

(i) It warns us against the danger of presenting the gospel in 'psychologising' or 'historicising' terms, a danger, moreover, which is at its greatest in the context of the festival of Christmas. Round the infancy narratives has grown up a whole host of ideas which have their origin in representations of the crib, Christmas plays and Christmas carols from both ancient and recent times. And if we allow the message that we preach to be conditioned by the pious accretions which have come to surround the biblical narratives throughout a long history of devotion, then that message will sink all too easily to the level of mere comfort for the emotions. In that case it will be 'no longer a witness to our belief in the glorified Lord, but at most a way of soothing and comforting ourselves, an occasion for reviving family feelings or a regression into some benign but childish world of dreams' (Frör, 286).

The preacher should be honest in testing his ideas about the origins of Jesus' life and making sure that they conform to the actual message of the gospel itself. Here the atmosphere is purified by the eschatological force latent in it, which derives from an ever present awareness of Easter. If he submits his mind to the gospel text then he will recognise that it is not his task to provide vivid representations of the holy family, the draughty stable and the shepherds numbed with the cold, after the manner of Christmas plays, but rather to give expression to the confession of faith in Christ the Lord and the redeemer.

(ii) It is when we recognise the essentially pastoral character of the infancy narratives that we can discern the dimension of saving history in them. Today Christmas has to a large extent been reduced to a private celebration, and this not merely in virtue of the fact that in the minds of many christians the festival has come to be thought of as a family celebration. In the spiritual sphere too the character it bears is chiefly that of a private festival. Its significance is determined by the characteristic images of the holy family in the stable at Bethlehem and the encounter of the individual believer with the child in the manger.

If we follow the mind of the gospel itself in viewing the birth of Jesus in the perspective of Easter, then all kinds of distortions are nipped in the bud and the broader perspective of history as guided and controlled by God is opened up. Christ is the fulfilment of the promises of the old covenant. In him the *eschaton* is made present, has become 'today'. He is the glorified Lord whose kingdom is without end. The task of confessing our faith in him is not a private affair but rather our witness before the world.

(iii) The dynamism of the Easter message latent in the infancy narratives makes it impossible to understand Christmas merely as a memory. It does not allow us to fall back into dreams of a world that is past as though all things, despite their transience, were still the same today as they were then. The early christian community has not achieved a historical reconstruction of the origins of Jesus' life, but rather interpreted and 'actualised' those origins in the light of their faith in their risen Lord. Their Christmas witness summons us to believe in the Christ who is present now. His presence among men contains, it is true, an intrinsic reference to a fact of the past. But it does not continue to be restricted to this. He is present 'today' and that too not as a child in the manger but as *Christos Kyrios* the redeemer (Lk 2:11).

2 Preaching as opposed to 'historicising explanations'

The infancy narratives are a proclamation of Christ. The early christian community's confession of Easter faith in their Lord has embodied itself in these narratives. It constitutes their heart and centre and should be the heart and centre of our preaching also.

The preacher, therefore, should not content himself with retelling the story as vividly as possible, especially as in this approach he can hardly escape the danger of introducing elements which are alien to the gospel text itself and which arouse in his hearers an interest which has nothing to do with that text. He should recognise that the evangelists do not present us with any exact description of the manner in which God entered into the world, that they were not composing the first section in a biography of Jesus. Rather they are presenting us with an interpretation of the birth of Jesus inspired by the primitive community's confession of faith in their glorified Lord. If the preacher acts as though he were retelling in his own words a precise eye-witness account of what took place, then he is leading his hearers into error. It would be irresponsible in him if he 'sought to impose upon them that they had to accept as *de fide* the historical reality of every detail in Luke's narrative...' (Stählin 1, 225).

But the preacher falls no less wide of the mark if he imagines that his function is to inform his congregation of the current position in the sphere of historical and critical research and to help them by attempting 'to "explain away" angels and other manifestations and ideas which represent "scandals" for our rationalistic thinking, or even to "apologise" for scripture because of its modes of thought' (Iwand, 204). The fact that in Jesus God has come to us—that is something that can and must be not 'explained' but rather proclaimed. It is something which is not to be measured by any standards of ours, not circumscribed by the categories of our thought, and finally not to be verified in terms of scientific history. It belongs to a dimension which exceeds our powers of critical analysis. The origins of Jesus remain undiscoverable and incomprehensible to us. He comes not from us but to us. In him the new world, the new creation begins. This is what scripture intends to express in its own terms. It intends to set before our eyes the inception of something new, something which has broken in upon our existence from the world of God. It intends not to analyse the mystery of God assuming a human nature, but rather to lead the hearers into that mystery and to involve them in it. The terms in which it does this are not an end in themselves. The scene as a whole (stable, shepherds, magi, angels) is not depicted for its own sake, and it follows that the preacher should not lose himself in these details. They serve to draw our attention to the event in which God in Jesus, by an act of radical condescension, bestows himself upon men. It is this that the preacher has to express anew in such a way as to make it have its due impact upon the lives of his hearers.

In preaching the message of Christmas we must turn away from all 'historicising' or 'psychologising' reconstructions, and concentrate on proclaiming the living and present Lord. This alone will bring our Christmas preaching back to its origin and its centre.

3 The manifold aspects of the biblical message of Christmas

In the minds of many preachers and congregations Lk 2:1–20 is accounted *the* text for the Christmas sermon. It has exercised a decisive influence on the actual shape of the Christmas festival, and many of the ideas and customs connected with this day have their origins in this text and are decisively influenced by it.

The dominating influence of the Lucan story of Jesus' birth is not something that should go unchallenged. It has given rise to the impression that apart from this, scripture has nothing else to tell us about 'Christmas'. This arbitrary concentration upon a single passage has led to a one-sided formation of our Christmas devotions, and must be held responsible for some of the excesses present in them. Not only does it imply an impoverishment of the new testament message of Christmas in terms of content, but also it fails to do justice to the multiplicity of its forms (narrative, instruction, confession of faith, hymn). Luke and Matthew, Paul and John have each in their own way something to tell us concerning the birth of Jesus. An appreciation of the riches of the biblical message will lead to a regeneration of our Christmas preaching and result in a purification of our understanding of Christmas.

4 The situation in which the message is proclaimed

Christmas confronts the preacher with a special task, which carries with it great opportunities but at the same time great dangers also. In the popular awareness of christians no festival has so great a significance as Christmas. On no other day in the church's year do men attend divine service in such numbers. Very rarely are they so ready and eager to receive the message of the sermon as on this festival.

Nevertheless—and this is a special problem entailed by the very situation in which the message is proclaimed—the minds of the hearers are already made up beforehand as to what they expect to hear. Christmas is enveloped in an atmosphere which in many cases is fed by questionable sources and which is neither easy to define nor easy to break through. A whole host of emotions and ideas are connected with this festival. It is felt to be the festival of children and of childhood, of the family and of the people, of giving and receiving presents, and not least as the festival of love and peace.

However vague and superficial such moods and expectations may for the most part be, however frequently they remain stuck fast at the level of sentimentality and cliché, it cannot be the preacher's task to take the field against the distortion of the festival of Christmas which they imply in barren polemics. Here too he has to make contact with his hearers in their existing situation, and not make them sink still deeper in the mire of their perplexities. We cannot expect salvation to come from reproaches. It is precisely those hearers who only still find their way to church at Christmas who will be put off by these, and strengthened in their dislike for attending mass and listening to sermons.

Admittedly it is just as important that the preacher should not simply confirm and intensify the expectations of the congregation and their 'Christmas mood'. He is a servant first and foremost of the word of God and not of the desires of his hearers. He will serve the interests of his hearers best precisely by faithfully and unreservedly submitting his mind to the Christmas message.

II Treatment of individual pericopes

Following the same plan as before we have selected from among the passages treated of in our exegetical investigation those four narratives which were prescribed in the previous arrangement of pericopes in the Roman liturgy for the Sundays and festival days of the Christmas season and the connected festival of the annunciation, with the place of use given in brackets

The annunciation story (Lk 1:26–38).
(The feast of the annunciation)
The Lucan narrative of Christmas (2:1–20).
(First and second masses of Christmas)
The story of the magi (Mt 2:1–12).
(The feast of the epiphany)
The story of Jesus in the temple at twelve years old (Lk 2:41–52).
(Feast of the Holy Family)

A list of the present positions of the passages discussed in the exegetical section follows in Appendix 1.

1 The annunciation story (Lk 1:26–38)

(a) ON THE SERMON LITERATURE

The suggestions for preaching were mainly concerned with the particular festivals being celebrated, and hardly enter into the gospel itself. Only in the case of the annunciation do they make this the essential point of their considerations. But even here the interpretation of this gospel is based not upon the actual sense of the text, but upon the contemporary understanding of the feast. The festival *In Annunciatione Beatae Mariae Virginis* came into existence in the course of the middle ages and is derived from an earlier one, the existence of which is attested about the year 740, known as the *Annuntiatio Domini* (Klauser, 64). The effect of the festival has been that in the hands of its interpreters this gospel has lost its christological character. The title 'All Look to the Virgin of Nazareth' is characteristic of the outlook of the composers of these sermons. It is rigidly mariological in orientation.

The portrayal of Mary
What the actual gospel text has to tell us about Mary is only seldom adverted to in the available sermon literature. Instead of this, free rein is given to the author's fantasies. 'How good, how unique the figure of Mary appears to us! She stands out among her people as far above the average.' 'She was descended from the royal house of David.' She is 'a privileged favourite of God', the 'chosen masterpiece of his creation'. 'The Holy Spirit has ... endowed her ... with the richest graces and the highest gifts ... has trained her throughout her sheltered childhood and youth in the deepest love of God.' 'How pure and spotless Mary must have been throughout all her previous life, full of dedication to God and men ...'. She is familiar with the holy books and has 'a profoundly religious disposition'. She already knows beforehand that the redeemer is coming to her. 'How the heart of Mary trembles at the thought that she will see him for whose coming she has prayed so much ... And already her lips murmur with ardent devotion "Behold the handmaid of the Lord". This surely must have been how Mary thought and prayed.'

This glorified portrayal of Mary runs counter to the text of the gospel. This has nothing to say in Mary's praise, either with regard to her origin or to any other factor already present in her from her past. It contains not a single word about her virtues and piety. In her case we are precisely not told, as we are in the case of Zechariah: 'Thy prayer is heard' (Lk 1:13), but instead of this 'Thou hast found grace with God' (1:30). She is chosen without any special prayer on her part. The encounter between her and the messenger of God takes place not in the holy city or in the hallowed sphere of the temple, but in the insignificant village of Nazareth and the half pagan district of Galilee. 'The extraordinary event takes place in an unexpected place and to an individual who, unlike the parents of John, has not previously possessed any very outstanding status' (Barth, 18). With her God initiates a new course of events in circumstances of complete insignificance. Unlike the parents of John she is not chosen by reason of her observance of the law or other virtues. She is endowed with grace (1:28). She is illumined not by any radiance which she possesses of herself, but rather 'because the light of God falls upon her' (Barth, 19). We do no service to the veneration of the mother of God if we make her a subject for our personal speculations and fantasies and, in defiance of the text, attempt to make value judgments about her from our own resources. No-one can accord her a more appropriate place than that assigned to her by scripture itself.

Reconstructions of the annunciation story
Many authors of sermons are exceedingly free in their reconstructions of the gospel. Since it fails to satisfy their bent for romantic elaborations they supplement it according to their own individual tastes. They find it possible to tell us far more than is contained in the text.

We should 'thank God for the fact that Luke, his conscientious chronicler, has acquired knowledge of the conversation between the angel and the mother of God which constitutes the source of today's gospel'. 'In the quiet of a humble house at Nazareth in the hidden land of the Jews kneels a maiden in the first bloom of her youth. She is Mary.' 'What she has been praying for so ardently over and over again is precisely the final coming of him who is promised by the prophets and eagerly awaited by the peoples. Then suddenly her chamber is suffused with an unearthly light, and as she raises her head she sees a prince of heaven bathed in sweet radiance.' 'She bends her ear to the revelation. She gazes upon him, hears and sees him.' 'What emotions and feelings must then have been aroused in Mary! But this is a moment which is wholly calculated to take away her breath and make her heart miss a beat . . .'. 'Here in this room in the life of this virgin, probably at her hour of prayer, world history is taking place.' More even than this, here 'without any exaggeration, takes place the most important event in the whole history of the world'.

Special interest is aroused by the angel. He is 'the one sent by God to woo the bride in order that the divine may enter into nuptials with the human'. He 'sinks upon his knees and adores the God hidden in the virgin's womb'. The whole world of angels is drawn into the reconstruction of this episode. Concerning their reactions to it opinions are divided: 'It is as though the angels in heaven had to interrupt their hymn of praise at this moment, as though all the heavenly choirs had to fall into silence in order to listen to what was taking place upon earth. The hour of destiny for humanity!' 'No music upon earth can render the jubilation which resounded through the heavenly spheres in that most blessed hour of the annunciation, a jubilation so loud and heartfelt that it seemed as though it was meant to conquer the entire world.' Emotional embellishments and extravagances of this kind betray a false focus of interest and one that is alien to the text. They trivialise the gospel and deprive it of its power of expression. The gospel itself is concerned neither with the idyll of a humble home in a little town, nor with the thunder of angelic music. The angel is the messenger, not the subject of the message. He claims our attention not for himself but for what he has to say. His message, therefore, must provide the focal point of the sermon.

The main underlying motive which prompts authors to indulge in historical reconstructions of the annunciation story is that they fail to recognise the literary form of the narrative. Its structure has been determined not by considerations of history, but by the pattern of the 'annunciations' so often to be met with in the tradition material of the bible.

The virgin birth
The virgin birth is to be numbered among the central assertions of the annunciation story. The composers of sermons show themselves ready to discourse upon it at length, but only exceptionally recognise the limits imposed upon them by the text. Whereas here the manner in which the virgin birth is brought about remains a mystery, they attempt to intrude upon it from curiosity and to illumine what they take to be its obscurities from the biological point of view.

Many preachers take Mary's question in Lk 1:34 as an expression of her vow of virginity and her resolute resistance to any demand for pre-marital intercourse. 'But she is already betrothed . . . and, from motives of loyal obedience to God, she is resolved to adhere uncompromisingly to the moral principles of her people, which regards every kind of sexual intercourse between those who have been betrothed as shameful. That which the angel promises her can take place not in the here and now, but only after the space of a year, when her espoused husband has already taken her into his home.' 'What man . . . would not be ready to receive an honour offered him, and what woman would not be susceptible to the seduction of a little flattery? Millions would have grasped at it with both hands in a transport of happiness and without much consideration. But Mary remains calm.' 'Is it not moving to see how even the message of an angel could not shake Mary in her basic principles . . . In all her joy at her election Mary keeps a clear head.' 'Her decision to preserve her virginity so long as she has not yet been brought into the home of her espoused husband is scrupulously respected by God.' Mary's encounter with the angel is taken to fix the point in time at which the conception would have taken place. In it the 'creative dialogue' finds its fulfilment. 'Now reverent silence. It is as though creation had been waiting for this moment, which is destined to change its fate for the better. Thoughtfully the virgin raises her head, full of interior emotion. Humbly she bows it once more and speaks the ever-memorable word in which all our salvation lies hidden ... Now fresh floods of heavenly light fill the chamber of the elect, transforming it into a cathedral ... And even while this God-man is resting beneath the heart of the virgin he is at the same time, according to his divine nature, everywhere ...'. 'What took place between Gabriel and Mary—the greeting, the moment of fear, the question and the answer, the commission and the assent—all this has brought together heaven and earth, God and man, time and eternity.' Some assertions lead, in various ways, directly to ideas associated with a theogamy. 'The Son of God wills to become man, true man with body and soul, flesh and blood. For this he, like every man, needs a father and a mother. A father he already has—his heavenly Father. This Father sends his angel to Mary in order that she may become the mother of his Son.' In another instance it is the Holy Spirit who has richly endowed Mary in order 'to make her capable and ready for the sacred moment when, as a divine bridegroom, he could lay the Son of God beneath her heart'. Mary is the bride of God, the bride 'of the Holy Spirit'. The climax of this tasteless approach is reached when the phenomenon of parthenogenesis among animals is adduced as an analogy to the virgin birth. 'In reality we modern men should feel less difficulties in this question. As no generation before us we have penetrated into the mysteries of how life comes to be. Today the biologist recognises a phenomenon known as parthenogenesis among animals, in other words virginal generation. By the application of certain chemicals he can cause egg cells to develop without sperm cells, and cause them to grow into adult beasts. Thus science provides a signpost for us ...'

Such misguided speculations are wholly alien to the annunciation story. In this the virgin birth is not taken as a prior condition in the biological sense for the existence of Jesus. There is no intention here of providing any physiological explanation of how the Spirit produces its effect in Mary. 'In no case should the power of the Spirit be understood as a divine seed of life... All too easily the danger arises of misunderstanding the virgin birth in a biological sense which is a distortion of the Chalcedonian doctrine of the two natures. This distortion, even if not directly expressed, is prone to influence our devotion in a manner which is all the more effective for being hidden, and to give rise to the impression that in Jesus we are dealing with something in the nature of a demi-god... To this the whole gospel of Luke is uncompromisingly opposed' (Voss 1964, 49). It is not a generating cause in the sense that a physical father is this. Ideas of God entering into marriage with a woman such as were widespread in the milieux which the early christians knew are foreign to the gospel. It has no interest in describing biological processes. Rather it proclaims that Jesus has his origin in God. It cannot, in the last analysis, be made to conform to our biological categories. God himself brings about the new beginning by the creative power of the Holy Spirit. This is expressed in sign and symbol through the virgin birth.

The question proposed by Mary (Lk 1:34) cannot be taken as indicating that she had taken a vow of virginity, or even as a sign of her faithfulness to her principles in the question of pre-marital intercourse. Such an interpretation distorts the emphasis of the pericope by transferring it to the moral sphere and obscuring its christological purpose. This verse has a stylistic function to perform in the structure of the narrative as a whole, and is used to bring out the full significance of the angel's message. 'Psychologising' conjectures about a conflict of conscience in Mary are quite alien to it.

On making the story relevant to the present
In the 'actualisation' of the annunciation story very different approaches are adopted, yet only few of them attain their goal.

Mary is presented as an example of undeviating steadfastness in the time of espousal. Over and above this she is accounted 'an example of virginity and motherhood'. The state of virginity is regarded as finding its basis in her and she is celebrated as 'the fairest flower in the garden of the church' and as 'an ideal ... by means of which all the hardships of life can be overcome'.

The angel's greeting is taken as an occasion to point out the importance of giving greetings, 'an old custom which must not be regarded as out of date'. '"God greet you". Every greeting that falls from our lips should be modelled on this wish.'

With regard to the first line of interpretation, this moralising and idealising approach cannot claim any support from the text. Any idea of providing a justification for the state of virginity is foreign to its intention. It is no part of the message of this text that it is only Mary's interior attitude of virginity that 'imparts to her motherhood soul, warmth, humanity, interior greatness' and that without this in the hour of the crucifixion she would have been broken with sorrow, 'and this precisely because of her motherhood'. Such an interpretation, which plays off the virginity against the motherhood of Mary, finds no basis in the gospel. It is not because of her virginity that Mary is called blessed, but because she has believed (Lk 1:45).

To the second line of argument it may be rejoindered that the importance of the salutation must not be denied. Yet in Lk 1:28 something more is implied. This verse is to be taken as something more than a mere greeting. It is a summons to messianic joy. What it asserts is that the *eschaton* has been inaugurated.

Several authors regard Mary not (or at least not only) as a private individual who has been endowed with grace, but as the representative of the people of God. This view is in conformity with the text. 'When God looked upon Mary then all of us were included in the regard of God and in his love.' When she answered his summons Mary did so as our representative. She acts from her own free decision in the surrender of herself as person. Her assent is not only an act of unconditional obedience, but an assent to Christ. Thus the claim upon us implicit in the annunciation story demands from us not merely submission to the will of God, but our assent to Christ. It is the content of her faith and of ours.

(b) SUGGESTIONS FOR PREACHING ON LK 1:26-38

The findings of exegesis are that Christ is the subject of the annunciation story. This is a fact of which we have to take due cognisance in our preaching. The text itself prohibits an interpretation that is primarily mariological. It demands that we shall preach on Christ. In our preaching Mary should assume that place which is accorded to her in the actual story.

The context in which this pericope is to be understood is not limited by the four walls of the quiet chamber at Nazareth. It is characterised by the messianic promise and expectation of the old covenant and the fulfilment of this in Jesus Christ. Every attempt at confining the message to the private circumstances of the individual misses the point of the text and deprives it of its dimension as an element in saving history. In interpreting the annunciation story in our sermons we might view it in the perspective of the structure of the Lucan infancy narrative as a whole and bring out the overriding importance of Jesus by including as a background the story of the annunciation of the birth of John. But an approach which would be no less legitimate would be to interpret Lk 1:26-38 as an independent story without referring in any direct sense to the immediate context. We shall opt for this latter approach. The first-mentioned approach, though perfectly valid, is more suitable for a congregation that is already acquainted with bible study. Such a wealth of different aspects arise from the comparisons involved in this approach that hearers who are not already thoroughly familiar with scripture will be confused.

Mary

Mary is presented as a virgin and as espoused. That is all that we are told about her—not her rank or royal descent, not any special achievements which single her out in God's eyes. She is as unknown as the village in which she dwells. Nazareth is a place which plays no part in the annals of Israel, much less in those of world history. It is to this place that the messenger of God comes, and to this insignificant individual, Mary. Precisely why she is chosen to be the mother of the Lord remains a mystery hidden in God which cannot be resolved by any facile formula. She is no superhuman figure, but a simple girl. She evinces no special quality making her apt for God's service, no extraordinary equipment for what he has in store for her. 'If in all that she is Mary is a witness to that which is extraordinary in God, this amounts to saying that this extraordinary element is the compassion of God which concerns itself with humanity' (Barth, 17). This quality alone can be praised. As it is with Mary so too it is with the christian community. 'God chose what is low and despised in the world, even things that are not, to bring to nothing things that are, so that no human being might boast in the presence of God' (1 Cor 1:28f).

'Rejoice thou who hast been endowed with grace' (Lk 1:28). This messianic call is not addressed to Mary in some sense as a purely private individual. She represents Israel. She stands for the people of God of the old and new covenants as she receives the message of salvation. In her person the church has found grace in God's sight and has been accepted by him. The church experiences in Mary that the bestowal of grace is the true basis for her joy.

Jesus

The grace becomes effective in the covenant which God seals with his people. This has been the pattern in the history of Israel right from the outset: 'the Lord is with thee'. The promise which is implicit in this reiterated message of God to his people attains its fulfilment in Jesus. He is the embodiment of the 'God with us', the Immanuel in person. His titles of dignity confirm this: 'Son of the Most High', 'Son of David', 'King over the house of Jacob', 'Son of God'. He is the goal of the expectations of the people of God. In him God enters into history.

In the annunciation story the centre of interest is Jesus, and Jesus as messiah. He is the subject of the angel's message, the focal point of the entire narrative. Without him it would be nothing, 'as absurd as a predicate suspended in mid air without its subject' (Barth, 23). He who sets himself to continue the proclamation of the angel must say 'Jesus'. Everything depends upon him. If he goes unmentioned then everything is suspended in mid air. 'The radiance of God's favour which lies over the mother is proper to her Son, and extended to the mother only because of him. In the same way it is solely and exclusively on account of this one man Jesus that God regards all of us with love' (Iwand, 206).

With Jesus the new creation begins. It does not lie within the sphere of human powers. Mary owes her son neither to her husband nor to her virginity, but to God alone. He fulfils his promises, he is the creator who summons the new life into being. It is in this that the miracle consists of which the virginal conception is a sign. Jesus is not brought into being through this miracle merely in order to become one more member in a genealogical list. In him God is at work in a quite direct manner right from the outset. The Spirit of God, present at the first moment of the old creation, presides over the new creation also. Jesus is brought into being by the Spirit. He owes his existence right from its origins to the Holy Spirit. In him the Spirit of God manifests itself, and through him the Spirit imparts itself to his church.

Faith
'Insofar as we men become sharers in this event, we become so

in the person of Mary, Mary who respects the limitations of her own nature, who allows God truly to be God' (Iwand, 204). The 'otherness' of God to man is not removed in this encounter, but asserted in all humility. 'Behold the handmaid of the Lord' (1:38). Mary is God's creature, his possession. She knows and acknowledges that what she is she has received from God. Her answer here is that assent to God's word, that assent to Jesus, which, in all freedom, she gives with her whole existence. 'Obedience and faith are the ultimate response which can be expressed from our side—from the side of humanity—to the message, the tidings which so much exceed all our preconceptions, all our understanding. This is Mary ... This is the true church which continues to stand by her response: Behold the handmaid of the Lord, be it done unto me according to thy word' (Iwand, 206).

2 *The story of Christmas (Lk 2: 1–20)*

The distortion of the festival of Christmas is widely deplored. Anyone who sets himself not merely to fall in resignedly with this chorus of lamentation, but rather to overcome the externalism involved, must begin by attempting to establish its root causes. He should not be too hasty merely to pillory profiteering business interests and advertising agencies. The roots of the evil lie deeper than this. Christian preachers themselves have to ask themselves whether they do not have to take a decisive share of the blame for the devaluation of this festival. If today they find themselves to a large extent helpless in the face of forces destructive to this festival, have not they themselves conjured up the spirits responsible for these forces? Is the effect of their preaching to arouse merely the sentimentality associated with Christmas, or do they bear witness to the gospel of Christmas? Does their preaching grow from the central message of Christ, or does it remain stuck fast at the level of vague 'Christmassy' sentiment?

PREACHING THE CHRISTMAS STORIES

(a) THE SERMON LITERATURE

The sermon models available are very often governed by dogmatic considerations, or else treat in very general terms God's love, and our love for God and man, or condemn in somewhat violent terms the degradation of the Christmas festival. In comparison with these only very few attempts are made to interpret the text of the Christmas narrative. Admittedly individual sayings are frequently seized upon and treated in isolation from their context. On the basis of the various points of view presented in them the sermon models which we have examined may be divided into the following groups:

> The retelling of the Christmas story
> The child in the manger
> The birth of Christ and the eucharist
> Christmas joy.

The retelling of the Christmas story

Whereas in scripture the birth of Christ is of only secondary importance in comparison with his death and resurrection, in the sermon literature it is accorded the place of honour. The phrase 'celebrating the memory' may be taken as characteristic of the interpretation of Christmas presented by most authors of sermons. They insist upon the duty of remembering the birth of Jesus. They celebrate his 'birthday'. They look back into the past and eagerly bend themselves to the task of freely paraphrasing the gospel in their own language and trying to make the individuals mentioned in it live before their hearers once more. In doing this they very rarely restrain themselves from describing more than the actual text admits of. Many preachers cannot content themselves with using their own powers of imagination to elaborate upon the motifs of the biblical narrative. They base their considerations on legends which are totally foreign to the gospel text. Many preachers regard their task as consisting essentially in putting their hearers in a Christmas mood and constructing a world of unreality about them as though everything were now as, according to their ideas, it must have been then. An examination of a representative number of sermon models reveals the fact that all betray a single unambiguous tendency: they aim to produce the same effect as the Christmas plays and representations of the crib. They try to construct a scene as vividly as possible before their hearers, and do not hesitate to 'fill out' the gospel narrative, 'unfortunately all too brief', according to their own inclinations so as to give it a 'more effective' presentation. The original intention behind the narrative is suppressed, and arbitrary personal interests of the preacher's own are superimposed upon it. In this process the preacher's delight in romanticising and legendary embellishments bears fruit in the strangest forms. Personages, beasts and ideas which are wholly foreign to the text are introduced, which rather reflect a dubious chapter in the history of western devotion than bear witness to the gospel. All this is designed to induce a temporary Christmas mood in the hearers, or to intensify this mood when it is already present. As in a certain type of film, they are introduced into a dream world which is neither the world they live in nor that of the gospel. This provides us with an essential part of the answer to the question of how the festival of Christmas has come to be distorted. The way to a renewal of it can only succeed when a halt is called to certain customs in the practice of preaching which are extremely widespread right up to the present day, and if we concentrate afresh upon the gospel.

The treatment here is in complete contrast to the loquaciousness of so many sermons. For the birth of Jesus is related with astonishing restraint 'as though the narrator was afraid that if he were to spend too long in relating the circumstances in any closer detail and in mentioning special points of interest, he would merely draw attention away from the event itself' (Schürmann, LUM 29). All the strands in the narrative lead up to the proclamation of the message. Those who seek to lend emphasis to it with highly coloured descriptions after the manner of baroque representations of the crib, produce the opposite effect. So soon as they set the scenic elements in the foreground the actual message is either suppressed or distorted. We can indicate three specific ways in which this comes about:

(i) There is a tendency to depict the characters of the shepherds in accordance with a preconceived pattern. This dictates that precisely those to whom the advent of the messiah is first proclaimed must be especially suited for the privilege: men of faith who know their bible, devout and incorrupt. How could God call persons of ill repute or 'undevout' persons to the crib?

In the actual story the shepherds are introduced primarily as a messianic motif. If over and above this they represent a specific class, then this is precisely not that of the devout but that of the poor, the insignificant and the despised. God breaks through the patterns imposed by our human expectations. When he calls the shepherds he does not require any prior dispositions already present in them in the form of special virtues. They have nothing to recommend them. From the social and religious point of view they are *déclassé*, the last who become the first. Their election is a grace. The saviour of the poor and sinners has been born.

(ii) The emphasis on descriptions designed to evoke subjective atmosphere and mood leads inevitably to the event of Christmas being treated as a matter of private feeling (the idyll of the crib, the Christmas of the soul, Christmas as a specifically German institution). This approach runs counter to the entire message of the gospel of Christmas, which bears witness to the fact that the event of Bethlehem is something that affects the entire cosmic order (2:1). The messiah is the Lord not merely of the individual's soul, but of the world (2:11, 14).

(iii) Christian preaching remains essentially rooted in the history of Jesus, and in this sense has constantly, amongst other things, a commemorative character (see below p 337). But it is not the sort of commemoration that the celebration of a birthday is, in which we cast our minds back to the joys of the past. It is of the essence of *anamnesis* that it affects the present also. When in our preaching we call to mind the salvation which was achieved once and for all, we do so in the power of the Lord as present to us in the here and now, and in a manner that summons men and lays claim upon their present lives. Thus the scene of Luke's Christmas story is no longer merely Bethlehem but the church. The message goes forth *today* (2:11), 'and we must not, from the perspective of our own times, change that "today" into "at that time"' (Bertsch DW 1, 223).

In many sermons ideas are put forward which are quite unrealistic. They encourage congregations to indulge in the fantasy that everything is still the same as it was then. Instead of drawing the message into our 'today' they attempt to transfer the hearers back to a realm of 'at that time' which, for the most part, has merely been conjured up by their own subjective fantasies. This leads to theological falsifications, and is, in the last analysis, impossible of achievement.

Neither the birth of Jesus nor the congregation of the present must be withdrawn from their respective places in history. The faithful of today achieve contact with the event which took place then not through an artificial regression which represents the greatest possible danger to faith, but solely by believing in the Lord actually present to them, who is none other than that Jesus Christ who was born at Bethlehem. Bethlehem constitutes a stage on his journey which certainly must not be overlooked. But it is not the goal of that journey, to which we have to return. The Christmas gospel summons us to a fresh awareness of the presence to us of *Christos Kyrios*.

The child in the manger
The message of the angels has the effect of setting the child in the manger in the centre of the Christmas story. It follows that this must constitute the centre of our preaching also. For this reason we can only welcome the fact that so much attention is

paid to this in the sermon literature. Unfortunately many sermons indulge in idealisations of childhood and attempts to carry their hearers back to a childhood paradise. This treatment of the child in the manger in terms of a romantic idealisation of childhood is quite unworthy and reveals a total misunderstanding of the real message of the text.

(i) The child in the manger has come to be surrounded with an aura of the miraculous in which, as we have seen, the factor of sentimentalising plays its part. But side by side with this a further factor makes itself manifest, namely that mysterious undercurrent of monophysitism which runs through our average christological interpretations. This continues to make itself felt in our preaching and devotions right up to the present. Against this what we are told of in the Christmas gospel is an event which belongs in the fullest possible sense to this world. No angel guards the crib. No halo of glory is to be discerned. Mary's son is no prodigy, but an ordinary child. The intention underlying the text is precisely the opposite of any kind of docetism ('veil', 'enveloped'), namely to emphasise that in becoming man God had endured the ultimate in self-abasement and lack of recognition, that he has become fully a man of this world and not a golden child of heaven. The message to the angels, as presented by Luke, is already stamped with the Easter confession of faith in Christ the king, and does not speak of God as a child who is merely all smiles and lovability.

(ii) The regression to the paradise of childhood is just as unworthy and as dangerous as the false idealisation of the crib. No support can be claimed for this approach from the dominical saying of Mt 18:3: 'The purpose of the comparison with a child is to point not ... to any particular intrinsic quality in childhood, as, for instance, its openness, kindness, innocence etc, but rather to that which a child is always and of its very nature, namely small' (Haenchen 1966, 346). Childhood possesses no special attribute or disposition in virtue of which the kingdom of God is bestowed upon it. It is precisely because it is insignificant and of no account that it is suitable for this in the eyes of God. This is the *tertium comparationis*, the common factor in the comparison. The exhortation that the hearers shall become as children leads immediately into infantilism. By concentrating our conscious faith exclusively upon a specific phase in human development the opportunity which each new phase in life opens up to the believer is lost. Furthermore the idealisation of childhood springs from wishful thinking, and betrays a deficient knowledge of the true mentality of the child.

The birth of Christ and the eucharist
Since Christmas preaching takes place almost exclusively in the context of the celebration of the eucharist, many preachers try to establish a connection between the birth of Jesus on the one hand, and transubstantiation and communion on the other. Yet neither the gospel of Christmas nor any other part of the biblical message provides any grounds for such a connection.

It is suggested that there is a parallel between Jesus being born in Bethlehem then and being 'born' in us now. But this is misleading. In effect it does away with the fundamental difference between the life of Jesus of Nazareth as a unique and unrepeatable event and our encounter with him in the sacrament which is not identical with this, for it fails to express the fact that this sacramental encounter goes beyond that earthly life. The gospel knows nothing of any birth of Jesus in our souls. What it records is that he was born of Mary. Certainly according to the witness of the bible Christ does bring about a new birth in us. But this is derived not from his birth but rather from his death and resurrection.

Any approach in which the eucharist is traced back to the birth of Jesus is in principle to be challenged. The eucharist is a sacrament of Easter. Its connection with Christmas is based upon the doctrine of the incarnation and leads to a static interpretation of the eucharist, as though it were mainly an ontological projection of the hypostatic union. If, on the other hand, the paschal mystery is recognised as the centre and starting-point of the eucharist, then its dynamic character stands revealed. This vision is in accordance with the understanding of the eucharist found in the early church and in the constitution on the liturgy.

Peace

The theme of peace figures prominently in sermons on Christmas, and rightly so for the proclamation of peace is a central factor in the content of the Christmas gospel. But the peace spoken of in the angels' hymn (Lk 2:14) signifies not a specific interior attitude on the part of the individual ('peace of soul'), but that eschatological salvation which has its basis in the coming of the messiah. 'What is in question here is not *eirene* in the sense of peace both as between individuals and between mankind and God. What is meant by peace in the angels' message is rather that now salvation has come to be upon the earth' (TWNT II, 411). This peace is no mere wish which still awaits its fulfilment. Its presence among men is just as real as that of the messiah himself. Christ is our peace (salvation) in his own person.

It is through him that God has chosen men. It is because he is present in whom the Father is well pleased (cf Mk 1:11 par) that there are 'men of God's favour', men who have been endowed with peace (salvation) in Jesus. This peace is not delivered into their hands in such a way that they can dispose of it as they will. Their enjoyment of it is not due to any moral qualifications on their part, not to their own good will but to that of God.

The translation 'to men who have good will . . .' fails to do justice to the text. It ascribes to our human will what belongs to God alone. Unfortunately this rendering still persists in catholic sermon literature with the interpretations arising from it, a sign of how little influence exegesis has had up to now. A translation of Lk 2:14 which is faithful to the actual text is urgently needed in our preaching and liturgy alike (cf the *Gloria*). Obedience to the word of God demands this.

(b) SUGGESTIONS FOR PREACHING ON LK 2:1–20
The Christmas narrative of Lk 2:1–20 falls into three parts. It comprises the birth of Jesus in Bethlehem (2:1–7), the message of the angels (2:8–14) and the tidings brought by the shepherds (2:15–20). The arrangement of the sections prescribed for public reading still assigns the first two parts to the first Christmas mass, while the third section is assigned to the second mass. Our preaching will follow the development of the gospel itself.

The hearers will have been familiar with the text from their youth upwards. It is so well known to them that all too easily they will fail to notice what it says. They already 'know' beforehand what is coming next, and what the text has to say. There is a real danger that right from the first sentence onwards their minds will be guided into familiar paths and preconceived notions which are not in accordance with the gospel. A fixed 'Christmas pattern' very easily imposes itself, which represents an obstacle to real living attention. Many hearers expect this, but not all of their expectations should be fulfilled. The preacher is ruled primarily and essentially by the text, and not by the wishes of his hearers.

(i) The gospel of the first mass of Christmas Lk 2:1–14

The birth upon earth
Lk 2:1–14 appropriately combines the birth of Jesus and its interpretation through the heavenly revelation as the gospel of the first Christmas mass. The first section (2:1–7) goes beyond the ideas which have become familiar to us. It is challengingly earthly, of this world, realistic, without any glorification. 'It happened'—these are the opening words of the sober narrative. What follows next is not a statement such as 'that the Son of God came down to assume our flesh and blood', but 'that a

decree went out from Caesar Augustus'. The tone is set by the mention of Augustus and Quirinius. This is a story concerned with the world in which they rule and exact tribute. They make the arrangements. Joseph and Mary conform their lives to the commandment of these and so journey to Bethlehem. The part they play is that of humble people without privileges or connections in the vast ramifications of the Roman world-empire. There is not a single word in the text to suggest that they realise the true significance of their journey. They act in obedience to Caesar and his representative. On arriving at the goal of their journey Mary brings forth her firstborn son into the world—into *this* world! The event is mentioned without any special emphasis—almost in parenthesis. Nothing extraordinary is happening here. The newborn child, like any other child, is wrapped in swaddling clothes and, because there is no other place available, laid in a manger. That is all. What we expect is angels and a heavenly light. What we find is the civil authority, tax-gathering, a journey, birth and swaddling clothes—everyday factors in our world. God goes altogether unmentioned. It is as though in this whole episode he were absent.

Proclamation in heaven
The scene changes. The story moves on to the second act (2: 8–14), to its centre and climax. The scene opens with the shepherds—people, therefore, who are of no account and do not enjoy any good repute. And there is nothing particularly remarkable about those mentioned here. They do what all shepherds do—they care for their animals, they watch over their flocks. There is nothing to indicate that they are particularly well equipped and prepared for an encounter with God. In the midst of their daily and quite ordinary work in the fields they are surrounded by the radiance of God's glory. How could they fail to be overcome with great fear, when they were touched so immediately by his presence? How could they not be terrified to find the old world, so defined by their own expectations and

human resources, at an end, and a new world beginning? Without this profound fear at the advent of God we cannot understand the significance of Christmas.

It is to those upon whom great fear has fallen that the messenger of God proclaims great joy. No words are capable of describing this. This joyful tidings, this gospel, is the centre of the whole narrative, the central point of our preaching too. It comes not from man, but to him. It is not something that he discovers for himself, but rather something that he receives. God himself proclaims himself in it, and makes known what has taken place. Every word here is important. 'You'—so runs the form of address. It refers not only to the shepherds but to 'all people' (2:10), the people of God.

This 'you' lays claims upon the preacher, directing him to instruct those whom he is addressing in the message of Christmas and to explain this in terms of their own thought and their own language. He must not withdraw himself into the realm of 'then and there', but must rather engage himself in the context of 'today'. Where the gospel is proclaimed, there is this context of 'today', the 'today' of the coming of the Lord. God proclaims the newborn child as the promised messiah ('in the city of David'), the saviour and Lord, and thereby reveals that he himself has come to us in him.

The sign
The royal proclamation is followed by a reference to the sign. The shepherds and all those who hear the message are directed to turn to the child in the manger.

In this way the connection is forged between the first part of the story and the second, and this connecting link is itself momentous. God who has seemed to be silent in this episode which belongs so utterly to the real world (2:1–7) brings its true significance to light. He points to the sign which, without his intervention, would have been overlooked. In the light of his words the events begin to assume a fresh meaning for the

PREACHING THE CHRISTMAS STORIES

hearers. Admittedly the word and the reality pointed to seem to contradict one another: here the royal proclamation, there the crib; here the saviour and Lord, there the child in swaddling clothes. Who can unite the two? Only the believer can find the connection. He sees that here the mysterious paradox by which God abases himself, empties himself and takes the form of a servant (cf Phil 2:5–11) begins. It is his way into our world, a way which ends at the cross. God is man, 'overturning all our ideas of God, poor and ungodlike, yet by the very fact that he ceases to remain in the heaven that is his not ceasing to be himself, bringing himself to us' (Gollwitzer GPM 11, 24). The real God is real man, wrapped in swaddling clothes (this is mentioned twice over lest anyone should fail to notice it), not a miracle child but a child of this earth. He does not merely assume an earthly veil soon to pass away. He puts himself wholly in our place, becoming so insignificant, belonging so wholly to this world that we can fail to recognise him, can deny him, and only by listening to a revelation from heaven can we see him for what he really is and understand aright the events attendant upon his birth.

It appears, then, who the 'Lord' of this story really is: not Augustus or Quirinius, who initially appear and exercise their authority, but God. He directs their actions. He has them so much under his control that they set in motion the entire Roman civil service in order that Jesus may be born in the city of David in accordance with God's own will and in conformity to his promise. Step by step the story advances from Augustus in Rome to the child in the manger at Bethlehem. Whereas Caesar may extol himself as Lord and saviour of the world, the real ruler is he whom God proclaims to be Lord and saviour, and whom the church confesses to be such, Jesus. He was born in our world (in the world of Augustus, Quirinius and Pontius Pilate) in order that in it he might enter upon his dominion. In him there is glory in the highest (for God) and on earth peace (salvation) for men of (God's) good favour.

(ii) The gospel of the second mass of Christmas (Luke 2 : 15–20)
The angels have gone. The shepherds are left alone with their flocks in the fields, and yet they are not abandoned. Certainly it seems at first as though now they alone occupy the stage. They speak and come to decisions, they come and find, see and make known, return and pray. Yet all this is dominated by the 'thing that the Lord has made known' (2:15). They do not 'find' him of themselves. They have listened to his word. They have been seized by the glory (*doxa*) which radiates about them, and they prove themselves to be men of his good favour (*eudokia*). In them is 'described the Christmas faith of the christian community precisely in this process of summoning one another and hastening, seeking and finding, seeing and bearing witness. It finds expression in the way in which many individuals react in astonishment to the Christmas event, above all in the way in which that particular individual (Mary) reacts who keeps the word in her heart and ponders it there . . .' (Hamel, GPM 15, 26).

The shepherds set out
The shepherds speak to one another and summon one another. 'Come, let us go to Bethlehem . . .' (2:15). Their departure is the outcome of no isolated decision. Here is the christian community which rouses itself to dare the challenging journey which leads from the place of God's revelation to the earthly reality of the child in the manger (at this initial stage these are two distinct factors). They set out in haste, take the gospel at its word. For them there is nothing more important. Because they set out they arrive at their goal. They find what they seek. But who is it, precisely, whom they find? Two young parents and the child in the manger—nothing superhuman in this! What can all this have to do with God? Yet it is in this way and in no other that God intends events to develop. Thus they are promised 'You will find the child wrapped in swaddling clothes and lying in a manger' (2:12). There alone is he to be found.

What they see they connect with what they have been told. It is in this that their faith is made manifest and authenticated. They see where in literal fact there is nothing particular to be seen, no glimmer of that glory which shone about them. They 'see' in this child the redeemer, the Christ, the Lord. When they have seen it they make known what has been proclaimed to them. They become messengers bearing the tidings which they themselves have received. They, quite ordinary insignificant men, laymen, are the first messengers of the gospel. They continue the mission of the angels. For this there is no need of any pulpit or any special level of education. He who hears the message hands it on. He who seeks to use it merely for his own edification and religious satisfaction has surely never heard it at all.

The tidings evoke astonishment. Who could receive such tidings as this as a matter of course? Mary—the type of the christian community which hears and believes—keeps these things (words) in her heart and sees the connection between them. She unites what she hears with what she sees.

Return to the flocks
The shepherds return to their flocks—but not in weary disillusionment. They praise and extol God for everything which they have heard and seen. Reflection gives rise to thanksgiving.

It is natural to extend the application of this statement in our preaching, applying it to the eucharist, the great thanksgiving for which the christian community gathers itself together. Yet this should be no isolated event, an island, as it were, of praise offered to God. The situation should not be one of glorifying God here while outside the drabness of everyday continues. The shepherds turn their steps not to the temple but back to the fields. The praise of God resounds in the mundane circumstances of their everyday lives. It is there that they were touched by God's presence, thither that their way leads, and it is not pursued any further. 'What we are told of here is not an exodus, a flight from the world, but the redemptive intervention of God into this world of ours . . .' (Eichholz, 33), his faithfulness and the faithfulness of those who are his own to the earth. This is the theme which dominates the Christmas gospel.

3 The story of the magi (Mt 2:1-12)

The festival of the manifestation of the Lord has its origins in the eastern church. It arose almost at the same time as the Roman festival of Christmas—c 300—and, like this, was primarily celebrated as the festival of Christ's birth. This was combined with the commemoration of his baptism in the Jordan and of the miracle at the marriage feast of Cana. In the course of the fourth century the festival of the epiphany became known in the West, while the celebration of Christmas was disseminated in the East. The juxtaposition of the two festivals led to a division of their earlier content. The eastern church followed the western in the celebration of Christ's birth on the 25th December, while Rome separated the adoration of the magi from Christmas and made it the central point of the festival of the epiphany. While the commemoration of the baptism of Jesus and that of the marriage festival at Cana were accorded a place here also, they nevertheless remained in the background. As a result of the translation of the presumed relics of the 'three holy kings' from Milan to Cologne, the veneration of these became, to an increasing extent, the dominant theme of the festival of the epiphany, especially in the German-speaking sphere, so that in the popular estimation it assumed more the character of a saint's day ('the three holy kings') than a festival of the Lord.

(a) THE SERMON LITERATURE
This historical development of the festival finds its counterpart in the overall impression offered by the sermon literature. Whereas scant attention is paid to the epiphany of the Lord and the commemoration of his baptism and the marriage feast

at Cana, the support of the gospel is invoked for ever-fresh variations on the motifs of the 'three holy kings', their journey and their gifts. Even Israel and the foreign missions do not go unnoticed.

The magi
'... then the magi came from the East to Jerusalem...' (Mt 2:1). This is the brief and sober statement of fact which we find in scripture. Plainly it is quite different from the fantasies which flourish in the sermon models which are proposed. Scripture contains not a single adjective which would characterise the magi in any greater detail. The story mentions neither the number of them nor the colour of their skins. It speaks neither of their royal status nor of their princely caravan, neither of their traits of character nor of their knowledge of scripture. The attempt to interpret them as representatives of the academic class as opposed to the workers (the shepherds) in order to make Christ and christendom acceptable in higher circles has its basis not in the text but in the inferiority complex of the preachers themselves.

The intention of the text is not to make the magi the focal point of interest, but rather to concentrate our attention upon the 'newborn king of the Jews' (2:2) whom they proclaim. This fact is overlooked in most sermon models. Here attention is fixed so exclusively upon the magi and upon all that has been made of them down the centuries that the central figure of the whole episode is almost overlooked. Yet what we say about the magi in our preaching should be what the story tells us—no more, while conversely what we say about Christ should be what the story tells us and no less. Only so will the festival of the epiphany too be brought back to its true origins.

The theme of the magi and its relevance to the present
(i) It is no part of Matthew's intention to include a vivid record of the journey as part of his story of the magi. He does

not let fall a single word about the hardships of the journey or the mockery endured at the hands of their fellow men. 'Historicising' embellishments of this kind are alien to the gospel and should be rejected. They turn the hearers' attention away from the message of the text itself, and arouse an interest that is false. The message of the 'newborn king of the Jews' (2:2) constitutes the focal point of the story.

(ii) Another approach adopted by preachers is to make the story relevant to the present by taking the journey of the magi as a model of the way to be travelled by believers. Against any such approach the following considerations should be borne in mind. Certainly the presentation of faith as self-commitment, as the accepting of a challenge, as a break with the past and a state of being on a journey is firmly rooted in the bible and hence is a legitimate approach for the preacher, the more so since as a result of certain changes which have taken place in the church's understanding of her own nature she has arrived at a new awareness of herself today as the people of God on pilgrimage. In proclaiming such a message preachers are fully justified in pointing to certain central passages of the old and new testaments. But whether they can claim such explicit support from Mt 2:1–12 is doubtful. The exegesis of this pericope suggest that a different line of argument must be followed. The narrative is not so much a story of faith as one of epiphany. It is not the magi and their journey that occupy the centre of the stage but Jesus and the message of his messiahship. And however justified it may be to bring out secondary features in a given pericope in order to make it actual and relevant to the present, it is vital never to lose sight of the central point of it in the process. This must remain the determining factor in the total message we draw from it. It seems that all too often the interpretations of preachers proceed not from the text itself but from the preacher's own preconceptions of what his beliefs must entail, which he has read into the text.

The gifts

The symbolic interpretation of the gifts which the magi bring to the child is greatly enlarged upon in the sermon literature. On the one hand a symbolic value is attached to these gifts. They are regarded as preliminary indications of who Jesus is and how his life is to end. On the other hand they serve to 'express the inner convictions of the wise men' and—this is how their present relevance is brought out in conformity with this—to show how we should come to Christ. Each gift, considered as symbol, has an ambivalent force. On the question of what precise function of Christ the particular gifts point to, or alternatively what attitude on the part of the magi and of christians they signify, there is a wide divergence of views. Generally speaking gold is taken to signify Christ's kingship, but also his divinity. It is meant to remind us of our duty of faith, of loyalty, love and the sacrifice of our possessions.

The incense is meant to point to Christ's divinity, his priesthood and his sanctity. It summons us to adoration and to participating in the liturgy, to reverence, honour and hope. The myrrh is intended to signify the humanity of Jesus, his cross, his role as redeemer and his immortality, and it acquires a significance that is almost universal. It calls upon our willingness to sacrifice and endure suffering, our readiness to bear the cross, our love and self-surrender.

The individual gifts are taken together and interpreted as an expression of faith, self-giving, the sacrifice of wisdom, obedience and love, and the acknowledgment of the king.

The wide variation between these suggestions enables us to recognise how questionable the symbolical interpretation of the individual gifts is. It is inspired not by the text but by ideas which are foreign to the text and not infrequently adopted for quite arbitrary reasons. The interpretation which refers the individual gifts respectively to the kingship, the divinity and the burial of Jesus can indeed claim support from the Fathers, but has no basis in Mt 2:11. Taken together with the gesture of worship, the handing over of gifts is an act of homage to one recognised to be king. We should adhere to the meaning of the text and reject all interpretations which go beyond this; above all we should avoid making them the sole subject of a sermon.

Israel and her messiah
Exegetical examination reveals that what lies in the background of Mt 2:1–12, as in that of the gospel of Matthew as a whole, is the confrontation between the early christian community and the judaism of its time. This story serves to indicate how the representatives of Israel deny the messiah right from the very outset. Many authors of sermons advert to this problem because it finds expression in the text itself. But their manner of presenting it is in many cases questionable. First the assertion that Israel condemns the Gentiles wholesale as rejected and accursed contradicts what we are told by scripture. Certainly the old testament does contain severe warnings and oracles of judgment against the peoples, but side by side with these it proclaims in unmistakable terms that they will also be sharers in the messianic salvation (cf Jeremias, ET 55). Mt 2: 1–12 takes the homage of the wise men precisely as a fulfilment of this promise.

Israel expects that salvation will come to all peoples, and is herself the mediator of this. She shows the Gentiles the way to the messiah. This point is clearly expressed in the story of the magi, and must not be neglected. The sharp antithesis between the disbelief and rejection of the Jews on the one hand, and the faith of the Gentiles on the other, makes the message all the simpler. Certainly Israel does not escape serious condemnation on the grounds that she has denied the messiah although she herself is the bearer of the promise. But side by side with this, witness is borne no less clearly to that which is her inalienable function. Without Israel the Gentiles would never have found the messiah.

Thus to present Jerusalem alone as the great obstacle to finding the way to Christ is wholly to distort the objective meaning of the text. This contains not a single word to suggest that the holy city put the magi to the test by placing such immense obstacles in their path. On the contrary, what is stated is surely that it is only by means of the information given them there that they arrive at their goal. This is a point which must not be overlooked. The fact of Israel's vocation and the fact of her denial are set side by side as her destiny and the burden of guilt which she has to bear. Both factors are included in Matthew's presentation of her.

Second, kerygmatic aspects: our exegetical analysis warns us not to indulge in any one-sided or distorted presentations, and forbids us to resolve the dialectical tension between the election of Israel and her denial of her messiah by opting for one of these factors at the expense of the other. This means that the preaching of the message of this gospel entails no easy task for the preacher. It is rendered all the more difficult by the fact that our contemporary situation is quite different from that envisaged by Matthew, in which the early christian community had to assert its own independence and justify its own existence against the Jewish community. The centuries which have elapsed between then and now are filled with denials of Israel on the part of christians, and make it impossible for us to speak of their guilt without first acknowledging our own. A further point is that while it is certainly true that the Jews who are alive today are, as 'Israel', involved in the denial of the chosen people, their share in this denial is different from that for which those who actually crucified Jesus are responsible. Just as the catholic church finds herself today in a different position with regard to the protestant churches than at the time of the reformation, so too the situation in which the christian message is to be preached has changed in relation to Israel. And finally the preacher has to reckon with the fact that the concepts 'Jews', 'Jerusalem', 'Israel' have today acquired secular connotations in the minds of the hearers, and have a different content than that which they bear in scripture. Precisely at this point a mere repetition of individual words and phrases would fail to do justice to the message of the bible itself. It is of primary importance that a fresh awareness should be awakened of the special position of Israel—a position which she still enjoys to this day— precisely in the sense conveyed by scripture.

These considerations show that today more than ever it is illegitimate to indulge in wholesale condemnations of 'the' Jews of a discriminating kind. And it is just as illegitimate to represent Jerusalem, without further qualification, as the type of unbelief. We must reject as vigorously as possible that attitude which stigmatises the 'holy city' as the arsenal of all those weapons which are characteristic of a world grown hostile to God, and in which the Jews are scornfully referred to as the 'Jewish tribe' and condemned as the type of the unprincipled and of those lacking in moral concern. This is an attitude which is totally indefensible either on the basis of scripture or on that of the spirit of christian preaching, and which is in contradiction to the *Constitution on the Jews* of the second Vatican Council.

The homage of the Gentiles
Many sermons interpret the magi as the 'first fruits' and representatives of the Gentiles. Their homage is regarded as a sign 'that Christ has come as redeemer not merely to the people of Israel, but to the Gentile world as well'. He is the king of the world and the epiphany is taken as the missionary festival of the church. It is true that it is part of Israel's expectations that at the end of the days the peoples will come in streams to Zion, and become sharers in the salvation of Israel. The story of the magi announces the fulfilment of this promise. The Gentiles come in order to do homage to the messiah. Yet at the same time Mt 2:1–12, in common with scripture in general, entertains a conception of the Gentiles which is different from that of many preachers. Magi are not poor pagan children who need to be

ransomed by any alms of ours. They appear as anything but poor and disconsolate individuals. The narrative does not refer in any direct sense to the mission to the Gentiles. No mission is being sent to the magi in their own homeland. By means of his sign God summons them to Jerusalem. This is in accordance with the expectations of the old testament from which any idea of missionary activity is absent. The coming of the Gentiles is an eschatological deed of God.

Admittedly it is noteworthy that the story of the magi is set at the beginning of the gospel which ends with the missionary precept. Christ, to whom the Gentiles do homage even at this stage by their very coming, sends out his disciples as risen Lord, in order to proclaim his kingdom. His commission in Mt 28:18–20 is the logical outcome to which the story of the magi points, and in some sense it counterbalances it. Hence it is legitimate to connect it with the church's missions. Admittedly here, as in the biblical message in general, a strong impetus is given to missionary work. God brings about the coming of the Gentiles. Right from its very origins missionary work is the eschatological act of God and not the work of men. All ideological strategies in missionary work which are inspired by anti-communism or other polemical attitudes, and which betray themselves in their militaristic vocabulary, stand condemned by the gospel. The Gentiles come—this is the message of the story—to do homage to Christ. That is the goal of missionary work. It is concerned with the recognition of his dominion.

(b) SUGGESTIONS FOR PREACHING ON THE STORY OF THE MAGI

The manifestation of Christ
There is a certain parallelism between Mt 2:1–12 and the Lucan version of the Christmas narrative. In both cases the theme of the story is the revelation of Jesus, his 'manifestation'. But how is he made manifest? In such a way that he enters into

history, into this world of ours, in which Herod (or alternatively Augustus) is the ruler. He does not come in the dazzling epiphany of a Caesar, but unnoticed, in a manner so everyday that he would almost have passed unnoticed if God had not revealed the true significance of him, in the Lucan narrative (Lk 2) through the message of the angels, here by giving the magi a sign, and then by making them in turn become a sign. For their journey—initially with Jerusalem as its goal—is the fulfilment of the old testament promises of salvation. Their coming reveals the advent of the messiah. He is the central point of the story, and should be the centre of the sermon too.

The magi, representatives of the Gentiles, respond to 'the call which comes from God first in their own way and according to their own understanding in the miraculous star which for them is the sign of God' (Eichholz, 45). They come to Jerusalem, the holy city with the holy mountain, the goal of the Gentile pilgrimage (Is 2:2f). Here they find no knowledge of the event which has prompted their journey. King and city react with fear. So soon as the question is put concerning the 'newborn king of the Jews' straightway we find a presage of the cross. Jerusalem does not leave the magi alone with their question. She has an exact knowledge of the answer to it and tells them what it is. She shows the Gentiles the way to their goal and thereby does them a service that no other could provide. But no one of those who supply this information goes with them to Bethlehem. Thus the wise men are led by the star in order that they may find the child in that dismaying state of obscurity which is his. Through the star God brings to light the true significance of the child, so insignificant as he seems. And so the sight of him fills them with indescribable joy.

In the reality of Mary's child no deeper significance is manifest, yet this 'king of the Jews' is 'manifested' to them as their king, as the king of the world. This invisible glory of God causes them to fall down before him in order to adore him. In this gesture, in which no words are spoken, yet which says so much, in which they submit themselves together with their gifts to their king, their journey achieves its goal.

The reaction of men

The theme of the story of the magi is the 'manifestation' of Christ, which draws the Gentiles to him and is an occasion of downfall to the elect. Our preaching upon it, therefore, should be primarily christological in orientation, and should bring out the significance of this story as a part of saving history. The universality of the salvation bestowed in Christ and the fact that the ways to him are manifold must be expressed. If the preacher begins with the theme enunciated in the pericope itself of the transition from the old to the new covenant, and passes on from this to speak of Israel, he should bear in mind how far the situation in which he has to preach has changed from that in which Matthew wrote. We have seen that in the gospel text the magi on the one hand and Herod (here taken as a second pharaoh) and Jerusalem on the other, are viewed not so much in individual terms as in their function in saving history. But while this is true, it is still made clear in the treatment of them (as a secondary and subordinate theme, so to say) how individuals react to the message of the coming of the messiah. In his task of making the gospel message relevant to the present the preacher could make a fruitful use of this secondary and subordinate theme in the pericope. When the message of the 'newborn king of the Jews' reaches his ears Herod is alarmed. He thinks only in the categories of power politics. The key word 'king' unleashes his elemental insecurity in the face of this rival. He fears for his own power and his thoughts turn to a solution of the conflict by force. 'The world is thrown into panic at the manifestation of the Lord because the manifestation of itself is so precious to it' (Eichholz, 45). And yet however hard it tries, it cannot prevent his manifestation.

To this world also, which denies the messiah, belong the high priests and scribes, the experts in questions of religion. They have made a pact with the powerful and paid their tribute to him. They have the relevant literature at their finger-tips and can provide the appropriate answer straight away. Yet they themselves fail to draw any of the practical conclusions from it. They are 'the ominous forerunners of all those theologians who provide specialist answers to every question in the field of exegesis and dogmatics yet make no use themselves of the teaching they give to others: the bridge-builder who never crosses the bridge he himself has built' (Stählin, 3). Manifestly one can have exact information concerning the messiah without being thereby moved to action, without coming to any encounter with him. The magi, those foreigners from far distant regions, represent exactly the opposite attitude to this. They pay heed to the sign which God gives; they listen to his word and do it. They set out upon the journey and follow where God points. Like the shepherds they come and see. The end of their journey is marked by the homage they do to the king. This is the goal of their encounter with God.

This development, which is intended to make the gospel 'actual', is far from corresponding to the main emphasis of the passage itself. For this reason, however tempting it may seem to make them the dominant theme, or even the sole theme of our sermon, we must resist this temptation. Mt 2:1–12 is not a moral tale providing us with an example to follow but the story of an epiphany. Its primary concern is not with Herod, the scribes or the magi, but with the manifestation of Christ in our world. Where is the newborn king? This is the question that is put at the opening of the story and in their act of homage the magi provide the answer to it. Christ is the king of the whole world.

4 The story of Jesus in the temple at twelve years old (Lk 2: 41–52)
Lk 2:41–52 is prescribed in the liturgy as the gospel for the festival of the holy family. This festival owes its origin to the spirituality of recent times. It was Leo XIII who promoted the

veneration of the holy family and instituted a liturgical festival in its honour because he regarded this devotion as an effective means of preserving the ideals of christian family life. Under Pius x this festival was abolished, but subsequently it was reinstated by Benedict xi in 1921.

Right from its very origins this festival has been predominantly pedagogical in character. Although this in fact represents a departure from the original understanding of the liturgy itself, it does reflect the underlying intention of those who instituted it, and this intention has had a quite decisive influence upon the sermon literature. It is accounted as a festival 'for the education of the people'. It has become customary to portray contemporary family life in forbidding colours, and to contrast this with the ideal portrait of the holy family of Nazareth in order to recommend people to model their family life upon this. In all the support of the gospel is claimed in order to extol above all Jesus' submission to the will of God and his obedience.

(a) THE SERMON LITERATURE

A survey of the relevant published sermons reveals a tendency to re-tell the story with embellishments of the preacher's own in which the pericope is deprived of its level of significance as a part of saving history and reduced to a family idyll which is essentially petit-bourgeois in outlook. The story of the epiphany is turned into a piece of private family history. The messiah in his moment of self-revelation is made to figure as a model child, and the holy family as the epitome of all virtues. Attempts are made to compensate for the 'lack' of information supplied by the bible with regard to the hidden life at Nazareth by giving free rein to personal fantasies, and thereby filling out the alleged gaps with embellishments of the preacher's own. The various presentations are influenced far more by the apocrypha and the imitations of these in the portraiture of the last century than by the gospel. The unbiblical way of speaking in superlatives is especially significant. Everything is depicted as perfect, incomparable and ideal. Yet all the time the preacher is attempting in this way to conform his ideas to the pedagogic aims of the 'family Sunday' he is departing more and more from the text of scripture. 'In very truth to make the story of this gospel a pretext for holding a "family education" Sunday is, in effect, to read into it a message which is the very opposite of its true meaning. Even the fact that great authorities can be cited in support of such a proceeding should not prevent us from evaluating it at its true worth as a misunderstanding and a misuse of this story' (Stählin, 235).

The sermons we have examined, therefore, to a large extent fail to reproduce the meaning of the text of the bible itself. But a further question over and above this is whether the pedagogic aims pursued in these sermons are in fact achieved. A family which is presented as a model of every kind of virtue, as unique and unequalled in its excellence, will be viewed as a lifeless ideal, alien to this real world. It will appear innocuous but boring to the hearer, and he will find it more repellant than attractive.

The obedience of Jesus

'And he was subject to them' (Lk 2:51b). This verse is the subject of great interest to preachers. It is regarded as an expression of Jesus' 'absolute obedience' towards his parents. But against this interpretation it must be pointed out that Jesus is neither the model for christian pedagogy, nor yet an abstract ideal of what education should be, but rather the messiah. The context of Lk 2:51 is the story of an epiphany, not a moral tale for children. This verse has affinities not so much with the fourth commandment of the decalogue as with the message of Phil 2:5-11. The intention behind it is to emphasise the fact that the messiah has 'emptied himself' and taken the form of a servant, and the fact that he has entered into the everyday circumstances of human life. Its true message is lost if Jesus is depicted in the hues of a miracle of childish virtues and set before the children as an ideal to be striven after.

Jesus remains behind in Jerusalem

The circumstance of Jesus remaining behind in Jerusalem, and the way in which he reacts to his mother's question (Lk 2:43–49) raise numerous problems for the composers of published sermons. This is reflected in the wide range of explanations which they suggest. An examination of the relevant sermon literature on this point shows the lengths to which interpreters of the gospels can go when they make the historical and psychological aspects their primary centre of interest, and allow their minds to be governed exclusively by the desire to make moral applications. What extravagant notions they find it necessary to put forward, for instance, in order to rule out the least suggestion of any culpable disobedience on Jesus' part! They enable us to recognise how mistaken it is 'to concentrate one's whole interest upon questions of the psychology of youth or of the biographical details... involved in this episode... Here there is no mention whatever of any kind of "development". A certain psychological curiosity makes some all too eager to occupy their minds with aspects which, from the very nature of the story itself, are intended to remain undisclosed. But these will find little material here suitable to nourish their ill-directed interests' (Stählin, 235). The centre of the pericope is found in Lk 2:49. Right from the outset (and not merely at the end of some kind of spiritual development) Jesus stands in a unique relationship to God. He calls him his Father and thereby reveals himself to be his Son, the messiah. It is only from this, the mid-point in it, that the story as a whole can be understood. Its central message, so far from pointing to some psychological phenomenon, is a witness of faith. Jesus belongs so intimately to the Father that no human individual can have control over him. He must be where his Father is. The necessity implied in this 'must' is something far more than a requirement of the first commandment of the decalogue. Hence any explanations which regard it merely as an expression of the fact that the first commandment takes precedence over the fourth fail to do justice to the text. This 'must' is an expression of the necessity governing the messianic mission of Jesus from first to last. It cannot be limited to any commandment or any category of human thought, but is based solely on his unique union with the Father, which transcends all human understanding.

The point of the story is missed if we interpret Jesus and his basic attitude merely as providing an example, and hold it up for imitation. In the mind of the author of the text Jesus is so utterly unique that in the last analysis there can be no question whatever of imitating him. Hence it is for the hearer to identify himself in this episode not with Jesus but with his parents. Like them he does not comprehend the message of Jesus' messiahship. It is something that must be proclaimed in his ears again and again.

(b) SUGGESTIONS FOR PREACHING ON LUKE 2:41–52
In the course of the Lucan infancy narrative first angels (1:26–38; 2:8–14) and then human figures (2:25–38) bear witness to the coming of the messiah. In Lk 2:41–52 it is Jesus himself who speaks. The story as a whole is focused upon him to such an extent that it does not contain a single verse which does not refer explicitly to him. 'Truly a reason for adhering to the same singleness of vision in our preaching' (Eichholz, 48).

Jesus' own self-revelation
How is the self-revelation of Jesus conveyed? Once more he does not appear as the centre of any particular 'spectacle', against a golden background, as it were, but in the everyday circumstances of human life as a member of the people among whom he is growing up. Like all Israelites he is subject to the law (cf 2:21–39; Gal 4:4), and it is this that brings him here to

the festival of Passover with his parents. In this he is following universal custom, 'the custom of the feast' (2:42). The hidden reality of what he is doing—for at this point he still seems merely to be complying with the law—is brought to light in the temple. God accompanies the boy on his journey and so this pilgrimage to Jerusalem, so unremarkable as it seems, culminates with the 'manifestation' of Jesus. The story leads us stage by stage up to this point by showing us how Jesus breaks through the accustomed pattern of events. Ultimately speaking his destiny cannot be contained within the dispositions of the law. While his parents, following the universal custom, return home 'after they have accomplished the days' Jesus remains behind in Jerusalem (2:43). He withdraws himself from them because he is subject to another law. This is shown in the temple. Here he reveals himself not indeed as a wonder-child who knows everything—he listens and asks questions (2:46—all elements of the miraculous are avoided) but still in such a way that all who hear him are astonished at his understanding and his answers (2:47). He is not subject to the limitations of the ordinary and the familiar. This becomes plainly apparent in the reaction of his parents. They cannot understand what is taking place before their eyes. When they see him they are amazed (2:48). All their preconceptions are utterly overthrown when they hear his answer to Mary's question. They would like to bring their son back into the family circle, to bind him with family ties. But they have to experience the fact that his life is subject to other ties, that their claims upon him have to give way to another claim. 'Did you not know that I must be about my Father's business?' (2:49). His life and his mission are subject to that 'must' implied by the Father's will. From his first words (2:49) to his last (24:44–49), from his first journey to Jerusalem for the Passover right up to that last journey in which the Passover achieves its consummation in him, in his final self-surrender to his Father (23:46), his life and mission are dominated by that 'must'. So radically is he consecrated to God and subject to him that his significance can no longer be understood in terms of custom and law. The fact that he can say 'my Father' distinguishes him from all others, and it is because of this that he is designated as 'my beloved Son in whom I am well pleased' (3:22).

'Did you not know ...?' This question contains an implicit rebuke to his parents. They should have known it, and yet they failed to understand it (2:50). 'They are the representatives of the blindness of all humanity.' For who could ever arrive at a stage when he can say that he knows and understands the mystery of Jesus. Who does not need to have it revealed to him ever anew?

In spite of this 'otherness' of his, which makes Jesus so different from the rest of mankind, he does not recede into an 'otherworldly' realm. He who, in the last analysis, withdraws himself from the control of his parents, goes down to Nazareth with them into their world and is subject to them (2:51) 'so that the Son may become like in all things to those on whose behalf he has come from the Father'. This is what it means for God to have descended to us, to have entered into our flesh and blood, our process of growing and developing (2:52). This is what it means for him to have emptied himself and taken the form of a servant (Phil 2:7). It is here that we find the most startling point in the whole episode. The Son of God identifies himself wholly with man, is God in man, God as man. The beginning and end of the pericope insist with great emphasis upon the fact that the emergence of Jesus from obscurity to epiphany takes place in our world, that Jesus appears in the flesh. So far as Mary is concerned the episode does not end with the return to Nazareth. She 'kept all these words (events) in her heart' (2:51). In that part of the story to which 'we' belong she is the principal figure. She is the type of the believing community which keeps the word in its heart (cf 8:19–21; 11:27f).

The application to the present
The pericope bears witness to the manifestation of the Lord,

and at the same time shows us how men bear themselves towards this. From ancient times, therefore, it has been assigned an appropriate place in the liturgy near the epiphany.

In applying it to the present the hearers might be drawn into the story in such a way 'that they, so to speak, undertake this journey together with the parents and then go on to experience the "other-worldly" elements in these events stage by stage' (Smauch, GPM 15, 60). How often this is the case, that we set out upon the way 'supposing him to be in the company' (2:44), and he does not go with us so that we seek him sorrowing (2:48) and find him in quite different circumstances from anything we had imagined. Is not this exactly our position, that we circumscribe him with our habitual preconceptions, subordinate him to our plans and unreflectingly fail to recognise his true significance? Do we not then have to experience that he is different —does not fit in with our calculations, that he is not ours to control, not measurable by any standards of ours? And finally it is not only the parents who fail to understand the revelation of Jesus. Jesus' question is directed to us: 'Did you not know . . . ?' 'It is a grave judgment upon the thoughtlessness and forgetfulness of those who have heard this truth: this Jesus is the salvation of God' (Kraus, GPM 9, 47). It reminds us of the fact that Jesus' emptying of himself even to the cross, however shocking and alienating it may be, 'must' be in order that his Easter 'transition' into the glory of the Father may be accomplished. In this way it directs our gaze to the central point of the eucharistic celebration.

8
SERMON COMPOSITION

The catholic sermon literature of the last two decades has shown hardly any awareness of the findings of biblical scholarship with regard to the gospels. Although in the course of this period catholic bible study has made great advances in opening the doors to the conclusions and methods of historico-critical exegesis, and although the importance of these has been explicitly emphasised in the church's official directives, and catholics have been required to pay due heed to them, in practice preachers have so far to a large extent followed the accustomed paths and neglected the new insights which have been gained. So strongly do the sermon models of the last few years resemble those of the period between the wars that one might imagine that no advances had been made in the interpretation of scripture in the meanwhile. Certainly there has been an increase in the number of quotations from the bible which are employed; often, indeed, these have been used to introduce the observations which the preacher has to offer. Yet not infrequently they serve merely as illustrations, and only give a superficial impression of a preaching that is based on the bible. Out of 1500 sermons examined for this study, less than 15 offered an objectively accurate exposition of the relevant passage from scripture.

By way of contrast with this disappointing state of affairs we have attempted to show how greatly contemporary study of the gospels can help the preacher to unfold the meaning of the relevant texts. Whenever he takes this as his guide, the points he makes by way of exhortation and instruction in his preaching gain in theological force and clarity. All this underlines the fact that in any renewal of preaching the findings of biblical scholarship cannot be ignored.

SERMON COMPOSITION

It is not only that a deeper and more comprehensive understanding of the individual sections of scripture is opened up through the study of the gospels. We have made a series of detailed analyses of individual passages drawn from the different areas of subject-matter with which the preacher has to deal. And these have given rise to observations of a similar kind, which enable us to recognise more clearly the nature and function of preaching and to avoid aberrations. In the pages which follow we shall present a summary of our conclusions on this point.

I Hearers of the word

1 The necessity of historico-critical exegesis for the preparation of sermons

God reveals himself in history. His revelation is not imparted to us in the form of sacred pronouncements couched in lapidary formulae, but in the form in which it has been experienced by men. His word and his deeds come down to us in the response of those whom he encounters. Holy scripture is the record in writing of this response. It is an historical witness of events and experiences belonging to the past. Its language is not our language. Its thought-forms and ways of formulating its ideas are not immediately accessible to us without further translation. It is a witness that belongs to a world that is past, and is intended to be taken seriously on its own terms, different though these are from our own. It is only when the historical context is taken into account in which these ideas were initially worked out that they express what they were then, and still are now, intended to express. Historico-critical exegesis strives with all the means available to it, in the form of truly discriminating historical scholarship, to recapture the essential quality of the original message and to make an objectively accurate understanding of it available to contemporary hearers. In this it recognises the obligation of being faithful to the text of scripture considered as an historical document, and regards this as no less binding upon it than the critical outlook of our own times, with its demand for honesty. 'In this kind of approach to the text, in which we take due cognisance of those elements in it which are historically remote from, and alien to ourselves, our attitude to it is not one of arbitrariness or arrogance, but rather one of respect for the fact that God has revealed himself in history and tradition, and one of willingness to acknowledge his revelation simply for that which it is in objective fact' (Schlier 1964, 51). Christian faith remains orientated towards the word of God which, uttered in the past, has embodied itself in scripture, there to become the enduring norm of preaching. To the extent that it represents an attitude of paying heed to the exact meaning of this word, historico-critical exegesis constitutes a standard by which to regulate our living faith.

Hence it is frequently not merely an irresponsible failure to take pains, but a sign of deficient faith as well when preachers presumptuously thrust aside the findings of exegetical research as so much ballast, unnecessary or even positively an obstacle so far as practical purposes are concerned, upon the pretext that they are going to devote themselves to the 'homely words of scripture'. The consequences of such an approach have become apparent in the course of this work. Instead of devoting themselves to the word of scripture as it actually exists they devote themselves to their own whims and their own ideas. The text is turned into a springboard for fantasy. It sets in motion all kinds of associated ideas which, nourished by general religious preconceptions, replace the ideas latent in the text itself and suppress its real message. Finally the text is used as mere 'illustration'. The roles are inverted. Instead of the sermon being subordinated to the message of scripture, scripture is wrongly forced to serve as a quarry to supply materials for the preacher to build up his own ideas. Behind the façade of a vague 'spirituality' lie concealed a failure in reverence towards the word of God and a lack of theological responsibility. 'It is a

SERMON COMPOSITION

very great error, into which many so-called practical men fall, to suppose ... that they can give free rein to any ideas they choose to put forward in their preaching, or that provided only that these ideas are in line with the mind of the church, and put forward under the aegis of the church, they must in all cases work to the church's advantage' (Schlier ^{3}1962, 245).

The practice of reading out texts from scripture before the sermon should not remain at the level of a mere ritual or only give the superficial impression that it is the message of the bible that is being preached. In all logic this practice should have the effect of ensuring that it is the message of the passages adduced that is expressed in the sermon. It is the text first and foremost that determines what the subject of the sermon should be. It is not enough, therefore, to remain in general terms within the bounds of the church's teaching. It is the message of that specific passage from scripture which is adduced here and now that is meant to be reproduced in the preacher's words. From the particular passage involved issues a claim which God makes upon men, and it is this, and not the preacher's own ideas, or religious ideas in general, that is important. The first and most decisive service which exegesis renders for the performance of this task, therefore, is 'to exercise the preacher in an attitude of listening, an attitude which simply accords its due value to that which belongs to past history, and therefore at first seems alien; an attitude, therefore, which does not regard the basic form in which our encounter with God is achieved as something to be forced into a shape which is quite alien to it' (Käsemann II, 106f). The historical circumstances in which the passage was written have conditioned its meaning to such an extent that we cannot penetrate to that meaning without taking due cognisance of those historical circumstances. We shall do full justice to the message of the passage involved only if we allow ourselves to be shown how to achieve this instead of trusting to the vague promptings of a 'catholic instinct'. We shall only arrive at the true message of the passages we preach upon if we do not assume beforehand that we already know everything, and refuse to advance any further from what we have previously learned. Instead of this we must learn how to listen better and be prepared for surprises.

Certainly historico-critical exegesis often leads to surprises which are alienating and disquieting, and which seem at first to make the task of preaching more difficult. It is not the function of this exegesis to make this task easier at all costs, but rather to create the prior conditions in which we can discharge it aright. Even though in this process rigid preconceptions may be shattered, still, despite the momentary disquiet which this may entail, it can, in the last analysis, only be beneficial. Even if our presentation of the passage seems strange, still this very fact guards us against an unthinking recitation of it, as though it consisted of mere empty formulae. It shows that the truth it contains is not immediately obvious to us in such a way that we have it completely at our disposal and can manipulate it in any way we like. 'It compels us not simply to repeat the great messages of the new testament as self-evident truisms . . . to ask ourselves very earnestly what we really mean when we call Jesus the Son of God or Christ or Lord' (Schweizer 1963, 137). Thereby it paves the way for us to a new encounter with the living word of God which reaches us in the word of scripture.

2 The relationship between exegesis and preaching

Historico-critical exegesis regards scripture primarily as an historical document belonging to an age that is past, one, therefore, the interpretation of which is not immediately obvious to us, but which is intended to be taken on its own terms, terms wrought out once and for all in an age that now lies far behind us (in the same way Jesus too cannot, in fact, be withdrawn from that specific place in history which belongs to him). It does no service to preaching to underestimate the gap which has to be bridged between then and now. A sound, methodical, scientific research should not be stigmatised as the 'relics of an exaggerated preoccupation with history' or as the 'judaism of methodology'. Such verdicts are refuted by the results of the enquiry: Historico-critical research has, 'as a result of its long and toilsome journey, arrived not, as it originally hoped, at the historical Jesus, but at the early christian kerygma as the original datum of gospel tradition' (Käsemann I, 194). It is precisely the methods of form-criticism, so often rejected and the object of suspicion, that have brought to light afresh the kerygmatic character of scripture. Carried through to its logical conclusion, it points beyond itself and finally arrives at the word that is preached. Scripture is not sufficient to itself, but demands preaching as its complement. This is not to deprive it of its objectivity. On the contrary, it is only by recognising this that we can retain a firm hold on its objective nature. For the texts which are explained by the form-critical method were, as that method has proved, originally preached and are intended to provide material for further preaching. These texts are the outcome of preaching and lead on to preaching.

However true it may be that exegesis points us back to preaching while preaching, for its part, needs exegesis as its point of reference, still it must not be overlooked that each of these disciplines has its own distinct function to fulfil. In working out what the message of a given pericope is the exegete has in view the individuals to whom it was originally directed. As a result of his investigation he decides 'this was the way in which the evangelist preached then. This was the message which he sought to convey to his congregation.' The preacher bridges the gap between the situation then and now in order that the message of the text may make its due impact upon his hearers. Certainly it would be inadmissible for him to devote his attention to establishing the precise meaning of the pericope by means of a thorough and searching exegesis. This is a task for the stage of sermon preparation, and one with which he should not occupy the minds of his hearers during the sermon itself. The function of the sermon, therefore, is to cause a message which has already been listened to to be listened to afresh. 'The transition from the text of scripture to the sermon can therefore be characterised as follows: the preached word actually in the process of making its impact has to be developed from a preached word which has already made its impact' (Ebeling 1960, 345).

Preaching and exegesis are mutually interconnected though each has a distinctive function of its own. No exegesis is objectively accurate if it remains sufficient to itself and if, together with all the various methods of research employed in it, it does not contribute to preaching. On the other hand everyone in the church who sets himself to preach the word of God responsibly must pay constant heed to the work of exegesis. Exegesis is the 'goad' of preaching and preaching is the 'goad' of exegesis.

3 The limitations of historico-critical exegesis

The fact that we have to recognise the importance of historico-critical exegesis does not mean that we must close our eyes to its limitations. Its value is always called in question whenever it is tied to a philosophical system. No doubt it is true that there is no such thing as an exegesis without any presuppositions. The encounter between our minds and the biblical text takes place (like other encounters) in each case in a preconditioned context of ideas. This 'prior understanding' must, nevertheless, be open to modification in our dialogue with the text. As we examine it we must be ready to revise our ideas and to allow them to be replaced by new and more relevant ones. There are no categories of thought (whether those of the scholastic or the existentialist systems) which are, without further qualification, totally adequate to express the message of scripture (or of theology in general). To confine this message within the limits of any one fixed system is to do violence to its kerygmatic openness. And if we still persist in doing this then our approach is vitiated beforehand by weaknesses which render a completely open encounter with the text difficult or even impossible. In such a case we approach it not in a spirit of questioning or with a readiness to listen to its message, but rather already know beforehand what it has to say and read our own intentions into it. Its real messages are suppressed by the system. 'A historico-critical view of the bible which derives from any such close system will easily develop into a "judge" with dictatorial claims which, so far as any genuine "learning" and "listening" is concerned (and it is precisely these that we must and will be concerned with in historico-biblical bible study) is ruled out' (Zimmerli, EV TH 19). We shall have more to say on this point at a later stage.

A further point which cannot be contested is that other approaches, side by side with and independent of that offered by a methodologically exact exegesis are possible. These open up a short cut to us, as it were, by which to find our way to the true meaning of scripture. The situation is similar to that which we find in the sphere of art. An analysis of a given painting in terms of the history of art is not the only way of achieving an 'encounter' with it. The fact that this is so does not imply that we have 'a blank cheque for any private devotions we may choose to be guided by, or that we can imagine that ideas which happen to suit our particular fancy can be any substitute for methodological interpretation' (Schlier 1964, 56). They do not dispense the preacher from his task of recognising in all seriousness the fact that scripture is foreign to our modern minds and that a considerable gulf divides us from it. Thus the preacher has to use all the means at his disposal to explain the special meaning which a given text acquired in its original historical context. At the same time, however, these other approaches cannot be set aside as 'unscientific' without serious loss. The 'short cut' is not discredited by the fact that it can be misused through over-enthusiasm or dilettantism any more than historico-critical exegesis is deprived of its value because it is sometimes misused in the manner indicated above. The importance of this other approach should not be denied any more than that of methodological research. It serves to remind us that however acute our exegetical methods may be the reality with which scripture is ultimately concerned cannot, in the last analysis, be fully comprehended by any methodological approach and is rather to be received as a gift than worked out as a piece of research. It warns us further to guard against any tendency to make historical research an absolute end in itself, and draws our attention to the fact that we can only achieve an 'encounter' with the true method of scripture 'if we achieve a meaningful contact with the truth that summons us from scripture and a penetration into its deeper meaning for us . . ., if in interpreting scripture an understanding of it emerges in our minds which at once grows out of the real content of scripture and itself draws out that content still further in a constant and reciprocal interplay of mind and message. This is to understand it at a level which inspires us to open ourselves to it in a living and unconstrained response of total obedience. Now this is something that goes beyond the initial process in, through and by means of which we bridge the gulf between scripture and ourselves by bringing to bear upon it the light which philological and historical investigation can supply' (Schlier 1964, 55). Only a concept of science in which it is taken as an absolute and seeks to assert its authority to the point of rejecting everything which is not susceptible of analysis by it could describe this as unacceptable, and disqualify it on the grounds that it 'lacks objectivity'. A passage belonging to a remote historical context only begins to yield up its message to us when the enquirer ceases to close his mind against it in the effort of striving for an alleged objectivity, and allows it instead to enter into the historical context to which he himself belongs. And if this is already true of those who are engaged with historical questions in general, much more is it true of our encounter with sacred scripture. Only an exegesis which pays due heed to this and integrates its methodology with the broader context from which

SERMON COMPOSITION

alone our understanding can emerge is capable of receiving preaching as its complement.

II The kerygmatic structure of the gospels in its significance for preaching

The Easter narratives, the miracle stories and the infancy narratives are—this has consistently been shown to be the case —to be understood as kerygmatic narratives. The intention of the evangelists is not merely to give their hearers and readers information about what Jesus once said and did. They have not presented his life as belonging exclusively to the past. They tell the story of that life in such a way as to proclaim the message of who he is now and what he signifies for the community that belongs to him. They are concerned, therefore, with something more than merely keeping his memory alive. They seek to give expression in contemporary terms to that claim of God which he embodies and conveys. They not merely record, they preach, they bear witness to faith in Jesus Christ and summon others to that faith.

The effect of the rediscovery of the kerygmatic structure latent not only in the gospels but all through the scriptures has been to orientate our preaching towards its true goal. Nevertheless kerygma and history are not set side by side as alternatives. They belong together. In the light of scripture itself the 'kerygmatic Christ' is as much an abstraction as the 'historical Jesus'.

1 Preaching as address

The gospels are not conceived of as providing sermon texts for the age of the church. They are not intended to supply material which can be utilised in sermons. They have themselves the character of sermons. Prior to serving as a basis for new sermons they themselves were preached to a specific community. The fact that they were addressed to particular definite hearers (even though they do not have the same direct impact upon hearers today) is something that belongs intrinsically and permanently to their nature right from their inception. To the extent that he submits his mind to the text the preacher is himself caught up in the urgent vitality of this proclamatory function in the gospels, and has to direct it towards his own hearers. He must make the message intelligible in the claims it makes upon men in the contemporary situation. In its essential function as proclamation the gospel carries him along with it. On this showing, therefore, his task is not to preach about the gospels but to preach the gospel itself. He has not to preach a given text, but rather to proclaim Jesus Christ as the living Lord, though admittedly he is guided in this by the text (just as Matthew and Luke too did not preach about the gospel of Mark but, guided by the gospel of Mark, proclaimed Christ). Preaching should not remain at the level of mere information or instruction *about* salvation. It is a proclamation *of* salvation. From this basic insight the following consequences follow.

(i) The preacher falls wide of the mark if he attempts 'to fill in the gaps' which the gospels have left, through a deficient interest in chronological details, with his own conjectures, or to expand the stories with edifying embellishments in order to present a vivid picture of the life of Jesus before the eyes of his hearers and to make it comprehensible to them at the psychological level. So soon as he ceases to concentrate upon the word of scripture and instead gives himself up to his own fantasies he abandons the vital character of scripture as proclamation and has cut himself off from the gospel. The claim which this makes is surrendered for the sake of the uninspired requirements of a purely private edification.

In the course of this work it has become apparent how far the sermon literature has departed from the gospel precisely in this respect. The gospel has been withheld from the christian community in the interests of a deceptive clarity. In view of the church's rejection of the apocrypha there can be no mistaking the attitude she has adopted towards all such embellishments of the life of Jesus of a 'historicising' or 'psychologising' kind.

SERMON COMPOSITION

(ii) The preacher must not content himself merely with repeating the biblical text. He must find new words in which to express it, and that too in such a way that it is felt to be addressed to his own hearers. The mere imparting of the contents and ideas of the bible, however much we may base ourselves on science in doing this, still does not constitute preaching. Just as the gospels themselves did far more than merely inform their hearers concerning Jesus' life, so too the preacher cannot stop short at the merely informative level in which he points out to his hearers how the given text fits into its general context. Otherwise the sermon is reduced to a mere instruction upon textual and historical problems of the bible. It becomes a mere record of a vanished past instead of unfolding the future which has been bestowed in Jesus upon his hearers in the present. It tells us about the gospel instead of proclaiming it.

(iii) In the light of this the division of the sermon into 'explanation of the pericope' and 'application to the hearers' so much favoured by preachers must be called in question. The idea behind this is that we must first supply an objective exposition of the text before we can then go on to adapt it to the subjective needs of the hearers. But this is to do justice neither to the special character of scripture itself nor to the task of preaching. It seeks to view and to explain the gospel first simply 'in itself', and thereby fails to recognise the fact that of itself and of its very nature it has from the first a constant tendency to achieve contact with the present in virtue of the kerygmatic quality latent within it. Because of this, so long as it is presented as an abstract entity belonging to the past its true nature as gospel can never be expressed. The sermon is taken to be, at least in part, the explanation of a text, notwithstanding the fact that at every stage in its development it should be orientated towards the proclaiming of a message. For this reason the address should not merely be added on afterwards in the form of a moralising appendix ('Let us, therefore . . .'). It is its goal, and as such determines the nature of every element in it. It follows that instructional explanations of the text are justified only to the extent that they contribute towards this goal.

(iv) Concrete instances of this occur, for example, where congregations have come into contact with current questions of biblical criticism. Not infrequently they are thrown into disquiet and confusion in these circumstances by the proffering of inappropriate information, and this has the effect of preventing the real message of scripture from reaching them. It is not the function of the sermon to enlighten those who hear it as to the methods and findings of biblical science in the field of historico-critical research. A wide range of resources is available for this apart from preaching, and up to the present these have been far too little used. Only in exceptional cases should the preacher have occasion to speak of problems of interpretation, and that only to the extent that this is absolutely necessary in order to convey the essential message. His task is not to enable his hearers to come to decisions with regard to problems of biblical criticism, but to bring them to the decision of faith.

2 *Preaching as a disclosing of the truth of the gospels*

There can be no doubt that the question of the truth of the gospels is one of the most burning problems with which those engaged in the task of proclaiming them are confronted by historico-critical exegesis. The chief reason why the study of the gospels has caused disquiet is—as has been shown in the course of this work—that it has thrown doubts upon the historicity of many of the stories contained in them. This gives rise to the alarming question 'In that case are the gospels true or not? What can we still be sure of?'

Against all the misunderstanding and mistrust which gospel study may incur at this point, so painful as it has come to be, it must be emphasised that precisely here it has done a signal service to the task of preaching.

(i) It has broken through the limitations of that narrow-minded outlook which equates truth with historical accuracy in this field. Certainly some may be shocked at this breakthrough, but in reality it has a liberating effect. That conception of truth which is derived from the idea of accuracy in the sphere of sheer material fact is inapplicable to the truth of scripture. It has the effect of causing its truth to be artificially reduced and restricted so as to mean that the mere statements of fact and assertions contained in scripture are verifiably accurate. Scripture itself is reduced to a mere history book which supplies information about situations and questions affecting our human faith. According to these ideas the authority of scripture stands or falls by whether it can be verified in purely historical terms. By undermining this authority to some extent the scientific study of the gospels has drawn attention to the fact that their truth is not to be sought within the limits of a system of thought which is restricted to material facts. That is its negative side. It is frequently viewed in isolation and therefore condemned as destructive. In reality it removes obstacles to the path leading to a rediscovery of deeper dimensions.

Scientific research into the gospels has brought to light the original intention underlying them. They are intended to give fresh expression to the claim of God which was embodied in and issued from Jesus. That is their truth. It is no abstract entity, not something to be taken 'in itself' as an objective fact waiting, so to say, to be dug out. It has its basis in the living address of God, which takes effect in the words and actions of Jesus. It is for this that we are meant to enquire of the gospels. The truth they proclaim lies beyond any merely positivist interpretation, and is one 'which we can only bear witness to, by which we can take our stand, for which we can live and die, but which we cannot demonstrate to our fellow men. Hence the very fact that the evangelists seem almost carefree in their manner of relating the historical facts enables us to recognise that the real truth which they are seeking to convey is something more than the truth of simple assertions of fact' (Schweizer 1963, 142).

If we allow ourselves to be guided by a recognition of these facts in our preaching, then we shall conclude first that it will be preserved 'from the oversimplified historical materialism which leads to the superficial idea that a simple retelling of past events is *ipso facto* preaching' (Zimmerli, EV TH 30). Preaching in the true sense begins at that point at which the claim of God comes to be expressed. The task of the preacher, therefore, cannot consist in making historical reconstructions of the narratives and giving the impression that he is basing himself on mere records of factual history. This is not to say that the historical element is to be eliminated. In the event of faith it has its own inalienable place. (We shall have more to say on this point at a later stage.) But for all its importance it is not to be considered as a neutral sphere, distinct from and superior to that of faith, from which faith itself can be confirmed or even proved.

This insight affects not only the content of the sermon, but also something which is indivisibly connected with this, namely the attitude of the preacher. It makes a difference whether somebody feels it to be his task to speak as an expert instructing the unenlightened and able to adduce proofs in support of the accuracy of the gospel, or whether he conceives of this task of his rather as one of bearing witness to the truth. Second, the sermon has a function (this point has been brought out by research into the gospels) of finding fresh words in which to express the claim of God which has been preserved in the words of the gospel. 'For it is this and nothing else that is the truth of scripture. It is our encounter with this, and with nothing else that causes truth to be in us. To make this claim of God emerge from scripture and make its impact upon human minds—this is what it means to bring about the truth of an event' (Schlier 1964, 53).

Today the task of preaching is affected by the whole question of our understanding of truth. It is rendered more difficult in this regard by the fact that in contemporary thought pride of place is accorded to the natural sciences. The approach corresponding to this in the religious sphere is that of traditional apologetics, which has taken over the same 'objectivising' mode of thought and outlook, and in which truth value is therefore measured by the same criterion of objective accuracy. This has emerged particularly clearly in the sermons we have examined on the miracle stories. This mentality, which has to a large extent been brought about by the traditional forms of preaching themselves, has to be reckoned with but not supinely acquiesced in by the preacher. The counsel recommending him to keep quiet and not to disturb the faithful in their 'simple childlike faith in sacred scripture' is foolish and a betrayal of truth. It is foolish because it involves closing one's eyes to the fact that the faithful have become aware of the problems raised by historico-critical research to a greater extent than many pastors suppose, and are already deeply disturbed by these problems. It is irresponsible because it involves a betrayal of the truth of scripture and the task of preaching. The function of the preacher is not to vindicate a positivist concept of truth, but to make known the truth of the gospels to his hearers. He has to pursue this aim even when it means upsetting their allegedly 'simple faith'. If this faith is based only upon the face-value of the gospels, on their historical accuracy, then it is only 'ostensibly' faith and rests upon fragile foundations. It seeks assurances and certainty from sources outside itself and in an unrealistically neutral realm which it imagines to be that of pure history, even though it is only in the light of its own (personal) certainty—admittedly not one that transcends history—that it can survive here. 'For historical facts can never as such provide a basis for faith. There are indeed witnesses, signs and experiences supporting the truth of faith, but in no case do these constitute proofs governed by a positivist concept of truth' (Schweizer 1963, 142).

In view of the mentality which predominates today a process in which the hearers are brought to re-think their ideas and re-trace their steps is necessary in order to introduce them to the truth of the gospels. The preacher must maintain contact with his hearers at every stage throughout this process. But if he is to fulfil his responsibilities to the truth of the gospels and of faith this process *must* be gone through. In achieving this the preacher must not allow himself to be influenced by any pleasure he may take in overthrowing false ideas as a matter of personal temperament. The only pleasure which should move him in this is pleasure in unfolding the truth.

The task which has consciously to be undertaken in order to overcome the 'objectivising' interpretation of truth is one that is not only theological but also, and pre-eminently, anthropological. If we take factual accuracy as our sole model in shaping our concept of truth, then this concept, 'taken as a definition of truth in the absolute, implies a loss of those deeper levels in man which alone constitute him as what he really is. The effect of this is to allow man to be dominated by bare facts and so depersonalised' (Kasper 1965, 58).

3 Easter as the fountainhead of preaching
Our exegetical investigation has shown that in all the narratives we have treated of, including even the infancy narratives, Easter provides the initial inspiration. Biblical scholars are unanimous in telling us that this is true of the gospels in general. By their mode of presentation they convey to us that the place assigned to Jesus' resurrection in the total span of his life is such that it cannot be conceived of as a temporary interruption in his career, after which life continues as it was before the interruption took place. In the gospels the resurrection is conceived of not as a postscript to his career, but as its all-dominating centre. 'It is only through the resurrection that the salvific meaning and salvific coherence of all the rest of the salvific event becomes manifest. For it is only in this that that which provides the basis for all other salvific acts is disclosed. Now this means that the resurrection itself is recognised as the funda-

SERMON COMPOSITION

mental action of all history considered as meaningful' (Schlier 1964, 88).

This is not to deprive the work of Jesus prior to his crucifixion of its value, or to imply that it can be set aside as of no account for faith. But Easter constitutes first and foremost the gateway which, according to the conviction of the evangelists, provides the sole legitimate means of access into Jesus' earlier life. Their procedure is not simply to trace the course of Jesus' life in its historical sequence in order finally to celebrate the victory of Easter which falls at the end of it. Rather they interpret this history of his right from its initial stages in the perspective of what takes place at its end. It is only through Easter that it becomes 'fully recognisable and able to be proclaimed as the decisive eschatological event' (Vorgrimler, 180). Easter provides the foundation of the *kerygma*, sustains it in being and is the supreme message implicitly present in everything else that we are told. The word of preaching derives its vital force from the fact that Christ is present in it. That is why it constantly finds expression anew in the present, and constantly has a fresh message to convey applicable to fresh situations. In their whole shape and structure the gospels confirm that saying of Paul, 'If Christ is not risen then is our preaching vain' (1 Cor 15:14).

The conclusion of this for our preaching is that so far as the preacher is concerned Easter must not remain at the level of one saving event among others, or one that is preached about merely when this is prescribed in the festal calendar. It is true that the specifically Easter sermon, as compared, for instance, with the sermon for Advent, Christmas or Lent, has an overriding importance of its own. It is true that, as has been shown above, there is need for a renewal of specifically Easter preaching. But however true this may be, still the nature of the gospels themselves demands far more in the way of preaching than merely the specifically Easter sermon. Our preaching as a whole must have its basis in the Easter event. Obviously this is not to say that every sermon must contain explicit references to

Easter, but it must be implicitly present in every sermon just as it is throughout the gospels. And wherever this truth is recognised there the way is blocked to any attempts at merely re-enacting Jesus' life at the level of pure historical fact. It is the presence of the Lord to us that makes it possible for the truth of scripture to become the truth of our preaching. Our preaching lives because, and to the extent that, he lives in it. It is not in any sense a mere discourse about him. He himself speaks in it. Its function is not simply to relate the word that he once uttered, the action that he once performed in the past. It is the word that issues from him today, and the act that he performs today. It is meant (this is something that the gospels themselves point to with all possible clarity) to be addressed to the hearers in the present as the living word of the living Lord. It would be of great value for the renewal of preaching if preacher and hearers alike were to become aware of this fact.

III The significance for preaching of the quest for the historical Jesus

The gospels preserve the address which God has uttered to man in Jesus Christ. That is their truth. The effect of scientific study of the gospels is to recall preaching to its task, namely to explain this truth to men in the form of a witness of faith. In doing this scientific research points out the way to a renewal of preaching. This first decisive step forward must be combined with a second: that which leads us to the historical Jesus. This is prescribed by the gospels themselves, and in the more recent research on the gospels is widely recognised as necessary. To omit it is to allow the first step forward to carry one into a void.

1 Attempts to exclude the historical question

The existential interpretation of the gospels
The recognition that the gospels are in essence sermons inspired by the faith of, and addressed to the faith in believers is funda-

SERMON COMPOSITION

mental. But in the more extreme forms of 'kerygmatic' theology it has led to the suggestion that the whole question of the historical 'content' of this *kerygma* should be eliminated as theologically irrelevant, if not absolutely dangerous, and that the *kerygma* itself should be understood exclusively in its existentialist significance. So far as Jesus is concerned it is only the 'existential impact of his having come' (cf Bultmann [4]1961, 45) which is of interest, because it is this that initiates the 'existential impact' of the *kerygma*. The *kerygma* finds its authentication independently of any reference back to the historical past, and solely in the act of relating the understanding of existence which it offers to modern man's understanding of himself. It confronts him—this is its unique function—with the eschatological decision which is capable of liberating him from the false security of the controllable (that which can be 'objectivised', the merely 'thing-like', that which belongs to the material world), and which can lead him in faith into the uncontrollable (non-'objectivising', not of this world) openness of 'authentic existence'. By acting in this way the *kerygma* replaces Jesus. It makes him superfluous: 'Now if the position is that the *kerygma* proclaims Jesus as the Christ, as the eschatological event, if it claims that in him Christ is present, then it has itself taken the place of the historical Jesus. It is a substitute for him' (Bultmann [4]1965, 26). The historical Jesus is given up in exchange for the 'Christ *kerygma*'. The continuity between the two attested in the primitive christian credal formula 'Jesus Christ' is surrendered. The quest for the 'basis' in history for what is proclaimed is rejected as an unworthy striving for 'confirmation' of one's faith, and cannot be allowed any place in preaching.

It will become plain when we enlarge on this point below that this exclusively kerygmatic interpretation is too one-sided to represent correctly the message of the gospels. Our initial task at this point must be to draw attention to certain acute dangers for preaching which ensue from this kerygmatic approach.

Certainly it is true that, as has been shown above, the scientific study of the gospel does supply preaching with 'a formal definition of its task' (Stallmann, 51). It is essentially an address, a summons to the decision of faith. But if this important formal principle is accorded an absolute value, and if all questions of the material content of the gospels are thrust aside in favour of the sheer 'existential fact' of the gospels as summons to faith (the sheer fact that this summons has been posited and has been 'uttered into reality'), then the formal principle itself is elevated into a tyrannical power and made the sole content of our preaching. In that case, just as the whole gospel tradition is crammed into the straight-jacket of a hermeneutical principle, so that none of the actual content of what it tells us is adverted to but solely and exclusively the summons it conveys to us to the eschatological decision, so too our preaching itself is subject to the dictatorship of the same claim that it shall confine itself purely to an abstract *kerygma* cast in the form of a permanent monotonous (or even monomaniac) monologue. All ideas which are illustrative, or designed to appeal to the imagination must be excluded from it. Old and worn-out formulae are replaced by new ones, but these new ones themselves are already dead as they come to birth because it has been made a rigid principle that they shall be devoid of content.

Finally the categories of thought involved in this rigidly kerygmatic interpretation of the gospels are such that they are no longer capable of sustaining the idea of God as self-subsistent being. To a large extent they exclude the social (ecclesiastical), worldly and historical dimensions of faith.

(i) If instead of according due value to the *kerygma* being founded in historical fact we regard its authentication in terms of existentialist theory as the sole point of importance, then in the last analysis we are identifying the problem of existence with the problem of God. All statements about God, to the extent that they are not shown to be existentially significant, are excluded as mythological (pertaining to this world, 'objectivised'). Revelation is confined within the concept of man's understanding of himself. The concept of Jesus as a subsistent being in his own right loses its significance. Jesus is reduced to the level of the initiator of a new (the 'authentic') understanding of the self, and, since this is the only 'role' accorded to him, he is banished from the *kerygma*.

(ii) Preaching itself is pent up in the ghetto of the individual's own private decision. The community is no more than a necessary prior condition, making it possible for the kerygma as address to make its impact upon the individual man (the 'understanding subject'). Everything is concentrated upon him, and upon his decision, constantly renewed. Community signifies 'the process by which man becomes absolutely alone before God' (Bultmann ³1963, ET 188). If such ideas are carried to their logical conclusion, then preaching is distorted to the point where it becomes a monologue which has nothing to do with reality, and 'the church is turned into an amalgam of individuals constantly renewing their own personal decisions' (Bohren, 59).

(iii) In their anxiety to avoid any kind of 'objectivisation' the exponents of this theory restrict faith to the purely private sphere of the individual's own 'authentic existence', and remove it from that of the external world. As a result the whole sphere of material realities in the world is set aside as irrelevant. Now as soon as the world is regarded as alien to faith it necessarily follows that preaching too must be regarded as having nothing to do with this present world. Certainly it can still attempt to interpret the world from outside, and to bring men to a new understanding of the world, one in which it is viewed as extrinsic to faith itself. But preaching on this basis is quite incapable of penetrating into the world, or attempting to alter it.

(iv) With the surrender of the world goes the surrender of history as well. The existential interpretation loosens its hold upon history as that which has taken place, and leads—and this is a point that no amount of talking about the meaningfulness of history can explain away—to a concept of existence in which history plays no part, one in which the decision involved is concentrated exclusively on the present moment and which is cut off from past and future alike. The consummation is achieved in the eschatological decision in the 'now', and beyond this there is nothing. Against this 'the question imposes itself from the theological point of view whether it really can be the case that man comes "to himself" precisely in the event of revelation as embodied in preaching and faith, arrives, that is to say, at that state of authentic existence in which that which pertains to the origins and that which pertains to the end are both combined. If that were the case then evidently faith itself would be, in practice, the end of history as planned by God, and the believer would himself, by the mere fact of believing, have achieved the state of perfection intended. There would be nothing left for him to achieve, no goal still lying before him to which he had to make his way in the physical, worldly and historical dimension of his life' (Moltmann, ET 67f). On this showing preaching loses its character as that which is preliminary and provisional, and is accorded an absolute value in itself as the summons to eschatological decision.

The 'de-historicising' of the gospels and 'preaching that transcends the dimension of time'
A distinct movement, independent of that involved in the existential interpretation of the gospels, and still more directly and inextricably involved than this in idealistic ideas is that which attempts to 'liberate' the *kerygma* from history. The process of 'de-historicisation' is elevated into a law of interpretation which has 'everlasting validity' for the preaching of the gospel. The *kerygma* 'is thereby transferred to a dimension which is permanent and immutable, and which we too can enter into'. 'The gospel is raised to a plane in which it is everlastingly in force . . . It is emancipated from history, it is a timeless preaching' (Fesenmeyer 1963, 51–66). The author regards the 'de-histori-

cising' process as realised in the Johannine gospel as a 'splendid release', and therefore holds it up as a 'pattern for preaching the bible'. Against this we have the testimony 'precisely of the fourth gospel, which in fact stems from the period of the conflicts with docetism . . . that revelation takes place on earth and in the flesh' (Käsemann, 201). Fesenmayer's claim to the support of the Johannine gospel must be resisted just as strongly as his demand for a 'de-historicised' preaching. Here we have no difficulty in recognising ideas which are characteristic of Greek thought 'which experiences in the *Logos* the epiphany of the eternal presence of Being, and in this finds the truth' (Moltmann, ET 41). This means that historicity is surrendered to truth as attested by the gospels. The implications for preaching which arise from this correspond to those set forth in the foregoing section. Preaching cannot dissolve the link with history. It is not 'timeless' or 'transcending time', but on the contrary belongs to time and history because it bears witness to that salvation which in Jesus has taken place and will take place in history.

2 *Kerygma and the historical Jesus*

The cleavage between kerygma and history which has grown up from philosophical premisses is quite foreign to the gospels. Every system of interpretation which implicitly involves this, and which, in the name of the *kerygma*, declares history to be irrelevant, misses the true message of the gospel altogether and grasps at a void. The distinctive quality of the gospels consists precisely in the synthesis they achieve between *kerygma* and history. The very fact that they have come into being at all is to be attributed to the special interest which faith takes in history. The gospels themselves already have before their eyes the dangers entailed by a 'pure' *kerygma* theology. For this reason they bring their hearers (or readers) back to an encounter with the historical Jesus. They remain constantly in union with those whom he once called to be his disciples, and take their stand side by side with these. They give renewed expression to the words of him, the earthly master, and relate the works he performed. Naturally this process does not extend beyond Easter in such a way as to adduce a historical proof designed to confirm the faith of believers. 'The Easter perspective in which the history of Jesus is presented to the early christian community must certainly not be forgotten for a single moment. But it is no less important to bear in mind the fact that now it is precisely the history of Jesus before Good Friday and Easter that we are viewing in this light. If it were otherwise the community would have surrendered itself to a timeless myth . . .' (Bornkamm, 20). The gospels combat this danger which threatens by showing that *kerygma* and faith are not closed in upon themselves, and are not sufficient to themselves, but are related to a history which has already taken place and with which they are indissolubly connected. The Christ who is present once and for all is none other than that Jesus of Nazareth in whom God acted at a specific point in the past, and of whom, accordingly, we must also speak in the past tense. The past history which belongs to him is not merely incidental and so an unimportant supplement so far as our present faith in Christ is concerned, but rather a constitutive element of that faith.

The historical Jesus cannot be replaced by the Christ of faith. He is indispensable. Each aspect modifies the other and both are held together in the credal formula 'Jesus Christ', which bears the gospels within it. There are two distinct sides to its message: the basic *kerygma* of the Easter faith, 'Jesus is the *Christ*, is complemented by the further witness, '*Jesus* is the Christ'. From this the following conclusions can be drawn for preaching.

(i) Certainly 'the theological standpoint for the question of the historical Jesus . . . lies not before but after the post-Easter *kerygma*' (Schweizer 1963, 146). But this standpoint must not remain unoccupied. The question must not go unanswered. However true it may be that our preaching lives by the Easter faith, it is no less true that it is precisely this same Easter faith that points us back to the history of Jesus. Deprived of this reference to the past, this Easter faith finds itself suspended in mid-air without connection. It remains permanently subordinated to the 'once and for all' of the historical Jesus. In the *kerygma* of Christ his name must not be reduced to a meaningless sound (a mere cypher). It must be made plain who bears this name. The history involved is not merely incidental or supplementary to the revelation of God, not something which can be dispensed with, but that in which the revelation is realised. Considered as a whole it is not in any sense the mere form in which revelation is expressed, an outward figure of it (cf the expressions 'temporal garment', 'historical clothing'). On the contrary it belongs to its actual content and is an integral element in the *kerygma* and in faith. Preaching finds its basis in the primitive credal formula 'Jesus Christ'. It has, therefore, a twofold function: 'Against an a-historical gnosis it has to proclaim the earthly Jesus as the glorified one. In other words it must preserve the connection with the historical tradition. But the continuity asserted here is meant to lead to an assertion of identity. In preaching the earthly Jesus, as he who has now been exalted, he himself becomes present through his Spirit as the power of the new aeon' (Filthaut–Jungmann, 28).

Theological statements do not imply a historical background in every instance, nor may we deny that scripture does contain 'historicisations' of theological statements. Both of these factors have been illustrated sufficiently clearly in the course of this work. But it certainly is maintained here that history and faith do not, in principle, exist on different planes, so that they are merely juxtaposed to one another, or that whatever contacts there are between them are merely superficial. W. Marxsen (^{2}1965, 7ff) rightly draws attention to the fact that in the present-day discussion concerning the objective interpretation of scripture the problem of faith and the natural sciences has been detached from the question of the relationship between faith and historical fact. In order to throw light upon the questions with which we are currently preoccupied he adduces as 'the best possible example' the controversy which in the meantime has to a large extent been resolved concerning the creation narrative and the conclusions arising from this. Certainly parallels are to be drawn between the two cases, both with regard to the matter under discussion and the form in which the respective discussions developed. But in recognising this we should not fail to recognise also the essential difference between the problems involved in each case. There can be no conflict between the findings of the natural sciences and the assertions of faith, because each supplies answers to different questions. To the extent that scripture makes statements belonging to the province of the natural sciences it should be understood that these seeming assertions have been formulated according to the conditions of the age in which they were written. So far as science is concerned no binding force is claimed for them (cf the discussion concerning the creation narrative). But when we turn to the case of the relationship between faith and historical fact we have to recognise that this is different from the former instance. The problem that confronts us here is different in certain specific essentials. The questions involved can intersect one another so that it is not possible in all cases to follow the requirements laid down by Marxsen (1965, 39), 'To maintain a clear distinction between these two planes, the historical and the theological...'. We cannot draw any radical distinction between the statements of faith in scripture and the historical assertions it contains (in such a way that these latter are in *all* cases to be taken as couched in the form of assertions, though certainly this would apply to many instances of such historical statements). On the contrary these historical statements enter into faith itself and occupy a central place in it, and so belong integrally to its content. If it could be proved historically that Jesus was not crucified, or even that he never lived at all, this would destroy our faith. This is a point on which the findings of historical research are supremely relevant for theology. The statement 'I cannot allow historical research to dictate to me what can and what cannot count as a theologically correct statement' (1965, 30) is certainly applicable to many statements in scripture, but as soon as it is presented as a definition of one's universal attitude it becomes untenable.

(ii) If the history of Jesus (his words and works) belongs to the content of the *kerygma*, then preaching cannot be considered in isolation as a summons issuing at one particular point purely in the present to the eschatological decision. It is also—indeed essentially—a commemoration (*anamnesis*). This does not mean merely the preservation of some kind of spiritual testament. Still less is it a question of preserving an 'honoured memory' of the person of Jesus. He is the Christ who is present. But however true it may be that his word issues in the here and now, it is, nevertheless, not born of this present moment. It has a history of its own. In the act of calling to mind the message uttered and the things done in the past christian preaching becomes, by the power of the Lord present to his church, a summons to and a claim upon christians in the present and, as a word of promise, opens the future to them also. The act of remembering is not a mechanical process to be worked out methodically. It enters integrally into the very act of preaching.

(iii) This implies that for christian preaching there can be no such alternative as 'either *kerygma* or narrative'. Both belong inseparably together. The narrative is reduced to the level of mere information if it is not given its due value as the word of the living Lord and so made an address uttered in the here and now. Christian preaching remains suspended in a void if it does not refer back to the past by relating the events in which salvation was achieved. However justified criticisms may be of the 'historicising' and 'psychologising' presentations of the christian message, which deprive preaching of its true character, this further point must not be overlooked. To say that the narrative elements must not be distorted is in no sense to say that narrative itself must be excluded from preaching. 'To the extent that *kerygma* does not include this narrative element it becomes the proclamation of an idea, and to the extent that the element of proclamation is not constantly recaptured anew in the telling of the narrative it becomes a historical document' (Käsemann, 95).

3 The unity of works and word in Jesus
The foregoing study has been particularly concerned with the narrative material of the gospels, and in the light of this we must now attempt to define in concrete terms the relevance of the history of Jesus.

The address of God to man issues in the word of preaching, and faith is taken to be the response of man to this word of God as it is uttered. This can lead to a theology purely of the word. This danger is immediately incurred when the enquiry into the earthly Jesus 'is approached solely from the aspect of the connection, and at the same time the distinction and tension which exists, between the preaching of Jesus himself and that of the community he founded' (Käsemann, 213), an approach, therefore, in which his works are not also taken into account. Manifestly, according to the information supplied by the gospels themselves, it is not enough to emphasise that God has spoken in Jesus. No less important a part of the witness they are intended to bear is that God has acted in him. Matthew's way of bringing this out is to relate the messiah of actions to the messiah of words.

In the course of this work it has repeatedly become apparent that in view of the notable variations in the narrative material as it has been handed down it is difficult to arrive at answers which are historically reliable. The outlines of the visible works of Jesus are blurred, and it is hardly possible that they can be made to stand out more clearly in any essential respect in the future either. It would be quite illegitimate, however, to conclude from this finding that we can hold ourselves completely dispensed from investigating the facts of Jesus' life, and concentrate our historical interest 'solely' upon the preaching of Jesus. The wrongness of this course appears all the more clearly if we find confirmation of the hypothesis that the tradition of the works (above all that of the miracles) generally provides earlier data in terms of tradition history than that of the words. But for all the historical problems which may arise in particular cases, the very fact that in general the gospels contain historical and narrative material, and do not merely transmit doctrines and ideas—this fact taken by itself is, on a general view of the whole, significant. However important it may be not to misinterpret the narratives by taking them as historical records, they do show at all events that God has established salvation in Jesus not merely in his words but in his works as well.

Hence in the gospels the exhortation to 'hear' has its counterpart in the exhortation to 'see'. Certainly this is not intended in any sense to signify a purely optical process, but it would be just as incorrect to say that the optical element is totally excluded. (In this exhortation we are precisely not told: 'Close your eyes and ears, turn inwards upon yourself'.) So far as witness and faith are concerned this element is manifestly not irrelevant. However true it may be that the command 'See' is intended to point us on to the command 'Hear', still the latter is not totally independent of the former. The intrinsic unity of revelation as word and revelation as act also finds expression in the fact that the Hebrew *dabar* signifies both. The words and actions of Jesus cannot be played off one against the other. They are mutually complementary. Just as his actions have a verbal quality in them, so too his words have the quality of acts. Certainly the act of 'seeing' on the part of the witnesses has entered into the word of the gospels. But in this process it has not been lost to us, but on the contrary preserved. From the point of view of preaching what has been said so far serves to put us on our guard against two mistaken courses.

(i) If the quality of revelation as things done is suppressed, then an absolute value is accorded to the significance of the word. In the effort 'to preserve the faith in its purity' a one-sided theology of the word 'expects salvation to be made present in no other way ... than in preaching, in which God himself bears witness to himself in his word' (Stallmann, 48). All ideas of mediators or intermediary means of salvation are eliminated, and the relationship between saviour and saved is asserted to be precisely immediate and direct once the proposition is formulated that faith can only be achieved in the 'word that happens' and 'event that is uttered', ie when there is no other medium whatever between speaker and hearer, nothing which can be treated of as an entity in its own right, nothing except the sheer immediacy of the word. On this showing the event of the word and the event of salvation are identical. The present is made a source of God's revelation.

Certainly faith is not ours to control. But the category of 'that which cannot be controlled' does not extend so far as to include what is stated in the gospels. In Jesus God has, so to say, made himself available by entering into a specific history and a specific form of words. He has divested himself of his 'otherness' to the external world, and in consequence of this it is precisely not by 'by-passing' the external world that we can attain to him. Sheer immediacy to God, a sheer state of 'not being able to control or dispose of' what God brings to us—these are the postulates of a prior system of thought which is idealist and personalist in character, and they fail to do justice to what we are told in the gospels. They prescribe a course for divine revelation to follow, instead of examining the actual course it has followed in actuality, and listening to the actual words which God, of his freedom, has chosen to utter. With regard to the gospels it is not permissible to view all elements of the objective and factual as so many external confirmations, designed to bolster up one's faith. Nor is it permissible to condemn them as odious on the grounds that they represent a decline to the level of magic. 'Pure faith does not consist in the

SERMON COMPOSITION

fact that the believer lets the visible go by and commits his whole existence to the invisible, but rather in the fact that he accepts things belonging to the visible world as signs of God, and so surrenders himself to God's revelation in this present life' (Müller-Schwefe, 199). Sheer immediacy, elevated into a principle, is actually degraded by the fact of itself being made the most sublime of media, one which has power to control the freedom of God himself. It turns out to be a modern variant of the *theologia gloriae*. Preaching no longer has the force of an act of salvation which is provisional and conditional. It acquires a definitive character and is made an end in itself. The word is deprived of its nature as an element in the historically contingent. It is no longer viewed as a means, but as the ultimate goal.

(ii) If conversely the history of Jesus is not accorded a corresponding value as having an eloquence of its own, a message of its own to convey, then too much weight comes to be attached to the dimension of visible and external event. Moreover this second danger is no less great than the first. One way in which it manifests itself is that the revelation of the works of Jesus is adduced as a proof of the revelation of his words, and thereby reduced to the level of mere blunt fact and nothing more. But we also come across this approach in that kind of theology which seeks to understand 'revelation as history' and to gain knowledge of Jesus primarily 'from the language of the facts' (Pannenberg, 100). The logical development of this idea is to present 'preaching as ... a record of history as conveying revealed truth, and as an explicitation of the language of the facts implicitly contained in this history' (Pannenberg, 114).

Against this it must be emphasised that events cannot be recognised *ipso facto* as deeds of salvation by everyone who has eyes to see without any further enlightenment. Every historical fact is of its nature ambivalent. It is capable of acquiring an unambiguous meaning only when it is combined with the interpreting word. Every event of salvation is to be viewed in the perspective of the word and is to be understood only in the light of this. The pure 'language of the facts' taken by itself is incomprehensible to us.

We cannot by-pass the word so as to withdraw to a position of objectivity where we take our stand upon demonstrable facts belonging to this world, using this as neutral territory from which to evaluate the situation. If the revelation of works is, in the last analysis, taken to be a proof that is sufficient to itself, then no room is left for the free decision of faith. In that case here too the provisional nature of revelation is suppressed in favour of a *theologia gloriae*.

(iii) The alternative 'either word or deed' is just as inadmissible as that between faith and history. The truth of christian revelation is neither restricted to that which has found utterance in Jesus' words, nor exclusively to that which he has accomplished in his works. Both belong integrally together. 'The character of revelation as event safeguards revelation from being misunderstood in a one-sidedly doctrinal sense, and serves to remind us that revelation is not only instruction, does not only provide a basis for a dialectic of existence. It assures us of the *ante et extra nos* of faith, just as the character of revelation as word gives expression to the *in nobis et pro nobis* of it' (Kasper, ThQ 144, 163). The word is aimed at personal address, while the action involves the cosmic sphere in the event of salvation. Word and act are the two complementary aspects of one and the same revelation of God in history. This co-ordination foreshadows the connection between the proclamation of the word and the visible act in the christian church. It is doubtful whether this latter element should be restricted to the sacraments. The element of act here signifies not merely the sacraments but the whole range of the visible ministry of christians, and the service of God in everyday life in the world.

(iv) It is not open to the preacher—this is the conclusion of what has been said—to by-pass the statements of objective fact in the narrative tradition or to resolve them into abstract propositions. They have a significance of their own which cannot be dispensed with. But how is he to do justice to his task in view of the fact that the historical problems involved are almost impossible to solve in any precise detail? Should he present all we are told in the narrative sections, without further ado, as historically reliable? Should he interpret them solely as a witness of faith, and by-pass the historical question? Should he take his stand upon a nucleus of 'genuine' historical fact as assured by the present findings of contemporary research? All three ways are inadmissible. The first must be avoided at all costs, because it involves constructing a pseudo-history and thus leads to dishonesty. The second way involves leaving the world and God's history with mankind out of consideration. The third leads to a 'history' in the abstract which is set side by side with the history attested in the gospels.

We cannot expect to find a solution to this problem through any alternative which draws a rigid line of separation between the historical fact and the confession of faith. On the contrary, the solution can only come from a synthesis which holds both together in a fundamental unity. Just as the *kerygma* is not something that is set alongside the events of Jesus' life, but has a radical and intrinsic reference to them, so too the works of Jesus are not 'objective facts of salvation' with an independent existence of their own, but rather live in the light of the word that interprets them and bears witness to their meaning, and can be understood in their significance as acts of God only in virtue of this. Right from their very inception event and confession of faith belong together. The situation is not that in the beginning a historical record was handed down—for instance in the form of a diary kept by the disciples—and that unfortunately in the course of time further and rather dubious embellishments were superimposed upon this in the interests of faith, so that today we have first to pare away the 'inauthentic' layers of encrustation in order to extricate the nucleus of 'genuine' historical material. On the contrary, right from its very origins the tradition can only be understood as the response of faith to the action of God in Jesus.

This response is not given in so absolute a manner as to be incapable of further adaptation. The original event, the action of God in Jesus, is open to the future. Its effects continue. By being enquired into afresh and interpreted afresh and expressed in fresh terms it itself creates history. The gospels themselves already enable us to recognise three great stages in this history: the works of the earthly Jesus and the response of the group of his disciples as the first 'setting in life', the confession of the post-Easter community as the second 'setting in life', and thirdly the respective redactions of each of the evangelists.

Only in the broader sphere of this troubled history of tradition or 'history of action and reaction' can we achieve any adequate encounter with the event in which all originated; it belongs integrally and inseparably to this history. The point at which the preacher stands is (provisionally) at the end of this history of tradition, and he has to expound the truth preserved in it to his hearers in such a manner that it holds good in this present day.

IV The task of making the witness of the gospels relevant in the present

Under the influence of the findings of scientific study of the gospels it has become apparent to us that the tradition they embody is to be viewed from two distinct aspects. On the one hand this tradition preserves an integral connection with the unique and unrepeatable history of Jesus. On the other it is made a living and vital force by faith in the abiding presence of the glorified Lord. These two factors are fundamental, and only on the basis of these can we understand a further phenomenon which form-criticism has discovered: the evangelists combine an attitude of faithfulness to tradition with an astonishing freedom in interpreting its content. They do not understand their function as that of handing on a rigidly defined system of unalterable teaching and timeless truths. They are conscious of being witnesses called to be such in that particular historical situation which belongs uniquely to them, and which no system could have laid down beforehand, and they are bold enough to express the tradition that is handed on in a manner appropriate to meet the special needs of their particular age. One and the same narrative, as re-told in the differing situations in which preachers find themselves, is constantly being enquired into anew for its message, and constantly acquires a fresh eloquence such that its message 'has a place' in the life of the particular community to whom it is addressed. The hearers of the message are not mere dumb recipients of the word, they join their voices with it. With the questions they raise and the experiences they undergo, with their faith and their trials, they are themselves totally involved in the message. So deeply have they entered into the gospels that to this very day the structures and inter-relationships within the communities they belonged to can still be discovered there. So true is this indeed, that it is absolutely necessary to throw the fullest possible light upon their particular circumstances in order to be able to understand the message at all.

In this connection due attention must be paid to the sometimes very considerable theological differences which the gospels display in the witness they bear to one and the same history of Jesus (cf for instance the different interpretations in each of the gospels of the same group of miracle stories). No attempt should be made to minimise or 'smooth out' these differences. We should not adopt the approach and outlook of that kind of traditional biblical theology which lumps the gospels together and reduces them all to a single common denominator, taking no account of the differences between them. Approaches of this kind lead to falsifications of the specific statements of the particular gospels. The fact that in preaching the same objective state of affairs has been presented in manifold ways does not imply any weakness to be eliminated as far as possible. On the contrary it implies a strength deriving from the nature of the witness to Christ itself, a rich quarry which repays excavation. The gospels constitute a single complex of preaching, dynamic and full of internal tensions, and one which must be viewed in all its manifold historical connections. The common centre to this complex consists not of an immutable system of doctrines (however true it may be that it does also contain doctrines) but Jesus Christ.

The approach which we should adopt in our interpretation of scripture is the opposite of these leanings towards superficial harmonisations. Precisely with preaching in view we should work out as accurately as possible the structure and development of each individual passage. The more clearly we manage to bring to light the message which each particular biblical witness proclaimed to his own community in his own situation and at his own time, the more deeply we shall make the preacher aware of the fact that he too is called to be a witness today and in his own community, and the more clearly we shall be able to show him how he can fulfil this task.

1 Preaching as a living mode of handing on the gospel tradition
The dynamic process by which tradition is handed on, as attested in the gospels, is open to further developments, and cannot be held back by any exaggeratedly doctrinal restrictions. It is in this same dynamic process that preaching has its place. It stands in the central current of the movement in which the christian message is proclaimed, a movement which has its origins in Jesus Christ, and which lasts so long as his church endures. It is true that the initial stage in this movement has been declared particularly sacred, but this does not imply that the movement itself is arrested at this stage, that thenceforward it is enough to travel that particular section of the way which has been, in this sense, 'canonised'. Certainly the bible, considered as the crystallisation in writing of the *kerygma* of the origins, has a normative significance for all time. But it is not

simply the word of God and nothing more. The gospels are not the gospel in the singular. Rather they are the supreme witnesses to this gospel. They proclaim it in the historical context of the apostolic origins, a situation rendered unique and unrepeatable by the fact that it is so close to Jesus himself. But as historical witnesses of the eschatological event they point on beyond themselves, and are open to ever greater developments in the future. The eschatological event which took place in Jesus Christ has indeed left its impress upon them (to that extent their character as definitive and normative is proper to them alone). But the process is not exhausted with them. Unique and unrepeatable as they are, they are at the same time provisional, the pledge of the promised fulfilment. They are caught in the tension which exists between that which has *already* been achieved, and that which belongs to the stage of 'not yet'. For this reason they are intended to be constantly interpreted anew, and that too in such a manner that the community of the interpreter's own contemporaries can enter into the 'history of action and reaction', into the actual process by which the tradition of the eschatological event to which they bear witness is transmitted.

It follows from this that the tradition of the church is to be understood neither as a mere handing on of a series of truths formulated as propositions, nor yet as a mere repetition of the words of scripture. It is brought to realisation in the *viva vox evangelii*. The living preaching of the gospel sustains and prolongs the tradition by addressing it afresh to the contemporary world at each particular age, and in doing this it injects a forward impulse into it, pressing it on towards its eschatological fulfilment.

Scripture and tradition, therefore, do not stand side by side as two distinct accumulations of truth. It is not left to the preacher to decide whether he will base himself on scripture or on the church's doctrine (tradition). For him the basic point of reference is surrendered if it is maintained that he should not limit himself to the content of the new testament, but that he has to develop and enrich this. What has happened here is that the idea of an alternative (*partim partim*) has been developed from the dubious theory of the two sources of revelation, and this has had a damaging effect precisely for our understanding of the preacher's task as well. It has led to the position that side by side with the biblical homily, regarded as the pure preaching of scripture, there is also a thematic sermon which is concerned with the church's teaching. This latter should then enlarge upon specific subjects which have come to be of particular concern in the context of our own times.

The result of setting these two distinct kinds of sermon side by side is to cause both forms to develop along erroneous lines. Whereas the biblical homily (as will be shown later) to a large extent stops short at the stage of an explanation of scripture, and so remains orientated towards the past, the thematic sermon loses contact with scripture altogether. The only way of overcoming these mistaken developments is to relinquish the doctrine of the two sources of revelation developed in the narrow-minded atmosphere of the counter-reformation, and to bring back to the forefront of our minds once more the intrinsic unity of scripture with tradition. The word of God which went forth in Jesus Christ, and which is attested in scripture, constantly finds fresh expression in the living tradition (preaching) of each particular age. Over and above this 'content' to which scripture bears witness, namely Jesus Christ, there is nothing. And in this respect every alleged 'enrichment' is in reality an impoverishment. This original witness must be the standard by which every sermon is measured, and in this sense all preaching has at all times to be a preaching of scripture.

From what has already been said so far it should already be apparent that we are not advocating here any kind of exaggerated biblicism. On the contrary it is precisely this approach that represents a perversion of that element in scripture of which we have been speaking, namely a forward impulse and an openness to the future which defies any kind of systematisation, and orientates it towards God on the one hand, and to a constant renewal of the vital impact of his word upon mankind on the other. The gospels do not offer us a collection of timeless stories, intended to act as examples supplying answers to every question, with a plan ready to hand for every situation. The mere recitation of the words of scripture does not make a scriptural sermon. On the contrary, not infrequently it represents a positive hindrance to this. What scripture has to say can only be orientated and applied to the present in such a way that it is not simply repeated but stated in 'fresh' terms in order to arouse a renewal of faith. The 'content' of scripture is precisely not an immutable system of doctrine but a person, the living Lord who wills to make himself present in words in the here and now. Obedience towards the witness of the gospel requires the preacher in all freedom so to bear witness to what he has heard in his own particular circumstances and his own particular age that it achieves an 'integral place' in the life of the community to which he belongs. The freedom is the logical outcome of his obedience. Faithfulness to scripture demands faithfulness to the present.

2 Attempts at applying scripture to the present which are inadequate

The biblical homily
It is often expected today that the renewal of preaching will take its rise from a revival of the 'biblical homily'. In Germany this term is generally used to designate 'that form of preaching which consists of an explanation of a section of holy scripture and an application of the knowledge thus acquired to the religious and moral life of the hearers...' (Tillmann–Goedeke, 49). It can be further subdivided. In the 'exegetical homily' the way of analysis is chosen, and the prescribed text is explained

sentence by sentence, while the 'thematic homily' begins by setting forth the theme of the given pericope and, with this as its starting-point, seeks to understand the individual verses it contains. In both cases it is a question first of explaining scripture and then of making a 'practical application'.

Biblical preaching of this kind is incapable of achieving a renewal of preaching. It is the outcome of an unhistorical line of thought, the exponents of which imagine that today the task of preaching can be fulfilled 'all the more easily in view of the fact that the religious and moral needs and demands remain constantly the same in all ages and for all christians' (Tillmann–Goedeke, 47–58). The preaching, therefore, which belongs to the time when the scriptures were written—this is the underlying presupposition—must also become the preaching of today by a mere process of repetition. No serious consideration is given to the special circumstances of the hearer, any more than it is to the dynamism of history which is the special quality inherent in scripture. Nor can we allow ourselves to be deceived on this point by the questionable, and for the most part moralising, element of the 'practical application'. The words of scripture are handed down like so many minted coins, and finally fall out of circulation. They cannot simply be repeated like the answer to a sum that has been worked out. A word-for-word repetition is precisely not capable of sustaining in being the true meaning which scripture is meant to convey. In the altered conditions of the particular age this is lost sight of, or is stated too briefly to be understood, and so distorted that it leads to grotesque misunderstandings and does positive harm. This message retains its true identity only if it is expressed 'differently'. For the historical situation constitutes an integral element contributing to its effectiveness.

The exaggerated attempts of biblicists to recapture the pristine form of the text signifies not faithfulness to the word of God but a departure from it. It is not enough to 'continue the proclamation' of consecrated cyphers in the hallowed sphere

SERMON COMPOSITION

and behind closed doors. The word of God attested in scripture is meant to be expressed anew.

On this showing a further tendency, widespread in the sermon literature, is also to be rejected, that namely which attempts to lead the hearers back into the past and to represent to them what the situation was at that time. The deceptiveness of this regressive tendency appears from the fact that the hearers are placed for the time being in an alien world artificially constructed for the purpose, and also that not infrequently contemporary attitudes are unconsciously 'read into' the biblical stories. The proclamation of the christian message in the gospels points in the opposite direction. Certainly it remains firmly rooted in the history of Jesus. But it presses forward, as it were with this history to support it from behind, in the awareness of the presence of the Lord, in order to become engaged in the new set of circumstances before it. This is the direction which preaching has to follow.

Effects of a rigidly systematic separation between the mode of expression and the content which is expressed

In our efforts to arrive at an objectively accurate interpretation of the bible it becomes vitally important to pay due heed to the literary *genre* of a given pericope or a given document. The distinction between the mode of expression and the content which is expressed, customarily drawn in this connection is, it is true, not altogether unjustified. But at the same time the limitations of such a purely abstract distinction must not be overlooked. If we allow ourselves to be influenced in this by the scholastic concept of distinction, taking over and applying this purely in terms of a rigid pre-existing system, then precisely with regard to preaching it can only lead to the most serious misconceptions. The content of what is expressed will then be understood as an essential or 'non-variable' truth which can be detached from the original circumstances and made use of in the context of today. The early christian community and the world in which it actually lived are not taken seriously. Its function is merely to lend colour to this essential truth, to act as its external façade. The outer covering changes, the content endures. Only on the outward surface is it altered. The task of the preacher is to impart to it the outward presentation that is appropriate to each particular age. This is varied according to the taste of each particular preacher. Reference may be made to two 'types' of sermon held up for imitation.

(i) Not infrequently in our investigation of the sermon literature we have met with certain frenzied efforts at achieving 'relevance' at any price. Sermon titles such as 'Madonna or teddybear' and 'Sex bombs at the cross' arouse the suspicion that they are dictated by the quest for sensationalism, that the preacher does not trust the real subject, which such devices are meant to lead up to, to have much power in itself to attract interest, and that he takes it no more seriously than the audience to whom he is addressing himself. Preaching follows in the wake of advertisements for branded goods. It is dominated by the question 'What will sell?' (or 'How can I make a sale?'). Slanginess of this kind, which is prompted by a consciously assumed attitude of modernity, is intolerable and fails to achieve its purpose. The task of pointing out the relevance of the gospel to the present is not accomplished by using slovenly colloquialisms and adopting the jargon of the gutter. This approach reduces the gospel to the triviality of the fashions of the moment. It is quite evident that it is precisely not possible to draw a simple and facile distinction between the content of a message and the form in which it is conveyed.

(ii) The concept of 'decking out' the message with the 'trappings of the age' leads, in the last analysis, to an attempt to manipulate the world and mankind like so many puppets. The world serves as a storehouse of illustrative materials. It is turned into a sort of theatrical workshop. The events of human life are deprived of their true and proper meaning, and are seized upon by the preacher as though the only reason for their

SERMON COMPOSITION

having taken place was to provide the trappings in which an enduring and immutable 'essential truth' could be clothed for the time being, as though they had no truth proper to themselves to sustain, as though they did not have an eloquence of their own in which to convey it. Here a dangerous perversion stands revealed. 'Men with their destinies are made the tools and instruments of the sermon instead of being the hearers to whom it is addressed. The worldly circumstances in which they live are not the field in which and upon which preaching has to prove itself effective. Instead the circumstances and conditions of human life serve merely to provide "illustrative material" for a faith which is already sufficient to itself in developing its ideas. Instead of the word of faith seizing upon the world and mankind and transforming them, it takes its fill of the world of appearances and leaves these realities untouched' (Jutzler, 236).

We see the full depths to which preaching can sink through this radically wrong approach above all in those cases in which the needs of others are mercilessly exploited as 'illustrative material', and in which they are 'used' as a matter of routine as an instrument ('formal expression') for preaching. 'What a fruitful field for preaching is provided simply by the catastrophes which follow one upon another at ever shorter intervals! What possibilities they offer of striking terror into the world of men, of shaking their confidence in the greatness of the world they live in, and of bringing out the radical dependence of all that is upon God' (Kirchgässner, 13).

So long as history is taken to be the 'outward covering' in which a universal 'essential truth' is decked out 'for the time being', any application to the present in the sense intended by the gospels is impossible. In them we are confronted with the history of the world and of mankind not as the external façade which covers a permanent and immutable doctrine, but on the contrary as something that belongs to the very essence of the gospel itself.

353

Demythologising
The term 'demythologising' is used to designate the most significant and most stimulating attempt in recent theology to translate the message of the new testament into contemporary terms in such a way that it will be listened to and understood by men of the modern world. Its object, therefore, is to eliminate from preaching those images and ideas which occupy the foreground and which represent obstacles to modern man, being shaped by a conception of the world which is alien to him. By doing this it is sought to uncover the real stumbling-block, that with which christian faith is truly concerned as its 'proper' object.

In its presentation of the event of salvation the new testament avails itself of the mythical conception of the world evolved in its own cultural environment. It uses mythological language so that it '. . . speaks of the other world in terms of this world, and of the gods in terms derived from human life'. This way of speaking is 'incredible so far as modern man is concerned because for him the mythical picture of the world is obsolete'. It is incapable of being revitalised 'since our every thought has irrevocably been shaped by science'. Today the preacher can only still count on being understood when he succeeds 'in divesting the truth of the faith from the mythological ideas in which it has been formulated', in demythologising it' (Bultmann, KUM, ET 10; 3ff).

But this is merely to show the negative aspect of a much broader development of ideas, culminating in the existential interpretation. The aim is, in preaching, to avail oneself of a language which, in contrast to myth, does not speak of otherworldly and divine realities as though they belonged to this world and were at one's disposal, but precisely in an 'otherworldly' way and with a recognition of one's limitations in their regard. This alone corresponds to that which is most essential to the mind of the new testament and brings it to light. This language is initially formulated where human existence comes to be spoken of and expressed, for this precisely is not under our control. It is realised in act. All the statements contained in scripture must be liberated from the sphere of, 'divested of' the 'objectivising' mythological thought in which they have been couched, and the understanding of existence expressed in them must be investigated and interpreted existentially. Only so, in the dimension of existence, is their true and essential meaning arrived at. Only so can the word of scripture make its due impact upon modern man, that word which is addressed to him on the basis of the act of God in Christ and which liberates him from the sphere of material and merely disposable things, and thereby 'from his own self, bringing him to his authentic life'. Faith in this redeeming and saving activity on God's part is not a 'remnant of mythology'. 'The transcendence of God is not as in myth reduced to immanence. Instead, we have the paradox of a transcendent God present and active in history' (Bultmann KUM, ET 44). Here lies the crucial stumbling-block at which all is decided.

It is not the task of this work to provide a comprehensive evaluation of the theory of interpretation set forth here, or to point out its limitations in detail. For our purposes, however, the following points are of special importance.

(i) It has repeatedly been brought home to us that the need to make the gospel message relevant to the present is a demand imposed by the gospels themselves. We are indebted to 'demythologising' for the fact that, bearing in mind the changes which have taken place in the conception of the world, it has drawn attention to the need for this in the most decisive possible manner. From time immemorial it has been the concern of a living and vital tradition to make the witness of scripture comprehensible to the minds of contemporary believers, and it has grappled with this task down the centuries in all kinds of ways with some degree of success. All through this process a kind of demythologising has been being achieved (for instance in the formulation of dogmas). But whereas up to the present this development has been to a large extent unconscious and unreflecting, today it has been worked out as a methodological principle and incorporated into a comprehensive system of interpretation. The intellectual honesty which is brought to bear upon this task of tradition deserves to be respected and copied.

Finally the existential interpretation which is connected with demythologising offers one advantage too great to be surrendered. It enables us to recognise that from the moment that revelation finds expression in words man himself is actively involved in it, that if he wants to encounter it fruitfully he cannot either initially or at any point exclude himself from the process. He is touched in his own personal existence and brought to the point of decision.

(ii) The existential interpretation of the mythological modes of expression of the new testament is designed to penetrate the symbols and images and to 'divest' the truth which is indicated in them of its figurative mode in order that man may encounter it pure and direct (devoid of imagery) and may be set free for 'authentic living'. Demythologising is the necessary prior condition for establishing an identity between history and *eschaton*, an identity which can be maintained only by a paradox. It is the prior condition for the stark 'affirmative' of faith as postulated by the existential system, an affirmative that finds its achievement in the now of the eschatological decision, and that surrenders the horizontal dimension of history (the state of progressing from a given starting-point to a given goal) in favour of a vertical orientation which is achieved in sheer immediacy to the present (in the summons of God which reaches man in the *kerygma*). By demythologising faith is 'purified' from all reference to worldly realities and the imagery to which they give rise. The stumbling-block of faith is reduced to a single point, the pure 'reality' of the eschatological act of God in Christ. But the price for this process of narrowing down faith to a single point is a surrender of history; the linear and horizontal development involved in it is telescoped into a single point.

If we are not ready to pay this price, if instead we recognise the obligation which the new testament lays upon us of maintaining the eschatological tension between the 'already' and the 'not yet', then this mythological language appears in a different light. It becomes apparent that it is the only proper mode of parlance for the new testament, and one for which there can be no substitute, to the extent that it preserves the provisional character of revelation, and is open to the promised future which looms ever larger before us. It accords due value to the vision which is 'in a glass darkly' (that is, expressed in image, in symbol), and does not seek to grasp at that vision which is 'face to face' before it is time (cf 1 Cor 13:12). It is able to point to something about God, the world and man which can hardly be expressed in any other way.

Again in the case of demythologising it becomes apparent that while it is indeed true that a distinction must be drawn between the form and content of a given statement, still in the last analysis the two cannot be separated from one another. It is impossible to arrive at the pure *kerygma* by stripping off the outer covering of mythology. History is the 'form' in which God has embodied his message, 'emptying himself' in order to enter into it. In consequence of this it is a constitutive element in the content of revelation. The alteration involved in stripping away this element of history signifies not some kind of purely formal modification, but a loss of the very pith and essence of revelation.

The task remaining for the interpreter is not one of demythologising, but rather 'that which has been his special preoccupation from ancient times, namely translation, though admittedly a process of translating that leads from the language to the actual truth itself which is expressed in it' (Schlier 1964, 95). The mythological mode of expression, with its images and archetypal symbols, can only point to the mystery of God. It cannot adequately express it. This too requires constantly to be interpreted afresh. But this can only be done in an objectively accurate way if it is not confined to a rigidly anthropological (existential) approach, but remains theologically orientated. It is useful to reflect 'that the new testament frees us first and foremost from ourselves, from looking at ourself, from an individualism which causes us to regard ourselves and our faith as more important than the action of God' (Schweizer 1963, 147). A theological interpretation of this kind does not exclude the existentialist and cosmic relevance of the new testament, but rather includes it.

(iii) Demythologising misses its mark. It leads not only to abstracting what is essential to scripture, but also to an oversystematised concept of 'modern man'. The existentialist interpretation bound up with it is intended to make the biblical message relevant to the present by taking as axiomatic that certain specific existential elements in biblical man's understanding of himself are identical with those of modern man's understanding of himself. But in this the existential elements which are asserted to be present point not so much to scripture as to gnostic systems of thought. Certain elements which are essential to the biblical portrayal of man, such as the part played by the physical in human personality and the factor of social intercourse, are to a large extent suppressed. Finally a question which still remains unanswered is whether it can ever be possible at all to arrive at an application to the present which does justice to the sense of scripture so long as one adheres to a system of philosophy of man which is at basis unhistorical. The idea of the 'essential' man, or 'man in himself' is a lifeless figment of the imagination, a piece of docetist jargon. Just as there is no such thing as a 'pure' *kerygma*, so too there is no such thing as the 'pure' man emancipated from the world to be met with in the world. This state of emancipation from time and from the world is only to be acquired at the cost of ignoring time and the world in the development of one's ideas, and con-

SERMON COMPOSITION

juring up the image of a man who does not exist. The existentialist interpretation fails to do justice to the realities of the situation. While recognising that it raises questions which are both urgent and necessary with regard to the basic outlook and attitude of mind which condition modern man's judgment of things, we still feel that this system is more interested in outlooks and attitudes of mind than in man himself.

3 A preaching which measures up to the realities of the existing situation

The word of God—this much has become clear—does not confront us 'in itself' (divested of all human presuppositions). It is completely human in its orientation. The very definition of the word of God is such that man is integrally involved in it. The gospel is truth 'in itself' to the extent that it is truth 'for him'. This truth is achieved in its encounter with him. It has its point of intersection (not point of contact) with reality as it exists in the world, not merely outside it. In preaching, truth can only be achieved if it cuts across the realities of the world and the situation of those who hear it.

Encounter with the community
'The task of proclaiming the word of God to a society grouped in masses and dominated by the technical achievements of modern life is undoubtedly difficult. But this makes it absolutely necessary as a prior condition for such proclamation that we shall achieve a knowledge of man thus situated which is realistic and devoid of illusions' (HTG II, 768). This is not to be thought of as an additional duty for the preacher, one from which he might, under certain circumstances be dispensed. In the mind and meaning of the gospels it belongs directly to the message itself. The conditions for a preaching that is biblical are only half fulfilled (and that means, basically speaking, not fulfilled at all) if the preacher merely confines his attention to the prescribed text, and does not turn with the same degree of

openness and concentration towards his hearers. His encounter with the relevant passage in scripture demands a further encounter with the community. In this second encounter, just as in the process of working out the meaning of the text, the preacher should avail himself of the resources and findings of the appropriate sciences of the day. Just as historico-critical exegesis helps to elucidate the meaning of the prescribed passage in scripture, so too such disciplines as sociology and psychology help him to appreciate the circumstances and attitudes of his hearers. But as in the first instance so also here methods are not an end in themselves. They serve to sharpen our eyes and ears, so that we can enter more deeply into the question, but are not intended to be viewed as the actual object under investigation. They do not offer any ready-made prescriptions, applicable to any possible set of circumstances that might arise. They remain necessarily at the level of general principles. The moment we allow our preaching to become dominated by blueprints drawn from anthropological disciplines we incur the same danger as in the existentialist interpretation: we are speaking of man 'in himself', and letting slip the opportunity of addressing our actual hearers. Our access to them can be blocked just as much by rigidly imposed systems of thought drawn from secular science as by religiosity both old and new. Analyses of the present state of the world, books, newspapers and television, however helpful they are capable of being, are never any substitute for direct contact with the individual hearer.

For the achievement of personal contact of this kind the practice of discussing the sermon is especially important and in this respect may be compared with parish visiting. This should not be taken to imply that critical evaluations of the various preachers should be indulged in. In preaching it is necessary to view self-critically the limitations of one's own viewpoint, and to take in all seriousness the needs of the community as a whole. The members of this should no longer be condemned to the role of mere dumb recipients, or be thought of as mere 'objects to be preached at'. At some point after his sermon the preacher should throw the question open to free discussion among his hearers, and when he does this he should listen primarily not to those who uncritically fall in with his opinions, but to those who raise doubts and make demands upon him. Such discussions have a contribution to make in the preparation of future sermons. They can have the effect of ensuring that these have the character of a dialogue rather than a monologue, that the work of preparation is done not by the preacher in isolation, but by the community as a whole. The sermons must originate in the community and maintain a living contact with the community as they are developed. This presupposes that the preacher lives in the community and does not lead a life apart, that he is aware of being solidly at one with it, not merely knowing the life it leads but actually sharing in that life himself.

All these developments are not simply a matter of tactics and method, and are not simply dictated by the rules of psychology and language. Certainly the insights offered by these disciplines are not to be estimated lightly. They include elements which have an integral part to play in the process of preaching. But over and above these it belongs to the very nature of the word of God that it shall achieve expression in the context of a dialogue, in the response of the community, that it achieves its goal only at the stage at which the community defines its own attitude in its regard. The sermon is not simply the word of God and nothing more. It is the 'counterword' or response of one specific and accredited witness. For this reason it must not be presented as *ipso facto* the readymade answer to all questions. There are experiences which the hearer must be allowed to undergo for himself, and decisions which he must be allowed to make for himself. The sermon bears witness to faith. It cannot, of itself, 'manufacture' it. There can be no substitute for the response of the hearers.

These theological insights demand that we shall conform our

practice to them in such a way that the community is no longer condemned to the role of passive recipients of the word; that its members recognise as their goal the task of working out what their own attitudes of response should be, and actively contribute to this end. These theological insights once acquired demand to be put into practice in a way that takes seriously into account the fact that the community is not made up of the ignorant and the unknowing, whose prime need is to be enlightened. Rather it must be recognised that the community itself is endowed with the Spirit and has a word of its own to utter (something which must not be confused with an uninspired repetition of what has been said by others).

Encounter with the world
The community of Christ does not constitute some kind of enclave set apart from the world. 'It is not an ideological entity which stands "over against" or "above" the world, and which, from its home in cloud-cuckoo land in some sense "condescends" to the world' (Filthaut, 326f). It is that in which the encounter between God and the world is achieved. It is the community of those who live by the promise of God in the world and with it, but *for* the future which that promise holds out. Our preaching, therefore, should not be conducted behind closed doors or in a manner which leaves the world out of our calculations. It is a 'this-worldly' proclamation of the christian message. If it is set apart from the world then it is not fulfilling its function and is failing to bear witness to the gospel.

Let us have no misunderstandings on this point: a proclaiming of this message which keeps the world in view does not imply adopting an attitude of exaggerated and self-complacent clericalism, and from this basis abusing those 'worldlings' who do not come to church. In other words it does not mean addressing the world from the window of a tower. 'World' here means the hearers actually assembled. Precisely with these in view the sermon can succeed only if it is addressed to them as men of the world, as men living in the world and the meaning of whose existence is bound up with the world, men who, more than any others, bear the responsibility for the world's future.

If God encounters the world in such a way that he shows himself to be on its side, if the gospel is not presented as sufficient to itself but rather applied in the response of human individuals, if it cannot be arrived at as a pure supernatural essence by a process of abstraction, but always manifests itself as integrally embodied in the process of history, if it is not timeless but subject to time, not emancipated from the world but in the world and of it—if all this is true then preaching must constantly renew its openness to the questions which time and the world (and not only the community itself!) raise for it, and allow itself to be disturbed and troubled by such questions. 'It is not by remaining on some imaginary "shores of eternity" that we rescue those drowning in the stream of time; the only way to do this is ourselves to plunge boldly into mid-stream and swim' (Rahner 1964, 224). In the light of these truths the world no longer appears as a supplier of needs, still less as providing a dark background to some stage on which sham contests are enacted. It is experienced in its own unique nature. No longer is it discussed in the ghetto. It is included in the discussion as a partner, and stamps our preaching with its own distinctive nature. For a discussion is not a monologue delivered from a high watchtower. On the contrary it is an exchange, a process of give and take, of putting questions ourselves and having them put to us. Preaching can only achieve authenticity and remain true to its real nature if it enters into the mind of its partner instead of talking over his head. The word of preaching will convey truth only if it bears witness to that truth in such a way that it can be understood and lived in the contemporary world, if it establishes itself in a faith that transforms the world.

The 'worldliness' which preaching must have is anything but a capitulation to existing circumstances. The gospel does not merely answer questions or serve simply to ratify *de facto* findings. It raises fresh questions, calls in question the world and mankind. It is not subject to the categories and laws of the world, but transcends these and points beyond them to an ever-greater future. 'The proclamation of it always serves at the same time as a warning that that which already exists, that which has already been achieved, is soon to be brought to an end' (Filthaut, 313). From this aspect there are certain limits to be observed in any dialogue (including the particular kind of dialogue which preaching involves). Preaching is not one contribution in a general free discussion, but a summons to the decision of faith. The standard by which it is regulated is not some particular understanding of the self or of the world, but rather Christ. Its purpose is to reconcile mankind and the world not to itself but through itself to God. Mankind and the world are not ratified in their existing state. On the contrary this state, insofar as it involves being closed in upon themselves, is broken into. The stumbling-block of faith is not set aside, but, on the contrary, brought so conspicuously to the fore 'that it is experienced by the world in general as a reiteration of the claim that provokes contradiction and so appears as anything but a relic of a bygone age, too ineffective to carry any weight' (Filthaut, 31).

The language of preaching
The gospels are not the gospel. They were written to bear witness to the gospel in a specific situation. A further projection of the gospel is achieved in the *viva vox evangelii*, in proclamation by the living word. It cannot be imprisoned within the walls of a specialist religious vocabulary. It has an intrinsic forward impulse to encounter a new world and a new age and to find fresh expression in the language belonging to these.

Every language is conditioned by the age to which it belongs. As history advances so it changes. The fact that it is being employed to communicate the truth of the gospels does not render it immune to the influence of time in this sense. Even here it is an expression of the actual experiences of one particular group of men. It makes articulate their particular attitude to, and relationship with the realities of the faith. As worldly attitudes and relationships change the insights and experiences which faith provides change with them. And when this happens the earlier language of faith no longer meets the needs of the altered situation. If this language is to remain living, and not to be frozen into dead formulae, then it must undergo a process of regeneration. If it is banished to a sort of consecrated limbo, then it fails to retain its hold on reality and ceases to give utterance to the gospel, which achieves concrete reality precisely in being integrated into a dialogue with the men of the present age. Conventional formulae and empty husks of words are handed on in place of the *kerygma* itself. These become incomprehensible and untrue. They no longer express any articulate message (they are expressions of nothing), and therefore have no power to move their hearers. They do not make them listen, but lull them to sleep instead. Preaching as envisaged in scripture itself demands a constant renewal of language. The concepts and images that have been handed down must constantly be subjected to reappraisal, to decide whether they still correspond to the experiences and modes of thought of modern men, or whether they have already outlived their usefulness and should be withdrawn. They do not remain true merely in virtue of being rigidly adhered to through thick and thin. They must be translated in such a way that they continue faithfully to express the original content of the message and at the same time point to the contemporary realities of the world as it exists.

We cannot expect the renewal of preaching to come from some specialised language evolved from within ecclesiastical circles. Neither a 'consecrated language' nor a 'sacred mode of parlance that is in some sense "secular", nor yet a style that hovers between eternity and everyday life . . . between incense-smoke and cigarette-smoke' (Fesenmayer 1962, 363) meets the exigencies of the situation. If the preacher is to be understood he must speak a language that men can understand. In executing his commission no other language is available to him than the language current in the world of his own contemporaries. He must, in all honesty, familiarise himself with this. And he will not achieve this by attempting to 'cut the cloth' of language in shapes that seem to him appropriate, or to subordinate it to the fashions of the moment. It is not only the external form that is in question, but the actual message itself. Language is not the outward clothing in which a truth accidentally happens to be expressed, but an expression of the reality itself. The only way in which the preacher can achieve a sufficiently deep understanding of it is for him to give himself to the actual reality involved, and to the world. 'The word which the church addresses to the world must proceed from the deepest possible knowledge of the world, and so make contact with this same world in all its reality as it exists in the present' (Bonhoeffer 1, 144). Otherwise it is powerless to take effect.

The responsibility of the preacher

The implications for preaching which must be drawn from a deeper insight into the tradition of the gospels *ipso facto* affect the preacher also. Either explicitly or indirectly he too has been included in the foregoing remarks, so that at this point it only remains for us to consider a little more fully what his actual function consists in. In conclusion, however, two vital elements in our understanding of the contribution he has to make are worthy of particular mention.

(i) The preacher is one who has been commissioned by the church to proclaim the word of God to the community of his fellows. It follows that he is not solely and exclusively bound by the authority of the church. Like her he is subject to the authority of the word of God, and is a hearer of this. Obedience to this word lays a further claim upon him, namely that he shall pay heed to the voices which reach him from his own community and from the world in which he lives. This obedience

SERMON COMPOSITION

itself calls him to exercise freedom in bearing witness to the word of God in the place and time allotted to him, and to do so in such a way that the word will 'belong' integrally to the context of his hearers' lives. The freedom to interpret afresh, and so to exploit to the full the many levels of truth present in the witness, does not in any sense mean giving the preacher licence to give free rein to his own subjective caprices. This freedom is a freedom exercised in submisson to the word of God and within the sphere of the church.

The preacher cannot circumvent the risks entailed in this freedom by timidly falling back on readymade formulae. This would be to betray his inalienable responsibilities. The proclaiming of the christian message is a charismatic activity in which he cannot withhold the fulness of his own self-commitment. Admittedly he cannot sustain this responsibility of his as an individual in isolation. He is referred to the dialogue with the 'fathers of the faith', with his 'brothers in the ministry of the word', with the community to which he belongs and with the world.

(ii) Closely connected with the element of charismatic freedom is the further element of truthfulness. 'Nothing that has happened in the last few decades, and perhaps the last few centuries, has done so much harm to preaching as the lack of credibility which has been brought about by the handing on of empty formulae which were no longer invested in a vivid and vital manner with the spirit of those truths which they were originally designed to proclaim' (Ratzinger, TThz 70, 14). In the manifold forms of tradition which they contain, the gospels draw our attention to the fact that the *kerygma* cannot be treated as though it consisted merely of an objective set of facts, and so projected on in the christological titles employed in credal formulae. Rather it cuts across the lives of the witnesses themselves. The preacher neither can nor should proclaim that which he himself has not made deeply his own, or that which remains an empty formula and is not reinforced by any reference to the experiences of human life in which it is made real. He cannot bear witness to that of which he himself is not convinced. Responsibility for the task of bearing witness to the gospels prohibits that 'empty talk in which we cease to be witnesses. For in his gifts and in his failings, in the religious and irreligious elements in his character, a witness lives what he utters, whereas one who merely repeats the word of the Lord, adhering to every letter and every stress, is no more than a parrot which has not the least inkling of what it is saying when it utters its squawks' (Schweizer 1963, 137f). Honesty is not only a demand of our particular age, but a sign of the truth of christian preaching. Where it is accorded its due value there, and only there, will a genuine renewal of preaching be achieved.

BIBLIOGRAPHY

The following books and articles are quoted from in the text. Text references are to the author and, where necessary, to the date of the German edition used, even where English translation (ET) is referred to.

BARTH K. Vier Bibelstunden über Luk 1. München 1935
BOHREN R. Predigt und Gemeinde. Zürich–Stuttgart 1963
BONHOEFFER D. Gesammelte Schriften. München 1958
BORNKAMM G. Jesus von Nazareth. Stuttgart ^{6}1963
  ET Jesus of Nazareth. London 1960
BORNKAMM G.—BARTH G.—HELD H. J. Überlieferung und Auslegung im Matthäus-Evangelium. Neukirchen ^{3}1963
  ET Tradition and interpretation in Matthew. London 1960
BULTMANN R. Glaube und Verstehen I–IV Tübingen 1952–1965
  Das Verhältnis der urchristlichen Christusbotschaft zum historischen Jesus. Heidelberg ^{4}1965
  Das Evangelium des Johannes. Göttingen ^{9}1964
  Theologie des Neuen Testaments. Tübingen ^{4}1961
  Die Geschichte der synoptischen Tradition. Göttingen ^{6}1964
  ET History of the Synoptic Tradition. London
  Das Urchristentum im Rahmen der antiken Religionen. Zürich–Stuttgart ^{3}1963
  ET Primitive Christianity in its Contemporary Setting. London 1956
CAMPENHAUSEN H. V. Der Ablauf der Osterereignisse und das leere Grab. Heidelberg ^{3}1966
CONZELMANN H. Die Mitte der Zeit. Tübingen ^{5}1964
  ET The Theology of St Luke. London 1960
CULLMANN O. Petrus. Jünger—Apostel—Märtyrer. Zürich ^{2}1960
  ET Peter; Disciple, Apostle, Martyr. London 1962
DIBELIUS M. Botschaft und Geschichte I. Tübingen 1953
  Die Formgeschichte des Evangeliums. Tübingen ^{4}1961
DINKLER E. (Hrsg) Zeit und Geschichte. Tübingen 1964
DODD C. H. Historical Tradition in the Fourth Gospel. Cambridge 1963

DREHER B. Die Osterpredigt von der Reformation bis zur Gegenwart. Freiburg 1951
EBELING G. Das Wesen des Christlichen Glaubens. München u. Hamburg ²1965
Wort und Glaube. Tübingen 1960
EICHHOLZ G. (Hrsg) Herr, tue meine Lippen auf 1. Wuppertal-Barmen ⁷1964
FESENMEYER G. Bibelpredigt im Aufbruch. Freiburg 1963
In *Oberrheinisches Pastoralblatt* 63. 1962
FILTHAUT T. (Hrsg) Umkehr und Erneuerung. Mainz 1966
FILTHAUT T.—JUNGMANN J. A. (Hrsg) Verkündigung und Glaube. Freiburg 1958
FISCHER B.—WAGNER J. (Hrsg) Paschatis Sollemnia. Freiburg 1958
FLENDER H. Heil und Geschichte in der Theologie des Lukas. München 1965
FRÖR K. Biblische Hermeneutik. München ²1964
FUCHS E. Gesammelte Aufsätze II. Tübingen 1960
GNILKA J. Die Verstockung Israels. München 1961
GRASS H. Ostergeschehen und Osterberichte. Göttingen ³1964
GRUNDMANN W. Das Evangelium nach Markus. Berlin ²1965
Das Evangelium nach Lukas. Berlin ²1964
HAENCHEN E. Der Weg Jesu. Berlin 1966.
Das Johannesevangelium und sein Kommentar in ThLZ 89 (1964)
HAHN F. Christologische Hoheitstitel. Göttingen ²1964
HEISING A. Die Botschaft der Brotvermehrung. Stuttgart 1966
HENNECKE F. E. New Testament Apocrypha. London 1963
IWAND H. J. Predigt-Meditationen. Göttingen ²1964
JEREMIAS J. Jesu Verheissung für die Völker. Stuttgart 1956
ET Jesus' Promise to the Nations. London 1958
JUTZLER K. Privatisierte Verkündigung in *Medium* 2 (1965)
KÄSEMANN E. Exegetisches Versuche und Besinnungen I, II. Göttingen ³1964, 1964
KASPER W. Dogma unter dem Wort Gottes. Mainz 1965
Grundlinien einer Theologie der Geschichte in ThQ 144 (1964)
KIRCHGÄSSNER E. Worauf sollen wir warten? Paderborn 1965
KLAUSER T. Das römische Capitulare Evangeliorum. Münster 1935
KOCH G. Die Auferstehung Jesu Christi. Tübingen 1959
KOCH K. Was ist Formgeschichte? Neukirchen 1964
LANG A. Die Sendung Christi. München ³1962
LAURENTIN R. Structure et Théologie de Luc I–II. Paris 1957

BIBLIOGRAPHY

LOHFINK G. Der historische Ansatz der Himmelfahrt Christi in *Cath* 17 (1963)
LOHMEYER E. Das Evangelium des Markus. Göttingen ⁷1963
LOHMEYER E, SCHMAUCH W. Das Evangelium des Matthäus. Göttingen ³1962
LOHSE E. Die Auferstehung Jesu Christi im Zeugnis des Lukasevangeliums. Neukirchen 1961
Martyrer und Gottesknecht. Göttingen ³1963
MARXSEN W. Die Auferstehung Jesu als historisches und theologisches Problem. Gütersloh ²1965
Der Streit um die Bibel. Gladbeck 1965
MOLTMANN J. Theologie der Hoffnung. München 1957
ET Theology of Hope. London 1962
MÜLLER-SCHWEFE H. R. Die Sprache und das Wort. Hamburg 1961
NINEHAM D. E. (Ed) Studies in the Gospels. Oxford 1957
OLIVER H. H. The Lucan Birth Stories and the Purpose of Luke–Acts in NTS 10 (1963/64)
PANNENBERG W. (Hrsg) Offenbarung als Geschichte. Göttingen 1961
PASCHER J. Das liturgische Jahr. München 1963
RAHNER H. Griechische Mythen in christlicher Deutung. Zürich 1957
ET Greek myths and Christian Mystery. London 1963
RAHNER K. Schriften zur Theologie. Einsiedeln 1956ff
ET Theological Investigations. London 1967ff
Handbuch der Pastoraltheologie I. Freiburg 1964
RATZINGER J. (Hrsg) Dogmatische Konstitution über die Kirche. Münster ⁴1965
SAHLIN H. Der Messias und das Gottesvolk. Uppsala 1945
SCHIERSE F. J. Weinachtliche Christusverkündigung in BiLe 1 1960
SCHLATTER A. Der Evangelist Johannes. Stuttgart 1930
SCHLIER H. Besinning auf das Neue Testament. Freiburg 1964
Die Zeit der Kirche. Freiburg ³1962
Die Osterbotschaft des Evangelist Markus in *Der christliche Sonntag*. Freiburg 1949
Das Mysterium Israels in *Studien und Berichte der katholischen Akademie in Bayern* H.33 (1966)
SCHMID J. Das Evangelium nach Lukas. Regensburg ⁴1960
Das Evangelium nach Markus. Regensburg ⁵1963
SCHMITT J. Jésus ressuscité dans la prédication apostolique. Paris 1949
SCHNACKENBURG R. Das Johannesevangelium I. Freiburg 1965
ET The Gospel according to St John. London

SCHÜRMANN H. Aufbau, Eigenart und Geschichtswert der Vorgeschichte von Lukas 1–2 in BiKi 21 (1966)
'Sie gebar ihren erstgeborenen Sohn' in LUM H39 (1966)
SCHWARZ H. Das Verständnis des Wunders bei Heim und Bultmann. Stuttgart 1966
SCHWEIZER E. Das Evangelium nach Markus. Göttingen 1967
Neotestamentica. Zürich–Stuttgart 1963
SMITMANS A. Das Weinwunder von Kana. Tübingen 1966
STÄHLIN W. Predigthilfen I, II. Kassel ²1961, ²1962
STALLMANN M. Die biblische Geschichte im Unterricht. Göttingen 1963
THÜSING W. Die Erhöhung und Verherrlichung Jesu im Johannesevangelium. Münster 1960
TILLICH P. Systematische Theologie I. Stuttgart 1955
ET Systematic Theology I, Welwyn 1951
TILLMANN F., GOEDEKE P. Die sonntäglichen Evangelien. Düsseldorf ⁹1965
TRILLING W. Fragen zur Geschichlichkeit Jesu. Düsseldorf 1966
Hausordnung Gottes. Düsseldorf 1960
Das wahre Israel. München ³1964
Das Evangelium nach Matthäus I, II. Düsseldorf 1962, 1965
VÖGTLE A. Ekklesiologische Auftragsworte des Auferstandenen in *Sacra Pagina* II. Paris Gombloux 1959
VORGRIMLER H. (Hrsg) Exegese und Dogmatik. Mainz 1962
VOSS G. Die Christologie der lukanischen Schriften in Grundzügen. Brügge 1965
Geboren aus Maria der Jungfrau in *Lebendiges Zeugnis* H4 (1964)
VAN IERSEL B. Die Wunderbare Speisung und das Abendmahl in der synoptischen Tradition in NOVT 7 (1964/65)
WELTE B. Auf der Spur des Ewigen. Freiburg 1965
WILCKENS U. Die Missionsreden der Apostelgeschichte. Neukirchen ²1963
ZIMMERLI W. Die historisch-kritische Bibelwissenschaft und die Verkündigungsaufgabe der Kirche in EVTH 23 (1963)

BIBLIOGRAPHY

Sources of sermon material

The quotations in the sections 'On the sermon literature' in chapters 3, 5 and 7 were mainly taken from the following collections:

Ambrosius, Zeitschrift für Prediger Donauwörth
Praedica Verbum (a continuation of *Ambrosius*) Donauwörth 1955ff
Gottes Wort im Kirchenjahr Würzburg 1940ff
Der Prediger und Katechet Freiburg 1850ff

Abbreviations

Authors writing in lexicons etc are not usually included in the bibliography. The following abbreviations have been used:

BiKi	*Bibel und Kirche*, Stuttgart
BiLe	*Bibel und Leben*, Düsseldorf 1960ff
DW	*Dienst am Wort*, Freiburg 1966f
EvTh	*Evangelische Theologie*, Munich
GPM	*Göttinger Predigt-Meditationen*, Göttingen 1946ff
GuL	*Geist und Leben*, Würzburg
HtG	*Handbuch theologischer Grundbegriffe* ed H. Fries, Münich 1962/63
KuM	*Kerygma und Mythos*, hrsg H. W. Bartsch, Hamburg ⁴1960
LTK	*Lexicon für Theologie und Kirche*, Freiburg ²1957–67
LuM	*Liturgie und Mönchtum*, Freiburg
NovT	*Novum Testamentum*, Leiden
NTS	*New Testament Studies*, London/New York
TthZ	*Trierer theologische Zeitschrift*, Treves
ThLZ	*Theologische Litteraturzeitung*, Leipzig
ThQ	*Theologische Quartalschrift*, Tübingen
TWNT	*Theologisches Wörtebuch zum Neuen Testament*, Stuttgart 1933f

TABLES OF READINGS

Appendix 1

Position of the selected gospel readings in the current Roman lectionary. Figures after the day show the yearly cycle. Brackets indicate a weekday.

(1) The resurrection narratives (pp 70–71)

Mk 16:1–8	Easter vigil 2
Mk 16:15–20	Ascension 2
Mk 28:1–10	Easter vigil 1
Mt 28:16–20	Ascension 1
Lk 24:1–12	Easter vigil 3
Lk 24:13–35	Easter evening 1, 2, 3; 3 Easter 1
Lk 24:36–49	3 Easter 2
Lk 24:50–53	Ascension 3
Jn 20:1–9	Easter day 1, 2, 3
Jn 20:11–18	(Easter Tues)
Jn 20:19–23	Pentecost 1, 2, 3
Jn 20:24–29	2 Easter 1, 2, 3
Jn 21:1–14	Easter 3

(2) The miracle stories (p 176)
(a) The paralytic

Mk 2:1–12	7 Sun 2
Mt 9:1–8	(13 Thurs)
Lk 5:17–26	(2 Advent Mon)

(b) The stilling of the storm

Mk 4:35–41	12 Sun 2
Mt 8:23–27	(13 Tues)
Lk 8:22–25	—

(c) The feeding stories

Mk 6:30–34	16 Sun 2
Mk 6:34–44	(Jan 8th)
Mk 8:1–9	(5 Sat)
Mt 14:13–21	18 Sun 1
Mt 15:32–39	(1 Advent Wed)
Lk 9:10–17	Corpus Christi 3
Jn 6:1–15	17 Sun 1

TABLES OF READINGS

(3) The infancy narratives (p 267)

Lk 1:26–38	4 Advent 2, March 25th, Dec 8th
Lk 2:1–14	Christmas midnight 1, 2, 3
Lk 2:15–20	Christmas dawn 1, 2, 3
Lk 2:21–40	Holy family 2, Feb 2nd
Lk 2:41–52	Holy Family 3, March 19th
Mt 1:1–25	(Dec 24th)
Mt 1:18–25	4 Advent 1
Mt 2:1–12	Epiphany 1, 2, 3
Mt 2:13–23	Holy Family 1

Appendix 2

Sundays and feast days in the Roman lectionary for which the gospel readings belong to the type of resurrection, miracle, or infancy stories dealt with in the exegetical chapters 2, 4, and 6. Figures after the day show the yearly cycle.

Day	Chapter
4 Advent 1, 2, 3	6
Christmas night	6
Christmas dawn	6
Holy family 1, 2, 3	6
Dec 29th	6
Dec 30th	6
Octave of Christmas (Jan 1st)	6
Epiphany 1, 2, 3	6
4 Lent 1	4
5 Lent 1	4
Easter vigil 1, 2, 3	2
Easter day 1, 2, 3	2
2 Easter 1, 2, 3	2
3 Easter 1, 2, 3	2
Ascension 1, 2, 3	2
Pentecost 1, 2, 3	2
2 Sun 3	4
3 Sun 1	4
5 Sun 2, 3	4
6 Sun 2	4
7 Sun 2	4
9 Sun 3	4

TABLES OF READINGS

10 Sun 2, 3	4
12 Sun 2	4
13 Sun 2	4
14 Sun 2	4
17 Sun 2	4
18 Sun 1	4
19 Sun 1	4
20 Sun 1	4
23 Sun 1	4
28 Sun 3	4
30 Sun 2	4
Trinity Sun 2	2
Corpus Christi 3	4
Feb 2	6
March 19	6
March 25	6
May 31	6
Aug 15	6
Dec 8	6

Appendix 3

Sundays and feastdays in the lectionary of the Church of England, Series 3, for which the gospel readings belong to the type of resurrection, miracle, or infancy stories dealt with in the exegetical chapters 2, 4, and 6. Figures after the day show the yearly cycle.

Day	Chapter
1 before Christmas (4 Adv) 1, 2	6
Christmas day 1	6
1 Christmas 1, 2	6
2 Christmas 1, 2	6
5 Christmas (3 Epiphany) 1	4
8 before Easter (Sexagesima) 1, 2	4
7 before Easter (Quinquagesima) 1, 2	4
5 before Easter (2 Lent) 1, 2	4
Easter day 1, 2	2
1 Easter 1, 2	2
2 Easter 1	2
3 Easter 1	2
3 Easter 2	4

TABLES OF READINGS

4 Easter 1	2
Ascension day	2
6 Easter (Sun after Ascension) 1, 2	2
3 Pentecost (2 Trinity) 2	4
9 Pentecost (8 Trinity) 2	4
17 Pentecost (16 Trinity) 2	4
19 Pentecost (18 Trinity) 1	4
22 Pentecost (21 Trinity) 2	4
Jan 1st (Circumcision)	6
Jan 6th (Epiphany)	6
Feb 2nd (Presentation)	6
Mar 25th (Annunciation)	6
July 2nd (Visitation)	6
Dec 28th (Innocents)	6

INDEX OF BIBLICAL PASSAGES

Genesis
1:2   233, 234
2:7   53, 99
17:15–22   230
18:2   38
26:3   232
28:15   232
35:21   238

Exodus
3:12   232
16   136
18:25   140
40:35   234

Leviticus
12   242

Numbers
11   136
11:25   233
27:17   139

Deuteronomy
18:15–18   136

Joshua
1:5   232

Judges
3:15   239
6:11–24   230
6:12   232
6:16   232
6:34   233
13:25   233

1 Samuel
2:21   244

2:26   244
10:6f   233
12   232
16:1–13   237
16:13f   233

2 Samuel
5:10   232
7   232
7:3   232
7:9   232
7:12–16   233, 250
23:5   232

2 Kings
2:1–18   47
2:11   106, 110
4:42–44   136

Psalms
23:2   140
72:10f   254
78   136
107   136
110:1   105, 110

Isaiah
2:2   254, 300
7:14   232
9:6   233
42:6   243
49:6   243
51   122
52:10   243
53:9   74
60:1–6   254

Ezekiel
36:25–27   233
37:1–14   42

INDEX OF BIBLICAL PASSAGES

Hosea
13:4–6   136

Joel
2:21–23   232
3:1–5   233

Micah
4:8   238
5:1   237

Zephaniah
3:14   232

Zechariah
9:9   232

Matthew
1   249–252, 258
1:1   237
1:1f   257
1:16   259
1:18–25   259
1:21   180, 188, 190, 249
2   252–257
2:1   227, 237
2:1–12   249, 253–5, 259, 267, 292–302
2:23   259
3:23–25   188
5:1   33
8:1–9:34   124, 130
8:18   127
8:19ff   131, 133
8:20   202
8:23–7   127, 130–3, 176, 192–203
8:26   129, 132
8:30   132
9:1–8   120, 124–126, 176, 188, 189–200
9:6   183
9:7   178
9:8   187, 188
9:36   146
11:2–6   174
11:5   190
12:28   174, 190
12:39   116, 166
12:40   117
13:53–17:23 143
14:6   145
14:9   145
14:12f   135, 143–146
14:24   131
14:31   132
15:29   33
15:32–39   136, 143–146
16:8   132, 145
16:12   145
16:17–19   57
16:18   201
16:19   188
17:1   33
17:20   132
18:3   283
18:15–18   188
25:5–7   30
26:20   145
27:62–66   22
28:1–10   22–24
28:7   25, 33
28:9f   13, 30
28:10   14, 33
28:11–15   23, 29, 40
28:16   14
28:16–20   12, 13, 15, 33–36, 43, 59
28:17   14, 34
28:18–20   299
28:19   16
28:20   49, 59, 126, 155, 187

Mark
1:11   285
1:13   20
1:15   139
1:34   130
1:35–39   121
1:44   130

380

INDEX OF BIBLICAL PASSAGES

2:1–5	124–125	6:52	144
2:1–12	120–124	7:36	130
2:1–3:6	126	8:1	152
2:6	124	8:1–9	135, 137, 138, 141–142, 176, 203–17, 220–223
2:7	126		
2:10	125		
2:12	125	8:1–10	142, 147
2:13–17	120	8:2	152
2:16	221	8:6	222
2:18–22	120	8:7	146
2:23–28	121	8:9	223
3:1–6	121	8:12f	116
3:6	139	8:13	117
3:9	127	8:14–21	147
3:12	130	8:17	129, 145
3:22	160	8:17–21	60
4:1	127	8:18	138
4:11f	128, 130, 138	8:21	129, 138, 141
4:12	139	8:22	147
4:33	120	8:22–26	139
4:35–41	127–130	8:26	130
4:35–5:43	134	8:29	130
4:36	131	8:30	130
4:37	131	8:32	120
5:43	130	8:32f	130
6:1–6	128	9:9	130
6:6–13	138	9:24	202
6:14–16	138	9:32	130
6:17–29	138	11:13	112
6:30	147	13	127
6:30–33	142, 144	13:27	20
6:30–44	135, 137–141	13:32	20
6:32	147	14:22	141
6:34	142, 146	14:22–25	137
6:34–44	139–141, 143	14:25	222, 223
6:35	151	14:28	13, 21
6:35f	142	14:62	46
6:36	210	15:42–7	19
6:37	144, 147, 150	15:46	19, 20, 80
6:39f	145, 146, 147	15:47	19
6:41	142, 145, 222	16:1	24
6:41–43	145	16:1–8	19–22, 71–83
6:45–51	138	16:5–7	30
6:45–8:26	147	16:6	29–30, 66
6:51ff	138	16:7	25, 33

381

INDEX OF BIBLICAL PASSAGES

16:8	14, 24, 26, 33	2:25–38	25, 306
16:9–20	19, 58–61	2:26	240
16:11–14	34	2:27	45
16:14–20	103–113	2:29–32	248
16:16	16	2:30	240
		2:37	45
Luke		2:39	227, 244, 259
1–2	228, 258	2:40	244
1:5	237, 242	2:41–52	25, 242, 243–246, 267, 302–309
1:6	231		
1:11	230	2:46	45
1:12	230	2:49	25
1:13	230, 231, 268	2:50	308
1:13ff	45, 230	2:51	259, 308
1:15	231	2:52	308
1:15–17	230	3:22	127, 235, 247, 308
1:18	230	3:23–38	234
1:20	230	3:38	237
1:26	228, 259	4:9–13	242
1:26–38	228, 230–236, 257, 258, 259, 267–278, 306	4:18	247
		4:21	127
		4:36	126
1:27	259	5:1–4	134
1:28	239	5:1–11	56
1:32	237	5:17–26	126–127
1:33	257	5:26	190
1:35	247, 259	7:18–23	174
1:37	240	8:1	134
1:39–56	228	8:4–18	134
1:45	236, 274	8:10	135
1:57–80	228	8:19–21	308
1:67–69	241	8:22–23	127
1:78ff	242	8:22–25	134–137
1:80	242	9:6	239
2	300	9:10–17	135, 147–149
2:1	257	9:13f	150
2:1–20	236–241, 265, 267, 278–292	9:16	37
		9:22	25
2:4	228, 259	9:30	25
2:5	259	9:44	25
2:5–7	259	9:45	244
2:8–14	306	9:51	46
2:10–14	248	9:51–19:27	25, 36
2:11	127, 259, 263	9:57–60	131
2:21–40	241–243, 306	10:1	131

382

INDEX OF BIBLICAL PASSAGES

10:8	135, 174	24:47	16, 49
11:20	135, 160, 174	24:49	36, 37
11:22	174	24:50–53	45–49
11:27f	308	24:52	239
11:29	116		
11:29f	117	*John*	
11:30	117	1	51
11:31	244	1:1	56
13:1–5	124, 180	1:59–80	241
15:17–26	120	2:18	117
17:14	185	3:3	99
18:31–34	25	3:18f	99
18:34	244	3:18	53
19:28–48	242	3:73	51
19:38	240	4:7	218
19:45–48	26	4:37f	218
22:19	37	5:22	185
22:69	45, 46	6:1–15	135, 176, 203–219
23:46	307	6:1–58	149–154
24:1–12	24–26	6:4	219
24:4–7	30	6:14f	219
24:5	30	6:30f	117
24:7	244	6:35	213, 219
24:9	14	6:51	219
24:11	34, 40	6:54	219
24:13–35	15, 36–39, 59, 83–90	6:62	51
24:16	56	7:37–39	53
24:21	244	8:23	154
24:22–24	29, 40	9	124, 180
24:23	93	9:39	99
24:24	14	12:23–33	154
24:25	34, 244	12:24	219
24:26	244	12:32	51
24:27	34	14:27	53
24:29	148	15:5	57
24:30	148	16:8	99
24:34	12	16:8–11	53
24:34f	60	16:22	52, 53, 98
24:36–49	12, 39–45, 52, 59	17:18	99
24:37	15	18:15–18	58
24:37f	34	18:25–27	58
24:41	34	19:19–29	40
24:44	25, 244	19:34	52
24:44–49	307	20	33, 49–56
24:46	49, 244	20:1	19, 59

383

INDEX OF BIBLICAL PASSAGES

20:1–6f	40	*Romans*	
20:1–10	14	4:17	80
20:1–18	26–29	15:19	115
20:11–18	50–52, 59		
20:12f	30	*1 Corinthians*	
20:13	29	1:22–24	116
20:14–17	30	1:28f	276
20:18–29	44	9:1	18
20:19–23	52–54, 59	13:12	357
20:19–31	90–103	15	75
20:19–29	40	15:3–7	12
20:20	15, 34, 41	15:3–8	62
20:22f	15	15:5	12–13
20:23	16	15:5–7	13
20:24–29	13, 14, 34, 54–5	15:14	11, 327
20:30f	102–103	15:36–37	18
21	12–14, 49f, 56–58	15:44	43
21:1	33		
21:1–19	56–58	*2 Corinthians*	
		5:18	191
Acts		12:12	115
1:2	46, 49		
1:4	36	*Galatians*	
1:8	26, 37, 49	4:4	251, 306
1:9–11	15, 47, 49		
1:10	25	*Philippians*	
1:11	46, 109, 112	2:5–11	289
1:21f	46, 224	2:7	308
1:22	46		
2:22	135	*2 Thessalonians*	
2:33–36	45, 46	2:9	115

INDEX OF AUTHORS AND EDITORS CITED

AUGUSTINE 214

BARTH, K. 269, 276, 277
BOHREN, R. 331
BONHOEFFER, D. 366
BORNKAMM, G. 12, 35, 117, 124, 125, 131, 140, 145, 146, 157, 334
BULTMANN, R. 27, 28, 52, 57, 62, 64, 119, 165, 329, 331, 354-355

CAMPENHAUSEN, H. V. 19f, 32
CONZELMANN, H. 26, 48, 147, 230, 233, 242
CULLMANN, O. 58

DIBELIUS, M. 22, 129, 224, 231, 232, 234
DINKLER, E. 35, 89, 236, 243
DODD, C. H. 149
DREHER, B. 67-68

EBELING, G. 45, 316
EICHOLZ, G. 80, 300-301, 306

FESENMEYER, G. 332, 365
FILTHAUT, T. 79, 335, 362ff
FISCHER, M. 69f
FLENDER, H. 247
FRÖR, K. 173, 257, 262
FUCHS, E. 239

GNILKA, J. 129, 134, 141
GOLLWITZER, H. 289
GRASS, H. 15, 31, 55ff
GRUNDMANN, W. 20, 59, 138, 231, 234, 238, 241

HAENCHEN, E. 54f, 122, 141f, 283
HAHN, F. 123

HEISING, A. 141, 149, 152f
HENNECKE, F. E. 235
HIPPOLYTUS OF ROME 67

IWAND, H. J. 190, 264, 277f

JEREMIAS, J. 296
JUTZLER, K. 353

KÄSEMANN, E. 114, 166, 170, 313, 315, 333, 338
KASPER, W. 326, 342
KESSLER, H. 64
KEUCK, W. 222
KIRCHGÄSSNER, E. 353
KLAUSER, T. 268
KOCH, G. 30
KOCH, K. 32
KRAUS, H. J. 309

LANG, A. 162f
LAURENTIN, R. 226, 242
LEO the Great, Pope 67
LOHFINK, G. 47
LOHMEYER, E. 19, 59, 121, 125, 128, 132, 256
LOHSE, E. 18, 40

MARXSEN, W. 158, 335-337
MELITO of Sardis 67
MOLTMANN, J. 65, 332f
MÜLLER-SCHWEFE, H. R. 341

NINEHAM, D. 33

OLIVER, H. H. 230, 234, 243

PANNENBERG, W. 341
PASCHER, J. 111

INDEX OF AUTHORS AND EDITORS CITED

RAHNER, H. 261
RAHNER, K. 43, 188, 363
RATZINGER, J. 110, 112, 202, 367

SAHLIN, H. 234
SCHIERSE, F. J. 225, 236, 248, 258
SCHLATTER, A. 154
SCHLIER, H. 5, 29, 45ff, 76, 79, 81, 83, 158f, 246, 255, 312f, 317, 324, 327, 357
SCHMID, J. 226
SCHMITT, J. 11, 123
SCHNACKENBURG, R. 115, 151
SCHÜRMANN, H. 229, 238ff, 260, 280
SCHWARZ, H. 165
SCHWEIZER, E. 61, 81f, 139, 314, 323, 325, 334, 358, 368
SMITMANS, 150, 153
STÄHLIN, W. 90, 264, 302, 304f

STALLMAN, M. 330, 340
SURKAU, H. W. 234

THÜSING, W. 51, 52ff
TILLICH, P. 165f
TILLMANN, F. 349f
TRILLING, W. 36, 144, 188

VÖGTLE, A. 16
VORGRIMLER, H. 327
VOSS, G. 246, 273

WEBER, O. 112
WELTE, B. 165, 168
WILCKENS, U. 11

ZENO of Verona 67
ZIMMERLI, W. 317, 324